IN THE SHADOW OF VIOLENCE

This book applies the conceptual framework of Douglass C. North, John Joseph Wallis, and Barry R. Weingast's *Violence and Social Orders* (Cambridge University Press, 2009) to nine developing countries. The cases show how political control of economic privileges is used to limit violence and coordinate coalitions of powerful organizations. Rather than castigating politicians and elites as simply corrupt, the case studies illustrate why development is difficult to achieve in societies where the role of economic organizations is manipulated to provide political balance and stability. The volume develops the idea of limited access social order as a dynamic social system in which violence is constantly a threat and political and economic outcomes result from the need to control violence rather than promoting economic growth or political rights.

Douglass C. North is co-recipient of the 1993 Nobel Memorial Prize in Economic Science. He is Spencer T. Olin Professor in Arts and Sciences at Washington University in St. Louis and Bartlett Burnap Senior Fellow at the Hoover Institution at Stanford University. He is author of eleven books, including *Institutions, Institutional Change, and Economic Performance* (1990).

John Joseph Wallis is a professor of economics at the University of Maryland and a research associate at the National Bureau of Economic Research. Professor Wallis is an economic historian who specializes in the public finance of American governments.

Steven B. Webb worked at the World Bank for twenty-one years as an economist and adviser on policy research, evaluation, and operations for Latin America and the Caribbean and other regions. He currently serves as a consultant to the Bank.

Barry R. Weingast is the Ward C. Krebs Family Professor in the department of political science and a senior Fellow at the Hoover Institution at Stanford University. A member of the National Academy of Sciences, he has been the recipient of the Riker Prize, the Heinz Eulau Prize, and the James Barr Memorial Prize.

To Christine Leon de Mariz

In the Shadow of Violence

Politics, Economics, and the Problems of Development

Edited by

DOUGLASS C. NORTH

JOHN JOSEPH WALLIS

STEVEN B. WEBB

BARRY R. WEINGAST

CAMBRIDGE
UNIVERSITY PRESS

CAMBRIDGE UNIVERSITY PRESS
Cambridge, New York, Melbourne, Madrid, Cape Town,
Singapore, São Paulo, Delhi, Mexico City

Cambridge University Press
32 Avenue of the Americas, New York, NY 10013-2473, USA

www.cambridge.org
Information on this title: www.cambridge.org/9781107684911

First published 2013

Printed in the United States of America

A catalog record for this publication is available from the British Library.

Library of Congress Cataloging in Publication data
In the shadow of violence : politics, economics, and the problems of development / edited by
Douglass C. North, John Joseph Wallis, Steven B. Webb, and Barry R. Weingast.
pages cm
Includes bibliographical references and index.
ISBN 978-1-107-01421-3 – ISBN 978-1-107-68491-1 (pbk.)
1. Developing countries – Economic conditions. 2. Developing conditions –
Social conditions. I. North, Douglass Cecil. II. Wallis, John Joseph.
III. Webb, Steven Benjamin, 1947– IV. Weingast, Barry R.
HC59.7.I47 2012
338.9009172'4–dc23 2012015678

ISBN 978-1-107-01421-3 Hardback
ISBN 978-1-107-68491-1 Paperback

Contents

List of Contributors   *page* vii

Acknowledgments   ix

1. Limited Access Orders: An Introduction to
    the Conceptual Framework   1
    Douglass C. North, John Joseph Wallis, Steven B. Webb,
    and Barry R. Weingast

2. Bangladesh: Economic Growth in a Vulnerable LAO   24
    Mushtaq H. Khan

3. Fragile States, Elites, and Rents in the
    Democratic Republic of Congo (DRC)   70
    Kai Kaiser and Stephanie Wolters

4. Seeking the Elusive Developmental Knife Edge:
    Zambia and Mozambique – A Tale of Two Countries   112
    Brian Levy

5. Change and Continuity in a Limited Access Order:
    The Philippines   149
    Gabriella R. Montinola

6. India's Vulnerable Maturity: Experiences of
    Maharashtra and West Bengal   198
    Pallavi Roy

7. Entrenched Insiders: Limited Access Order in Mexico   233
    Alberto Díaz-Cayeros

v

8. From Limited Access to Open Access
   Order in Chile, Take Two   261
   Patricio Navia

9. Transition from a Limited Access Order to an
   Open Access Order: The Case of South Korea   293
   Jong-Sung You

10. Lessons: In the Shadow of Violence   328
    Douglass C. North, John Joseph Wallis, Steven B. Webb,
    and Barry R. Weingast

Index   351

Contributors

Alberto Díaz-Cayeros is an Associate Professor of International Relations and Pacific Studies and Director of the Center for U.S.-Mexican Studies (USMEX). His current research interests include poverty, development, federalism, clientelism and patronage, and Mexico.

Kai Kaiser is a as Senior Economist with the World Bank, currently in the Phillipines. His research focuses on economic development, notably public finance, inter-governmental relations and sub-national growth, extractives (oil, gas, and mining-related growth), and the application of various forms of new technology and media to enhance public sector accountability.

Mushtaq H. Khan is a professor of economics at the School of Oriental and African Studies, University of London. He is an institutional economist specializing in developing countries with interests in technology policy, property rights, the relationship between governance and growth, and developmental state policies.

Brian Levy worked for twenty-three years at the World Bank, including stints as leader of the Africa Region public sector governance unit, and of the organization-wide governance and anti-corruption secretariat. He currently is a senior adjunct professor at the School of Advanced International Studies, Johns Hopkins University, and the University of Cape Town, South Africa. He has a Ph.D in economics from Harvard University.

Gabriella R. Montinola is an associate professor of political science at the University of California, Davis. Her research focuses on governance in developing countries. She has written several articles on corruption and the rule of law in the Philippines. Her recent work examines the impact of foreign aid on governance across developing countries.

Patricio Navia is an associate professor of political science at Universidad Diego Portales in Chile and a Master Teacher of Liberal Studies at New York University. He specializes in electoral rules, political parties, public opinion, and democratic consolidation in Chile and Latin America.

Pallavi Roy has worked for more than a decade as a business journalist in India for *Businessworld* and *Financial Express*. She covered industrial and mining sectors and the political economy of reforms. She is currently completing a Ph.D. in the economics department at SOAS on growth and governance issues in India.

Stephanie Wolters has been working as a journalist, researcher, and political analyst in Africa for twenty years. She specializes in political and economic research in Africa, journalism, and media management, focusing in particular on conflict zones, post-conflict reconstruction, governance, electoral processes, and media in conflict zones.

Jong-Sung You (유종성) is Assistant Professor at the Graduate School of International Relations and Pacific Studies, University of California, San Diego. His research focuses on the political economy of inequality, corruption, and social trust, and he is writing a book on inequality and corruption in South Korea, Taiwan, and the Philippines.

Acknowledgments

The World Bank has supported this project from the beginning in several different ways. A grant from the Governance Partnership Facility, run by the Bank with funding from government donors, financed the conferences and the case studies that make up this volume. Piet Hein Van Heesewijk of the GPF Secretariat has helped us in managing the grant since 2009. Prior to that, the Bank's research committee provided two grants to prepare the proposal, enabling us to bring the team to Washington and to meet with groups interested in the Bank.

We received useful suggestions from many people inside and outside of the Bank along the way. We thank our colleagues and friends: James Adams, Doug Addison, Junaid Ahmad, Ahmad Ahsan, Anna Bellver, Francois Bourguignon, Carole Brown, Ed Campos, Ajay Chhibber, George Clarke, Maria Correia, Robert Cull, Augusto de la Torre, Jean-Jacques Dethier, Shanta Deverajan, Francis Fukuyama, Saurabh Garg, Alan Gelb, Marcelo Giugale, Carol Graham, Isabel Guerrero, Stephen Haber, Stefan Haggard, Scott Handler, Gerald Jacobson, Dani Kaufmann, Phil Keefer, Ali Khadr, Stuti Khemani, Lili Liu, Beatriz Magaloni, Nick Manning, Yasuhiko Matsuda, Stephen Ndegwa, John Nye, Alison Poole, Francesca Recanatini, Dani Rodrik, Fernando Rojas, David Rosenblatt, Mary Shirley, Michael Walton, Deborah Wetzel, and Yong-mei Zhou. A team from Agence Français de Development, including Robert Peccoud, Nicolas Meisel, and Jacques Ould-Auodia, has started a parallel project using the same analytic framework, and have been tremendous intellectual partners over the last four years. Lee Alston and Bernardo Mueller provided a careful reading and important suggestions in the editorial phase, as did several anonymous referees.

Christine de Mariz and later Carmen Machicado handled administration of the project, with important assistance from Gabriela Calderon Motta.

The department of political science at Stanford University hosted a conference of the team in January 2010. We thank Eliana Vasquez and Jackie Sargent who did a great job of hosting.

When the GPF grant was approved in early 2009, Christine de Mariz took charge of administering the project's most intense phase of contracting consultants, monitoring preparation of case studies, and organizing the team meetings. Christine was a full intellectual member of the team and also did a wonderful job of organizing, coordinating, and inspiring. In May 2010, however, Christine was seriously injured in a car accident while on a World Bank mission in Haiti. We dedicate the volume to Christine, in thanks for her assistance in 2009–10 and in hope for her swift and complete recovery.

ONE

Limited Access Orders

An Introduction to the Conceptual Framework

Douglass C. North, John Joseph Wallis,
Steven B. Webb, and Barry R. Weingast

1.1 The Problem of Economic and Political Development

Success in economic as well as political development depends primarily on improving institutions. This has become the consensus among economists over the last twenty years, as the world has witnessed many development failures in spite of abundant capital, natural resources, and educated populations, who emigrate or stagnate if institutions do not put them to good use. The question now is: What institutions are right? As elaborated later in this chapter, some argue that developing countries should emulate the institutions of the most successful, high-income economies of the OECD. We and others, however, see evidence that most low- and middle-income countries are not ready to utilize many Western European or North American institutions or that these institutions function very differently if transplanted into these low- and middle-income economies.

The purpose of this volume is to develop and apply an alternative framework for understanding the dynamic interaction of political, economic, and social forces in developing countries, which was first laid out by North, Wallis, and Weingast (2009, hereafter NWW). The standard approach begins with neoclassical assumptions that growth will occur whenever profitable opportunities present themselves unless the intervention of political or social impediments prevent markets from working. In contrast, the alternative perspective presented here begins with the recognition that all societies must deal with the problem of violence. In most developing countries, individuals and organizations actively use or threaten to use violence to gather wealth and resources, and violence has to be restrained for development to occur. In many societies the potential for violence is latent: organizations generally refrain from violence in most years, but occasionally find violence a useful tool for pursuing their

1

ends. These societies live in the shadow of violence, and they account for most of human history and for most of today's world population. Social arrangements deter the use of violence by creating incentives for powerful individuals to coordinate rather than fight. The dynamics of these social arrangements differ from those described in neoclassical models, and this difference limits the value of the neoclassical tools for understanding the problems of development.

Our framework builds on the exciting work of a range of scholars studying the political economy of development. Some draw heavily on international contrasts of historical experience through detailed analysis of cases (Abernethy 2000; Bates 1981, 2001; Haber et al. 2003, 2008; Herbst 2000; Fukuyama 2011; La Porta et al. 1999; Landes 1998; Mokyr 1990; Spiller and Tommasi 2007; Tilly 1990). Our framework tries to take account of the events portrayed in those case studies. Other authors use econometric analysis to test for the historical origins of institutional differences (Acemoglu and Johnson 2005; Acemoglu and Robinson 2006; Engerman and Sokoloff 2008). Our framework aims to provide a new institutional explanation for why patterns of political economy have persisted for centuries. Another group of studies elaborates theoretical models of political interaction that give explanations for the dysfunction that plagues developing countries (for example, Buchanan et al. 1980; Bueno de Mesquita et al. 2003; Cox and McCubbins 2000; Levi 1988; North 1981; Olson 1993; Przeworski et al. 2000). Our framework takes more account of the issues of violence and of organizational structures within the elite. The studies closest to our approach not only look directly at institutions in developing countries today but also argue that no simple or linear relationship exists between institutional and economic development (Collier 2009; Easterly 2001; Grindle 2007; Khan 2004; Khan and Jomo 2000; Rodrik 2007; Shirley 2009). Our approach provides a more systematic explanation for some of the nonlinearities that they identify.

Others have also discussed how the institutions of developing countries differ qualitatively from those in developed economies. Marx, of course, noted how capitalist societies differed from their predecessors. Huntington (1968) and more recently Collier (2009) see the importance of the problem of violence in these societies, suggesting that they may not be ready for some of the institutions prevalent in more economically developed countries. Grindle (2007) and Rodrik (2007) see the need for developing countries to strive for "good enough governance," with the implication that the institutional needs in these places is qualitatively different from in developed countries. Alston et al. (2010), Khan (2004), Khan and Jomo (2000),

Moore (2010), and Shirley (2009) also see an institutional agenda for developing countries that is not the same as an incremental and linear adoption of the institutions in developed countries. Compared to these earlier analyses, our integrated conceptual framework enables us to think about the interaction of economic and political behavior, explicitly considering the problem of violence as an entry point.

The problem of violence has increasingly become a concern of the World Bank. The central message of the 2011 World Development Report on *Conflict, Security, and Development* "is that strengthening legitimate institutions and governance to provide citizen security, justice and jobs is crucial to break cycles of violence" (World Bank 2011, p. 2). The report offers many dimensions of analysis within the theme that creating widespread trust in institutions and popular satisfaction with outcomes – like employment and rising living standards – are integral to reducing the threat of violence. Our approach puts more emphasis on the nature of organizations and the relations between their leaders – the elite, broadly defined. The WDR acknowledges a role for elite bargains, but sees them as a temporary solution at best for the problem of violence. Our framework sees elite bargains as the persistent core of developing societies and seeks to understand which types of elite bargains have contributed to positive economic and social development and which have not.

1.2 The Logic of Limited Access Orders

The conceptual framework emphasizes that developing societies limit violence through the manipulation of economic interests by the political system in order to create rents so that powerful groups and individuals find it in their interest to refrain from using violence. We call this way of organizing a society a *limited access order* (LAO), and this section explains the logic of these societies.

LAOs are social arrangements – simultaneously political and economic – that discourage the use of violence by organizations. Even in a world where violence is a viable option that cannot credibly be deterred by a third-party or central authority (like a government), some or all potential violence can be discouraged so that it remains latent, allowing individuals and organizations to have some confidence of peace in dealing with other organizations with violence potential. The LAO framework builds on the importance of organizations, both as a way of coordinating individuals and as a way of generating rents and shaping incentives consistent with individual behavior.

We develop the underlying logic by starting with a simple example that focuses on two groups and two leaders. Real societies are much larger and more complicated. The story begins with self-organizing groups that are small and that have no way to develop trust between individuals beyond ongoing personal relationships. Members of one group trust others within their group but distrust members of the other groups. Because they recognize that disarming will lead the other group to destroy or enslave them, members of neither group will lay down their arms. To avoid an outcome with continual armed conflict, the leaders of the groups agree to divide the land, labor, capital, and opportunities in their world among themselves and agree to enforce each leader's privileged access to their resources. The privileges generate rents, and if the value of the rents the leaders earn from their privileges under conditions of peace exceeds that under violence, then each leader can credibly believe that the others will not fight. The leaders remain armed and dangerous and can credibly threaten the people around them to ensure each leader's privileges.

An important feature of the agreement between the leaders is the ability to call on one another to help organize and discipline the members of each leader's group. Especially they *limit* the possibility for others to start rival organizations. Limited access to opportunities for organization is the hallmark of LAOs. The arrangement is represented graphically in Figure 1.1, where individuals A and B are the two leaders and the horizontal ellipse represents the arrangement between them. The vertical ellipses represent the arrangements the leaders have with the labor, land, capital, and resources they control: their clients, the a's and b's. The horizontal arrangement between the leaders is made credible by the vertical arrangements. The rents leaders receive from controlling their client organizations enable them to credibly commit to one another, since those rents are reduced if cooperation fails and there is fighting. The rents from peace that are lost if violence occurs create incentives that curtail violence.

A reciprocal effect also exists. The agreement among the leaders enables each leader to structure their client organizations better, because they can call on each other for external support. In effect, the ability of the leaders to call on one another can make their individual organizations more productive. The rents the leaders enjoy, then, come not only from their privileged access to resources and activities, but from the leaders' ability to create and sustain more productive organizations.

We call the coalition among the leaders the *dominant coalition*. The dominant coalition provides third-party enforcement for each of the member organizations. The vertical organizations might be organized as political

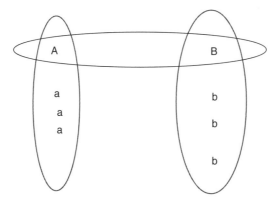

Figure 1.1 The logic of limited access.

parties, ethnic groups, patron-client networks, or crime families. The combination of multiple organizations, the organization of organizations, mitigates the problem of violence between the really dangerous people, creates credible commitments between the organizations with violence capacity by structuring their interests, and creates some belief that the leaders and their clients share common interests because they share in the value of rents.

The figure is a very simple representation. It portrays the dominant coalition as an organization of individuals, when the coalition in reality is usually an organization of organizations. They are often portrayed as patronage networks. The LAO framework calls attention to their function not only as the distributors of spoils but also as essential institutions to bring about cooperation rather than violence among organizations with violence capacity.

In a functioning limited access society, members of the dominant coalition include economic, political, religious, and educational leaders (elites) whose privileged positions create rents that ensure their cooperation with the dominant coalition and create the organizations through which the goods and services produced by the population can be mobilized and redistributed. Among the most valuable privileges members of the dominant coalition enjoy and the primary source of rents within the coalition is the ability to use the dominant coalition to enforce arrangements within the organizations of the coalition members. The rents created by those exclusive privileges are part of the glue holding together the agreements between the organizations. Limiting access to enforcement of rules by the coalition creates rents and shapes the interests of the players in the coalition.

The creation and structuring of rents are the heart of the logic of limited access. The framework focuses attention on rents to elucidate how a coalition of organizations provides order, but it differs in two ways from the uses of the term *rents* in recent economic literature. One difference is terminological, but the other difference illuminates how the LAO framework depicts the dynamic interaction between political and economic institutions.

Ricardo classically defined rents as a return to an asset or action higher than the return to the next best opportunity foregone. The neoclassical proposition is that individuals maximize net benefits: the difference between total benefits and total costs, where costs are defined as opportunity costs. Net benefits are rents, therefore rational individuals maximize rents. A smoothly operating market achieves the maximum amount of rents, the sum of consumer and producer surplus.

In the last few decades, a relatively narrow use of the term *rents* has come to dominate both academic and policy discussions about development. Krueger (1974) and Bhagwati (1982) extended the ideas of public choice economists like Buchanan, Tollison, and Tullock (1980) that individuals not only maximize rents, but that rational individuals are willing to devote resources to gain rents for themselves, an activity called *rent seeking*. The problem, from society's point of view, arises because individuals devote resources to pursuing rents that have no socially useful purpose. For example, suppose the government is deciding whether to impose a tariff on imports, which will create winners and losers. Both sides devote resources to gaining their desired end, spending up to their expected value of winning. The resources expended by winners and losers are directly unproductive rent-seeking activities (DUP), since the expenditure of resources creates no value for society as a whole. When rent seeking leads to outcomes that make society worse off, it creates DUP rents.

Common practice has dropped the *DUP* qualifier. A popular element of recent development policy, including the governance and anticorruption agenda, is the elimination of DUP rent seeking. Unfortunately that often is stated simply as eliminating rent seeking. Defined in the classical way, however, rent seeking is a ubiquitous characteristic of human behavior. Adam Smith pointed out how individual rent seeking could benefit society. We want to be explicit that the LAO framework uses the term *rents* to mean classical rents, not just DUP rents.

Our thinking about elites and dominant coalitions emphasizes that rents make people's behavior more predictable. An individual willing to work for ten dollars an hour but is paid fifteen dollars an hour receives a rent of five dollars an hour. A small change in circumstance will not lead that person to quit his or her job. In contrast, if the worker is paid $10.05 an hour, he or she receives a rent of only $.05 an hour and may quit the job if even a small change in circumstances raises the value of his or her alternatives or reduces his or her benefits from working.[1]

Following the logic of limited access, rents are critical to coordinating powerful members of the dominant coalition because rents make their behavior predictable. But not all rents make behavior with respect to violence more predictable. The rents can limit violence within the coalition only if rents are reduced when violence breaks out. The logic of limited access therefore emphasizes a kind of rent creation effected by violence that can serve to coordinate members of the dominant coalition.

This logic also shows why organizations are so important to the dominant coalition. In Figure 1.1, A and B enjoy rents that will be reduced if they are violent, creating a credible incentive for both of them to be peaceful. But A and B also receive rents from their organizations that depend on their continued cooperation. If A and B serve as credible third parties for each other, then their vertical organizations become more productive. The gains from making their organizations more productive are the rents from cooperation. If A and B do not coordinate, the rents from their organizations are reduced.

This understanding of rents distinguishes the LAO framework from other schemes that focus simply on the maximization of elite rents from any source.[2] The DUP approach ignores violence and implicitly assumes that the creation of rents is unrelated to the underlying nature of the society in which the rents appear. The LAO focus on violence and instability highlights the trade-off between stability and efficient growth. Specifically, when is it better to allow some costs to the economy, and perhaps to civil or political rights, in order to maintain or strengthen stability? The conceptual framework shows that the appropriate counterfactual about eliminating rents is not a competitive market economy (as the DUP perspective suggests), but a society in disorder and violence. To the extent that rent creation in LAOs is the means of creating stability, rents are a symptom of the development

---

[1] This is the logic of "efficiency wages" laid out by Akerloff and Yellen (1990).

[2] In a stable LAO (effectively motivating restraint of violence), everyone in the dominant coalition is getting a efficiency wage, which means that they are dividing the pie so that no one individual or group is maximizing its rent. If someone were maximizing in the neoclassical sense, it would mean pushing someone else close to the edge and ready to change loyalties if there were a marginal change in prices. Limited access allows all the members of the dominant coalition to enjoy extra rents and not be at their lower margin. Of course, sometimes a big change in relative prices precipitates discontinuous changes in the LAO dominant coalition. But the more robust LAOs have enough excess rents in the system to avoid this most of the time.

problem, not the cause of it. Attempts to remove institutions and policies that support economically unproductive rent creation and corruption need to be done in ways that avoid recurrence of instability and violence, which derails development in a LAO.

Combining the dynamics of rent allocation within the dominant coalition with the neoclassical idea that individuals seek to maximize rents allows us to understand the uncertain dynamics of limited access orders. One important implication is that limited access orders do not have a strong tendency to adopt arrangements that increase rents in the aggregate by making social organizations more productive. Individual elites usually have a complicated mix of rents, and their interests in maximizing rents through the dominant coalition is not wholly predictable. As a result, limited access societies are not characterized by steadily increasing stability or productivity. Rather, they have periods of rapid growth and periods of stagnation or collapse.[3]

LAOs are not static. When a crisis hits a limited access society, the dynamics of the dominant coalition lead it to focus on the rents – old or new – that sustain coordination and limit violence, and the creation of new rents that do sustain coordination and limit violence, as in the cases of Mexico in the 1930s, Chile in the 1970s, Korea in the 1960s, and Zambia in the 1980s. Or a crisis may lead to a free-for-all, as in Mozambique in the 1980s or in the DR Congo since the 1990s. A lot depends on the personality of the leaders in these times of crisis (Alston et al. 2010). Whether the new rents are good or bad for economic growth is not predictable. In some cases, new rents seem to cause social decline, as in Marcos's crony capitalism in the Philippines. In other cases, the new rents move societies forward, as when privileges were granted to conservatives in the 1980 Chilean constitution. The mixed role of rents in limited access orders explains why these societies do not inevitably improve over time.

Another implication of the framework is that limited access to organizations and economic rights necessarily limits competition and economic productivity. In other words, the solution to the problem of violence may become an impediment to long-term economic development, although it does not set an absolute limit to economic growth.

To summarize, LAOs constrain violence by limiting the ability of groups to form political, economic, social, military, and other organizations to engage in social activities. The rents created from those limits on access form the incentive structure that controls violence: powerful groups and individuals understand that their rents will fall if violence erupts, so they

---

[3] See NWW, chapter 1.

are more likely to be peaceful. At the center of all but the most fragmented LAOs is the dominant coalition, an organization held together by the interlocking interests of its members. A valuable privilege for members of the dominant coalition is that it provides exclusive third-party services to enforce arrangements between and within the organizations in the coalition. The rents created by those exclusive privileges are part of the incentives holding together the agreements between the organizations and their leaders. Limiting access to enforcement by the coalition creates rents and shapes the interests of the players in the coalition.

The logic of how LAOs solve the problem of violence has striking implications for economic development. Limits on the rights to form organizations and numerous privileges for rent creation necessarily mean extensive political constraints on the economy. Local monopolies and restrictions on economic entry hinder competitive markets and long-term economic growth. Put simply, the means by which limited access orders solve the problem of violence is part of the development problem.

Before the twentieth century, the problem of development was really the problem of human history. For roughly ten thousand years after the first large societies emerged in the Middle East, the long-run growth in the material standard of living of most of the population was essentially zero. The field of economic development largely ignores the long expanse of human history, focusing almost exclusively on the last century of relatively slow or zero per capita economic growth of societies outside the twenty-five or so countries that achieved high incomes by the late twentieth century. Viewed in the context of long-run history, the developed world was decidedly abnormal while the slow or nondeveloping world appeared normal.

By the end of the twentieth century, however, the LAOs of the world, including many newly liberated former colonies, were in a world economic and political system dominated by OAO economies and organizations. This has had many effects (North et al. 2007), but an important one for long-term growth was that the LAOs could access technology, markets, and even institutions from the OAO part of the world, especially Western Europe and the United States. This has allowed many developing countries to have significant per capita GDP growth over several decades while maintaining LAO institutions to restrain domestic violence as well as to benefit the elite in the dominant coalition. While some countries have had major reversals of growth, taking productivity and living standards temporarily back to levels of past centuries (like the DRC and Mozambique in our sample), other LAOs do not seem likely to have huge reversals and could plausibly keep growing. Even without making the transition to open access they are growing in the wake

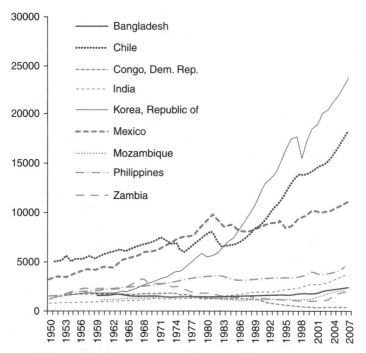

Figure 1.2 GDP per capita in nine countries (2007 prices).
Source: Heston et al. 2009.

of the OAOs – Mexico, India, and Zambia in our sample, along with Brazil, China, Indonesia, Malaysia, Vietnam, and South Africa.

Figure 1.2 shows the last half century of per capita GDP in our sample countries – usually but not always growing. There is a lot of room for most developing nations to grow economically and improve their institutions while remaining LAOs. To properly advise developing countries, we need to understand better how the LAOs work.

1.3 The Spectrum of Limited Access Orders

How do LAOs improve or regress? Although all low- and middle-income countries today are limited access orders, they have per capita income levels that differ by a factor of twenty or more, reflecting wide differences in the quality of institutions. To differentiate limited access orders and to think about the process of change within them, we developed a spectrum (not categories!) of fragile, basic, and mature LAOs. The three labels are not distinct stages, but variants of an ideal type: points on a continuous spectrum of societies differentiated by the structure of their organizations. The formation of organizations as a means of creating rents lies at the root of the logic of limited access. The nature of organizations that a society can sustain also defines the dimensions of the LAO spectrum. Whereas the LAO/OAO distinction reflects a fundamental difference in the dynamics of social orders, the different types of LAOs are shorthand terms for ranges that are not clearly distinct.

In the *fragile LAO* range of societies, the dominant coalition can barely maintain itself in the face of internal and external violence. These societies find it difficult to sustain organizations that persist through time. Most organizations are closely identified with the personality of their leadership, and leaders are personally connected in the dominant coalition. Contemporary examples include Afghanistan, Haiti, Iraq, the DR Congo, and several other places in sub-Saharan Africa. Among the powerful individuals and organizations that make up the coalition, a distinct organization called the government may or may not exist, but if it exists it has no monopoly on violence, and – as in the DR Congo – may control only a small fraction of the country's nominal territory.

The bottom billion described by Collier (2007) live in fragile LAOs, in which each faction in the dominant coalition has direct access to violence, and violence capacity is the principal determinant of the distribution of rents and resources. If the allocation of these rent flows is out of alignment with the balance of power, factions demand or fight for more. Because of their instability, fragile LAOs have simple institutional structures for the government. Individuals in fragile LAOs may perceive the potential benefits from better institutional structures, but the inability to maintain the coalition over long periods creates pervasive uncertainty about outcomes and prevents individuals and organizations from credibly committing to observe rules in many possible circumstances.

In the *basic LAO* range of societies, the government is well established compared to a fragile LAO. A formal government is often the main durable organization (or more accurately, an array of government organizations), although nongovernment organizations often exist within the framework of the dominant coalition.[4] Elite privileges and organizations are closely identified with the coalition and often with the government. Contemporary examples include Burma, Cuba, North Korea, Mexico at the height of PRI hegemony, and many Arab, former Soviet, and sub-Saharan African

---

[4] One of the clearest implications of the framework brought out in the case studies is the large number of nongovernment organizations that exercise substantial power and sometimes have violence capacity in LAOs.

countries. In twentieth-century socialist countries and other one-party states, almost all organizations were embedded within or closely linked to the ruling party. In contrast to fragile LAOs, basic LAOs create and sustain fairly stable organizational structures for the government.

As the society develops a more sophisticated internal institutional structure, it may provide more organizational forms to citizens, but usually within the direct orbit of the dominant coalition, including ruling parties. Basic LAOs do not support organizations outside the orbit of the coalition itself, even for elites, for several reasons. In some cases, independent private organizations potentially threaten the dominant coalition. In other cases, the coalition cannot commit to honoring the private organizations' rights and privileges, so members of the elite as well as the non-elite are reluctant to create economically significant private organizations for fear of expropriation. As a result, private elite organizations are closely and often personally tied to the coalition, even the branches of multinational companies operating in the country. Basic LAOs differ in the extent to which they tolerate (even without supporting) organizations outside the dominant coalition. As these LAOs mature, organizations start to proliferate and compete to gain acceptance in the dominant coalition.

The specialization and division of labor within a basic LAO government mainly involves its ability to create organizations (such as ministries, public enterprises, and banks) to provide public and private goods for the dominant coalition, such as managing trade, education, religion, tax collection, and economic infrastructure. Violence capacity in basic LAOs usually remains dispersed among government organizations, such as police, secret security, and branches of the military, each with a way to extract rents through corruption or monopolies. Sometimes nongovernment organizations also have significant violence capacity. Although not every organization in a basic LAO has violence capacity, those that survive have connections to some organization with violence capacity; in case violence actually erupts, members of the elite know they will need protection.

In the *mature LAO* range of societies, the dominant coalition supports a large variety of organizations outside the government, as well as within it, but still the LAO limits access to private organizations that the government allows and supports. In this way, the dominant coalition limits competition and creates rents to maintain itself and prevent violence. Mature LAOs include most of Latin America, China, South Africa, and India. Mature LAOs have durable institutional structures for the government and can support a wide range of elite organizations that exist apart from the government. A mature LAO, therefore, has a body of public law that specifies the offices and functions of the government, the relationship between the offices and functions, and provides for methods of resolving conflicts within the government, and by extension, within the dominant coalition. The law may be written or unwritten, but it must be embodied in a government organization, such as a court or bureaucracy, that articulates and enforces the public law. The Chinese Communist Party, for instance, recognizes this need and is attempting to create such institutions in a manner consistent with the Party and its many goals.

As LAOs mature, a two-way interaction occurs between increasing the sophistication and differentiation of government organization and the parallel development of (nonviolent) private organizations outside the state. In a mature LAO, the government's commitments to policies and institutions can be more credible because elite private organizations are in a position to put economic pressure on the government to abide by its commitments. This ability arises as private organizations act to protect their interests in the differentiation and autonomy of public institutions, such as courts and the central bank.[5] In this way, independent elite organizations are not only a source of economic development, but their presence also allows more sophisticated institutions and organizations to mature within the government. On the other hand, without more complex public sector institutions, like courts, independent private organizations cannot prosper.

Mature LAOs are more resilient to shocks than fragile or basic LAOs. The public institutions of a mature LAO are capable, in normal circumstances, of lasting through both a range of changing circumstances and changes in the makeup of the dominant coalition. Nonetheless, strong shocks always have the possibility to cause breakdowns, and mature LAOs typically face intermittent crises. The extent to which mature LAOs have more durable government institutions than basic ones is a matter of degree rather than of kind.

Table 1.1 summarizes the spectrum of LAOs. Although the types can be ordered in a progression from least to most developed, the progression does not imply a teleology; societies do not inevitably move from fragile to basic or from basic to mature; indeed, many societies regress instead of progress while others stay as one type for decades or centuries. Further, some societies exhibit a mix of types – Colombia appears mature in Bogota and Medellin but fragile in many rural departments. Ecuador, Venezuela, and Russia seem to be regressing as they nationalize, inhibit, or outlaw

---

[5] The same process plays a more visible role in open access orders, where sophisticated private organizations in a market economy serve as a counterbalance to the government and other political organizations.

Table 1.1 *Types of limited and open access orders*

Type (Examples)	Economic Organizations (EOs)	Political Organizations (POs)	Violence Capacity (VC)
Fragile LAO (Afghanistan, the DR Congo, Haiti)	EOs and POs are not clearly distinguishable, except perhaps for multinational firms present in fragile LAOs.		All surviving organizations have VC. Civilian and military not clearly distinguished.
Basic LAO (USSR, Saudi Arabia, Tanzania 1970–90s, Mexico 1940s–80s)	All EOs – public or "private" – are linked with the coalition; some are also linked with multinationals.	Most POs are controlled by the state, for example, a one-party state or dictatorship. Opposition parties are under threat.	Many VC organizations are part of government, yet significant nongovernment organizations possess VC.
Mature LAO (Mexico since 1990s, Brazil, South Africa, India, China)	Many private firms, some multinationals. Effectively limited entry, requiring political connections.	Multiple POs, but dependent on central permission. Democratic process, if present, cannot challenge major economic powers.	Government controls most organizations with VC, but exceptions here are common.
OAO (Western Europe, USA, Canada, Japan)	Most are private. Nondiscriminatory rules for any citizen to start an EO and get government legal support.	Nondiscriminatory entry rules for any citizens to start or join a PO.	Civilian government controls all organizations with VC.

once independent organizations. Similarly, other societies fall into violence and regress, such as Somalia and Rwanda and the former Yugoslavia in the 1990s. Germany in the 1920s and 1930s regressed from a very mature LAO in 1913 to a basic LAO under the Nazis.

1.4 Development within LAOs

LAOs are not static. They often progress across the LAO spectrum, because the progression increases rents and elites can make themselves better off if they manage to retain power while moving from a fragile to a basic LAO or from a basic to a mature LAO. But many LAOs stagnate or regress. The reason is that all LAOs are vulnerable to internal shocks and to changes in the environment – relative prices, technology, demographics, external threats – that affect the relative power of elites. As relative power shifts, those gaining power naturally demand more rents. If all members of the dominant coalition agreed on how power has shifted, they would adjust the rents through peaceful bargaining. But when elites in an LAO disagree about relative power shifts, they may end up fighting, particularly if some elites believe they are stronger than others believe they are. Thus, LAOs often regress into disorder. At other times, changes in world prices that alter rent pools force or allow members of the dominant coalition to restructure their societies (as exhibited in the Philippines under Marcos and Venezuela under Chavez, both regressing). In short, LAOs frequently change even as they remain within the logic of limited access.

Three processes seem to be key for the maturation of an LAO; they are important advancements and are the basis for most of the recent reduction of world poverty: First, some LAOs bring more of the country's organizations with violence capacity into relationships that successfully reduce actual violence. This does not usually involve bringing all of them under the direct control of the government (in the Weberian sense of a state monopoly on violence).[6] Rather, it involves allocating the rent-generating activities in the LAO in a way that motivates organizations with violence capacity to refrain from actually using violence.

Second, other LAOs increase the scope of relationships in which rule of law is effectively maintained. Expansion of the rule of law is sustainable only when it is consistent with the arrangements that generate adequate incentives for organizations to restrain violence. Even when its scope is limited, having some rule of law seems to reduce violence and promote economic growth. Rule of law that covers all public relationships among elites arises late in the maturation process. It is even later that rule of law is extended to become effective for the wider population, and some aspects of rule of law may become universal before others.

---

[6] Complete consolidation of violence under control of the political system is an aspect of an LAO reaching the doorstep of transition to OAO. It means that only specialized organizations (military and police) may use violence and that these organizations are controlled by the government and follow explicit rules about the use of violence against citizens. This consolidated control over violence is a step in the separation of powers and purposes, which is a hallmark of stable and effective democracies (Cox and McCubbins 2000).

Third, LAOs also mature by increasing the reliability across time with which the government provides support for the organizations and enforces agreements among them. Strengthening organizations that make up the government – executive, legislative, military, police, dominant political parties, public sector unions – depends in part on strengthening organizations outside the state – private firms, opposition parties, and so forth. The organizations of the government achieve more coherence and credibility when the organizations independent of the state achieve enough strength and coherence to hold the state accountable for its commitments, independently of the individuals who initially made those commitments. As elaborated in the concluding "Lessons" chapter, a country is often at different stages on the three dimensions.

1.5 Open Access Orders, the Transition, and the Doorstep Conditions

To understand LAOs, we must also look at open access orders. OAOs are sustained by institutions that support open access and competition: political competition to maintain open access in the economy and economic competition to maintain open access in the polity. In OAOs, the Weberian condition holds, so that the government has a monopoly on violence, potential and actual. Organized violence is consolidated in military and police forces; other organizations are not allowed to use violence. Exemplifying the extensive credible commitments in OAOs, the political system controls the organizations – military and police – that have a monopoly on the legitimate use of violence.

An open access order fosters economic, political, and social groups that can organize and reorganize themselves at will to defend their interests in response to government policies and to pressure for change. In the presence of appropriate constitutional institutions, strong private organizations help to check the use of military and police force by the government.

Open access is sustainable in societies where entry into economic, political, religious, and educational activities is open to all citizens as long as they meet standard (impersonal) requirements. This access requires that the government supports forms of organizations in these areas and makes access to those forms open to all citizens. The rule of law must be enforced impartially for all citizens. The portion of the population enjoying open access need not be 100 percent in order to sustain open entry in economic and political systems, which points to the importance of defining citizens.

The *transition* from limited to open access orders has two features. First, within LAOs it is possible, following the logic of the LAO, for a mature LAO to develop institutional arrangements that enable impersonal exchange among elites. Second, the transition process begins when members of the dominant coalition find it in their interest to expand impersonal exchange and, therefore, incrementally increase access. The system changes from the logic of limited access rent creation to open access entry.

Historically, societies that developed sustainable property rights and rule of law began by making credible commitments to sustain those rights for elites. Later, as elite rights came to be defined impersonally, then it became possible to extend those rights to wider circles of society. Defining and enforcing legal rights occurred as societies developed sophisticated public and private elite organizations (i.e., becoming mature LAOs) and increased the range of credible commitments the state could make (NWW).

We identify three *doorstep conditions* that make impersonal relationships among elites possible:

1) Rule of law for elites.
2) Support for perpetually lived elite organizations (including the state), both public and private.
3) Consolidated political control of the organizations with violence capacity (including military and police forces).

These conditions are the culmination of the three dimensions of improvement within LAOs. Historically, the doorstep conditions built on one another in the first societies to move to open access. Although it is not clear whether the historical order of development is necessary, the two of our cases that are making the transition – Chile and South Korea – did achieve these conditions.

1) Rule of Law for Elites. The dominant coalition in every LAO is an adherent organization, a group of individuals and organizations bound together by mutual interests and threats. Their constant interaction inevitably gives rise to the possibility of regularizing behavior through rules, both informal and formal, governing specific relationships among the elite. Adjudicating disputes among elites is a fundamental part of sustaining relations among elites. In mature LAOs on the doorstep, these functions not only become formalized into a machinery of government and justice, but they also became operational for the elites. As mentioned earlier, the origin of property rights and legal systems is the definition of elite privileges in the LAO.

2) Perpetual Lived Forms of Elite Organizations. A perpetually lived organization lives beyond the life of its individual members. Because a partnership must be reformed on the death or withdrawal of any partner, a partnership is not perpetually lived. A corporation is a perpetually lived organization because its structure allows it to live beyond the life of the members who create it; no single member (excepting the case of a single individual with majority control) can dissolve the corporation at will. Organizations that exist at the pleasure of the current king or leader are therefore not perpetually lived. Perpetual life is not eternal life, but a life defined by the identity of the organization rather than the identity of its members. Perpetual life is a doorstep characteristic of both public and private organizations, and if a government cannot credibly commit to honor its agreements beyond the current dominant coalition, then it cannot commit to enforce the agreements of an elite organization whose life extends beyond the lives of its members. The second doorstep condition requires development of perpetual life for the government as the most important elite organization.

3) Consolidated Control of the Organizations with Violence Capacity. The third doorstep condition is consolidated control of the military, police, and other organizations with violence capacity. In LAOs, the government often lacks consolidated control of the military and the capacity for violence is dispersed throughout the elite. Consolidated control of the military requires the existence of an organization with control over all the military resources of the country; control over the various military assets is consolidated in that organization; and a set of credible conventions that determine how force is used against individuals and coalition members.

Consolidated control of violence capacity is a subtle problem. In some basic LAOs, a faction within the dominant coalition may gain monopoly control of military and police resources. But such an LAO is not a society on the doorstep, but is probably a tyranny, as Nazi Germany and the former Soviet Union illustrate. Moreover, societies where a single faction dominates the military are unlikely to sustain consolidated control for long, since the factions and groups in the dominant coalition without the means to protect themselves have no reason to believe that the commitments made to them will be honored. In most LAOs the absence of consolidated control of the organizations with violence capacity is simply a fact of life, as in Bangladesh, India, Mexico, and the Philippines. Therefore, one cannot expect these places to make a quick transition to open access. South Korea and Chile are the only ones among our cases that had achieved this condition by 2000, although each clearly had an earlier period when the civilian government did not control the military.

All three doorstep conditions are consistent with the logic of the LAO and arose historically within some limited access orders. The establishment of laws and courts is the means by which the dominant coalition regularizes relations among elites. Perpetually lived organizations are a vehicle for limiting entry and generating rents in a more systematic manner. Consolidating military power and other violence capacity under control of the political system creates a monopoly on violence that dramatically reduces the frequency of violence. Combined, the three doorstep conditions create the possibility of impersonal relationships within the elite.

Unlike the gradual distinctions among types of LAOs, the distinction between an LAO and an OAO seems to be a matter of substance rather than gradation. Unlike the historical pattern in which limited access societies move back and forth along the continuum between fragile, basic, and mature LAOs, the transitions from LAO to OAO have occurred rather quickly, usually over fifty years or less. So far in history none of the transitions to OAO has been reversed.

1.6 Case Study Countries

The concluding chapter discusses in detail the lessons from the nine country cases. Here we emphasize four commonalities that clearly stand out from the application of the LAO framework. The first commonality is the centrality of violence, its management, and prevention in the history of these countries. Violence is important not only in the interaction of formal military and police forces with the government but also in the presence of powerful nongovernment groups that threaten and use violence to affect the course of national affairs. In only three of the cases, Zambia, Mexico, and India, was the army under the control of the political system for the entire period under consideration; but violence capacity was not limited to the official organizations. Even in Korea and Chile, two of the more successful cases studied, the military at times took control of the government. In none of the societies considered has the government always maintained a monopoly on organized violence, although the degree to which nongovernment groups use or threaten violence varies widely.

The second commonality is the central place of organizations in structuring relationships within and between the polity, economy, and wider society. In every case, powerful groups enjoy the explicit and privileged support for their organizations – for example, unions and business elites in Mexico, *chaebols* in South Korea, and ruling families in Bangladesh and the Philippines. The privileges enable those organizations to act in the domestic and international economy under conditions that differ from their fellow citizens.

The third commonality is the pervasive use of rents to organize political and economic coalitions. Indeed the source of rents is often the privileges provided by the dominant coalitions of powerful interests. Social dynamics in limited access societies are driven by attempts on the part of dominant groups to seek rents, which efforts have important effects on growth and control of violence. Sometimes these goals are compatible and LAOs grow spectacularly, at least for a time; for example, the so-called Brazilian and Mexican miracles of the 1960s and the more recent East Asian miracles. At other times the institutions to reduce violence constrain growth. And sometimes the institutions that once reduced violence fail, with disastrous consequence for the well-being of all, as in Mozambique in the 1980s.

The fourth commonality is that none of these societies have been static. All of them have gone through significant changes, with some falling into violence. Nonetheless, except perhaps South Korea, they all remain limited access orders. The cases therefore illustrate the varieties of LAOs and how individual LAOs can exhibit remarkable change over time, sometimes being democratic, while at other times being authoritarian; sometimes growing and at peace while other times shrinking and mired in violence.

The case studies that make up this volume do not simply apply and confirm the existing LAO/OAO framework. They offer new insights that expand the framework. One set of comparisons results comes from the four regional groupings. We chose the comparison of South Korea and the Philippines in East Asia because they appeared to be in roughly the same circumstance in the 1950s, with the Philippines perhaps in a slightly better situation. Their courses have since diverged widely, as South Korea moved to become a more developed LAO and is now in the process of making the transition to an open access order. In contrast, the Philippines appears to have made some progress but then regressed toward the kind of LAO where personal connections and organizations play a larger role in a more unstable environment.

In South Asia, Maharashtra, West Bengal, and Bangladesh (former East Bengal) offer an intraregional comparison of different development trajectories coming from similar legal and institutional origins. Mexico and Chile have different outcomes today although they share the Latin American pattern of high inequality, important mineral export sectors, long histories of electoral processes, and periods of authoritarian rule. In Africa, Zambia, Mozambique, and the DR Congo all had periods of one-man, one-party rule starting shortly after independence, but they reached very different outcomes by the 2000s. Mozambique illustrates the difficulty and the possibility of achieving control over violence, while the DR Congo illustrates a situation in which violence and disorder have become more widespread. Zambia has had relatively little violence since independence.

Organizations provide a different set of comparisons. Some societies are capable of sustaining independent public and private organizations; South Korea and Chile have moved the farthest in this direction. They can be compared to societies with durable elite organizations that are, nonetheless, not independent of the ruling coalition – the *chaebols* in early Korea, Pemex in Mexico, and the sugar cane lobby in Maharashtra. These can be compared again to societies where powerful organizations require personal leadership and close coordination with the dominant coalition as in the Philippines, Bangladesh, or the DRC. In the cases, these differences in organizational characteristics appear to correspond with broader levels of economic and political development.

Another dimension of comparisons appears when we group countries by development outcomes. We have chosen this dimension to order the individual case studies. We begin with countries at the fragile end of the LAO spectrum – the DR Congo, Bangladesh, and Mozambique (along with Zambia). Then come the cases that are basic or mature LAOs but not yet on the doorstep – the Philippines, India, and Mexico. The last two cases – Chile and South Korea – have matured the most and achieved the doorstep conditions for transition to open access. The case studies represent societies moving toward better organized mature LAOs and perhaps toward open access, as well as societies regressing toward the basic and fragile, respectively, end of the LAO spectrum.

The concluding chapter draws lessons from the combined experience of the case studies. Readers may wish to go directly to the concluding chapter, or refer back to the introduction and "Lessons" chapters as they read the case studies. The development of the case studies, both individually and collectively, opened our eyes to the problem of development in limited access orders. We hope it will help you reframe the concept of development as well.

References

Acemoglu, Daron and Simon Johnson. 2008. "Unbundling Institutions," *Journal of Political Economy* (**113**): 945–95.

Acemoglu, Daron and James A. Robinson. 2006. "Economic Backwardness in Political Perspective," *American Political Science Rev.* **100**(1): 115–31.

Abernethy, David B. 2000. *The Dynamics of Global Dominance: European Overseas Empires, 1415-1980*. New Haven: Yale University Press.

Akerlof, George A. and Janet L. Yellen. 1990. "The Fair Wage-Effort Thesis and Unemployment." *Quarterly Journal of Economics*, **105**(2): 255–83.

Alston, Lee, Marcus Andre Melo, Bernardo Mueller, and Carlos Pereira. 2010. *The Road to Prosperity: Beliefs, Leadership and Windows of Opportunity: Brazil 1960-2010*. Manuscript.

Bates, Robert H. 1981. *Markets And States In Tropical Africa: The Political Basis Of Agricultural Policies*. Berkeley: University of California Press.

2001. *Prosperity and Violence: The Political Economy of Development*. New York: Norton.

Bhagwati, Jagdish. 1982. "Directly Unproductive, Profit-Seeking (DUP) Activities." *Journal of Political Economy*, **90**, 5 (October), pp. 988–1002.

Buchanan, James M., Robert D. Tollison, and Gordon Tullock. 1980. *Toward a Theory of the Rent-Seeking Society*. College Station, TX: Texas A&M Press.

Bueno de Mesquita, Bruce, Alastair Smith, Randolph M. Silverson, and James D. Morrow. 2003. *The Logic of Political Survival*. Cambridge, MA: MIT Press.

Collier, Paul. 2007. *The Bottom Billion: Why the Poorest Countries Are Failing and What Can Be Done About It*. Oxford and New York: Oxford University Press.

2009. *Wars, Guns and Votes: Democracy in Dangerous Places*. Harper-Collins.

Cox, Gary W and Mathew D. McCubbins. 2000. The Institutional Determinants of Economic Policy Outcomes," in S. Haggard and M. McCubbins, *Presidents, Parliaments, and Policy*. Cambridge: Cambridge University Press.

Easterly, William. 2001. *The Elusive Quest for Growth: Economists' Adventures and Misadventures in the Tropics*. Cambridge, MA: MIT Press.

Engerman, Stanley E. and Kenneth L. Sokoloff. 2005. "Colonialism, Inequality, and Long-Run Paths of Development," NBER Working Paper 11057.

Fukuyama, Francis. 2011. *The Origins of Political Order: From Pre-human Times to the French Revolution*. New York: Farrar, Strauss and Giroux.

Grindle, Merilee S. 2007. "Good Enough Governance revisited," *Development Policy Review*, **25** (5): 553–74.

Guinnane, Timothy W., Ron Harris, Naomi R. Lamoreaux, and Jean-Laurent Rosenthal. "Putting the Corporation in its Place," *Enterprise and Society* **8** (Sept. 2007): 687–729.

Haber, Stephen H., Herbert S. Klein, Noel Maurer, and Kevin J. Middlebrook. 2008. *The Second Mexican Revolution: Economic, Political, and Social Change in Mexico since 1980*. Cambridge: Cambridge University Press.

Haber, Stephen H., Armando Razo, and Noel Maurer. 2003. *The Politics of Property Rights: Political Instability, Credible Commitments, and Economic Growth in Mexico, 1876-1929*. Cambridge: Cambridge University Press.

Herbst, Jeffrey I. 2000. *States and Power in Africa: Comparative Lessons in Authority and Control*. Princeton: Princeton University Press.

Heston, Alan, Robert Summers, and Bettina Aten. Penn World Table Version 6.3, Center for International Comparisons of Production, Income and Prices at the University of Pennsylvania, August 2009.

Huntington, Samuel P. 1968. *Political Order in Changing Societies*. New Haven: Yale University Press.

Keefer, Philip and Razvan Vlaicu. 2008. "Democracy, Credibility and Clientelism," *Journal of Law, Economics and Organization* October 2008, **24**(2): 371–406.

Khan, Mushtaq H. 2004. "State Failure in Developing Countries and Strategies of Institutional Reform," in Tungodden, Bertil, Nicholas Stern, and Ivar Kolstad, ed. *Toward Pro-Poor Policies: Aid Institutions, and Globalization. Proceedings of the Annual Bank Conference on Development Economics.* Oxford: Oxford University Press and World Bank.

Khan, Mushtaq H. and K. S. Jomo, eds. 2000. *Rents, Rent-Seeking, and Economic Development: Theory and Evidence in Asia.* Cambridge, UK: Cambridge University Press.

Krueger, Anne. O. 1974. The Political Economy of the Rent-Seeking Society. *American Economic Review*, **64**, 3 (June), pp. 291–303.

Landes, David S. 1998. *The Wealth and Poverty of Nations: Why Some are so Rich and Some so Poor.* NY: W.W. Norton.

La Porta, Rafael, Florencio Lopez-de-Silanes, Andrei Shleifer, and Robert Vishny. 1999. "The Quality of Government," *Journal of Law, Economics, and Organization* (**15**:1).

Levi, Margaret. 1988. *Of Rule and Revenue.* Berkeley: University of California Press.

Mokyr, Joel. 1990. *The Lever of Riches: Technological Creativity and Economic Progress.* NY: Oxford University Press.

Moore, Mick. 2010. *An Upside Down View of Governance.* Brighton, UK: The Centre for the Future State.

North, Douglass C. 1981. *Structure and Change.* New York: W.W. Norton.

North, Douglass C., John Joseph Wallis, and Barry R. Weingast. 2009. *Violence and Social Orders: A Conceptual Framework for Interpreting Recorded Human History.* New York: Cambridge University Press.

North, Douglass C., John Joseph Wallis, Steven B. Webb, and Barry R. Weingast. 2007. "Limited Access Orders in the Developing World: A New Approach to the Problems of Development." World Bank Policy Research Paper No. 4359. Washington, DC.

Olson, Mancur. 1993. "Democracy, Dictatorship, and Development," *American Political Science Review*, **87**(3): 567–75.

Przeworski, Adam, Micael E. Alvarez, Jose Antonio Cheibub, and Fernando Limongi. 2000. *Democracy and Development: Political Institutions and Well-Being in the World, 1950–1990.* Cambridge University Press.

Rodrik, Dani. 2007. *One Economics, Many Recipes: Globalization, Institutions, and Economic Growth.* Princeton: Princeton University Press.

Shirley, Mary M. 2009. *Institutions and Development.* Cheltenham, UK: Edward Elgar.

Spiller, Pablo T. and Mariano Tommasi. 2007. *The Institutional Foundations of Public Policy in Argentina.* Cambridge: Cambridge University Press.

Tilly, Charles. 1990. *Coercion, Capital, and European States, AD 990–1990.* Cambridge, MA: Basil Blackwell.

World Bank 2011. *World Development Report 2011: Conflict, Security, and Development.* Washington, DC: World Bank.

TWO

Bangladesh

Economic Growth in a Vulnerable LAO

Mushtaq H. Khan

Bangladesh was born out of two violent partitions, each caused by elites' inability to agree about the distribution of rents. It has subsequently struggled to achieve political stability based on different mechanisms of rent distribution among its elites. In the midst of quite significant instability, its economic performance improved in the 1980s. Its experience therefore provides interesting case study material to examine and elaborate the LAO framework. The geographical territory of Bangladesh, then called East Pakistan, was first carved out of the eastern agrarian hinterland of Bengal in 1947 when British colonial rule ended. Unlike West Bengal, which remained in India and which was significantly industrialized at that time, East Bengal was almost entirely an agrarian economy growing rice and jute. In the 1960s, after very limited industrialization had been achieved, another set of violent confrontations between incumbent and emergent elites in Pakistan culminated in 1971 in the independence of East Pakistan, from that point forward known as Bangladesh. In more recent years, Bangladesh has emerged as a relatively high-growth developing country with a significant manufacturing base rooted in the garments and textile industries. But it has an apparently dysfunctional governance structure and political system with frequent political standoffs between the major political parties. We will examine the evolution of the LAO in Bangladesh as a transition between three variants of a basic LAO to a fourth and final version that has elements of maturity but is vulnerable and faces problems in enabling and sustaining sophisticated productive organizations. Indeed we will argue that there appears to be a tension between the capacity of LAOs in very poor countries to achieve sustainable political stability based on the accommodation of political organizations and their ability to assist the development of productive organizations.

This analysis confronts the good governance reform agenda, which has informed much of the reform efforts in the country but with very limited results in terms of achieving better scores on "good governance." The paradox of poor scores on the good governance criteria and sustained growth over two decades has generated two types of responses. The dominant response has been to argue that growth in Bangladesh cannot be sustained unless progress on good governance is achieved rapidly. On the other hand, the inaction and lack of commitment of the ruling elites to implement any of these reforms suggests that their private assessment is quite different. Their actions suggest that the good governance agenda does not address their day-to-day problems of accumulation and political management.

Both responses are partially correct but also wrong in important respects. Improving governance is clearly necessary for sustaining growth given the vulnerability of growth in countries like Bangladesh. But the governance priorities may not be the ones that the good governance agenda identifies. Equally, the good governance agenda clearly does not give elites a workable reform agenda because it ignores the problem of how to maintain political stability in developing countries. But business as usual is just as dangerous for elites because the social order that has emerged is vulnerable and critical weaknesses need to be identified and addressed. The LAO framework focuses on how rents are allocated to achieve a cessation of violence. Some of these ways of achieving political stability may be more successful than others in the context of particular countries, and some may offer more growth opportunities than others. These differences need to be explored from a policy perspective to develop policy priorities that simultaneously address the political requirements of controlling violence and the economic requirements of sustaining growth.

The difficulty of achieving improvements in terms of good governance has a lot to do with the fact that rent creation is necessary to satisfy powerful elites, often outside the structure of rules of the formal state. While the allocation of rents to achieve political stability is clearly vital, some methods of rent allocation have failed to achieve peace and stability, and some types of rents have been very damaging for the economy. Other methods of rent allocation have achieved some measure of stability, and some types of rents have enhanced growth or have at least been consistent with the continuation of growth. By examining some of these differences in the political and economic effects of different patterns of rent allocation we can improve our understanding of how the LAO in Bangladesh has performed and evolved in response to this performance. Reform strategies are likely to have a better chance of implementation if they are based on a proper understanding of the challenges facing the operation of an LAO in a specific country. The challenge is to design incremental institutional and organizational changes that improve the ability of competing elites to develop "live and let live" strategies that also allow growth to be sustained if not accelerated.

The evolution of the LAO in Bangladesh has gone through five major phases that are summarized in Table 2.1. The first phase was one of constitutional crisis following independence from British rule in 1947, a crisis that persisted until 1958. *Pakistan inherited a basic LAO but it faced a growing risk of a descent into fragility during this period.* The partition of British India created a truncated state of India and the unique state of Pakistan consisting of two wings separated by more than a thousand miles of India. The partition left the successor states, particularly Pakistan, facing a monumental human and economic crisis. There were sporadic outbursts of violence, but at the heart of the constitutional crisis in Pakistan was the absence of a power-sharing formula between East and West Pakistan. Elites in the two wings did not share a joint history of state-building aspirations. A viable ruling coalition that included representative members of the elites from the two wings simply could not be constructed. The ruling coalition that created Pakistan and its use of the state apparatus it inherited had many characteristics of a basic LAO but with significant potential for fragility. The threat of fragility undoubtedly assisted ambitious military and bureaucratic personnel to find an authoritarian solution to the constitutional problem.

The second phase that followed was characterized by military governance from 1958 until 1971, when Pakistan was again partitioned to create the new state of Bangladesh out of its eastern wing. For Bangladesh, much of the Pakistan period was this period of military rule. *We characterize this phase of the LAO from 1958 to 1971 as a "military-authoritarian" basic LAO.* Here the dominant coalition was tightly defined by a military-bureaucratic coalition and its close business clients and allies. The most important rents were access to critical subsidies to enter productive activities and these were allocated from above to a small number of business houses. Political rents were distributed to a broad group of rural political representatives, bypassing traditional political organizers. The opposition of the latter was countered with the threat of force. Rent allocation from above gave this military-authoritarian period a praetorian character. There was a significant improvement in the organizational sophistication of a small number of emerging capitalist sectors in the previously rather primitive economy. Many "learning rents" were created for infant industries and early industrialization was therefore rapid. However, the management of these rents was

Table 2.1 *The evolution of the social order in Bangladesh*

Partition and Constitutional Crisis (1947–58) (Basic LAO with risk of fragility)	• Birth of Pakistan in 1947 • Partition of India causes refugee and economic crisis • Constitutional crisis of power sharing between East Pakistan (Bangladesh) and West Pakistan
Military Authoritarianism (1958–71) (Basic LAO)	• Military-bureaucratic coalition controls rents • Electoral "Basic Democracy" with limited entry • Growth of industry based on rents for infant industries but long-term efficiency low • Unequal access for East Pakistani elites • Victory of East Pakistani Awami League in the 1970 elections leads to war and independence when West Pakistani elites prevent the formation of a government
Failed Populist Authoritarianism (1971–5) (Collapsing Basic LAO-Fragile LAO)	• Bangladesh born in 1971 • Weak dominant party begins to lose control over asset-grabbing party members and rebellions outside the party • Appropriation by powerful groups contributes to crisis but at the same time Bengali asset-owning class emerges • Widespread violence and uncertainty • Attempt t o institutionalize basic LAO in one-party state results in greater fragility and military coup
Authoritarian Clientelism (1975–90) (Basic LAO with features of maturity)	• Rent distribution within competitively formed parties constructed under military-authoritarian leadership • Controls over competing political organizations relaxed • Privatization and liberalization encourage setting up of economic organizations outside the dominant coalition • Growth led by new sectors like garments and textiles benefiting from global rent allocation (the MFA)
Competitive Clientelism (1990–) (LAO with more features of maturity but also vulnerable to fragility)	• Multiparty democracy without overall control by military-authoritarian leadership • Formal (and substantive) capabilities to set up economic and political organizations outside dominant coalition • Electoral crises and violence when "live and let live" compromises between competing factions collapse • Military-backed emergency government of 2007–8 wasted opportunities of reform by attempting to institutionalize Weberian good governance

not very effective because political organizers were becoming increasingly powerful and could protect inefficient industrialists even in the context of the praetorian LAO. But the real failure of the praetorian LAO was that by excessively limiting the access to rents it failed to maintain long-term political stability and Pakistan collapsed into catastrophic violence out of which Bangladesh was born in 1971.

The *third phase, from 1971 to 1975, was a period of intensely unproductive "primitive accumulation" and a failed attempt to institutionalize a one-party populist authoritarianism.* This period had the formal characteristics of a basic LAO, and in particular, the attempt to create a one-party state aimed to institutionalize a rigid version of a basic LAO. But in reality, this was a period of increasing fragility, with high levels of overt violence and a free-for-all in the economy as powerful groups grabbed resources abandoned by the previous regime. Primitive accumulation refers to the grabbing of assets and resources using political and organizational power. As a large number of previously excluded political organizers entered the rent capture game during this period, rent capture was extensive and damaging as asset stripping, overemployment, and other types of damaging rent creation accelerated. Neither economic nor political viability was achieved as the central leadership lost control over all rents. The belated response of nationalist leader Sheikh Mujibur Rahman was to attempt to control rent capture by constructing a more inclusive but still centrally controlled LAO in the form of a one-party "socialist" state. This too catastrophically failed as violence escalated and Mujibur Rahman and most of his family were assassinated. The support for and opposition to Mujib's one-party plan was couched in terms of a debate about planning and socialism, but more mundane issues of rent allocation underpinned these debates. While a broad sweep of political organizers were to be included in the state party under this plan, it was clear that there were not enough rents to satisfy everyone. There were too many powerful organizers relative to the available rents and all could not be accommodated using an inclusive populist strategy of constructing a one-party state. Most organizers, particularly those from other parties asked to join the new single party, feared they would permanently remain minor players. There was serious opposition to the plan not only from outside but also from within the ruling Awami League.

The *fourth phase, from 1975 to 1990, we characterize as "authoritarian clientelism" where military leaders formed parties and ruled through rent distribution within competitively constructed parties and with occasional elections.* The broad principles on which the competition for rents is organized in contemporary Bangladeshi politics began to emerge during this period. Ziaur

Rahman, president from 1977 until his assassination in 1981, was a popular freedom fighter and his presidency was quite different from that of his successor, Ershad, who ruled from 1982 until his overthrow in a mass uprising in 1990. Nevertheless, there are some common features of the period as a whole. These were basic LAOs, but with increasing characteristics of openness and maturity because the new military rulers realized that the earlier praetorian approach of defining a narrow dominant coalition from above would not work any longer. The new clientelistic logic was to selectively include enough political organizers in the dominant coalition to minimize the required threat of force to an acceptable level. And by not attempting to block organizational rights and capabilities of outside political organizers, they also avoided the mistake of inclusive populist authoritarianism. Dissatisfied organizers could build organizations outside the ruling coalition, biding their time. Earlier praetorian strategies of going over the heads of established political organizers to try and empower new layers below them through strategies of decentralization continued to be attempted.

The combination of these strategies ensured considerably greater access for political organizers and political organizations outside the ruling coalition compared to the praetorian phase of military rule in the 1960s. Zia reintroduced multiparty elections in 1979, which his Bangladesh Nationalist Party won. However, given presidential control over the army and the administration, politics in this phase was essentially about negotiating inclusion into the dominant coalition led by the ex-military leader. This model proved unviable under Ershad, who did not enjoy anything like Zia's popularity or legitimacy. The military clientelistic period came to an end in 1990 with the overthrow of Ershad after months of street protests and violence. This marked the transition to a version of multiparty democracy under which the opposition has a real chance of winning and establishing a new dominant coalition consisting of a different set of individuals and coalitions having privileged access to the most significant rents.

Another important characteristic of the 1980s was that a gradual economic turnaround began after the devastation of the war and the damage caused by destructive rent extraction from productive enterprises. Zia and Ershad began the process of privatization that slowly began to reduce asset stripping from productive enterprises. But given the weakness of regulatory agencies and property rights, the privatized enterprises were initially only marginally better in terms of economic performance. Nevertheless, the separation of economic from political rents reduced the most damaging types of predatory rents in the economy. It also allowed the emergence of the garment industry, which President Zia was directly involved in establishing.

Economic organizations in these new sectors could be set up without direct support from the dominant coalition and began to drive growth in the economy. Fortunately for Bangladesh, the garment industry was a beneficiary of accidental rents created for countries like Bangladesh by the quotas set by the MFA for more advanced garment exporters. These rents created the incentives and the opportunities for the transfer of critical technological capabilities to Bangladesh. The experience of the garment industry suggests that even low-technology sectors face market failures that constrain the transfer of technology. The accident of the MFA was particularly fortunate for Bangladesh because the dominant coalition was no longer attempting to assist the creation of new productive organizations. The rent strategies of the dominant coalition were mainly focused on political stabilization, in contrast to the strategies employed by leaders of the praetorian LAO of the 1960s, who directly allocated rents to emerging capitalists in an attempt to accelerate industrialization and growth.

The fifth (and current) phase, from 1990 onward, can be described as "competitive clientelism," which sustains a vulnerable semi-mature LAO. This has many characteristics of maturity as political organizations can be set up and operated to challenge the ruling coalition, and the support of the dominant coalition is not a precondition for setting up many types of economic organizations but there is simultaneously significant fragility at the margins. Competitive clientelism is our description of developing countries' democracies, though there are significant variations among developing countries (Khan 2010). Formally, and to a large extent in practice, the dominant coalition no longer controls the establishment of new organizations, including political organizations. Nevertheless, given the absence of a Weberian state enforcing a rule of law, the operation of organizations still requires assistance from political and state actors that has to be "purchased" on a personalized basis. Moreover, the elements of maturity may be limited for important rents (like the rents involved in major construction or power sector projects) that may be jealously controlled by the coalition currently in power. Similarly, the dominant coalition may keep tabs on and sometimes take steps against organizations (like television channels or organizations belonging to specific individuals or groups), often in very arbitrary ways. Nevertheless, for a broad range of organizations, there is a great deal of openness about who can set up these organizations, even though the support or nonintervention of the dominant coalition/state has to be indirectly purchased where required. Moreover, the dominant coalition can in principle and in practice be replaced by a new coalition if the opposition can organize a coalition with sufficient organizational power.

The latest phase of the LAO faces challenges in both the political and economic spheres. In the political sphere, party competition remains very vulnerable because "a rule of law for elites" has not emerged and parties periodically get locked in violent confrontations about how to conduct elections. In the economic sphere, greater openness has had some paradoxical effects. Since the dominant coalition can change, this can occasionally have negative results for investment. Where large and long-term investments are required, as in the power sector, investors are wary of the possibility that a new coalition may overturn previous contracts. On the other hand, sectors like garments, pharmaceuticals, and textiles can provide entrepreneurs and workers with opportunities to acquire the technological capabilities necessary to be globally competitive. Organizations in these sectors are also unlikely to threaten the rent extraction strategies of the dominant coalition. Setting up productive organizations in these sectors has elements of maturity. Support from the dominant coalition is no longer a precondition for setting them up. Interesting, these organizations are driving growth in contemporary Bangladesh. Nevertheless, acquiring technological capabilities in completely new sectors faces significant market failures. Without a strategy for addressing these market failures, the emergence of new medium-sized productive organizations in new sectors is effectively constrained. Since responding to market failures typically involves the creation of policy-induced rents, the failure here is essentially a failure to create and manage productive rents. In the subsequent sections we look at the five phases of the evolving social order in Bangladesh in more detail.

2.1 Partition and Constitutional Crisis: 1947–1958

Pakistan was created in 1947 out of some of the least developed agrarian parts of India. The deep political and economic crisis in Pakistan at the end of British rule was not accidental. The economic underdevelopment of the largely agrarian regions that became Pakistan was bad enough but, in addition, trade links with industrial areas elsewhere in India were severed as a result of the partition. The reasons behind the political crisis were even deeper. A constitutional crisis in the newly independent Pakistan was almost inevitable given the way in which the country was created. East Pakistan was poorer and less developed and had virtually no indigenous capitalists, and virtually no senior bureaucrats or army officers. West Pakistan too was underdeveloped compared to more advanced areas of India, but many of the immigrant Muslim businessmen and senior bureaucrats from other parts of India settled in West Pakistan as they were culturally closer to that region. The army too was largely drawn from the Punjab region of West Pakistan. *The basic LAO inherited by Pakistan/Bangladesh was threatened by a collapse into fragility as a result of intense disagreements among elites over the constitutional arrangements for sharing power between the two wings of the country.*

The irony behind the creation of Pakistan was that it had not been a significant aspiration for elites in *either* wing of what became Pakistan. Pakistan was carved out of the two most important Muslim-majority areas of India: Punjab (whose western part was to dominate West Pakistan) and Bengal (whose eastern part became East Pakistan). Neither had been strongly behind the idea of Pakistan before 1947 for good reason. The demographic dominance of Muslims in these provinces meant that Muslims already enjoyed substantial power under the electoral system introduced by the British in 1936. The demand for Pakistan came from Muslim political elites in central and western India where Muslims were a minority. In particular, Jinnah used the demand for Pakistan as a bargaining tool to try and achieve a guarantee of federalism, which he believed would ensure that Muslims all over India could exercise significant voice in an independent India (Jalal 1985: 258). When Nehru and the Congress Party failed to reach an agreement with Jinnah along these lines, and particularly after Nehru rejected the Cabinet Mission Plan proposal for a federal structure for India in 1946, Muslim elites all over India began to lose confidence in the intentions of Nehru and the Congress and Pakistan suddenly became inevitable.

But Jinnah's Muslim League was not organizationally strong in either Bengal or Punjab and faced serious problems in trying to cobble together a Pakistani state. West Pakistan's largely Punjabi elites soon discovered that they were the dominant group in the new state and this encouraged many of them to buy into the idea of Pakistan. In contrast, East Pakistan elites remained embroiled in conflicts with the central leadership. At its heart this conflict was over who had the power to create and allocate rents in the new state. East Pakistan had a majority of the population of Pakistan, and so its political organizers potentially had significant power, even the power to dominate Pakistani politics. But West Pakistan was dominant in terms of military, bureaucratic, and economic power. As a result of these tensions, the new state of Pakistan faced serious conflicts among elites from the outset, and a decade of constitutional discussions failed to resolve the question of how rents should be distributed among these competing groups.

The central problem was that the relatively poorer and less developed East Pakistan had a bigger population (at that time), making it difficult for the economically dominant West Pakistani elites to feel confident that they could ensure their political dominance through any electoral system. And though East Pakistan was relatively underdeveloped compared to the West, its political organizers were more organized as it had a longer history of political mobilization against colonial rule. Moreover, rich peasants in East Bengal had been in power in the British province of Bengal since the 1936 reforms that allowed political parties led by rich peasants (like the secular Krishok Proja Party) to win elections and form provincial governments. These asymmetries in the economic, political, and organizational capabilities of the elites of the two wings created insuperable difficulties in constructing a constitutional settlement. The military coup of 1958 was the almost inevitable result.

2.2 Military Authoritarianism: The "Praetorian" Basic LAO: 1958–1971

While both political stability and economic viability were of concern to the early civilian leadership of Pakistan, for the military leadership that took power in 1958, achieving economic viability was a priority. From their perspective, the survival of the country depended on military strength and that in turn required a viable economy (Jalal 1990). Political stability was to be achieved mainly through the suppression of organizational rights. As in the rest of South Asia, the fifties and sixties in Bangladesh/Pakistan were a period of catching up under ambitious industrial policies, but in this case under a tightly controlled dominant coalition. *The praetorian basic LAO kept in place a dominant coalition from 1958 to 1971 with a focus on creating more sophisticated productive organizations in modern industry. A secondary objective was to use rents to maintain political stability, but in a context where force was the primary mechanism for limiting access to rents to a narrow group.*

This strategy was ultimately misconceived because it did not adequately assess the strength of the opposition that could be organized by excluded rent-seeking groups. While there was a growing mobilization of excluded elites in both wings of Pakistan, the mobilization in East Pakistan was explosive because state policies during this period discriminated against East Pakistan as a whole. Rent allocation to East Pakistan primarily benefited non-Bengali entrepreneurs to set up industries in East Pakistan. Emerging Bengali elites were largely excluded from the dominant coalition and unsurprisingly perceived the state strategy as one of national suppression. Their distributive conflict with the dominant non-Bengali political, military, and business elites based in West Pakistan eventually erupted in a massive breakdown of the social order, an outbreak of significant violence, and the emergence of the independent nation of Bangladesh.

An important feature of the basic LAO that this experience reveals is that it can only be stable if, by accident or design, enough of the potential organizers of violence are included within the ruling group. Pakistan's military government in the 1960s was more concerned with accelerating development and less with stability, clearly because in its judgment potential violence by excluded elites could be contained by the state given its overwhelming asymmetry in terms of instruments of violence. This judgment could not have been more wrong. Power in the context of civilian confrontations depends on the relative ability to organize large numbers of people to protest or vote in particular ways and here a monopoly of violence is not a sufficient guarantee of political stability in the long term. Ignoring the claims of powerful political organizers in Pakistan resulted in a growing and increasingly violent mobilization in both wings that eventually brought down the military government and led to the emergence of the new country of Bangladesh.

The coup led by Ayub Khan in 1958 established a military-authoritarian regime that can be described as a tightly controlled basic LAO. Its praetorian character came from its explicit threat of violence to limit access to rents. Martial law was imposed to curtail organizational freedoms to set up political organizations. All significant rents were allocated from above. The dominant coalition consisted of the military-bureaucratic elites and their close business allies. For a while, the threat of force disrupted the ability of excluded organizers to pose a significant threat to the dominant coalition. At the same time, by controlling exchange and interest rates, setting tariffs and quotas, and controlling the access to foreign exchange, the state created rents for privileged business elites. The initial effect was not only the achievement of greater political stability but also a sustained growth spurt that lasted through much of the 1960s. However, much of the rents that the state created and controlled were focused on establishing and promoting relatively sophisticated enterprises in new sectors. Controls over imports, an overvalued exchange rate (that made machinery imports cheap), and export subsidies that compensated for the overvalued currency built a structure of rents that created strong incentives for investment. Both import substituting and export industries developed and incentives were created for absorbing and learning to use new technologies. The early import substitution was primarily in textiles, generally of low capital intensity, but growth followed in other industries like chemicals, food industries, and light manufacturing (Papanek 1967: 1–74).

Though the state did not yet have the resources to provide rents in the form of direct subsidies to industrialists, the combination of an overvalued exchange rate, import controls, and rationing of scarce foreign exchange amounted to very significant hidden subsidies to investors in new machinery. Papanek reported that profits of 50 percent to 100 percent a year were not uncommon in the early to mid-fifties (Papanek 1967: 33). Access to foreign exchange licenses was a critical part of realizing these rents, and this in turn required close relationships among business, political, and bureaucratic elites. The basic LAO was based on and further developed the personal contacts that existed between the ruling Muslim League leadership and a small number of traders, dating back to the pre-partition days. "Nation Building Companies" like the Mohammadi Steamship Company and Habib Bank Limited had been established by these traders in India in alliance with the Muslim League, and they provided obvious candidates when individuals or companies had to be offered industrial projects (Rashid and Gardezi 1983: 1–8).

The military regime built on a number of agencies set up in the very early years of the state. A month after independence in 1947 from Britain, an industries conference was convened where various forms of assistance were offered to businessmen but the response was very poor. Partly as a result of this disappointment, in 1952 the Pakistan Industrial Development Corporation was set up with the objective of establishing enterprises and then divesting them at attractive prices to risk-averse owners in the private sector. Four members on its board came from the leading business houses, and the first head of the corporation, an enterprising public servant named Ghulam Faruq, went on to become one of the leading industrialists of the country. This arrangement allowed businesses to capture rents by getting the state to absorb all the risks of setting up a new plant, in particular absorbing the costs of training employees in new skills. The relationship between business and government had always been close, and the levels of accumulation and growth in the industrial sector were commensurate.

Also established in the early years were the key financial institutions that would finance investments by new entrepreneurs in new industries that did not yet have a track record and therefore would not be standard risks for normal banks. These were the Pakistan Industrial Credit and Investment Corporation (PICIC) and the Pakistan Industrial Finance Corporation (later Industrial Development Bank of Pakistan, IDBP), which were to assume great importance in later years (Alavi 1983: 46–50; Amjad 1983: 235–50). By providing low-interest loans to entrepreneurs with inadequate collateral and experience, significant rents were allocated to businesses patronized by

Table 2.2 *Growth in East Pakistan/Bangladesh 1950–80*

	Manufacturing	Industry	Agriculture
1950–5	9.5	11.5	2.4
1955–60	8.5	8.6	0.3
1960–5	10.6	17.4	3.2
1965–70	5.3	7.7	2.8
1970–5	−9.8	not available	not available
1975–80	5.1	5.9	3.3

Sources: Alamgir & Berlage (1974: apdx C, table 4; apdx 14-A), World Bank (1984, 1986).

the dominant coalition. Although these two institutions allocated about a fifth of total investible resources, leading businessmen from the monopoly houses were represented on the boards of all the state financial institutions and the boards of directors of other monopoly houses (Amjad 1982: 30–60, 1983: Table 9.7).

These agencies grew in importance under military rule. A small number of monopoly houses with close links to the ruling coalition benefited enormously. From 1958 to 1970, PICIC allocated 44.7 percent of its loans to thirteen monopoly houses, and even the IDBP, which focused on loans below 2.5 million rupees, allocated 31.9 percent to thirty monopoly houses between 1961 and 1970 (Amjad 1982: 51). By the late 1960s, the top eighteen business groups controlled thirty-five percent of industrial assets while the top forty-four controlled around fifty percent (Amjad 1982: 47). As a result of family cross-holdings, the figure for the percentage of assets controlled by the top families was even higher. In the popular press, the top twenty-two families became the butt of attacks as according to some calculations these families controlled most of the new productive assets in the country. Thus, by the late 1960s, limited access in the economy had a figure: twenty-two families. Table 2.2 shows growth rates in different sectors between 1950 and 1980. The initially high growth rates proved to be unviable, largely because many of the higher technology firms supported with (learning) rents never graduated to self-sufficiency. Perhaps more of them may have survived if given more time, but political crises led to the abandonment of these strategies by the late 1970s.

The economic success of Pakistan in the 1960s led some observers, such as Gustav Papanek, a Harvard Advisory Group economist working on Pakistan, to publicize Pakistan as a new model of growth (Papanek 1967: 2).

With the benefit of hindsight, the weakness of Papanek's analysis was that this acceleration of growth depended on the political sustainability of the state's ability to direct vast quantities of resources into the hands of a tiny emerging capitalist class during the late fifties and early sixties. The early results of growth in Papanek's statistics concealed the fact that these accumulation strategies were based on a vulnerable basic LAO and the state had very limited capacities to govern these subsidies to ensure that productivity growth was rapid enough to make the investments viable.

First, as in India, the state's governance capabilities for limiting moral hazard problems were not sufficiently developed. The result was that even by the late sixties, new enterprises set up a decade ago had not graduated to the point where they could become globally competitive without the implicit rents continuing. The popular perception therefore was that this was a strategy for enriching privileged groups. The second weakness, closely connected to the last, was the failure to develop a broad-based Bengali capitalist class in East Pakistan/Bangladesh. The weakness of the Bengali bourgeoisie is reflected in Table 2.3 since much of the growth in industrial investments in East Pakistan initially took place through a growth in the public sector, peaking at fifty-three percent of total investments in 1968. With the benefit of hindsight, the praetorian LAO failed to allocate sufficient rents to potential organizers of violence and allocated too many rents to client capitalists, a group that included almost none from the eastern wing. An emerging alliance between excluded business interests and excluded political interests in East Pakistan proved to be devastating for the stability of the regime.

Nevertheless, there was some growth of a Bengali industrial capitalist class in this period, even if concentrated in medium enterprises. At the time of the independence of Bangladesh in 1971, one study found sixteen large Bengali business houses, each with assets of more than Rs. 25 million and with combined assets of nearly Rs. 700 million (S. Baranov, cited in Sobhan [1980: 15]). The Pakistani rupee was roughly equal to 4.8 dollars U.S. at that time. The bulk of the nascent industrial bourgeoisie was, however, small to medium entrepreneurs. Excluding the large jute and textile industries, state financial institutions funding the establishment of enterprises had, by 1971, given over three thousand loans to Bengalis, most below Rs. 400,000, helping to set up around thirteen hundred units (Sobhan and Ahmad 1980: 64–5). However, a much bigger group of the Bengali lower middle classes felt totally excluded. These classes provided the political entrepreneurs and organizers who led an increasingly successful mobilization against the dominant coalition.

Table 2.3 *Industrial investment in West and East Pakistan 1961–71*

	1961	1962	1963	1964	1965	1966	1967	1968	1969	1970
West Pak	852.94	846.15	757.05	1062.50	1221.43	1087.96	987.16	1013.79	916.87	1061.36
%Public Sector	5.1	3.9	15.6	3.2	9.8	10.8	10.9	11.6	8.3	3.2
East Pak	205.99	459.42	332.21	382.30	450.21	390.00	477.02	799.81	796.84	700.88
%Public Sector	21.7	13.8	29.8	24.3	24.3	25.0	24.8	53.0	50.7	45.7
All Pak	1058.9	1305.6	1089.3	1444.8	1671.6	1478.0	1464.2	1813.6	1713.7	1762.2

Note: Million Rupees in Constant 1960 Prices.
Source: Amjad (1982: table A.9). The Pakistan rupee was equal to USD 4.8 at that time.

The military-authoritarian regime misjudged the strength of these excluded groups and their ability to mount a significant challenge. The praetorian order had kept an eye on rent distribution for political stability but it was far too inadequate. The major institutional mechanism for purchasing stability was the so-called basic democracy system that Ayub innovated with the Basic Democracies Order of 1959, one of the first acts of his regime. This attempted to bypass the established political elites in the towns by creating a new constituency of rent recipients in the villages. Eighty thousand "basic democrats" were elected on a non-party basis and they were the electoral college for electing members of parliament. Authoritarian regimes have often used this tactic of going over the heads of their immediate opponents by appealing to the interests of those below them. The latter initially demand a lower price and the authoritarian leader often believes they will be easier to control. The basic democrats also directly elected the president. The provision of relatively limited rents to this large army of rural representatives through rural infrastructure construction programs and Food for Work programs was for a time sufficient to create a countervailing source of support for the regime that made it difficult to organize dissent (Sobhan 1968).

In the end, the basic democracy plan was self-defeating. As the rural basic democrats became more confident and ambitious, they saw obvious opportunities in throwing their lot in with the growing dissent in the towns. When this began to happen in the late 1960s, not only did the "hot house" development in this LAO come under threat, the social order was fundamentally challenged as there were no easy ways of incorporating enough excluded elites into the system quickly enough. Under pressure in both wings of Pakistan, the military government allowed elections in 1970 that gave the East Pakistan-based Awami League an absolute majority in the all-Pakistan parliament as the East had a majority of seats in the central legislature. This led to an even more serious constitutional crisis for Pakistan as West Pakistani elites were unwilling to let an East Pakistan party form the government. The last desperate act of the praetorian LAO was a bloody crackdown on political organizers and their intellectual supporters in East Pakistan in March 1971. As the conflict became increasingly violent, the basic LAO rapidly collapsed into a fragile one. Ultimately, the social order could not be sustained and as the civil war intensified and transformed into a war for liberation and independence, Pakistan's historic enemy India intervened to assist the Bengali struggle for independence and the independent country of Bangladesh was born in 1971.

2.3 The Rise and Fall of a
"Populist Authoritarian" Basic LAO: 1971–75

The political break of 1971 allowed the emergence for the first time of a direct relationship between upwardly mobile Bengali political entrepreneurs and the state. However, the long-excluded Bengali political entrepreneurs had an apparently limitless appetite for rents and as yet no entrepreneurial capabilities to productively operate any of the assets and resources they were capturing. The massive acceleration of asset and resource capture by politically powerful organizations was the "primitive accumulation" that had catastrophic consequences for economic rehabilitation after the war, which had been disruptive enough on its own. Nevertheless, it was through these processes that a new Bengali capitalist class was to emerge after a decade. *The third phase, from 1971 to 1975, was characterized by extensive and unproductive "primitive accumulation" and a failed transition to a one-party state. Formally the latter was an attempt to institutionalize a basic LAO but the period was marked by growing fragility.*

The huge upsurge in the numbers and demands of political entrepreneurs who now wanted a share of the rents made it difficult to construct a new social order. On top of the ravages caused by the conflict, the victory created a big gap between the aspirations of a multitude of organizers who had participated in (or claimed to have participated in) the freedom struggle and the rents available for them to capture. The Awami League as the dominant party had many features of authoritarianism from the outset as it was a broad coalition of powerful organizers, many of them armed, who used political and military power to capture abandoned assets, settle disputes among themselves, and prevent their collective power being challenged. Rent capture went beyond the usual forms of targeted subsidies to include very damaging types of "primitive accumulation" as abandoned assets were grabbed and sometimes stripped, and nationalized mills and factories were used to create rents in the form of unsustainable employment and pricing policies. Not surprising, this LAO suffered from growing fragility, with politically powerful factions and armed gangs grabbing resources openly. The last-minute attempt by nationalist leader Mujib to institutionalize his failing populist authoritarianism by creating a one-party state only served to exacerbate fragility and the basic LAO effectively collapsed.

Violence kept erupting because the distribution of rents between the vastly increased numbers of claimants could not be settled by any other obvious means. Central control over the party and the growing number of organizers outside the party could not be easily established. Individuals and groups who received less than they expected threatened to leave the party and engage in opposition or violence from outside unless they were accommodated on their terms. Unfortunately, accommodating all individuals and groups on their terms would add up to more redistribution than the economy could possibly sustain. The growing conflicts were expressed in a number of ideological debates between those who had fought or claimed to have fought in the war of liberation and those who for various reasons had not or could not, and between slightly different versions of the now dominant socialist ideological consensus. Behind these debates lay the concern about who would have the power to decide or limit the allocation of rents.

This situation was clearly unsustainable and the ruling party, the Awami League, attempted to reassert a basic LAO by creating a one-party state. In January 1975 the fourth amendment to the constitution was pushed through despite misgivings among many party members only when Prime Minister Mujib, leader of the liberation movement, threatened to resign (Karim 2005: 348). The constitutional amendment changed Bangladesh to a presidential system with power concentrated in the hands of Mujib, who became the president. The amendment also provided for the creation of a national party with the sole power to engage in political activity, and all members of parliament and the president had to belong to this party. In February all parties were suspended and the national party launched. This was the Bangladesh Krishok Sromik Awami League (Workers and Peasants Awami League) or BAKSAL (Mascarenhas 1986: 57). The plan had the strong support of the pro-Moscow faction of the communists as it fitted in with the blueprint of similar one-party experiments in other parts of the developing world then supported by Moscow. Socialist ideology aside, this was clearly also an attempt to reassert central control over rent allocation within a defined dominant coalition, in other words, to recreate an authoritarian one-party version of a basic LAO.

However, ideologies do matter. There was genuine disquiet about the plan from those who believed it was the thin end of the wedge that would convert the country into a planned economy of the Stalinist type. No doubt, the pro-Moscow communists' support for the plan was based on the same expectation. Nevertheless, the failure of this proposal to win the support of many of Mujib's key lieutenants was significant. Many people inside and outside the party saw the move as a logical culmination of steps toward an authoritarian protection of the rents of the ruling coalition. The 1973 election, though it resulted in a huge victory for the Awami League, had revealed the vulnerability of many of the top leaders of the party and their reelection was widely believed to have been achieved through interventions in the electoral process (Karim 2005: 305–8). Many of Mujib's henchmen and relatives were already deeply unpopular for their acts of appropriation and their blatant immunity from all legal restrictions.

As the opposition National Awami Party put it: "Pakistan's 22 families have become Bangladesh's 2000" (Karim 2005: 290). The party could have added that the rents of the two thousand were based entirely on expropriation and were not even remotely associated with learning new technologies or industrialization. The paramilitary Jatiyo Rakkhi Bahini (JRB) was increasingly used to protect Awami Leaguers from attack and also to intimidate voters during elections (Karim 2005: 273). The introduction of BAKSAL must be assessed in this context. While there was little public demonstration against the constitutional amendment, the climate of fear was not appropriate for the free expression of views. In secret, many different groups inside and outside the ruling party began to plot Mujib's violent removal (Mascarenhas 1986: 64). Mujib himself explained that the fourth amendment could not provide a permanent solution and was an emergency response to a situation going out of control: "This one-party arrangement is purely temporary. Once I have saved the country from counter-revolution I will restore multi-party democracy" (quoted in Karim 2005: 258). Mujib's most dangerous enemies were within his own party. Many rightist members of his cabinet and foreign embassies were aware that a strike was planned against him and his family (Lifschultz 1979; Mascarenhas 1986). And so it was that on August 15, 1975, less than four years after independence, the founding father and president of the new country was assassinated.

Independent of the betrayals and conspiracies, it is also clear that the plan to create a one-party state was deeply unpopular with many sections of the elite who were supposed to join together in an inclusive basic LAO. Since the viability of an LAO is that significant organizers of violence should have an incentive to desist from violence, the BAKSAL experiment was demonstrably a failure. The interesting question is why the attempt to define the dominant coalition in this way did not find broad support among the very group that it was trying to incorporate. The likely answers to this question have important implications for understanding the nature of the LAO that subsequently emerged in Bangladesh.

The essential problem with an attempt to impose order on rent allocation in poor countries using a one-party authoritarian structure is that there is no well-defined elite to begin with. Political accumulation in South Asia is a dynamic process in which sequential layers of political entrepreneurs are continuously emerging at all levels. One way of imagining this is to think of a multitude of patron-client organizations with conveyor belts in each taking enterprising individuals higher up and with individuals at higher levels occasionally making a transition from purely political accumulation to various combinations of political and economic accumulation as they begin to invest in productive enterprises of different types. A single authoritarian populist party is simply a coalition of a large number of patron-client organizations brought together in a larger coalition. Attempting to define rent allocation in a coherent way in this context faces two sorts of problems.

The first problem is to determine the distribution of rents between and within the different patron-client organizations that together constitute the bigger coalition. If each of these organizations generated its own rents and the question was only about protecting the rents of each, the problem would be a lot simpler and the organizations could collectively provide third-party enforcement and protection of their individual rents. This may happen if all organizations were productive organizations or if the patrons of each organization were extracting rents solely from their own clients. But if a significant part of the rents of organizations were based on "primitive accumulation," each coalition is targeting the same pool of social resources for capture. In this case, the distribution of rents between organizations cannot be guaranteed by the organizations themselves. Each organization can no longer provide third-party enforcement for the rents of other organizations because there is likely to be a conflict of interest. Only a very strong leader could handle the arbitration of rent distribution between organizations and only if that leader had the support of most organizations most of the time.

Prior to the one-party experiment, the Awami League was facing a growing crisis in managing its intraparty distributive conflicts. Significant numbers of leaders within the party were disaffected and some were leaving. This was happening as early as 1972. In particular, the departure of a significant section of the left wing of the Awami League to form the Jatiyo Shomajtantrik Dal (JSD) in 1972 was significant. If the distribution between coalitions depends on the decision of a supreme leader, all coalitions have to be confident of their access to that leader, and the leader has to have sufficient authority to impose decisions once taken. The transition to a one-party structure has to be understood in this context. It is not clear that Mujib had the authority or the physical concentration of force to ensure that all individual organizers would come into the single-party structure and then accept the distribution of rents that the leader imposed. Historically, a sustainable one-party system requires a considerable concentration of the control over rents and of the instruments of force at the center and this was not in evidence in Bangladesh in 1975. Since all coalitions cannot be sure that the leader will treat them fairly *ex post*, and since leaving a constitutional single party is not legally possible, only coalitions already close to the leader would voluntarily agree to join the new system.

The second problem is to define the limits of the dominant coalition. There are potentially an indefinite number of political organizers who believe they have enough capacity to challenge the dominant coalition to deserve inclusion and a share of rents. However, the more organizers who are included, the smaller the rents that existing organizers can capture. The problem for a formal and well-defined dominant coalition like a one-party state is that it defines insiders and outsiders clearly and creates strong incentives for outsiders to unite against insiders. In the praetorian order, the insiders were not formally defined, but it was clear that a very small group was privileged. The political rents were broadly distributed but to less powerful organizers and achieved stability for a while. But the support purchased from 'basic democrats' together with the threat of force could not prevent powerful excluded organizers from opposing the system over time. The proposed one-party state defined a broader group as potential insiders but it defined the borders very clearly. This created strong incentives for all those who felt they may be excluded or may get an insufficient payoff to oppose the arrangement.

Apart from the difficulty of organizing primitive accumulation through a one-party state in the context of rapidly emerging elites, a further problem for the populist authoritarian model was that some of the primitive accumulation was already resulting in emergent capitalists who did not want the limitations of socialism. By 1974, appropriation had created a potential capitalist class who wanted opportunities to convert some of their acquisition into productive enterprises. They wanted property rights over their potential investments to be protected. Pressure from this group had already resulted in a revision of the government's socialist industrial policy. In 1974 the ceiling on private investment was increased from 2.5 million to 30 million takas. Partnerships with foreign private investors were allowed, and the moratorium on nationalization was increased from ten to fifteen years. The emerging capitalists were obviously not too excited by the prospect of a one-party state under which these changes may have been reversed. Some of the most successful accumulators under the Awami League thus became alienated from the party they had benefited from and constituted an internal rightist source of opposition to the proposed LAO.

It appears that viable, well-defined dominant coalitions like one-party states require either the military dominance of a leadership based on its control over a significant immediate flow of rents coming for instance from natural resource rents or it requires strong, broadly based party organizations that offer credible career paths for organizers to rise up the party hierarchy to benefit from a growing economy. Where the leadership already controls a significant flow of rents from, say, extractive resources, this can provide it with the military ability to deal with outsiders and offer enough to insiders to achieve political stability. Some oil-rich one-party states provide examples of this variant. Still, the calibration of the frontiers of the party is critical to ensure that the available force is sufficient to deal with potential dissent. Of course, the degree of concentration of force and rents required to make a one-party system of this type viable is not defined in absolute terms, but rather in relation to the organizational strength of potential organizations who are demanding rents by threatening violence.

Another variant that appears to work is the single party that is very broadly based and therefore not immediately offering significant rents to individuals lower down the organizational chain, but that can provide stable and credible career paths for aspiring organizers to move up the pyramid. To be credible, a party offering its organizers increasing rents over time implies that the party has access to rents from a growing real economy. This kind of strategy may therefore work if a well-organized party is operating a version of a developmental state, as in contemporary China. Mujib's BAKSAL had neither feature. It did not control enough resources immediately to create a cohesive coalition based on the control of rents and instruments of force at the center. Indeed, the party did not even fully control the army as Mujib had to build paramilitary forces to protect him, thereby further alienating the army. Mujib's assassins were mainly junior ex-army officers, though the conspiracy to remove him involved many others. Nor did the party have a credible development strategy and a strong internal organization that could allow it to offer stable career paths to its own political organizers by assuring them of a fair share of future rents.

The rents that competing coalitions of elites were trying to capture in Bangladesh are therefore also relevant. The fragility of the LAO was both a cause and a consequence of the fact that political appropriation at this time was largely unproductive. It was based on grabbing abandoned assets, appropriating public resources through the creation of excess employment, construction contracts, import contracts, and so on. These types of primitive accumulation create zero-sum rents that at best have no positive effect on production, and in many cases can have a significant negative effect. A major target of the appropriation was the assets abandoned by departing Pakistanis. But in the chaos, the assets of many Bangladeshis were also targeted, including assets of any group associated with the Pakistanis, such as the Bihari (non-Bengali) population. Not only that, the assets of many Hindus (who had never been supporters of Pakistan) were also grabbed (Karim 2005: 283–90).

The significant productive assets of West Pakistani capitalists like major factories could not be immediately privatized given the absence of Bengali entrepreneurs, but were nationalized by the state resulting in an increase in the state's share in modern industry from thirty-four percent to eighty-one percent. But even this was not enough for the new political order. The Presidential Order of March 1972 brought previously Bengali-owned factories in the jute, cotton, and sugar sectors into public ownership. This raised the public sector's share to no less than ninety-two percent of the assets of modern industry with a corresponding increase in the economic resources and jobs the state could allocate to its core supporters (Murshid and Sobhan 1987: 3–4; Sobhan and Ahmad 1980: table 10.1). Employment in the public services witnessed a dramatic expansion. At the time of liberation in 1971, there were 450,000 employees of all grades in the public services, of which only 320 were officers at the level of joint secretary or above. By 1973, total employment in the public services had increased to over 650,000, with officers in the higher grades increasing to 660 (World Bank 1984: 109). Some of this growth was due to the change in coverage from the inclusion of new industrial units within the public sector, which brought their administrative staff within the ambit of the public services. But the number of white collar staff in Bangladesh's small industrial sector would only account for a fraction of the increase.

Coalitions within the ruling party used their political power to enrich themselves directly (E. Ahmed 1986: 27; Umar 1980). Nurul Islam, an economist in the Planning Commission at that time describes some of the processes:

By 1974 there were a number of factors which had contributed to an accumulation of surplus funds in private hands. For one thing, high profits were earned in domestic and import trading activities, including illegal trade such as trade in contraband goods and in smuggling jute and other exportables across the border. Since these transactions were illegal, the risk premium was high and hence profits, once realised, were high. In addition, many residential buildings and trading or commercial enterprises, abandoned by Pakistanis, were illegally occupied by private persons. The "caretakers" of such commercial enterprises, hastily appointed by the government in 1972 immediately after independence, made large fortunes through the undeclared sale of assets. Moreover, there were gains to be obtained from rental or sales proceeds of the abandoned houses which were illegally occupied by private persons. Those who had accumulated financial resources were pressing the government to commit itself to a more substantial and permanent role for private enterprise in the economy of Bangladesh. (Islam 1979: 225–6)

This accelerated primitive accumulation had the expected negative effects on economic performance. An assessment of 1970–5 is difficult because of the very real disruptions caused by the war and the short life of the regime. Productivity in manufacturing was on average less than fifty percent of the level reached in 1970 and real wages in manufacturing were on average around sixty percent of their 1970 level (World Bank 1978: vol. II, annex I.6, p. 173; 1984: vol. II, table 9.12, p. 118). In addition, in 1974 Bangladesh suffered from a serious famine that took place without any significant decline in aggregate food availability (Sen 1983). The causes were largely state failure in managing distribution and ensuring purchasing power in a context of hoarding and smuggling. More than a million people died in the famine, probably more than in the war of liberation (Karim 2005: 335–40; Sen 1983: 134–41). The state could not of course remain insulated from the political consequences of the collapsing economy. The impetus for the "Second Revolution" and the creation of a one-party state came from the economic crisis and the need to control the expropriation, speculation, and smuggling destroying the economy.

2.4 Authoritarian Clientelism 1975–90

The problems of the first two phases help to explain many features of the transition that happened subsequently. Mujib's assassination brought the military to power through a series of bloody coups and countercoups. But the military leadership knew by now that neither the Pakistani praetorian model nor the authoritarian populist one-party model would work in Bangladesh. General Zia, who formally became president in 1977, was a decorated freedom fighter and widely popular. Nevertheless, he took care to construct a strong constituency of supporters for his rule. He did this by constructing a political party that eventually became the Bangladesh Nationalist Party (BNP), which remains one of the two dominant parties in contemporary Bangladesh. *The period from 1975 to 1990 was one of authoritarian clientelism when military leaders formed parties based on internal rent distribution and encouraged political competition to identify the most suitable factions for inclusion.* This strategy for constructing the dominant coalition had a number of important features distinct from the earlier phases.

First, the terms on which individual coalition leaders joined the dominant coalition were individually bargained. Individual organizers could join or depart from the dominant coalition depending on calculations of net benefits by the supreme leader and individual coalition leaders bargaining for entry. The terms of the bargaining were simple: the national leader wanted to incorporate the largest number of the most important organizers into the party at the lowest price in terms of the rents that they demanded. A broad ideology of development and nationalism defining the new party allowed individual organizers from the far left and right of the spectrum and everyone in between to seek terms for entry into the new dominant coalition. The price that individual leaders could extract depended on their proven organizational capabilities and the significance of their departure for undermining their erstwhile parties. As other parties were no longer banned, organizers had the chance of proving their organizational abilities outside the ruling party before seeking terms for incorporation. Opposition parties were allowed to set up, operate, and contest elections to demonstrate their organizational power. The only limitation was that it was implicitly clear that the top job was not up for grabs because the dominant party was unlikely to be defeated at an election given its control over the administration.

Second, no attempt was made to define *ex ante* the boundaries of the dominant coalition. The regime maintained the right to calibrate the size of the dominant coalition, again through a competitive process of assessment and negotiation. This too ensured that excluded elites had an expectation that they may be included on appropriate terms in the future if they played according to the rules of the game. The combination of these two characteristics ensured that the required rents were competitively allocated to the most important political organizers and political stability was as a consequence achieved.

Finally, both Zia and Ershad attempted to check the power of established political organizers by creating new rural voices through processes of decentralization. These strategies were quite similar to the basic democracy strategy of the praetorian period, but now they were a complementary part of a broader strategy and not the exclusive source of redistributive rents for achieving political stability. Even so, these strategies, particularly Ershad's attempt to create political legitimacy for a new class of political representatives in the newly created "upazillas" (a tier of government constituting a small number of villages), was strongly opposed by urban political organizers. These strategies therefore had a limited effect in enhancing overall political stability during this period, and the attempt to force them through possibly had a negative effect.

This period remained on the whole a period of considerable instability. Violence continued for a while, particularly within the army, where coups were frequently attempted. Nevertheless, some signs of a viable LAO began to emerge that were later built upon in the fifth phase. First, the strategy of ensuring entry to political organizers through individual negotiations to determine the price being demanded proved a viable strategy for constructing coalitions. It remains the strategy through which competing political parties in the fifth "democratic" phase construct the coalitions that sustain their power in and out of office. By its nature, it means that the ruling coalition is turbulent, with constant negotiations, infighting, and sometimes violence, both within the coalition and with coalitions currently out of power. But in the absence of any better method of determining the distribution of rents within the ruling coalition, this has emerged as the operative default mode. After a fashion, it works.

Second, the openness in terms of defining the boundaries of the dominant coalition proved extremely useful in managing the perpetual entry of new aspirants into the ruling coalition. Authoritarian clientelism allowed new entry into the ruling coalition except at the highest level, which was reserved for the (ex-) military leader. This arrangement, however, proved unsustainable over time. On the one hand it created strong incentives for ambitious officers within the army to try and replace the supreme leader. There were very frequent coup attempts under Zia in particular, as the traditions of violent seizures of power were still very fresh. In fact, Zia was finally killed in a coup by army officers in 1981. On the other hand, the reservation of the top job for a single individual eventually resulted in strong opposition to the system as a whole. The futility of elections to replace the top leader became apparent under Ershad and resulted in a growing political mobilization against him. As the BNP (the mass party set up by Zia) was now in opposition, this mobilization brought together the BNP with the Awami League, the party that had tried to set up the one-party state under Mujib. Under a combined and increasingly intense and violent mobilization, Ershad was deposed in 1990, marking the end of clientelistic military rule.

During this period, economic and political organizations could be set up relatively freely, without the prior clearance and approval of the dominant coalition for most categories of organizations. However, since the most important organization was the ruling party and the coalition it constructed, and entry into this was foreclosed without the approval of the dominant coalition, the system at the highest level had all the characteristics of a basic LAO. There were also important changes happening in the types of rents that organizations were seeking and capturing at this stage. The most rampant types of primitive accumulation began to die down as most abandoned assets had been appropriated. However, economically damaging politically created rents continued to be created explicitly as part of political stabilization strategies. These included, for instance, rents distributed to supporters of the ruling coalition in government construction contracts or in import contracts for scarce commodities like sugar and cement.

An important change that took place around this time compared to the praetorian phase was that the dominant coalition no longer saw rents as having any potentially productive purpose and stopped trying to create or allocate rents as part of an explicit industrial policy. Subsidies, for instance to agriculture or on fuel prices, were justified on welfare grounds and the earlier market failure justification for infant industry protection or technology acquisition began to die down. This was partly because of the memory of the political fight against the twenty-two families of Pakistan and the sham socialism of the Awami League, and partly because the international climate of economic opinion had changed radically in the 1980s. Zia was an advocate of privatization for all these reasons. The rents that public sector industries and the newly privatized industries continued to receive was because the state was too weak to remove these rents as powerful clients were benefiting, not because the ruling coalition believed that this would accelerate the modernization of the economy. Indeed, given the capacities of the state to manage these rents, there was little chance that rents could play a productive role unless new capabilities and political arrangements were developed. But this was not part of the agenda. Nevertheless, an accidental set of rents and Zia's interventions did result in the introduction of the garment industry into Bangladesh that changed the economic structure of the country.

Between 1976 and 1983, a total of 217 public sector enterprises were wholly or partially sold to the private sector or returned to their former Bengali owners from whom they had been nationalized without compensation in the aftermath of liberation. However, significant denationalizations only began under the regime of General Ershad. Under the New Industrial Policy adopted in 1982, denationalizations of large-scale public enterprises were given priority. Privatization faced substantial and growing political opposition, particularly from the trade unions of white collar workers where the overemployment was most significant (Bhaskar and Khan 1995). Nevertheless, the government divested 110 large units in little more than a year, including jute mills previously owned by Bengalis, after which the program continued at a slower pace (World Bank 1984: 149). The privatizations were supported by international agencies, but in effect they had a very limited impact on the economy. The large-scale enterprises created under the Pakistani industrial policy of the sixties had never achieved full global competitiveness. After their nationalization in the seventies they built up vast additional liabilities because of overemployment, looting, and mismanagement. This did nothing to help their future viability when they were gradually privatized in the eighties. The new owners took over the liabilities as well, wrongly believing that political arrangements could be worked out to sustain subsidies into the future. Some of the privatized firms limped on and were lucky to become moderately profitable. Many eventually closed down, particularly in the jute and cotton textile sectors.

The net effect of the Pakistani industrial policy as well as the accelerated primitive accumulation that happened in the immediate aftermath of independence did not take the country to a significantly higher technological level. Rather, the main effect was to achieve the creation of a new moneyed class through a process of primitive accumulation that began in the fifties. By the mid-1980s, Bangladesh had a potential small to medium capitalist class who had accumulated relatively significant blocks of capital. There were by now hundreds and possibly thousands of individuals who could if called upon raise $100,000 or more of capital in the form of land, liquid capital, or collateralized bank loans for investment. These individuals began to look around for simple technologies to invest in, now as economic entrepreneurs. It was at this stage that a lucky accident involving internationally created rents had a significant impact on Bangladesh's prospects.

The MFA and the Acquisition of Garments Technologies

The growth of the ready-made garments industry in Bangladesh has often been presented as a vindication of the success of free market policies combined with the virtual absence of labor market protections in Bangladesh. But in fact investment even in the simplest of technologies involves significant risks for domestic investors when these technologies are new to the economy. The time it will take to become globally competitive is not known and entrepreneurs have no idea of what production in very specialized globalized production chains entails. Nor is it viable for foreign firms to invest in up-skilling labor in a poor economy in low-margin, low-technology industries unless there is some cost sharing and risk sharing for the foreign firm. This is of course why all global production does not rapidly shift to the poorest countries. A combination of factors made this transfer of technology feasible for Bangladesh in the early 1980s.

An important part of the story was the emergence of the Multi-Fibre Arrangement (MFA) in 1973. This was an arrangement administered by the General Agreement on Tariffs and Trade (GATT) that set bilaterally negotiated quotas on developing countries for textile and clothing exports. The aim was to satisfy U.S. objections to free trade in garments, which threatened its domestic garment and textile industry. As a concession to global opinion, at the same time as quotas were imposed on established garment-producing countries, the MFA did not put quotas on a number of the least developed countries like Bangladesh that did not have any garment industry at the time and were therefore no threat to the United States (Goto 1989). For Bangladesh, it was fortuitous that just at that time a potential investor class was emerging through the industrialization efforts and primitive accumulation that we have described. The MFA created "quota rents" for countries like Bangladesh that did not have quotas by allowing them to sell at a higher price than established competitors and at the same time created incentives for established garment producers to transfer their technologies to countries like Bangladesh. And finally, Bangladesh was lucky to have just then an investor-friendly leader in the form of President Zia, who saw the importance of underwriting investments in the sector using informal support at the highest level. The garment sector emerged only because of a concurrence of these favourable conditions and provides a good example of why the emergence of productive organizations even in low-technology sectors required a lucky allocation of rents that allowed significant market failures to be overcome.

The MFA created serious problems for established producers of garments in countries like South Korea that suddenly found themselves quantity constrained. They had a strong incentive to relocate production to countries that did not have quotas. But developing countries that did not have a textile and clothing sector were clearly relatively poor countries and suffered from market failures affecting technology acquisition and learning. To attract investors from more advanced countries who wanted to relocate, developing countries had to offer something more than their quota-free status. After all, many poor countries were quota free but only a very few benefited from MFA. Bangladesh was one of them and its success has to be explained in terms of specific mechanisms through which these market failures were addressed.

By the late 1970s, domestic primitive accumulation had created numerous potential investors for a sector like garments where the efficient scale of investment was at most in the hundreds of thousands or low millions of dollars. The agent of change in Bangladesh's transition was a joint venture between a retired Bangladeshi civil servant turned entrepreneur, Nurul Quader Khan, and a South Korean multinational, Daewoo. The joint venture set up Desh Garments in 1979, a partnership in which the Bangladeshi partner provided capital and arranged government support for a new potentially risky investment and the South Korean multinational provided the training and technology transfer. That a retired civil servant from Bangladesh could sit across the table with a global multinational and offer credible equity cannot be understood outside the context of the primitive accumulation that the country had just gone through. Daewoo's calculations were straightforward. Bangladesh's access to the United States and other markets through the MFA was an attractive business proposition, but they would probably not have been willing to take all the risks of investing in Bangladesh without credible commitments from the developing country.

Equity participation from a joint venture partner provided part of this commitment, but perhaps even more important was the explicit support provided by President Ziaur Rahman to the project. President Zia's support appeared credible because he took the initiative in linking up Nurul Quader with Kim Woo-Choong, the chairman of Daewoo. His support assured the South Koreans that unexpected problems would be dealt with or at least addressed. And in fact, political support at the highest level ensured that relatively small but critical institutional innovations like the back-to-back LC (which allowed Bangladeshi producers to borrow from local banks using export orders as collateral) and the bonded warehouse (which allowed complex customs duties on imported inputs to be avoided) were quickly introduced.

Desh was remarkably successful. Between 1981 and 1987, its export value grew at an annual average of ninety percent (Rahman 2004). The learning and transfer of technology unleashed by this single project was remarkable. By the end of the 1980s, of the 130 people first trained by Desh in Daewoo's factories in South Korea, 115 had become entrepreneurs and set up their own garment firms! From virtually a zero base in 1980, by 2005 there were around thirty-five hundred active firms in the garments sector employing well over 2 million people (World Bank 2005). Primitive accumulation continued to be an important source of entrepreneurial supply. In a survey carried out in 1993, twenty-three percent of garment factory owners responded that they had originally been civil servants or in the army (Quddus and Rashid 2000). We can assume that many others had close contacts with politics and had made their initial capital through political processes. From a country not much different from the typical African country in the 1970s, Bangladesh's manufacturing output today equals that of all of sub-Saharan Africa combined excluding South Africa.

Table 2.4 *Bangladesh garments: Growth rates of dollar exports 1985–2006*

Year	Woven	Knitwear	Total Garments Dollar Export Growth Rates
1985–90			45.9
1990–5			24.1
1995–2000			14.3
2000–1			11.7
2001–2	−7.1	−2.5	−5.7
2002–3	4.3	13.3	7.2
2003–4	8.6	29.9	15.8
2004–5	1.7	31.3	12.9
2005–6	13.5	35.4	23.1

Sources: Based on Mlachila and Yang 2004: table 1; World Bank 2005: table 1.

The rapid emergence of Bangladesh as a garment exporting country is shown in Table 2.4. Exports grew at double digit rates for more than two decades. By the early 2000s, the sector accounted for around seventy-percent of Bangladeshi exports. By 1985, so successful was the Bangladesh garment industry that Ronald Reagan imposed quotas on it (M. A. Rashid 2006). Though Bangladesh continued to benefit from preferential treatment, particularly in European Union markets, effectively, the first five years of quota protection were enough to trigger a major shift in the country's fortunes. This result had many contributing factors, but in the first instance the MFA provided substantial temporary rents that served to reduce the risks involved in financing learning and technology transfer. Setting up complex productive organizations requires a significant amount of tacit knowledge, and this is typically only acquired through costly and uncertain processes of learning by doing. The costs and risks involved in acquiring this tacit knowledge meant that even relatively simple garments production technology was not transferred to Bangladesh prior to the MFA despite its much lower wages compared to countries like South Korea (Khan 2000, 2009).

The MFA unintentionally provided "learning rents" for building productive organizations in the garments sector. The difficulty of financing an initial period of loss making, when the tacit knowledge involved in using new technologies is being learned, often prevents start-ups in developing countries. In principle, markets should enable organizational learning to be financed but there are significant market failures that ensure that without

Table 2.5 *Bangladesh: Sectoral shares in GDP 1980–2005*

		1980	1990	2000	2005
Bangladesh	Agriculture	31.6	30.3	25.5	20.1
	Industry	20.6	21.5	25.3	27.2
	Services	47.8	48.3	49.2	52.6

Source: (World Bank 2008).

access to some rents, takeoffs even in low-technology sectors are rare. The MFA rents and the specific conditions of joint investments by Bangladeshi and foreign investors ensured that the necessary period of learning could be financed and also that the different stakeholders put in high levels of effort so that the rents were not wasted as a result of moral hazard problems (Khan 2009). Bangladesh also had a favorable political regime able to make small but critical institutional innovations to support the project. The political regime could meet its political stabilization requirements with other rents, so did not have to devise ways of letting its political clients capture the MFA rents, for instance by setting up unviable garment factories with state assistance. The emergence of the garments industry, together with successes in a number of other manufacturing sectors like pharmaceuticals, ensured that industry has been steadily increasing its share in GDP in Bangladesh, shown in Table 2.5.

The history of the garments industry's success is important as Bangladesh attempts to move higher up the value chain. Much of its growth so far has been at the lower ends of the value chain, even though there is evidence of growing backward linkages and diversification. By 2005, roughly forty-five percent of export value was added in the domestic economy due to growing backward linkages in spinning, weaving, dyeing, and accessories (Bhattacharya et al. 2002; M. N. Ahmed and Hossain 2006; World Bank 2005). The story of the garment industry's success tells us that market failures in capital and knowledge markets were overcome through very specific policy and governance arrangements. The blocks of capital required for the next stage of upgrading are much larger and primitive accumulation cannot be relied upon to provide these investments. A survey of the garment sector in 2007 revealed that the available terms of financing were an important constraint to technology upgrading in the sector (Khan 2008). Banks were willing to lend, but the fixed return and collateral requirements deterred investors unsure about the length of time required to learn new technologies. The sharing of risks and returns across a number of investors could in theory address this problem, but organizations could not credibly commit to reveal profits or pay dividends in the future, making these market solutions fail.

As the problem of credible commitments to uphold contracts on sharing returns across multiple investors is a major problem constraining the growth in the technological and organizational sophistication of organizations, it is important to examine why this problem persists. Third-party enforcement by the state is too much to expect in a limited access order. But why do productive organizations and their associations (like the Bangladesh Garment Manufacturers and Exporters Association, BGMEA) not attempt to engage in third-party enforcement of contracts? In fact, the BGMEA, like other business associations, does engage in a limited range of arbitration activities but the limited nature of these activities needs some explanation.

Around 2010, the BGMEA had four arbitration panels, each specializing on a specific part of the business, constituted of well-known and respected businessmen who are active in the BGMEA and who voluntarily give up their time to engage in arbitration as a social service for the trade body. The BGMEA is the most active among the different trade bodies in engaging in the arbitration of disputes involving its members. The critical part of the relative success of arbitration under the aegis of the BGMEA is that a number of informal pressures are often used to get the parties to first sit around the table, and then subsequently to comply with the outcome. Even more interesting is that these methods are used *without formal BGMEA approval.* For instance, the BGMEA provides UDs (Utilization Declarations) and UPs (Utilization Permits) to its members to show that they have used duty-free fabrics and yarns in their exports. These certificates are potentially very valuable because otherwise the garment factory becomes liable for significant import duties on the inputs they have imported. The BGMEA has no formal powers to withhold these or other certificates from its members. Apparently the arbitration panels have asked the BGMEA for formal powers to sanction members in the context of arbitration, but the board has so far not conferred such powers to its arbitration panels. We do not know the full reasons behind this, but perhaps the BGMEA leadership was afraid of potential misuse of these powers, which could lead to lobbying by members to return powers of granting certification to the customs authorities.

Nevertheless, arbitrators on these panels told us privately that hints that the granting of certificates or other services may be delayed were usually sufficient to get reluctant parties to attend hearings and in most cases to comply with outcomes. The fact that the arbitrators were themselves in the business also meant that they knew the hidden practices relating to profit-sharing arrangements or norms of compensation that often involved sharing profits or compensating different parties from profit that had not been declared. It is also clear that foreign buyers were aware of these arrangements and happily participated in them. This meant that arbitration using formal procedures would have been difficult in these cases anyway, and informal arbitration had a great deal of credibility because industry insiders had the knowledge to find acceptable solutions. This could involve, for instance, suggesting how to split losses using undeclared transactions such that both parties were reasonably satisfied in the context of unexpected problems.

However, while we find many examples of arbitration in areas of trade (for instance how should losses be shared if a shipment is delayed or cancelled?), we do not find BGMEA arbitration in areas of disputes between investors in plants and equipment. In general, the stakes involved in investment decisions are too high for the standard instruments used as threats to ensure compliance. While all organizations have an interest in improving the credibility of their contracts, as individuals contesting the interpretation of particular contracts, all individuals and organizations also have an interest in challenging the judgment of an arbitrator if it goes against them. Without recourse to the threat of a formal enforcement procedure somewhere, the process fails when the stakes become too high relative to the informal threats. A trade body just does not have the credible threats to enforce contracts affecting major investments, even though it may have sufficient instruments to ensure compliance with judgments in the case of contracts affecting particular shipments. This is why investment in productive organizations is still almost entirely organized by the resources of individual investors or bank loans raised by individual investors pledging first-class collateral. The sources of available financing ensure high levels of risk aversion in investments. Organizational growth is therefore typically horizontal, replicating areas of already existing competence. Investments in building more sophisticated organizations that are appropriate for more complex technologies are constrained by individual investors being unable to absorb all the risks of learning new technologies and building organizations appropriate for their use.

There does not appear to be a strong relationship between the types of LAOs as they evolved in Bangladesh and the success of third-party enforcement that could allow organizational depth to increase in productive organizations. When authoritarian clientelism was later replaced by open party competition in competitive clientelism (with its greater aspects of maturity), the problem of third-party enforcement of investment contracts was not significantly reduced. This is because different forms of the LAO in Bangladesh have primarily described the autonomy of *political* organizations. Economic organizations in Bangladesh (and South Asia more generally) have in general not required personalized authorization or support from the dominant coalition to set up, but have always required the support of political organizations in a very specific sense. Getting state officials to perform their formal duties or to desist from obstructing, or to deliver particular privileges often requires an entrepreneur to have political friends who can ensure the required services for a price. But the political organization is not in general required to sustain the internal organization of the productive organization. Moreover, political organizations even during the period of authoritarian clientelism were coalitions of organizers so it was always possible for a productive organization facing third-party enforcement against its interests to buy protection from another political organizer. It would in general not be worth the while of even a military ruler to take on an important organizer within his coalition simply to enforce a particular contract. With the advent of more open political competition after 1990, the problem of contract enforcement has remained at least as intractable as before.

Our interpretation of the causes behind the rapid growth of the garment industry in Bangladesh also casts doubts on the argument that Bangladesh's success was based on cheap labor and labor market flexibility. It is true that Bangladesh scores higher than India on labor market flexibility (it is easier to fire workers compared to India) and indeed both Pakistan and Bangladesh score higher than India on the overall ranking of "Doing Business Conditions" of the World Bank. But the specific mechanisms through which the garment industry developed suggests that cheap and flexible labor by itself did not help Bangladesh very much *before* the market failures constraining investment in a new sector were overcome. Moreover, the persistence of cheap and flexible labor has not helped investment in the next stages of the value chain even though wages have remained low. The implication is that the development of more sophisticated organizations using more sophisticated technologies depends on solving specific market failures. The break provided by the MFA cannot be relied on for other sectors or for moving up the value chain in garments and textiles. It is possible to imagine the political organizations in Bangladesh reaching an agreement to develop mechanisms for financing risk and cost sharing for technology upgrading. This type of productive rent creation, if it was on a limited scale, would not necessarily compete with the political rents that political organizations were primarily concerned with. The institutional and political arrangements required to manage such strategies are, however, not on the policy radar screen at the moment.

Indeed, unlike the praetorian period, the period of authoritarian clientelism established a new consensus that politics should not concern itself with productive rent strategies. There was no attempt to use rents internal to the system to create more sophisticated organizations or to absorb more sophisticated technologies than the ones that already existed. Rather, the focus of rent allocation by the dominant coalition became much more about the management of political stability. The emergence of the garments industry, itself the product of a fortunate conjuncture of conditions that enabled MFA rents to have very productive effects, allowed the political leadership to focus on the capture of political rents. The calibration of force and the distribution of rents that emerged during this period had features that continued into the next one. But the absence of any strategy of productive rent generation is a significant challenge to the system, as is the periodic disruption implicit in this system of political management, which we discuss in the next section.

The clientelistic military period established that brute force could not be used to stay in power. The dominant coalition needed to have a significant section of civilian political organizers. But it could not absorb all potential aspirants either. The actual practice of clientelistic military rule paradoxically established the norm that the control of violence in Bangladesh has to be based on a competitive system of rent allocation to allow the most important organizational and violence specialists to be brought into the ruling coalition at the cheapest price. However, the implicit links of the political leader with the army meant that this process of bargaining and calibration had to permanently happen under a single leader. Other parties could at best expect some of their most important organizers to be bought off. But eventually the major political parties united to reject an arrangement that deprived them of access to the most significant rent allocation decisions. Ershad was overthrown in 1990 by a popular uprising when the army refused to continue to support him if it meant shooting at thousands of demonstrators. However, the return to "democracy" kept intact many features of the system established during this period. The major change was that the top position of the dominant coalition became contestable in a competitive multiparty system where the leadership was selected by periodic demonstrations of organizational power by rival coalitions during elections.

2.5 Competitive Clientelism and Vulnerable Semi-Maturity 1990–

The overthrow of Ershad was followed by elections where none of the contestants were in power and so could not directly influence the administration in charge of organizing the elections. An ad hoc interim government led by a chief justice organized these elections and created a precedent for organizing acceptable elections in the future. As the administration remained tolerably neutral, the outcome of the election was determined by the organizational power that the parties could mobilize on the ground. The actual numbers of votes cast were almost the same for the two main parties in the 1991 elections but the BNP won significantly more seats because of the vagaries of the first-past-the-post electoral system, but also because the BNP had at that time a more extensive distribution of organizational strength. Even so, the BNP did not gain an absolute majority and needed the support of the Jamaat-i-Islami, a religious party, to nominate most of the thirty women members of parliament that the constitution allows, thereby gaining an absolute majority. As the BNP was not in power and could not have influenced the police, the vote counters or any other administrative tool to influence the outcome, the electoral result was accepted by the losers.

A fair election has come to mean that the outcome reflects the balance of forces on the ground without the interference of bureaucratic or military officials who are administering the police, the polling booths, and the process of counting the votes. If these administrative tools are controlled by one side or the other, the outcome of the election may not reflect the forces on the ground. Note that the objective of a fair election in this context is not to discover the true preferences of the electorate, partly because true preferences may not exist given the absence of serious differences in the policies that the parties are likely to implement. Rather, elections are processes through which the organizational strengths of the competing clientelist coalitions are revealed. Stability is likely to be achieved if the party with a demonstrable superiority in organizational strength wins the elections. The requirement is that no party should be able to leverage its strength by using the administrative apparatus to give it an electoral advantage unrelated to its strength on the ground. *The final (and current) phase, from 1990 onwards, can be described as "competitive clientelism" where the LAO has characteristics of maturity in the sense that the establishment of competing political organizations cannot now be controlled by the dominant coalition nor can they ensure that a coalition of oppositional organizations cannot eventually remove them from power.*

The electoral process built on elements of the competitive determination of the membership of the dominant coalition established in the previous period. The military-backed parties during the military clientelistic phase had accepted that new entrants had to be included in the dominant coalition depending on their organizational power and the price they demanded. The difference after 1990 was that the leadership and composition of the dominant coalition itself was determined by an electoral test of the aggregate organizational power of contesting coalitions. Potential entrants into the dominant coalition now had two tasks. They had to demonstrate, as before, their ability to organize to deliver stability or violence in particular sectors or geographic regions. But now they also had to choose a party where they were most likely to get the best deal in terms of an offer of the highest rents for the organizational power they could deliver. Of course for well-known, ideologically committed leaders, switching parties was not an option. But for the vast majority of political organizers, party choice was and is determined by the offer of rents. Indeed, so blatant are these calculations that Article 70 of the 1972 constitution prohibits members of parliament from voting against their parties as otherwise the horse-trading and transaction costs before every parliamentary vote would make voting in parliament prohibitively expensive.

However, after the BNP won the 1991 elections, the next election would be unlikely to be fair according to what would be acceptable to clientelist parties if a particular party remained in charge of the administration organizing the election. The opposition demanded the institution of a permanent constitutional arrangement to set up an interim caretaker government to organize every election after a government's term was up. Intense pressure from the opposition and a failed attempt to hold an election that was boycotted by the opposition finally led the government to pass the thirteenth amendment to the constitution in 1996 that set up the permanent institution of a caretaker government. A neutral caretaker government was to be set up at the end of every government's term with the last chief justice of the Supreme Court becoming the interim head of government. This was a unique institutional experiment to create a rule of law for elites at the critical moment of electing the next ruling coalition.

However, this institutional arrangement was clearly not buttressed by a deeper set of credible threats that needs to underpin a rule of law for elites or even a "live and let live" agreement. Any institutional system can be undermined if the underlying political compromises can be violated. The ruling coalition at any time always has an individual interest in prolonging its stay in power or to undermine the opposition through institutional and organizational steps. The caretaker government system worked for two elections, despite minor attempts by both parties to interfere in the elections when they were in power. In both cases the ruling coalition was replaced by the opposition. But the hope that a new rule of law for elites had been institutionalized was short-lived.

The constitutional caretaker arrangements collapsed in the run-up to the 2007 elections when the incumbent BNP went too far and appeared to interfere with the dates of retirement of Supreme Court judges so that its preferred candidate could head the caretaker government. The result was an increasingly violent standoff that resulted in a series of general strikes (*hartals*) and violent street confrontations in which the opposition graphically demonstrated its violence capabilities. In a context of increasing uncertainty, a group of bureaucrats backed by the military and the international donor community took over power on January 11, 2007 as a new emergency interim government. Under the constitution, the caretaker government has to organize an election within two months, but this caretaker government stayed in power for two years under emergency powers it gave itself.

The emergency caretaker government turned out to be a significant wasted opportunity. The emerging system of competitive clientelism had clearly not yet acquired a set of internal checks and balances to be fully self-sustaining. The emergency could have been an opportunity for investigating and establishing further checks and balances and indeed for establishing that if the parties could not agree, other institutions in the country would intervene to break the deadlock. But instead, the caretaker government, headed by an ex-World Bank bureaucrat and backed by an army very close to the international community because of its lucrative involvement in international peacekeeping missions, took a "good governance" perspective on how to solve the problem. Its interpretation (no doubt strongly influenced by dominant Western policy perceptions) was that the political instability was caused by political corruption. The opportunity for political corruption (so the argument went) created the distorted incentives for politicians to interfere with electoral outcomes. This analysis suggested that if political corruption could be rooted out and if parties could be made to compete on the basis of alternative manifestos of delivering public goods (as in OAOs) the problem of electoral violence could be rooted out.

For the next two years, the emergency caretaker government attempted to address the problem through "good governance" reforms, in particular through a focus on corruption, believing that the source of the problem of political violence was the engagement of political leaders in corruption. Hundreds and possibly thousands of political activists were arrested and incarcerated on charges of corruption, including the leaders of the two main parties. Hundreds of businessmen were arrested and some of them handed over millions of dollars to the new government as "ill-gotten gains" under pressure (which turned out to include torture). Thousands of cases of corruption and extortion were introduced in the courts. The whole exercise was deeply flawed, not only from the analytical perspective of an LAO analysis, but also in terms of procedures. In the end, almost all the cases had to be abandoned on the grounds that the evidence was missing or inadmissible. The experience of anticorruption cases globally suggests that even a single successful prosecution is very difficult as the participants do not leave paper trails and bank transactions that can unequivocally be established as corruption. Not surprising, the military caretaker government's attempt to address the problem in this way failed dismally. The two arrested leaders of the main political parties had to be released, and one of them was elected prime minister in the 2009 elections.

The main effect of the two-year experiment was a collapse in investor confidence that did not recover even a year after the election of a new government. The two main parties whose intransigence and violence had caused the problem in the first place did indeed receive a shock, but whether this will result in any lasting positive effect remains to be seen. The new government elected in 2009 immediately began conducting business as usual, including harassing the opposition using administrative powers and removing anticorruption cases against its supporters but not those against the opposition. As in the past, the opposition did not bother to go to parliament. It is not clear how the two-year emergency helped, except in the most limited sense of helping to construct a better voter register during this period. In 2011 the government amended the constitution to do away with the caretaker system and provoked a new round of mobilizations by opposition parties demanding the reinstatement of this arrangement for conducting the next elections. A rule of law for elites that will allow the smooth operation of elections will only emerge when both major parties recognize that wiping out the opposition using administrative means is simply not a feasible strategy. How long this takes to emerge remains to be seen.

The failure to make incremental improvements in the mechanisms through which a competitive clientelism operates in Bangladesh has significant negative implications. First, the threat of political violence remains undiminished. The paradox is that while the LAO has aspects of maturity in the sense that the dominant coalition cannot prevent the setting up of new organizations, the absence of a system of implicit rules guiding the entry and exit of political organizations in and out of the dominant coalition also gives the LAO many characteristics of fragility. The LAO can collapse very rapidly into fragility but the relative sophistication of political and economic organizations means that outbreaks of violence are not likely to result in a cumulative decline into anarchy. This cannot be ruled out, but there are enough stakeholders in business and in the international community who will intervene to try and stop it. The takeover in January 2007 was clearly part of such an intervention even though it was seriously misconceived.

The problem for Bangladesh in terms of the LAO framework can be stated as follows. The explosion in the number of aspirants who want access to rents on the basis of their capabilities for political organization has meant that a basic LAO is no longer a viable political proposition. Even as early as the 1960s, the attempt of the Pakistani praetorian order to manage rent creation and allocation for a defined set of elites was very vulnerable and eventually blew up in violence. The populist authoritarian one-party state did not even take off properly before the leadership was assassinated. The subsequent history of the LAO in Bangladesh has been about how to square this circle. Different attempts have also had important implications for the types of productive rents that the system could manage, as we outlined earlier.

The clientelistic military period demonstrated that entry and exit cannot be permanently managed by a single individual as the rents controlled by that individual can become the target of a significant social mobilization by all political organizers. Therefore the emergence of competitive clientelism can be seen as a natural evolution of the LAO. However, making it work is not simple given the absence of third-party enforcement of the critical rules for entry and exit of political organizations into the ruling coalition. The political organizations themselves cannot enforce rules of entry and exit because the rents at that moment become zero-sum for some of the organizations. The institution of the caretaker government was an attempt to create an institutional third party, but history shows that it cannot be truly independent as governments can also appoint Supreme Court judges. Indeed, the government also appoints army chiefs, though the last army chief appointed by the BNP went against the party by supporting the takeover of January 2007.

Here a comparison with India is useful. India's transition to an LAO with significant characteristics of maturity has also been in the context of a competitive clientelism and is also subject to vulnerability. But in India, the organization of elections has not been a problem as in Bangladesh. Why is that the case given the many social similarities between the countries?

One possibility is that India's size and diversity helps it to organize third-party enforcement of the electoral rules through which competing political organizations can enter and exit the ruling coalition. At the level of each Indian state, an election result that is strongly contested by powerful coalitions within the state, or allegations of partisanship on the part of the Election Commission of India, can effectively bring in organizations from outside the state to assess whether formal rules have been excessively transgressed to the point that a party with inferior organizational power won. An impasse between warring parties at the state level also means that the federal government can impose president's rule and rerun the election. Therefore, while election fraud, violence, and rigging does happen in India as well, the parties know that an outcome out of line with the organizational strength of parties on the ground cannot be sustained. The problem with a small country is that neither the election commission nor the interim government under the caretaker system has the credibility of being a neutral third party. Therefore on top of the general problems of organizing the dominant coalition in a context of growing political demands from emerging intermediate classes, small countries have an additional problem of running elections that can produce acceptable outcomes for competing clientelist parties.

The challenge for Bangladesh will be first and foremost to revisit the rules of organizing elections such that all parties are satisfied that the ruling party will not use administrative power to shift the electoral outcome too much. The problem is not just of blatant stuffing of ballot boxes but also more subtle uses of police and administration to harass the opposition and to make their attempts to get their supporters out more difficult. Delays in sending out the police to deal with ruling party thugs combined with swift responses against opposition party thugs may be all that is required to swing critical marginal constituencies. Administrative bias has become more serious as a result of the growing tendency to replace top bureaucrats with party supporters when new parties come to power. Given all these constraints, the electoral process will remain imperfect in LAOs like Bangladesh, but the efforts of the ruling party have to be restrained if the outcome is to be acceptable. If this process is seen as a good governance problem, it cannot be resolved because any election in Bangladesh in the near future will not conform to those standards. If on the other hand, elections are seen as a problem of managing a restructuring of the ruling coalition in an LAO, and the outcome of the election has to reflect organizational power on the ground, a better discussion of the types of policing, third-party monitoring and enforcement, and so on can ensue.

One of the paradoxes of the increasingly intense political competition and the aspects of maturity that have emerged is that long-term investments have become more risky. If ruling coalitions can change every five years and if significant investments (in say power plants) requires rent sharing with ruling politicians, the investor cannot be sure that the subsequent regime will not punish them by changing or cancelling contracts. One consequence has been that ruling coalitions have found it increasingly difficult to attract investors in long-term investment projects like power and infrastructure projects whose revenue streams have to be guaranteed beyond the life of a government. Here too, the nature of the LAO is at issue, rather than solely issues of corruption that the mainstream governance agenda focuses on. A more open public discussion of these issues may assist the judiciary to take a different view on these matters over time. The judiciary in Bangladesh has had a healthy tendency to provide judgments at variance with the wishes of the ruling coalition. So far, the judiciary has not taken a properly public interest approach in judging which contracts should be struck down. They have been more concerned to knock down legally dubious contracts when new governments have brought cases against apparent wrongdoings by previous governments. But it is possible to imagine that the conception of the public interest may change with a better discussion of the dynamics of LAOs. If courts look for insider dealing and corruption they could knock out all contracts but a more discriminating approach may focus on contracts that will clearly reduce value for the public. If elites begin to understand that their search for rents needs to be more closely aligned with the public good that would be significant progress.

The emergence of relatively high growth from the 1980s onward in a context of ongoing political instability may have lulled elites in Bangladesh to think that the economy can perform despite the damaging games played by political organizations. The fortuitous accident of the Multi-Fibre Arrangement has been particularly lucky for Bangladesh and came at a time when little else worked in the country. This international accident created temporary rents and incentives for investment in learning in the garment industry. The effect was hugely positive because the MFA did not allow a permanent dependence on rents simply because they could not be expected to last forever. And the terms on which these rents were allocated to particular firms could not be significantly manipulated by domestic political mobilizations.

The conditions that allowed the emergence of the garments sector need to be understood because the replication of this successful technology acquisition is by no means assured in other sectors. The ability of the ruling coalition to manage a few productive rents is critical if growth is to spread to new sectors. The replication of these accidental conditions through deliberate, yet modest, development of governance capabilities is a necessary precondition for the replication of these successes and their extension to other sectors in the context of the specific LAO characterizing Bangladesh. A better understanding of the rents necessary for the political sustainability of the LAO, and the rents necessary for accelerating the growth of organizational sophistication in the productive sector is necessary for a better public debate on institutions and governance.

References

Ahmed, Emajuddin. 1986. "The August 1975 Coup D'etat," in S. R. Chakravarty and Virendra Narain (eds.). *Bangladesh: Domestic Politics*, Vol. 2. New Delhi: South Asian Publishers.

Ahmed, Muhammad Nehal and Muhammad Sakhawat Hossain. 2006. *Future Prospects of Bangladesh's Ready-Made Garments Industry and the Supportive Policy Regime*. Policy Note Series No. PN 0702. Policy Analysis Unit (PAU). Dhaka: Bangladesh Bank.

Alamgir, Mohiuddin and Lodewijk Berlage. 1974. *Bangladesh: National Income and Expenditure 1949/50–1969/70*. Research Monograph No. 1. Dhaka: Bangladesh Institute of Development Studies.

Alavi, Hamza. 1983. "Class and State," in Hassan Gardezi and Jamil Rashid (eds.). *Pakistan: The Roots of Dictatorship*. London: Zed Press.

Amjad, Rashid. 1982. *Private Industrial Investment in Pakistan 1960–1970*. Cambridge: Cambridge University Press.

   1983. "Industrial Concentration and Economic Power," in Hassan Gardezi Hassan and Jamil Rashid (eds.). *Pakistan: The Roots of Dictatorship*. London: Zed Press.

Bhaskar, V. and Mushtaq H. Khan. 1995. "Privatization and Employment: A Study of the Jute Industry in Bangladesh." *American Economic Review* **85**(1): 267–72.

Bhattacharya, Debapriya, Mustafizur Rahman, and Ananya Raihan. 2002. *Contribution of the RMG Sector to the Bangladesh Economy*. Paper No. 50. Dhaka: Centre for Policy Dialogue.

Goto, Junichi. 1989. "The Multifibre Arrangement and its Effects on Developing Countries." *The World Bank Research Observer* **4**(2): 203–27.

Islam, Nurul. 1979. *Development Planning in Bangladesh: A Study in Political Economy*. Dhaka: University Press Ltd.

Jalal, Ayesha. 1985. *The Sole Spokesman: Jinnah, the Muslim League and the Demand for Pakistan*. Cambridge: Cambridge University Press.

Jalal, Ayesha. 1990. *The State of Martial Rule: The Origins of Pakistan's Political Economy of Defence*. Cambridge: Cambridge University Press.

Karim, Sayyid Anwarul. 2005. *Sheikh Mujib: Triumph and Tragedy*. Dhaka: University Press Limited.

Khan, Mushtaq Husain. 2000. "Rents, Efficiency and Growth," in Mushtaq H. Khan and K. S. Jomo (eds.). *Rents, Rent-Seeking and Economic Development: Theory and Evidence in Asia.* Cambridge: Cambridge University Press.

   2008. *Technological Upgrading in Bangladeshi Manufacturing: Constraints and Policy Responses Identified in a Study of the Ready-Made Garments Industry.* Dhaka: UNDP. Available at http://eprints.soas.ac.uk/9961/1/TechnologicalUpgrading.pdf.

   2009. *Learning, Technology Acquisition and Governance Challenges in Developing Countries.* Research Paper Series on Governance for Growth. London: School of Oriental and African Studies, University of London. Available at https://eprints.soas.ac.uk/9967/1/Learning_and_Technology_Acquisition_internet.pdf.

   2010. *Political Settlements and the Governance of Growth-Enhancing Institutions.* Research Paper Series on Governance for Growth. London: School of Oriental and African Studies, University of London. Available at http://eprints.soas.ac.uk/9968/1/Political_Settlements_internet.pdf.

Lifschultz, Lawrence. 1979. *Bangladesh: The Unfinished Revolution.* London: Zed Press.

Mascarenhas, Anthony. 1986. *Bangladesh: A Legacy of Blood.* London: Hodder and Stoughton.

Mlachila, Montfort and Yongzheng Yang. 2004. *The End of Textile Quotas: A Case Study of the Impact on Bangladesh.* IMF Working Paper No. WP/04/108. Washington: International Monetary Fund. Available at http://www.imf.org/external/pubs/ft/wp/2004/wp04108.pdf.

Murshid, K. A. S. and Rehman Sobhan. 1987. *Public Sector Employment in Bangladesh.* Mimeo. Dhaka: Bangladesh Institute of Development Studies.

Papanek, Gustav F. 1967. *Pakistan's Development – Social Goals and Private Incentives.* Cambridge MA: Harvard University Press.

Quddus, Munir and Salim Rashid. 2000. *Entrepreneurs and Economic Development: The Remarkable Story of Garment Export from Bangladesh.* Dhaka: University Press Limited.

Rahman, Shahidur. 2004. "Global Shift: Bangladesh Garment Industry in Perspective." *Asian Affairs* **26**(1): 75–91.

Rashid, Jamil and Hassan Gardezi. 1983. "Independent Pakistan: Its Political Economy," in Hassan Gardezi and Jamil Rashid (eds.). *Pakistan: The Roots of Dictatorship.* London: Zed Press.

Rashid, Mohammed Ali. 2006. *Rise of Readymade Garments Industry in Bangladesh: Entrepreneurial Ingenuity or Public Policy.* Paper presented at the Workshop on Governance and Development organized by the World Bank and BIDS. Dhaka: World Bank and Bangladesh Institute of Development Studies (BIDS).

Sen, Amartya. 1983. *Poverty and Famines: An Essay on Entitlement and Deprivation.* Oxford: Oxford University Press.

Sobhan, Rehman. 1968. *Basic Democracies, Works Programme and Rural Development in East Pakistan.* Dhaka: Bureau of Economics University of Dhaka.

   1980. "Growth and Contradictions Within the Bangladesh Bourgeoisie." *Journal of Social Studies* **9**: 1–27.

Sobhan, Rehman and Muzaffer Ahmad. 1980. *Public Enterprise in an Intermediate Regime: A Study in the Political Economy of Bangladesh.* Dhaka: The Bangladesh Institute of Development Studies.

Umar, Badruddin. 1980. *Towards the Emergency.* Dhaka: Muktadhara.

World Bank. 1978. *Bangladesh: Issues and Prospects for Industrial Development.* 2 vols. Washington, DC: World Bank.

1984. *Bangladesh: Economic Trends and Development Administration.* 2 vols. Washington, DC: World Bank.

World Bank. 1986. *Bangladesh: Recent Economic Developments and Medium Term Prospects.* 2 vols. Washington, DC: World Bank.

2005. *End of MFA Quotas: Key Issues and Strategic Options for Bangladesh Readymade Garment Industry.* The World Bank Bangladesh Development Series No. 2. Dhaka: The World Bank Poverty Reduction and Economic Management Unit.

2008. *World Development Indicators Online.* Accessed through Economic and Social Data Service. Manchester: ESDS.

THREE

Fragile States, Elites, and Rents in the
Democratic Republic of Congo (DRC)

Kai Kaiser and Stephanie Wolters

3.1 Introduction

The Democratic Republic of Congo (DRC), formerly Zaire and Belgian Congo, was theater to one of the most extensive post-Cold War wars in Africa, following the collapse in 1997 of the long-standing Mobutu regime. Often seen as the archetypal African kleptocracy, Mobutu's formal ascension to the presidency in 1965 temporarily stabilized the Congo in the wake of political instability and regional secession attempts following independence in 1960. Throughout various regime phases, natural resource extraction has played a central role in the governance of this vast country of 68 million people and 250 ethnic groups, with four times the area of France and as many as 700 local languages and dialects.

By 2012, the international community had devoted significant resources to the stabilization of the Congo and the government of President Joseph Kabila. Following its initial deployment in 1999, the UN continues to maintain a force of almost twenty thousand troops in the DRC under the United Nations Stabilisation Mission in the Congo (MONUSCO). Despite its resource wealth, the DRC continues to be subject to large aid. At the same time, concerns linger over poor governance and a predatory civil and military apparatus (including extensive human rights violations and sexual violence), as well as over the army's inability to defend the country's

The views presented in this chapter are those of the authors and do not necessarily reflect those of their organizations. Special thanks goes to participants of the Developing Institutions in Limited Access Orders: Nine Country Case Studies, Launch Workshop for Case Studies, held in Washington, DC, September 16, 2009, Stanford University in January 2010, and again in Washington, DC, June 2010. We would also like to thank Han Herdeschee, Phil Keefer, Steve Ndegwa, and James Robinson for helpful comments on previous versions of this chapter.

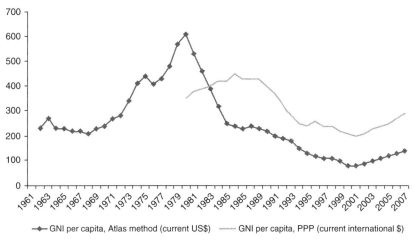

—◆— GNI per capita, Atlas method (current US$) ⸺ GNI per capita, PPP (current international $)

Figure 3.1 DRC economic performance (per capita GDP, 1960–2007).

population or its international borders. The latter phenomenon is most vividly reflected by instability in the country's east.

The DRC marked the fiftieth anniversary of its independence on June 30, 2010. Figures 3.1 and 3.2 summarize the growth collapse the DRC has experienced since 1960. While the seventies were relatively stable and provided some foundation for sustained economic expansion, these economic gains were subsequently wiped out by Mobutu's nationalization policy. The eighties and nineties were characterized by growing political instability, civil war, and economic decline, and economic growth only started to rebound timidly under the current regime of President Joseph Kabila and his ruling Presidential Majority (MP) coalition, elected in 2012. The DRC is currently going through another major economic crisis, and is surviving to a great extent thanks to the assistance of the international financial institutions and the influx of resources for mining rights from nontraditional partners such as China. Traditional cash cows such as Gecamines, the country's copper and cobalt mining company, as well as Minieres de Bakwanga (Miba), the diamond mining company, are no longer viable sources of rent and, moreover, are encumbered by significant levels of commercial and social debt; in the case of Gecamines, most of its assets have been sold off in long-term mining agreements, while Miba has been so badly managed that it has recently come to a complete production standstill.

The objective of this chapter is to review the evolution of elite bargains, stability, conflict, and access to rents in the Congo from the perspective

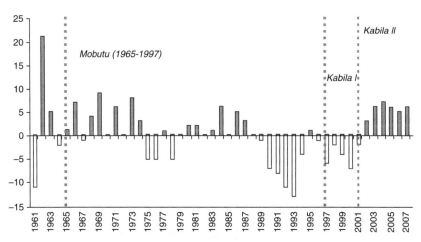

Figure 3.2 DRC economic performance (growth rates %, 1960–2007).

of the Limited Access Order (LAO) framework (North et al. 2009). The persistence of overt conflict in the DRC – notably in the immediate wake of independence in the 1960s and again since the mid-1990s – and prevailing political dynamics suggests that the DRC is best characterized as a *fragile natural state*: "the state can barely sustain itself in the face of internal and external violence ... commitments within the dominant coalition are fluid and unstable, often shifting rapidly, and dependent on the individual identity and personality of the coalition members ... [and] prevents the elite from credibly committing to observe the rules or laws in many possible circumstances (*NWW* 2009: 42)." In order to get some insight into the nature of this fragility, we examine the types of relationships and coalitions that have characterized elite power in the DRC for the past fifty-one years. Essentially, the three regimes dominating the country during this period have key traits in common: the personalization of power within an artificial ruling party, the reliance on ethnic and geographic allegiances, the use of incentives to sustain a small loyal ruling elite, and the heavy reliance on outside partners in moments of crisis. The downfall of all three of these presidents is the failure to understand the importance of widening the composition of the elite beyond narrow interests. In failing to allow a diverse group of actors to have a stake in the ruling elite's welfare, each regime – including that of incumbent president Joseph Kabila – has paved the way for its demise. The regimes have also shackled themselves to the arduous task of maintaining sufficient rents to sustain the existing elite, and thus their own hold on power, limiting their ability to engage in the types of prodevelopment activities that could underpin actual political popularity.

Finally, all three governments have relied heavily on key individuals to sustain support among ethnic and geographical constituencies, another set of relationships that must be maintained and whose political aspects have to be factored into all aspects of governing.

We proceed in four sections. Section 2 examines key elements of the nature of political authority in the Congo's three key postcolonial phases of leadership: Mobutu (1965–97), Laurent Kabila (1997–2001), and the governments of his son, Joseph Kabila (2001–present). Section 3 analyzes the rise and fall of the first Kabila government, and Section 4 studies the subsequent government. Section 5 assesses current prospects for transitioning out of a FLAO given prevailing elite bargains, rents, security sector reform, external agency, and the nature of center–region relations. Section 6 concludes.

3.2 The DRC's FLAO Narrative

Postindependence developments have been shaped by three presidents. This section will start with a look at the government of Mobutu Sésé Seko, who became president in 1965 and was overthrown by Laurent Kabila and his regional alliance after a nine-month war in 1997. Kabila's reign lasted only until January 2001, when he was assassinated by his bodyguard at his office in Kinshasa. During his time in office, he fell out with his regional allies, Rwanda and Uganda, and a second regional war broke out in 1998 that divided the country. Laurent Kabila's son, Joseph Kabila, took office following his father's assassination and restarted peace talks and engagement with the international community. In 2003, following the signing of an all-inclusive peace agreement in late 2002, a transition government was formed. It was composed of four vice presidents – one each from the two main rebel groups, the unarmed opposition and the government – and headed by Kabila. Kabila won a presidential election in a second round run-off in 2006, beating his main rival, Jean-Pierre Bemba, the leader of the Mouvement pour la liberation du Congo (MLC), a former rebel group.

Over the past fifty years, ex-Belgian Congo has been afflicted by two major cycles of extensive and overt violence: in the 1960s and again in the 1990s. The Mobutu regime provided for a notable degree of stability, but with devastating developmental consequences.[1] Since independence, the

---

[1] This contrasts with Indonesia, where roughly at the same time President Soeharto was establishing military rule, which was to last almost exactly the same length of time as that of Mobutu, but with very different developmental outcomes. Similarly, both Soekarno and Lumumba were characterized as leftist firebrands seeking to cement their relations with the Eastern bloc.

DRC has seen a number of shifting formal political arrangements, elites, and principal rents (see Annex 1). While a number stand out for being associated with stabilization, few could be considered markedly prodevelopment. When Mobutu Sésé Seko took power in 1965 following the instability after decolonization from Belgium in 1960 and secession threats from resource-rich provinces such as Katanga, it was no secret that his government was backed heavily by the Western powers that had felt so threatened by Patrice Lumumba's rise to power.[2] Although Mobutu attempted to disguise this link somewhat in subsequent years, Zaire's most stalwart and influential patron for the next three decades was the United States. France, Germany, the United Kingdom, and Italy played supporting roles. These links, based essentially on the political imperatives of the Cold War dynamic, were further consolidated as a result of Zaire's attractive natural resource base.[3]

In the short run the consolidation of the political authority of the New Regime somewhat reduced the permeability of the polity to external influences and diminished its need for continuous external backing. The rebellions were shattered, a large swath of the political spectrum co-opted into the government coalition and elements of the radical intelligentsia absorbed into the presidential staff. These factors permitted ... to momentarily define an international role of its own rather than being a mere object of external pressures.[4]

It is a telling fact that this quote describes a stage in the rule of every one of the country's last three presidents. Although it was written to describe the new Mobutu government shortly after it took power in 1965, it can just as easily apply to the government of Laurent-Désiré Kabila after he overthrew Mobutu in 1997 or the government of Joseph Kabila after he was democratically elected in 2006. In all three cases, the new president has consolidated power after a period of protracted instability due to military engagement with domestic and international actors, adverse relations with

---

[2] For one narrative concerning the United States' role in Mobutu's rise to power, particularly with respect to Lumbumba, see Devlin (2007).

[3] The Belgian colony of the Congo emerged out of the notorious and extraction-oriented personal fiefdom of King Leopold (Hochshild 1999). Putzel et al. (2008) provide a more comprehensive review of the literature on Congolese state formation. Ndikumana and Emizet (2005) focus on the role of natural resources in explaining the Congo's civil war in an international comparative perspective. Haskin (2005) provides for a general review of the chronology leading up to the present second Kabila government. The periodic updates through the UN Security Council provide a detailed perspective by the international community on events in DRC (cf United Nations Security Council 2009).

[4] Crawford Young, Thomas Turner, *The Rise and Decline of the Zairian State* (The University of Wisconsin Press, 1985), 365.

the international community and its financial and political institutions, and a decline in domestic economic activities.

In all three cases, these periods were characterized either by an actual strengthening of state capacity – arguably the case of the Mobutu government – or at least by the perception and certainly the hope that positive reform was the agenda of the new government – the case of the Laurent Kabila government and that of the 2003–6 transition government and the postelection government, both led by Joseph Kabila. Yet all three leaders followed the same pattern: a period of consolidation of state power, increased empowerment and leverage on the international scene, and buoyant domestic goodwill followed by a steady decline during which the state became ever more predatory, corruption spiked, domestic discontent was violently suppressed, and the economy suffered.

Each of these periods highlighted the precarious balance of maintaining elite coalitions, monopolizing violence, while at the same time sustaining a flow of rents. While much is made of the Congo's apparent resource abundance (copper, cobalt, diamonds, gold, forestry, and plantation crops), elites have been unable to effectively coordinate in the postindependence period around sufficient capital accumulation to underpin growing rent flows. Periodic cycles of aid and increases in natural resource rents due to international price booms have provided temporary and politically critical resource flows, but from an increasingly low base. Even after the end of the most recent cycle of conflict, absolute levels of production and extractive industry investment remains quite limited if normalized by population or area.

Nonetheless, the DRC has made some progress in postconflict stabilization over the last decade. While violence continues to afflict the eastern parts of the country, the 2006 elections and the adoption of a new constitution are in themselves milestones of significant progress. But the FLAO perspective can productively shift attention beyond stabilization at a national level to understanding shifts in patterns of elite behavior at both the national and sub-national levels. Informal if not illicit behavior has become a dominant feature of governance dynamics in the DRC. In such a context, it is often hard to discern a degree of collective interests or coordination within government beyond short-term individual enrichment. Viewed from an FLAO perspective, what are the main factors that could shape a transition from the current low-level fragile equilibrium to other intermediate (basic) equilibrium? How have elites historically managed coalitions, captured rents, strengthened the capacity for organized violence by the state, and balanced center-regional forces? We attempt to answer these questions in the following sections.

3.2.1 Joseph-Désiré Mobutu

As Young and Turner (1985) highlight, Mobutu's power was built on a complex system of patronage, the maintenance of which required a constant flow of resources. Under Mobutu's patrimonial rule, access to money and power came in exchange for personal loyalty and service to the president:

> The political elite are tied to the ruler by links of individual clientage. The reservoir of state offices forms a pool of prebends, whose attractiveness is a potent incentive to personal loyalty and service. In return, the client has the right not only to hold the office, but also to exploit it for his own benefit. All significant posts are held at the pleasure of the ruler: above all, constantly reaffirmed personal fidelity and services are indispensable. Any suspicion of a slackening of loyalty is grounds for instant removal.[5]

The client-servant was thus in a constant state of insecurity, always left to wonder how long a particular appointment or post would last. Not only did this mean that ministers and civil servants had little incentive to take independent initiative, but it also motivated people to accumulate as much money as possible while they were in office. In addition, as political control, not effective governance, was the order of the day, the apparatus of the state and its ability to deliver services to the Zairean population gradually eroded.

While popular lore has sometimes characterized Mobutu and his entourage as the archetypal billionaire kleptocrats, the overwhelming share of these resources is likely to have been deployed to sustain the extensive system of patronage spanning across all levels of Zaire and required to maintain this rule. Economically drained, adversely impacted by a serious of exogenous commodity price shocks, and seeing the end of the Cold War, Mobutu appeared to be accommodating some political opening in the early nineties, including through the reintroduction of multiparty politics in 1990 and the holding of the Conference Nationale Souveraine. However, Mobutu continued to skillfully play off the various competing interests to retain the reigns of power and there was no real progress toward a more democratic government.

The Mobutu regime resulted in a full-fledged rot of formal institutions, or alternatively, systematically precluded their development. The Mobutu regime also provided for the progressive breakdown of a number of the most lucrative rent extraction mechanisms inherited from the Belgians (notably the state-owned mining companies, plantation economy, and SOEs). The institutional legacy inherited from the Belgians arguably had already

---

[5] Ibid., 165.

been one of the weakest on the continent, with a systematic exclusion of Congolese from advancement and experience in higher positions. While Mobutu did appear to resort to a cadre of technocrats for some positions of government (including perhaps to appease counterparts in the international development community), the strategy of systematic politicization and fragmentation of those in the bureaucracy and security led to a full-fledged erosion of whatever institutional capacity may have existed.

As a result, the relationship between the government and population became perversely inverted: instead of the government, its institutions, and its policies serving the people, the state and its various apparatuses were forced to deprive the population of resources and services because these were needed to feed the patrimonial system that kept Mobutu in power.

By the mid-seventies, the first signs that the economy was in trouble started to emerge, notably in the steady decline in the performance of key state-owned enterprises, in particular in the mining sector, the country's main export earner. The Central Bank was another regular provider of funds; when more was needed, the governor turned to the printing presses and churned out the local currency, a process that ultimately led to massive hyperinflation. This was largely the result of a lack of management of these SOEs and the fact that Mobutu treated them as his personal treasuries. This practice ultimately led to the full-scale collapse of the Zairean economy.

Not only the productive entities of the state, but the state apparatus itself became a source of revenue for the maintenance of the regime. Defense contracts, infrastructure contracts, telecommunications contracts, and so on, were all transactions from which a bit could be skimmed; customs and tax revenue were commandeered, the state-run electricity company was looted – not a single entity avoided paying part of its revenues to the maintenance of the system.

In 1973, Mobutu's decision to nationalize the economy provided yet another important source of financing for his patrimonial system; the process of *Zairianisation* amounted to the expropriation of most commerce, plantations, small industries, construction firms, transportation, and property-holding enterprises. Although there is no doubt that Mobutu was at least in part motivated by the desire to "Africanize" the Zairean economy, the appropriation of the majority of the country's private holdings also provided a huge resource with which to sustain his political control. But this was to be short-lived – by 1975 the process had already been largely reversed through "retrocession" of most expropriated entities. Still, the economic damage had been done – few small business owners would again invest as significantly as they had.

Not long after the failed Zairianisation process, the country started to experience serious problems servicing its increasing external debt burden; by this time Zaire held debt worth $887 million with ninety-eight international banks. Mobutu's efforts to shore up the debts without having to involve the IMF were rebuffed, and after shunning the IMF for a decade, the government's inability to service its debt forced Mobutu to enter into discussions with the institution. This led to the disbursement of the first tranche of IMF credit in 1975. In the two decades that followed, the cycle of lending and bailouts would be repeated many more times; each time Mobutu would promise financial reforms and greater transparency, and each time, his governments would fail to make any substantive changes.

[T]he external world had become heavily implicated in the patchwork of expedients that kept the state lurching forward. The IMF became more heavily immersed in the internal processes of coping with the Zairean payments crisis than it had ever been in the internal processes of other countries. The private creditors silently endured a default in payments. But external support was at best half-hearted. The flaws of the new order were too deep-seated for ready remedy. The alternatives were unclear, and there was considerable uncertainty as to whether a new regime would, or indeed could, repair the corroded apparatus of the state.[6]

3.2.2 The Fall of Mobutu and the rise of Kabila

The secessionist movements of Katanga (and Kasai) in the initial post-independence period, and the interventions of various Cold War forces, highlighted the potential fractionalization of organized violence in the DRC and the emergence of various armed movements (Table 3.1). Under Mobutu, the Congolese security forces initially enjoyed a notable cadre of professional leadership, some members benefiting from American training. By the early 1990s, however, Mobutu's security forces had degenerated to a significant degree due to a number of factors, mainly irregular pay. At the same time, Mobutu had fractionalized the forces and its leadership to avert any direct challenges to his rule (cf Wrong 2001).

By the early nineties, the relationships between Mobutu and his key ally, the United States, and the international financial institutions such as the World Bank and the International Monetary Fund (IMF), had deteriorated significantly, and the latter had suspended all relations with Zaire. With Cold War imperatives fading in significance, the excesses of the kleptocratic

---

[6]   Ibid., 391.

Table 3.1 *Main armed groups 1996–2003*

Name	Description	Affiliation
Alliance des forces democratiques pour la liberation du Congo/ Zaire (AFDL)	Alliance of four Congolese groups created in 1996 to overthrow Mobutu. Led by Laurent Kabila	Backed by Rwanda, Uganda, and Angola
Forces democratiques pour la liberation du Rwanda (FDLR)	Congo-based political grouping of the Rwandan Interahamwe militia responsible for the 1994 Rwandan genocide	Allied with the Congolese government against Rwanda and Uganda
Mouvement pour la Liberation du Congo (MLC)	Congolese rebel group led by millionaire businessman and Mobutist Jean-Pierre Bemba	Heavily backed and militarily supported by Uganda
Rassemblement Congolais pour la Democratie (RCD)	Congolese rebel group set up by the Rwandan government and representing Congolese Tutsis and Banyamulenge interests	Heavily backed and militarily supported by Rwanda

Mobutu regime had become an embarrassment and direct engagement had waned significantly.

When the Rwandan-Ugandan-Angolan-backed Alliance des forces democratique pour la liberation du Congo (AFDL) emerged to overthrow Mobutu, his Western allies publicly turned a blind eye and, behind closed doors, essentially gave their support to the initiative. Meanwhile, for years a storm had been brewing in the eastern provinces, which created fertile ground for the AFDL and its foreign backers. The situation in the eastern Kivu provinces grew increasingly tense during the early nineties as a result of a number of issues. First, the question of granting Congolese nationality for Rwandophones – Hutu and Tutsis – was still unresolved. On the ground, meanwhile, ethnic tensions between Rwandophones and local ethnic groups had been on the increase and a growing number of ethnically based organizations were formed.[7] In addition, there was the fact that Mobutu's army had fought alongside the Rwandan Hutu army in the lead-up to the 1994 genocide, while many Zairean Tutsi and Banyamulenge had financed and fought with the Rwandan Tutsi Forces Patriotique Rwandais (FPR), which would win power after the Rwandan genocide. These positions would be

[7] Ndaywel e Nziem, (1998), *Histoire generale du Congo*, 790–4.

drawn to the fore with the arrival in July 1994 of hundreds of thousands of Rwandan Hutu refugees in eastern Zaire, many of whom were members of the Interahmwe militia responsible for the genocide.[8] The presence across the border of these elements was intolerable for the new Tutsi-led Rwandan regime, especially as Mobutu had been a long-standing ally of the Rwandan Hutu community. Out of this fertile mix of long-standing local and regional tensions grew the alliance that would overthrow Mobutu nine months later.

In October 1996, reports began to emerge from south Kivu of an unknown armed movement rapidly taking control of the province. Able to take advantage of the defeated and desperate nature of the poorly paid and undisciplined Zairean army, the AFDL quickly won ground and influence in the eastern part of the country. By early December, the group controlled most of the key cities along the country's eastern border.

Eventually the identity of the new armed group emerged: the Parti pour la revolution populaire (PRP) led by Laurent Kabila, the Conseil National de resistance pour la democratie (CNRD) led by Andre Kisase Ngandu, the Mouvement revolutionnaire pour la liberation du Zaire (MRLZ) led by Anselme Masasu Nindaga, and the Alliance democratique des peuples led by Deogratias Bugera. By New Year's Day 1997, the four groups formed the Alliance des Forces Democratiques pour la liberation du Congo-Zaire (AFDL). Kabila was appointed president of the coalition.

3.2.2.1 Kabila's International Coalition – An Elite Bargain

The AFDL's fighting forces were composed essentially of deserting FAZ soldiers and young boys and men recruited during its military campaign; on its own, the AFDL never had sufficient military might to achieve the military victories that it so rapidly did. The real fighting power came from a coalition of African countries: Uganda, Rwanda, and Angola, which had the tacit approval of key members of the international community, especially the United States, to overthrow the Mobutu regime. Without them, the AFDL and Laurent Kabila could never have seized power.

So what was the origin of these three country's interests in Zaire and its alliance with a little-known warlord? For all three (Rwanda and Angola in particular), the Mobutu regime and its foreign policy toward its neighbors had become an intolerable security risk. The solution was to mount an armed rebellion that had a Congolese face, but did not itself have strong popular support or a known identity. This is how the relatively unknown

[8]   Ibid.

leaders of the four groups that made up the AFDL were catapulted onto the national stage, and how Laurent Kabila, a man few Congolese had heard of, came to overthrow one of Africa's most entrenched dictators.

In choosing the AFDL as the Congolese vehicle for their objectives, the three regional allies expected to be able to exercise their military and political influence over the AFDL. This belief was based on the bargain they had struck with Kabila: to provide him with the military strength to go all the way to Kinshasa in exchange for the right to pursue their own security agenda in the Congo.

3.2.3 Regional Security Concerns

3.2.3.1 Rwanda

In mid-1994, up to a million Rwandan Tutsi and moderate Hutu were killed in the Rwandan genocide by the Hutu militia known as the Interahamwe. In the last weeks of the genocide, a vast number of Rwandan Hutu civilians, but also large numbers of Interahamwe, escaped across the border into neighboring Zaire, where they were later grouped into large refugee camps along the border with Rwanda (see map). Even once it had become clear that the Interahamwe were using the camps to regroup, the pro-Hutu Mobutu government refused to break them up and to assist Rwanda in capturing the Interahamwe. The Rwandan government's desire to see the destruction of the Hutu refugee camps is the primary reason why the Tutsi-led Rwandan government decided to create a Zairean proxy that would allow it to pursue its own security interests next door.

The destruction of the refugee camps was fairly rapidly achieved. But capturing members of the Interahamwe militia, a key Rwandan objective, was a far bigger and more complex job, one that would take the Rwandan army all the way across the country. Along the way, tens of thousands of Rwandan Hutu refugees – women and children as well as members of the Interahamwe – were massacred by the Rwandan army and their Congolese allies. .

3.2.3.2 Uganda

In addition to being closely aligned with the new Rwandan government, Uganda had its own security concerns in eastern Zaire, notably the presence there of two antigovernment rebel groups: the Allied Defense Forces (ADF) and National Army for the Liberation of Uganda (NALU), whose aim it was to overthrow the Museveni regime. Mobutu had allowed these two movements to use eastern Zaire as a base, and Museveni was hoping to neutralize these groups through his alliance with the AFDL and Rwanda.[9]

3.2.3.3 Angola

By 1996, the Mouvimento Popular para a liberacao de Angola (MPLA) had been in power in Angola since the 1992 elections, but was still engaged in a full-scale war against the Uniao para a independencia total de Angola (Unita), led by Jonas Savimbi. For years Mobutu had allowed Savimbi to use Zairean territory as a base from which to launch operations against the MPLA, to resupply with weapons, and to smuggle diamonds. Without Mobutu's support, Unita would have been in a significantly weaker position. The MPLA-led Angolan government therefore had strong incentive to support a regional military alliance to oust Mobutu. It also had an exceptionally strong, well-trained army.

3.3 The Kabila Government

Kabila came to power on May 17, 1997, inheriting a country that was on its knees and had been for close to a decade. International financial institutions had pulled out at the beginning of the nineties, most of the parastatals had been plundered and barely functioned, the apparatus of the state was destroyed, and the private sector was only a shadow of its former self.

The final years of the Mobutu regime had been so difficult that any regime change was considered an improvement by most, and Kabila was initially buoyed by this sentiment. The international community, which had contributed actively and tacitly to Mobutu's demise, welcomed the change at the helm of Africa's third largest country. Although he was relatively unknown, the hope was that Kabila might usher in a new era of democracy and good governance and build upon the gains made during the Conference National Souveraine. This uncertainty was the risk certain Western countries had taken when they stood aside and let him oust Mobutu. Meanwhile, his regional backers gambled on the fact that he would remain compliant, maintain his end of the bargain, and allow them to control the security forces in pursuit of their own interests. Kabila disappointed everyone, and the tide of international and domestic opinion soon started to turn against the former rebel leader. This would cost him his control over the country.

---

[9]   In the second war, both Rwanda and Uganda were to develop significant economic interests in eastern DRC, which motivated their continued military presence in the country.

With Kabila came a raft of Congolese from the diaspora, most of whom hailed from Katanga, Kabila's home province, and few of whom had any experience in government or in senior positions in any field. These people were to form Kabila's close inner circle and his cabinet. In the army, the same logic was applied; most experienced senior commanders left over from the Mobutu era were removed or sidelined and replaced with close friends or family members of Kabila's. For example Joseph Kabila, his son, became the head of the army in spite of the fact that he had scant military training or experience.. This new elite was quickly formed, and its main pillars would remain unchanged until after Kabila's assassination (although several had brief stints in jail at Kabila's whim). A deeply distrustful man, Kabila, who had spent the previous three decades in the bush and outside of the country in east Africa, made no credible attempts to expand his inner circle or to involve outsiders in governing the country. He shunned members of Mobutu's political, economic, and military elite and crushed the political opposition with legislation banning all political activities.

Upon arrival in Kinshasa, the new crowd also quickly started to appropriate public and private goods. Houses and businesses left behind by rich Mobutistes, the central bank, ministries, parastatals, and the armed forces were targets of plunder by the new elite. In the months that followed, Kabila and his close associates quickly fleshed out their own personal empires and started building private fortunes. Their behavior dashed hopes that the new elite would be less corrupt and bent on self-enrichment than the old. The population, civil society, and the political opposition quickly became disenchanted and public opinion turned against the new government.

3.3.1 Rent Seeking

For the private and the public sector, the end of the Mobutu era provided a welcome opportunity to reengage with the mineral-rich country that had fallen out of favor since the early nineties, and private companies were lining up to curry favor with the new president. This competition provided immediate, but short-lived access to rents to Kabila and his entourage.

But the shine was very soon off the Kabila government, and the massive inflow of public and private funds and investment it had banked on never materialized. The resumption of engagement by international financial institutions was dealt a final blow with the outbreak of a second war in August 1998.

As a result, the regime had to find different ways of sustaining itself. Gecamines and Miba, the country's diamond mining company, as well as the country's other resource parastatals, already severely damaged by years of plunder under Mobutu, were further bled by the Kabila government. The Central Bank, engaged in an ambitious attempt to align exchange rates across the country and to launch a new currency – the Franc Congolais – was enlisted to assist in the accumulation of wealth, printing money as and when it suited the new government.

Later on, as Kabila's intransigence in the peace negotiations grew, and prospects for a speedy resolution to the conflict receded, the Kabila government took to imposing ever stricter laws on foreign exchange, the diamond trade, and other key sectors, all of which provided lucrative rent-seeking opportunities for the government.

Finally, the Kabila government's failure to govern in any real way unleashed such a level of disorder in the various revenue collection services that private businesses used to high levels of corruption now found themselves prey to almost weekly assaults from agents of the government.

3.3.2 Security Forces

Close to one year after he took power, Kabila still did not have a unified national army. In early 1998, the Forces Armees Congolaises (Fac) reportedly consisted of five thousand ex-FAZ soldiers, three thousand Rwandan and Banyamulenge troops, and an unknown number of newly recruited and untrained Katangan troops.[10]

In the eastern part of the country the Kabila government faced an ongoing armed insurrection. The Mai Mai – a local militia composed mostly of baHunde and set up in the 1980s as a self-defense force in opposition to Rwandophones in eastern DRC – were fighting against the FAC alongside Hutu members of the former Rwandan army and the Interahamwe. Because Kabila and the AFDL had been aligned with the Tutsi-led Rwandan government, the Mai Mai considered them enemies. The situation was aggravated by the fact that the majority of the Congolese soldiers in eastern DRC were themselves either Rwandans or Congolese Tutsi to whom the Mai Mai were opposed.[11]

3.3.3 Kabila Breaks the Bargain

In 1997–8, the Kabila government's inability to control the east was the main cause behind his government's falling out with its Rwandan and Ugandan

[10] EIU (1998 Q2:25).
[11] EIU (1998 Q2:31).

allies, neither of whom felt that Kabila was doing enough to meet his end of the bargain to neutralize security threats against their governments. By the first anniversary of Kabila's arrival in power, the relationships with Uganda and Rwanda had deteriorated so significantly that neither the Ugandan nor the Rwandan president attended the celebrations or the regional security summit organized to coincide with them.

Kabila had further antagonized his allies by gradually reducing the influence of Tutsi in the government in favor of members of his own Katangan ethnic group – the Balubakat. Already by June 1998, the provincial balance of cabinet members was tilted strongly toward Katanga, with eight ministers of a total of thirty-one hailing from Katanga province. In addition, key positions in the military and the security services were also occupied by Katangans. But in choosing to trade the influence of the Congolese Tutsi and Rwandan allies who brought him to power for a group of inexperienced people who just happened to hail from the same province as he did, Kabila made a deal with the devil. The initial power coalition that had brought him to power was based on a coincidence of interests working in favor of all the elements of the coalition. In attempting to assert his independence from the Rwandans and the Congolese Tutsi, Kabila made a spectacular miscalculation – or simply a very arrogant one – alienating the very force that had allowed him to come to power and to maintain it. In breaking the regional bargain, Kabila certainly made a very personal decision that he no longer wanted to feel subservient to his allies' interests, even though these interests did not actually undermine his own. Had Kabila chosen to widen his circle and to form coalitions or links with other Congolese groups against Rwanda and Uganda, he would almost certainly have won over popular opinion, which largely disapproved of the foreign element in his government. Instead he cut off his allies without having built a domestic consensus, thus failing to lend his regime the legitimacy it so badly needed.

When Kabila announced in late July 1998 that all foreign troops – meaning all Ugandan and Rwandan troops – would have to leave Congolese soil by the start of August, Congolese Tutsi troops in Kinshasa and in the east mutinied. The rebels almost achieved their goal of overthrowing the Kabila government, however Zimbabwe, Angola, and Namibia's military intervention saved the Kabila regime. Meanwhile, rebels in the east were capturing control of one town after another and by late 1998 controlled much of the eastern part of the country.

It is hard to imagine that Kabila thought his allies would quietly accept his decision to expel all foreign troops from Congolese soil, especially given the reality of the situation in the eastern part of the country and the initial premise of their alliance. It is particularly difficult to understand how Kabila could have felt secure enough from a military point of view, given that the FAC remained a totally disorganized and disparate group of soldiers, many of whom were pursuing their own ethnic agendas. In the end, it was a new set of international players that would save him.

3.3.4 International Community

Upon coming to power, Laurent Kabila thought he could count on the strong support of the international community, both diplomatically and financially. In principle this was a fair assumption. But two key elements combined to lessen the international community's enthusiasm for the Kabila government and ultimately to isolate it. This lack of engagement would further entrench Kabila's anti-Western tendencies and have major repercussions on the evolution of the country and regional stability.

The immediate obstacle to a rapid resumption of international engagement in the Congo was the question of the fate of several hundred thousand Hutu refugees who had simply disappeared during the AFDL's military campaign. Shortly after Kabila came to power, the question of the fate of these refugees was raised by the UN and an investigative team went to the Congo to look into the matter. The team was repeatedly prevented from doing its work, and in April 1998 the UN withdrew the team. The subsequent UN report accused the Kabila government of the "systematic"[12] massacre of thousands of Rwandan refugees between 1996 and 1997. The report also concluded that Rwandan troops shared responsibility for the massacres, and recommended the establishment of an international tribunal to investigate individual responsibilities in the massacres. The Kabila government rejected the allegations, as did the Rwandan government. This question essentially blocked the international community from engaging with the new government in any significant manner.

Kabila's repressive attitude toward the political opposition, civil society, and the media in the Congo further isolated his government. Although Kabila had declared upon taking power that national presidential elections would be held in 1999, one of his first official acts as president was the promulgation of a law banning all political activity. In addition, the Kabila government rejected the draft constitution drawn up by the delegates of the 1992 Conference Nationale Souveraine (CNS), the national democratic conference in which the political opposition and the government mapped out a path toward democracy.

---

[12] EIU report, Q3 1998, 34.

Meanwhile, Kabila, whose attitude toward Western countries was heavily influenced by his quasi-socialist background, only became more defensive as a result of the international community's apprehensive attitude toward his regime. He could not believe that he, the person who had liberated the country from the corrupt Mobutu regime, was now being asked by the very same international community that had condoned Mobutu's behavior, to meet high standards on democracy and human rights.

3.3.5 Kabila's Foreign Allies – Take Two

Facing an imminent military overthrow, Kabila appealed to the Southern African Development Community (SADC), of which the Congo is a member, for military assistance and political support. Within days Zimbabwe and Namibia decided unilaterally to deploy troops to back Kabila's regime. At the same time, Angola deployed troops to the southwest of the capital. The intervention by the three countries significantly raised the stakes in the conflict, both for the Kabila government as well as for the rebels. Zimbabwe, Angola, and Namibia's military intervention recast what was to be a lightning strike military campaign into a long-term conflict requiring a significantly higher investment in time, resources, and military personnel. As a result of this decision and the war that followed, the Kabila government would spend the next two and a half years growing increasingly intransigent and isolated.

3.3.6 Kabila and the Interahamwe – A Lasting Bargain

Formed in 2001, the Forces democratique pour la liberation du Rwanda (FDLR) is the politico-military movement composed largely of former Interahamwe fighters responsible for the 1994 genocide in Rwanda. Following the RPF takeover of Rwanda, thousands of Hutu Interahamwe fled to the neighboring DRC. Not long after Laurent Kabila fell out with his Rwandan backers in 1998 and the second war erupted, Kabila formed an alliance with the Interahamwe, thousands of whom fought alongside the Congolese army (FAC) against Rwandan and Congolese rebel troops. This alliance was initially clandestine, but it became widely known over the following years that the Interahamwe had close military links to the Kabila government, and later that of his son, Joseph Kabila, and that the FDLR fighters were an important boost to the Congolese army's fighting power.

In 2002, while internal peace talks were taking place in South Africa, Joseph Kabila and Rwandan president Paul Kagame signed a bilateral peace accord committing Rwanda to withdrawing all troops from the DRC, and the Kabila government to disarming the Interahamwe. Rwanda subsequently withdrew its troops, but despite publically disavowing its links to the group, in practice the Congolese army continued to collaborate with Interahamwe forces.

Although the newly elected Kabila government did reduce its outright cooperation with the Interahamwe, on a localized level close contacts still exist between local military commanders from both groups. There is also evidence of collaboration on the extraction of natural resources and the sharing of profits from this collaboration. The bargain that existed between the central government in Kinshasa and the FDLR has certainly been weakened, but it cannot be ruled out that the relationship could be revived if the FARDC faced another significant military threat in the east and needed the FDLR to help defend itself.

3.4 Joseph Kabila

Joseph Kabila succeeded his father as president of the DRC at age twenty-nine, following Laurent Kabila's assassination in January 2001.[13] The key distinction between Laurent Kabila and Joseph Kabila, one that put the country back on track in the peace process, is that Joseph Kabila reached out to the international community upon becoming president, thereby kick-starting the stalled peace process. As a result, the international community rewarded Kabila with an ever-increasing flow of donor funds and significant public support throughout the 2006 election period. The various World Bank institutions are again engaged with the country, bilateral lending programs are again up and running, and the country became eligible for debt relief under the HIPC initiative.

3.4.1 Joseph Kabila – Pre-transition, 2001–2003

On February 25, 2002, just over a year after Kabila came to power, the Intercongolese dialogue was launched in Sun City, South Africa. The armed

[13] Laurent Kabila was assassinated by one of his bodyguards at his office on January 18, 2001. A number of Kabila's close allies were subsequently arrested, charged, and found guilty of plotting his murder, however, the real story of what happened and who ordered his killing remain shrouded in mystery. The bodyguard who killed Kabila was shot while trying to flee the scene. Born in 1971, Kabila attended primary and secondary school in Tanzania, with further military training, and university in Uganda. He became a commander of the AFDL during the march on Kinshasa in 1996 and 1997. Subsequently he also received training at the PLA National Defense University in Beijing, and served as chief of staff of the Land Forces from 2000 until his father's assassination.

and unarmed opposition, civil society, the Mai Mai, and the Kabila government participated. An all-inclusive peace accord was signed in December 2002. During the transition, the government was led by Kabila and four vice presidents – one each from the MLC, the RCD-G, the unarmed opposition, and the Kabila camp. Key ministerial positions were also distributed according to the strength of the individual component.

3.4.1.1 The Transition Government – A Bargain Kept

The agreement that emerged from the Sun City talks was cumbersome and the act of governing slow and ineffective, essentially because it required constant negotiations between parties that had compromised but nevertheless remained intense political rivals. As a result of this uneasy coexistence, progress on crucial matters such as the reform of the army, the disarmament of armed groups, the elaboration of a new constitution, and the planning of elections were all severely delayed.

At the same time, very few members of the government were in any way trained for the work they needed to execute in their various positions. This left much space for corruption and illegal influence buying. It also meant that government action was extremely poorly coordinated and that the various branches of the transition government were often at odds with one another or working at cross-purposes to one another because they were controlled by different factions within the government.

However, in spite of the cumbersome nature of the government during this period, the experience of the transition was an important one, as it was the first time in over four decades that the country's government had been an inclusive and, to some extent, a representative one. It was also a relatively productive period. Although key issues were unresolved, others such as the elaboration of a new constitution and the holding of a national referendum on it were achieved. The period was also characterized by a compact between the various parties, which was largely respected in spite of the fact that the actors remained political enemies (although there were frequent criticisms and almost constant fighting between the parties). It can therefore be considered a rare moment in which a real elite bargain was in place in the Congo that was neither betrayed by one of its partners nor fell apart.

The key was certainly the intense involvement of the international community, which played a key role in keeping the transition government together and in pushing it to ultimately meet key milestones such as the constitutional referendum in late 2005 and the national elections in 2006. A key instrument was the Comite international d'accompagnement a la transition (Ciat), a grouping of countries including South Africa, Belgium, the United States, and Angola whose mandate was to assist in the transition process. In addition, MONUC played a key role in organizing the national elections and in assisting the Independent Electoral Commission (IEC). There is no question that the national elections of 2006 would not have succeeded without this outside intervention.

Throughout this period, the international community, and MONUC in particular, were particularly supportive of Joseph Kabila. There seems to have been at this stage almost a tacit understanding between the international community and Kabila that if he cooperated with a UN-run election, he would receive significant moral support from the international community. Many MONUC officials have said "We supported him." This can be interpreted as the second successful elite bargain made since Joseph Kabila's arrival in power.

During this transition period, the political actors involved appear to have felt strong disincentives to not cooperating. There are a number of reasons why this may have been the case. First, as mentioned earlier, the international community closely followed the evolution of the transition government, and bad behavior by one or another actor did not go unnoticed.[14] Second, the specter of the country's first democratic elections in decades loomed, and political actors may have felt it unwise to appear to be a spoiler in the country's peace process. Most likely is a third option: all the players had a seat in government, and, therefore, an opportunity to access its resources. For most parties, and the individuals running them, this was a vast improvement on their previous circumstances, and there was therefore no incentive to rock the boat and risk losing a cushy position. Whatever the case, this phase of the DRC's history demonstrates that there is the possibility of elite cooperation, if the right set of incentives is made available to the various elite actors. Unfortunately, the most powerful players in the mix, that is the president and his political allies, appear to have calculated – rightly or wrongly – that this cooperation was not in their long-term interest.

3.4.1.2 The Democratically Elected Government of Joseph Kabila

In 2006, Joseph Kabila and his political alliance, the Alliance pour la majorite presidentielle (AMP), won the presidential elections in a run-off with the main opposition party, the Mouvement pour la liberation du

---

[14] There were a number of major disagreements, and various parties walked out at different times, most notably the RDC, which briefly abandoned the transition government in 2004 citing corruption and poor governance. It was convinced to return soon thereafter.

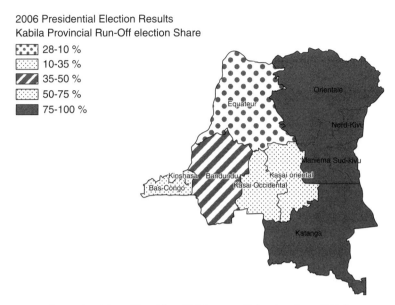

2006 Presidential Election Results
Kabila Provincial Run-Off election Share

- 28-10 %
- 10-35 %
- 35-50 %
- 50-75 %
- 75-100 %

Figure 3.3 Map of President Kabila run-off election share (2006).

Congo (MLC) and its Union National (UN) alliance. The MLC was headed by Jean-Pierre Bemba, a wealthy businessman and warlord hailing from the Equateur province in the north of the country, and one of the four vice presidents. The AMP also won the majority in parliament. The presidential party was able to win the second-round election as result of its alliance with the Parti Lumubiste Unifie (PALU), led by veteran Congolese opposition leader Antoine Gizenga. Gizenga, who hails from Bandundu province, was part of the postindependence government of the assassinated President Patrice Lumumba, and maintained his opposition credentials through the Mobutu and Kabila years. PALU's alliance with the PPRD allowed the Kabila camp to win support in the western provinces of Bas-Congo and Bandundu where its support was very weak. Nationally the AMP achieved 22.2 percent in the first round, while Bemba's MLC got 12.6 percent and PALU got 6.8 percent, with the rest of the vote fragmented between over eighty named parties and more independents. In the second round against Bemba, Kabila received a national majority, but his support, even with the PALU coalition, was heavily concentrated in the east (see Figure 3.3).

The presence of PALU in the ruling coalition is the most significant formal manifestation of political bargaining in the 2006 elections because it was an alliance based on an exchange of known benefits; the AMP needed PALU to align with it, not the MLC, or it risked losing the election, while

PALU calculated that it had a better chance of coming to power through an alliance with the AMP. The AMP won the election, and PALU was given the prime ministerial post and several key ministries. Although PALU has been frequently used as a scapegoat for all government shortfalls, the alliance remains intact, albeit somewhat strained.

The AMP was itself an umbrella grouping of dozens of political parties, including several larger, significant parties such as the RCD-K/ML led by Mbusa Nyamwisi; UDEMO, led by Mobutu's son, Nzanga Mobutu; and the ARC led by Olivier Kamitatu (see Table 3.2). The presence of such recognizable figures in the AMP contributed significantly to its appeal to voters.[15] Each of the main parties in the AMP was accorded a specific number of ministries, a formula from which the president has occasionally strayed, straining the relationship with his alliance partners and forcing him to make adjustments to underpin his political bargain.

The objective choices for individual voters in the 2006 election likely swung between embracing change and protest votes (Weiss 2007). But the 2006 elections were a moment of intense hope for the country and the Congolese people, who are generally extremely reticent to trust politicians or the political process.

The promises of large-scale and broad-based improvements in public goods have proven more sobering in reality. The Kabila presidency has prioritized his Cinq Chantiers (Five Construction Sites) developmental agenda, which emphasizes infrastructure, health and education, water and electricity, housing, and employment. But a significant part of the goodwill for the democratic government appears to have been largely squandered as a result of the government's failure to execute its program. While the DRC's security and socioeconomic challenges continue to be enormous, and the government continues to depend largely on international resources, there is not yet a political sense that stability and legitimacy of rule is best achieved primarily through improved public service delivery. By 2011, broad-based infrastructural increases in access to power, better transport, water, and sanitation remained limited, while improvements in the provision of health and education services remain wanting. Very few of the president's campaign promises have been met and there is little tangible change in the way the vast majority of people live. Both national and local authorities appear less driven by delivering on public service delivery and more interested in securing their often precarious positions in power and the benefits that control over parts of the state afford.

---

[15] Both Mobutu and Nyamwisi fell out with Kabila over the division of power in the cabinet before the 2012 elections. Nywamwisi supported the opposition, while Mobutu ran as a rival candidate to the President.

Table 3.2 *Main political parties since 2003*

Alliance pour la Majorite Presidentiel (AMP)[1]	Ruling alliance composed of many smaller parties
Mouvement pour la Liberation du Congo (MLC)	Party led by Jean-Pierre Bemba. Former rebel movement
Parti Lumumbiste Unifie (PALU)	Party led by Antoine Gizenga. In alliance with PPRD
Parti du people pour la reconstruction et le development (PPRD)	Presidential party in alliance with PALU. Leader of AMP
Parti du peuple pour la paix et le développement (PPPD)	Presidential satellite party created ahead of the 2011 elections. Member of the MP.
Mouvement Social pour le Renouveau (MSR)	Created in 2004, and allied with the ruling alliance in 2006 elections and in 2011 elections. Led by senior presidential advisor Pierre Lumbi.
Alliance des forces du changement (AFDC)	Led by former civil society leader Bahati Lukwebo. Created in 2011, member of the MP.
Rassemblement Congolais pour la Democratie (RCD)	Party led by Azarias Ruberwa. Former rebel movement
Rassemblement Congolais pour la Democratie – Kisangani / Mouvement de liberation (RCD-K/ML)	Party led by Mbusa Nyamwisi. Former rebel movement. Allied with Kabila in 2006 elections, but distanced himself from the MP in 2011.
Union des democrates Mobutistes (UDEMO)	Party led by Nzanga Mobutu, son of Mobutu Sésé Seko, in AMP.
Union pour la democratie et le progres sociale (UDPS)	Party led by veteran opposition politician Etienne Tshisekedi. Boycotted 2006 election, participated in 2011 election, the outcome of which it declared fraudulent. Tshisekedi has declared himself president of the DRC and ordered his MPs (the UDPS won forty-one seats) to boycott the National Assembly.
Union National (UN)	Alliance platform led by MLC and composed of many smaller parties
Union pour la Nation Congolaise (UNC)	Created in 2010 by Vitale Kamerhe, a former Kabila ally turned opposition leader
Alliance pour le renouveau au Congo (ARC)	Led by Olivier Kamitatu, ARC aligned itself with the AMP in 2006 and remains a member of the MP.

[1] Name changed to Majorite Presidentielle (MP) in 2011.

President Kabila's AMP[16] has increasingly sought to consolidate its formal grip on power in the wake of the 2006 elections. Following the violent clashes with Bemba's entourage in 2007, Bemba's flight into exile, and his 2008 arrest by the International Criminal Court, the MLC and the bulk of the formal opposition was in effect dismembered.[17] Despite not winning majorities in six of the eleven provinces, the ruling party secured the (indirect election) of AMP governors in five of these provinces, amidst some cloud of money politics (ICG 2007).

The government is already backpedalling when it comes to key democratic benchmarks such as holding elections. Local and municipal elections, originally due to be held in 2008, have still not been held. Having spent over $1 billion per year on MONUC since 2001, and having financed the 2006 elections at a cost of close to $1 billion, the international community will no doubt be deeply concerned by these delays and by Kabila's more recent amendments to the constitution, the most alarming of which is the elimination of the need for a run-off if the winning candidate does not get more than fifty percent of the vote in a first round.

By far the most obvious benchmark by which to measure the ruling party's waning commitment to the consolidation of democracy is the conduct of the 2011 election and its aftermath. Following the elimination of a second-round run-off, Kabila's second major blow to the credibility of the process was his appointment of a close personal associate and spiritual advisor, Daniel Ngoy Mulunda, to head the electoral commission – Commission electorale nationale independente (CENI). This appointment prompted widespread criticism that the CENI had already lost its political independence. Squabbles between the ruling alliance and the political opposition over the transparency of voter registration and other key procedures subsequently marred the pre-electoral period and the election campaign, with the CENI being accused of bias in favor of Kabila and his alliance partners (Wolters, 2011). By the time the election was held on November 28, it was

---

[16] The AMP was renamed the Majorite Presidentielle (MP) in 2010.

[17] In March 2007, Congolese government forces clashed with the several hundred MLC troops which had been Bemba's official guards during the transition period. Like the RDC, which also maintained troops in Kinshasa during the transition, the MLC guards were legitimate. However following the democratic elections of 2006, and the formation of a new government, all guards had to disarm within a certain period. When the MLC forces delayed their disarmament, they were provoked by the Congolese army, and the clashes ensued. The ICC indictment for Bemba was actually not focused on actions in the DRC, but rather those conducted in the Central African Republic in 2002 to help support the incumbent government.

clear that anything but a Kabila defeat would be contested by the political opposition.

Unfortunately, the conduct of the polls further undermined their credibility: local and international election observers noted incidents ranging from fraud, to intimidation of observers, disorganization at the polling stations, and missing or stolen ballots (see election observer reports from the Carter Center and the European Union, 2011, 2012). The subsequent vote-counting process in both the presidential and the legislative elections was chaotic at best and corrupt at worst. Although Kabila was ultimately recognized by the international community as the legitimate president of the DRC, the controversy around the elections has set the country back significantly.

Whether by way of the ballot box or other forms of elite bargains, the current environment does appear to significantly challenge the ability of any elites to make longer-term bargains with one another. Allegiances among politicians and elites remain particularly fickle. A telling joke (see Lee 1978) speaks to the difficulty of coming to a binding agreement with Congolese politicians: "Buy them? Why, you're lucky if you can rent them for the afternoon!" That said, this is the second electoral cycle in which the presidential alliance has remained intact.

3.5 The DRC as an LAO

3.5.1 Resources as Rents

Resource extraction, both in the formal and artisanal sector, continues to provide the most obvious source of rents. Additional sources to date include the exploitation of transit points and informal diversion of revenues notably in customs. Public expenditures, including the diversion of public sector wages and provincial budgets, provide another source of rents. While extractive resources in the DRC continue to receive significant attention, poor governance may be yielding aggregate rent streams well below potential. The World Bank (2007) estimates that the government currently collects less than twenty percent of revenues due under prevailing regulations. The government's review of mining contracts provides a vignette into ongoing negotiations concerning natural resource rents. In April 2007, the minister of mining established a forty-member Inter-ministerial Commission to revisit the contracts signed between the public sector and private firms in the mining sector. The impetus for this review was originally given by the Intercongolese dialogue, a resolution of which was to review all business contracts concluded by all parties during the 1998–2002 war. The initiative was initially welcomed by the mining sector and international NGOs concerned about the fairness of the contracts. However, it subsequently became increasingly opaque and subject to significant political influence and ultimately lost credibility. In the end, all reviewed mining contracts were renegotiated, one was cancelled outright, and one remained under negotiation until late 2010.[18]

Initially announced in 2008 by the minister of Infrastructure, a USD 9 billion (or just over ninety percent of the country's previous year's GDP) "infrastructure for resources" deal with the Chinese has attracted a significant degree of attention. Following initial objections from the IMF over associated sovereign guarantees, notably associated with a pending USD 13 billion HIPC debt reduction from largely traditional Western donors, the deal was restructured to provide for USD 3 billion in mining-related investments and USD 3 billion for infrastructure over the next five years (in addition to initial cash signing bonuses). The extent to which this model averts some of the "obsolescing bargain" risks encountered by traditional mining enterprises, and hence prospects for them being expanded in coming years, is uncertain. The deals do effectively bypass weak state capacity and offer the quick and highly visible delivery of infrastructure. At one level this may enhance the legitimacy and election prospects of the AMP through demonstrable infrastructure while also opening up transports routes across the country.

In the eastern part of the country, where the presence of myriad armed groups has discouraged most international mining companies from pursuing industrial operations, various armed groups, including the Congolese army, maintain illegal artisanal mining operations, frequently operating in conjunction with other armed groups in the area, especially the FDLR. In 2010, the Congolese government imposed a ban on mining in north and south Kivu, allegedly in order to put an end to illegal mining and the smuggling of minerals. This ban was lifted in 2011 in spite of the fact that illegal mining and smuggling by armed groups, the Congolese army and rebel groups continues. Attempts to regulate illegally mined ore from eastern DRC (e.g., the US Dodd-Frank Act) have focused on the ability to track exports bought by publically listed companies, which are accountable to institutions in their home countries. There is much controversy about whether such measures help or hurt small-scale local Congolese miners.

---

[18] The cancelled contract pertained to a USD 0.8 billion dollar investment about to start production by Canadian First Quantum, which also had a stake in the World Bank's private sector arm, the IFC. It become international in January 2010, and now sits idle. The second refers to US Freeport McMoRan's Tenke Fungurume operation in Katanga, which started operations in March 2009. Its capital costs approached USD 2 billion and made it the largest foreign investment in the history of the country.

The global recession and the collapse in commodity prices, combined with the Congolese government's diminished credibility due to the bungled mining review process, means that the Congolese mining sector is unlikely to see a renewed boom in the near future and that opportunities for rent seeking in the formal, industrial mining sector will be diminished for the time being. The government's current pattern of selling mining concessions to close business associates - notably Israeli businessman Dan Gertler - at below market value looks set to continue. It provides great opportunities for rent-seeking, although it comes at a price: the IMF has raised concern about opacity in the sector and is making transparency in all mining transactions a prerequisite of ongoing budget support. Given the high risks around sinking large amounts of capital for longer-term returns into the country, mining companies will likely demand access to very high-grade deposits and/or favorable deals to commit and operate large amounts of productive capital investments.

There has been growing interest in the DRC's oil sector. Although there are oil extraction operations in the west and the eastern part of the country, this remains a largely untapped resource. If the DRC were found to have significant oil reserves, there is no question that this would serve as a bonanza of rent-seeking opportunities for the ruling elite, and would also make it even more unlikely that prodevelopmental political coalitions and bargains will be formed. For now, more traditional sources of rents will be tapped – revenue services, the Central bank, and so forth, much to the detriment of efforts at national reconstruction and to the country's reputation.

3.5.2 Security Sector Reform

The Congolese state long ago lost its monopoly on violence, and security sector reform remains one of the country's most pressing issues. Without an effective, disciplined, and well-paid military that respects human rights, the DRC will remain vulnerable to regional military interventions and to the various well-organized armed groups already operating on its territory. In many cases, wage payment arrears in the Congolese army remain significant. In part, the failure to fully compensate troops in a regular manner may also be serving particular interests, not just in terms of diverting resources destined for military wages and ongoing operations. Even within the military, various commanders may be best placed to buy particular loyalty through the use of discretionary resource allocation rather than predictable wage payments. Building significant pockets of capacity in the FARDC could itself prove a potential threat to current elites, as it is not always clear to what ends this capacity could be used.

The result is that the FARDC today consists of a poorly disciplined, poorly trained military force that regularly preys on the civilian population, commits human rights abuses, and is incapable of protecting the country's borders from foreign incursions or ensuring domestic security. The Kabila government has failed to establish a monopoly over organized violence since the end of the war in 2002, and has, in fact, maintained at least casual links to nonstate armed groups, such as the FDLR, who are operating on its own soil.

Similarly, the failure over many years to complete the ongoing military integration processes, notably those involving the Mai Mai and other armed groups in the east, represents a far greater immediate security and political threat to the stability of the regime than their integration and professionalization could. From a security perspective, many disgruntled troops who have voluntarily joined the military integration process, but who have not yet integrated, are deserting and linking up with the various armed groups in the region or creating new groups. Given the many economic and geopolitical dynamics at play in the east, this merely serves to multiply the credible military threats the government faces, in particular as these groups are allowed to remain intact in areas where they might enjoy some degree of popular support. If they were integrated into the army, and redeployed as individuals throughout the country, any threat of organized violence from them would be significantly diluted.

The steadily degenerating security situation since 2006 has already eroded the support for Kabila in these areas, and yet the government is undermining the success of the military and political processes, the latter by not keeping up its end of the bargain, that is, the inclusion of the political wings of the various armed groups in the current government. In spite of this Kabila was able to win north and south Kivu provinces in the 2011 election and to be reelected. However the legitimacy of the election has been undermined by allegations of fraud, corruption, and incompetence, and domestic and international observers have cast doubt on the quality of the election exercise. In the aftermath of the controversial poll, which also included legislative elections, Kabila has again had to cobble together a fractious coalition built on promises of lucrative positions in government and the National Assembly. The overall sense that the elections were fraudulent has also stoked further resentment and anger in the east, where the government's failure to meet its military commitments is baffling. The longer the many armed groups here maintain their military capacity, the more political bargains they can extract from the government, and the more overcommitted the government becomes.

3.5.3 Region-Center Dynamics

International commentators (see Herbst and Mills 2009) have argued that the Congo needs to be engaged with less as a nation state, and more as an agglomeration of self-standing regions. While the Congo has been characterized by significant regional diversity, notably in the incidence of violence, and sub-national authorities have related in different ways to central authorities, this idea betrays the prevailing sense of national identity in the Congo. It is clear that the road to power in the DRC is still through Kinshasa.

The present MP elite coalition reflects a continued balancing act of interests at the national level. In 2006 the president's party drew its base mainly from the east, but was weaker in the urban agglomeration of Kinshasa and the western provinces, including the oil-endowed coastal province of Bas-Congo, which is one of PALU's political bases. Oddly, given the geographical elements in its alliance, the regime rarely addresses the concerns of potential sub-national elites, preferring to service those that maintain the national coalition, although even these are often neglected in face of the interests of power within the presidential circle. Even if provincial elites would like to pursue their independent interests, they remain both vulnerable to and dependent upon interests outside of their provinces. Students of the DRC's politics will be familiar with the web of particular informal power holders and shifting alliances, Part of this dynamic has been associated with varying sub-national natural resource endowments, for example, copper/cobalt in Katanga, colombo-tantalite and gold in the Kivus and Orientale, and diamonds in the Kasais. The capital, Kinshasa, has played a particular role as the country's commercial center, whereas provinces such Bas-Congo are strategically placed owing to their location of international ports.

Consequently, a central dynamic of the DRC's elite coalitions and rent extractions has hinged on dynamics within particular provinces (in particular in mining, but also other natural resources). Being able to capture rents from various sources (natural resource related, sovereign rents, other mechanisms including seignorage, exchange rate markets) remains a key challenge in the DRC. But regional sources of rents do not seem able to sustain a high degree of local elite consolidation, certainly not since the thwarted secession attempts of resource-rich Katanga and Kasai in the sixties, given high levels of predation from the central government. That this dynamic persists is evident in the current debate about the constitutional requirement that the central government return forty percent of provincial revenue to its source, a requirement yet to be implemented.

Center - Kinshasa	Rents	Elites	Violence Potential	National Links
(1) Katanga - Lumbumbashi *(Elizabethville/Sha ba)*	Copper and cobalt Customs, Transport, etc.	Balubakat ethnic clan close to Kabila Provincial governor, Babemba, President of the Provincial Assembly, Business	Presidential guard Katangans vs Luba North vs South	President, business
(2) South Kivu - *Bukavu*	Illegal Mining, Customs/Border Rents	Local and regional militias Congolese army Government/business	Local and regional militias Congolese army Neighboring countries	Military, senior members of government
(3) Orientale - *Kisangani (Stanleyville)*	Illegal and legal mining Forestry Customs/Border Rents	Local government and business Local, sub - provincial militias	Local, sub-provincial militias (Ituri) Congolese army	

Figure 3.4 Center-region dynamics (2009).

Figure 3.4 summarizes differences in rents, elites, violence potential, and associated links with the national elite coalition for three eastern provinces.[19] As of 2010, provincial political elites remained largely dependent on the center. If local leadership is considered as insufficiently collaborating with central authorities, or even risks being a threat, the MP in Kinshasa has the power to deploy various means to destabilize regional elected leaders. In no provinces, with the important exception of Katanga,[20] do sub-national elites appear

[19] Fieldwork as part of a World Bank Country Economic Memorandum (CEM) by Stephanie Wolters, researched the patterns of rent generation and capture for the national government/Kinshasa and selected provincial governments in provinces with significant resource endowments. The provinces for this research are Katanga, South Kivu, Province Orientale, as well as supplementary materials for the eastern Kasai.

[20] An interesting dynamic is the popularity of Katangan governor Moise Katumbi, a member of the AMP and a hugely popular politician in his own right. Katumbi is a Babemba from southern Katanga, while most of Kabila's associates are Baluba from northern Katanga. Given the traditional rivalry between north and south Katanga, this is a risky business which has already escalated into isolated incidents of violence, and in which Kabila is now increasingly caught in the middle. The stakes are high, as they are related to the process of decentralization – in which the two new southern Katangan provinces would emerge as winners, as this is where the copper is. There is also the dynamic of Katumbi's own popularity in Katanga and on a national level. He has the funds to operate his own campaign machine, and is hugely visible as a result of his ownership of the DRC's hugely successful TP Mazemba soccer club. He has also made a point of appearing very charitable and has gained a large following in Katanga and the country. Kabila therefore has to treat Katumbi with some respect and certainly cannot afford to alienate him. In some respects this may be another example of an elite coalition that actually works.

to have established coalitions that are resilient or impervious to national intervention. The president's power base also currently resides in Katanga, because that is from where his father hailed, as do many of his close associates. Ironically, many people in Katanga feel that the AMP government is ignoring them in favor of other parts of the country. This is perhaps because there were high expectations of receiving special treatment, as Katanga has in the past. Kinshasa's heavy hand in provincial politics has thwarted provincial development of more stable and longer-term relations with investors, in part under the knowledge that these are subject to central/external predation.

At the same time, most of the newly created provincial assemblies are dysfunctional, with one internal battle after another distracting from the business of administering the province. In many cases, these squabbles emerge as a result of battles over resources available to the provincial deputies – not to execute the provincial program, but for their own earnings packages. As a result of these distractions, provincial programs have barely been implemented, and very few reform initiatives have been undertaken. Finally, very few efforts to sanction corruption or poor performance are successful unless they are supported by the AMP in Kinshasa. This has led to a significant weakening of the provincial assemblies only five years after they were instituted.

Governors are indirectly elected, but as of a constitutional amendment passed in January 2011, governors can now be removed from their posts by the president, and national assemblies can be dissolved by the president as well. By May 2010, four governors in three out of eleven provinces had been replaced.[21] A number of these changes are attributable to corruption scandals, while others have apparently been the result of shifts in individuals' political alliances in Kinshasa. Although procedures were followed in the removal of the governors, that is, the provincial assemblies voted the governors out, the influence of key politicians in the ruling party was frequently cited as playing the deciding role. This would indicate that the newly developed decentralization framework has already been gutted of its independence, while also demonstrating that provincial elites cannot make credible bargains with national elites unless they are willing to toe the Kinshasa line.

Under these circumstances, a key question in the DRC is where more sustainable forms of elite coordination with longer-term time horizons around prodevelopmental outcomes are likely to evolve. Are these likely to emerge bottom up in the context of certain sub-national interests, or

---

[21] Two governors of South Kivu have been replaced.

be imposed on a grander scale top down? The recent China resource-for-infrastructure deal has offered the president a welcome commitment device with national reach, while at the same time bypassing the various vested interests associated with working through the normal public sector investment channels (Chevallier and Kaiser 2010). However, this came late in his first mandate and at a time when the electorate is already disappointed with the government's failure to deliver on key campaign promises. No doubt the Chinese infrastructure works are a useful campaign image, one that Kabila successfully leveraged to sustain a dominant position in the 2011 election.

In the presence of uncoordinated, short-term, and frequently non-binding elite interactions, elite actions that promise some significant scope of larger private goods (e.g., sustained industrial mining operations) or public goods (e.g., health clinics) are confronted with problems of incentive alignment and credit taking. For example, the delivery of malaria bed nets with the support of international donors arguably provides constituencies such as those in Kinshasa with tangible benefits. However, behind the scenes, this has already evoked spats between various national and provincial authorities as to who should receive credit for these measures. While there are some examples of success (often with the support of external donors), the challenge for improved elite coordination around security, the generation of greater sustainable rent streams, and public good provision remains significant in the context of the country's very weak institutional endowments. A key challenge moving forward will therefore be to seek to identify the most promising "islands of collective action" – be it in the area of security, sustainable rent generation, or public service delivery provision – which could in turn add up to a change in the direction of the country's national and sub-national developmental trajectories.

3.6 Conclusions

If the State was a person, I would kill him with a machete. The authorities maltreat us with their fields we always have to cultivate. We want to live without the State.[22]

Our survey of DRC's Fragile Limited Access Order (FLAO) has sought to better understand the evolution of governance and rule in Zaire/Congo over the last five decades, focusing in particular on the current regime.

---

[22] Selected quote from World Bank (2005) survey question.

Looking back, we have also suggested that there have been a number of notable milestones in the DRC's history. These could be seen as important watersheds for the DRC's developmental trajectory, but raise the question of whether they are more "virtuous" or "vicious" cycles in terms of stability and prospects for the greater welfare of the Congolese population. These include the Constitutional Congress (CNS) of the early 1990s, the 2002–3 peace process and transitional government, and the 2006 constitution and national elections. We would suggest that how elites managed rents and violence in each of these junctures sheds lights on some of the deeper underlying dynamics of Congolese state–society relations.[23]

In its first mandate, the Kabila regime can be associated with a small degree of stabilization in the Congo, essentially through the establishment of basic democratic structures such as the national and provincial assemblies, and some degree of process in governing. However the country is far from being stable, and outbreaks of violence will likely continue to feature in the social order in the DRC. In addition, there are worrisome indications that the transparent and organized elections held in 2006 may have been a one-time phenomenon. The 2011 presidential and legislative elections are a clear demonstration that the ruling party's commitment to democracy is weak at best.

At the same time, the DRC's institutional fabric and state capacity are by all accounts weak. Whether the existing elite coalition has either the interest or the capability to strengthen these institutions remains doubtful, especially after the experience of the 2011 election. To date, the experiences from the public and security sector reforms are not wholly encouraging. Continued dependence on traditional international development partners is likely to see continued negotiations and occasional standoffs with parts of the international community. At the same time, the resource-for-infrastructure deal with nontraditional partners such as the Chinese highlights the attraction of bypassing the more rigorous processes associated with receiving international development assistance.

Recent MONUSCO engagement and most political analysis have invariably focused heavily on dynamics in eastern DRC, which have played a disproportionate role on the national stage since Laurent Kabila overthrew the weakened Mobutu regime in 1996. Since then, the key ethnic and security

---

[23] The role of international aid during the seventies and eighties and pressures for structural adjustment have also come under increasing scrutiny. One argument suggests that international community reduced aid flows in the early 1980s when it could have tilted the country toward reforms, and therefore averted the subsequent welfare losses (Kiakwama and Chevallier 2010).

issues in the east have become even more complex and remain unresolved in spite of successive military campaigns, peace processes, and regional accords. There is no doubt that until the questions in the east are substantially resolved (including the more vexed issued of group nationalities in the broader Great Lakes context), this part of the country will prevent any real stabilization of the country as a whole.

The analysis suggests that the situation in the DRC will continue to demonstrate significant aspects of fragility and fluidity. Ongoing developments place the DRC in a steady state of fragility, which neither recent transparent elections, nor reengagement with the international community, nor the establishment of basic democratic institutions has been able to advance. The FLAO lens does raise the potential of a number of scenarios that may be more or less consistent with what would on its face present a trajectory of consolidation of electoral democracy, stability, and a prodevelopmental orientation of the regime. We conclude by examining two major questions: the prospects of a second democratic poll, and pressures to actually yield a more developmental orientation of the state in the DRC.

While beset by a number of fractures, the public face of the AMP coalition has managed to sustain itself. Incumbents elites decided to remain largely united to contest the 2011 poll. As the passing of the constitutional amendment in January 2011 indicated, the government prepared to use all means possible to skew the electoral process in its favor. According to the amendment, there will be no run-off election if the winner of the first round fails to garner a majority. This smoothed the way for Kabila to win, especially as he faced a divided opposition. There is no doubt that the government did this because it was aware that it had failed to make a positive impact on the population, while it also faced a number of very viable and popular opposition candidates. Contestation strategies included claims of having already or intending in the future to deliver gains to key parts of the electorate. In this category the delivery of high-profile infrastructure, notably through the Chinese contracts, has been a very symbolic gesture by the president. They also involved efforts to generate resources that could be deployed in advance of the polls in order to sway key local elites and vote banks. Even with significant resources, elites cannot ensure that voters will in an open vote cast ballots their way unless there is deliberate manipulation, which there appears to have been (European Union and Carter Center election observer reports, 2011).

The strength of Kabila's power base in the east, particularly if put to a more or less open ballot test, is subject to a significant degree of uncertainty.

In 2006, Kabila won significant majorities in the east (see Figure 3.3), where the populations considered him a hero for ending the war and relieving them of the presence of Rwandan and Ugandan troops. However, Kabila was pushed to a pact with Kagame to allow Rwandan troops back into the DRC to pursue the FDLR. The mitigated success of that and other ongoing military operations against the FDLR cost him some support among key constituencies. The PPRD lost significant numbers of MPs in the 2011 election and Kabila only won by three percent in South Kivu, where a key rival, Vital Kamerhe garnered forty-one percent against Kabila's forty-four percent. In North Kivu, the opposition lost because it failed to unite. The UDPS' Tshisekedi won twenty-one percent and Kamerhe twenty-three percent, against Kabila's thirty-eight percent (Commission Electorale Nationale Independante (CENI), www.ceni.gouv.cd). High levels of conflict and internal displacement therefore appear to have been an Achilles heel for the president.

Political jockeying in the West is another significant aspect of the formal trade-offs within the elite coalition. Without the support of PALU, whose traditional political base is Kinshasa and Bandundu province, the PPRD would not have succeeded in winning the election in 2006. The prime minister, following his previous post as minister of finance, has previously sought to control key parts of the discretionary investment budget (including through the national distribution of tractors), which governors claimed was their right under decentralization. This resulted in some of the more overt conflicts between the core PALU faction and governors from the presidential camp, notably Katanga.

The president has sought to appear above the fray of these more open political skirmishes, but increasingly has also sought to cast blame on the PM for the government's overall failings. This would seem to indicate that the dominant presidential elite still either does not understand that it is essentially in its interest to cement links with its ally, does not feel secure enough to do so, or holds out the prospect for alternative alliances. Both at this level, and in terms of access and use of various on and off-budget rent banks afforded by the positions of power, the political trade-offs are likely to be continuous and fluid. At the same time, few of the political parties have been able to significantly expand, or even consolidate their bases.

Against this political backdrop, the incentives to the overall MP coalition and its individual components to face another open poll are uncertain. Certain members such as the PALU may feel that another poll would promise them more leverage, especially if the president is exposed in the east (and west). But alternatively, elites could be tempted to avoid the DRC's potentially fickle electorate and seek a more closed pact to retain power (especially in the face of a formal opposition). An early worrying sign ahead of the 2011 elections for those vested in the consolidation of democratic process in the DRC was that the IEC distanced itself from the international community and decided to take the lead in the organization of the 2011 poll. This was an early indication that the government may have felt that it could not withstand the scrutiny of an internationally organized poll and at the same time win the elections.

A second, particularly vexing, question concerns the actual mechanisms by which a longer term and potentially prodevelopmental orientation among elites could emerge. The need to maintain alliances within the MP was a key dynamic in government before the election and has become even more acute in the hefty bargaining that succeeded Kabila's presidential victory and the MP's patchwork legislative majority of 341 seats. There is no evidence at this stage that the MP is motivated to pursue a prodevelopmental agenda. The post-electoral negotiations appeared to be centered on crude calculations of access to power in return for a good performance in the election. The newly-formed government, which is dominated by MP members and does not include a single opposition politician from a significant party, does not indicate that the President intends to change old governance patterns. The presence of just over 100 opposition MPs in the National Assembly and the general political imbalance and crisis of legitimacy caused by the controversial elections has exacerbated the tendency toward coercion and political pressures at the expense of real coalition building. At the same time, even if the presidency were inclined to each out to the opposition in order to heal the rifts caused by the election, it is essentially hostage to the promises of positions made before the election.

By all accounts, historic sources of rents have declined as a result of the collapse of key productive entities, although natural resources continue to be important. Especially in the east, there is some evidence that informal minerals rent extraction is potentially sustaining conflict and hampering security sector reform (cf Garrett 2009). The completion of the recent round of contract renegotiations and the continued stand-off with significant large mining operators raises the question of where and how significant future rent streams to stabilize the elite coalition will be identified. Anecdotal evidence from the investor community suggests that elite rent seeking has become increasingly short-term and opportunistic. This potentially dampens the overall size of the potential pie and growth prospects from the current low levels. The DRC has experienced some rebound due to postwar stabilization, but now must confront where the potential future sources for sustained growth lie. At the moment the principal elites appear more focused on extracting rents quickly to sustain a fragile coalition and enrich themselves, rather than on setting the conditions for medium to longer-term prospects. A more nuanced set of LAO trajectories could help identify junctures that see a changing set of behavior on the part of elites; not just how they capture rents in fragile settings, but how they seek to sustain them.

As the DRC achieves postconflict stability following a decade and a half of full-fledged violence, do its elites have the will and capacity to begin tackling the starkest aspects of its dysfunctionality? The factors of external intervention and/or engagement have clearly played an important part in the various phases of the DRC's fragile order. Current developments indicate that the ruling elite remains largely disengaged from the government–citizen compact which would guide its policies and behavior. Whether a transparent electoral contest may impose this is very much an open question. There may be some areas (including provinces) where such an orientation could be built from the bottom up, but these in turn remain prone to national (and external) intervention and rent seeking.[24] The prospects for the development of more elite coalitions remain elusive for as long as the ruling elite lacks the confidence to genuinely believe that its interests are served first by a consolidation of existing political alliances, and second, by genuine attempts in the long run to govern the country in a developmental manner.

References

Carter Center (2011). "First Carter Center Pre-Election Statement on Preparations in the Democratic Republic of Congo" (Carter Center, October 17, 2011).

(2011) Mission d`observation internationale du Centre Carter en RDC, Elections présidentielle et législatives du 28 Novembre 2011, Déclaration Post – électorale de la compilation et annonce des résultats provisoires del`élection présidentielle (Carter Center, December 10, 2011).

Chevallier, Jérôme and Kaiser, Kai-Alexander. (2010). *The Political Economy of Mining in the Democratic Republic of Congo (DRC)* (Washington, DC: World Bank).

---

[24] While the 2006 constitution is not federalist but unitary, it assigns the provinces significant roles and responsibilities, although on either dimension it diverges from reality. The "second generation" federalism literature has focused on the dejure and above all defacto institutional checks and balances between levels of government in decentralized governance, and the types of scope these provide for stable "market preserving" arrangements (Weingast 2006). Given prevailing elite incentives and fluid coalitions across levels of government, it remains to be seen under what circumstances and thought a more prodevelopment set of provincial behaviors can be produced and sustained.

Collier, Paul. (2009). *Wars, Guns, and Votes: Democracy in a Dangerous Place* (New York: HarperCollins).

Devlin, Larry. (2007). *Chief of Station, Congo: Fighting the Cold War in a Hot Zone* (Cambridge, MA: Public Affairs).

EIU. (1998). *DRC Country Report* (London: Economist Intelligence Unit [Quarter 2]).

Garrett, Nicholas and Harrison Mitchel. (2009). *Trading Conflict for Development: Utilizing the Trade in Minerals from Eastern DR Congo for Development* (London: Resource Consulting Services [April]), 50.

Haskin, Jeanne. (2005). *The Tragic State of Congo: From Decolonization to Dictatorship* (New York: Algora Publishing).

Herbst, Jeffrey and Mills, Greg. (2009). "There Is No Congo," *Foreign Affairs* March (Web Edition).

Hochschild, Adam. (1999). *King Leopold's Ghost: A Story of Greed, Terror, and Heroism in Colonial Africa* (New York: Mariner Books).

International Crisis Group (2007), *Consolidating the Peace*, Africa Report No 158, July 5. (Brussels: ICG).

Kaiser, Kai, Mulumba, Jean Mabi, and Verheijen, Tony. (2010). "The Political-Economy of Decentralization in the DRC" (Revised Paper Prepared for "Obstacles to Decentralization: Lessons From Selected Countries" Andrew Young School of Policy Studies, International Studies Program, Georgia State University).

Kiakwama, Gilbert and Chevallier, Jerome. (2010). *Aid and Reform: The Case of the Democratic Republic of Congo* (Washington, DC: Development Research Group, Project on World Bank on Aid and Reform in Africa).

Lee, Armistead M. (1978). "The Congo Desk," *The New York Review of Books* **25**(19).

Ndikumana, Leonce and Emizet, Kisangani. (2005) "The Economics of Civil War: The Case of Democratic Republic of Congo," in Paul Collier and Nicolas Sambanis (eds.), *Understanding Civil War: Evidence and Analysis (Africa)* (Washington, DC), 63–88.

North, Douglass C., Wallis, John Joseph, and Weingast, Barry. (2009). *Violence and Social Orders: A Conceptual Framework for Interpreting Recorded Human History* (Cambridge: Cambridge University Press), 326.

Nziem, Ndaywel e. (1998). *Histoire generale du Congo* (Afrique-Editions).

Putzel, James, Linderman, Stefan, and Schouten, Claire. (2008). *Drivers of Change in the Democratic Republic of Congo: The Rise and Decline of the State and Challenges for Reconstruction* (London: LSE Crisis States Research Centre, Working Paper No. 26), 55.

Union Europeenne, Mission d'Observation Electorale, Republique Democratique du Congo (2011). *Communique de Presse*, December 13, 2011.

United Nations Security Council. (2009). *Thirtieth Report of the Secretary-General on the United Nations Organization Mission in the Democratic Republic of Congo* (New York: December 4).

Weingast, Barry R. (2006). "Second Generation Fiscal Federalism: Implications for Decentralized Democratic Governance and Economic Development," *Decentralization and Democratic Local Governance Programming Handbook* (Washington, DC: USAID).

Weiss, Herbert F. (2007). "Voting for Change in the DRC," *Journal for Democracy* **18**(2), 138–51.

Wolters, Stephanie. (2011) *"Elections in the Democratic Republic of Congo"*, Okapi Consulting Briefing (Johannesburg, November 2011)

World Bank. (2005). *Governance, Service Delivery, and Poverty* (Washington, DC: Public Sector Reform and Capacity Building [AFTPR], Country Department 9, Africa Region, AFTPR, Report No: 32205-ZR).

Wrong, Michaela. (2001). *In The Footsteps of Mr. Kurtz: Living on the Brink of Disaster in Mobutu's Congo* (New York: Harper Collins).

Young, Crawford and Turner, Thomas. (1985). *The Rise and Decline of the Zairian State* (Madison, WI: The University of Wisconsin Press), 365.

Annex 3.1 Stylized Governance Features DRC

	Colonial Era (<1960)	Post-Independence Transition	Early-Mobutu (1965ff)	Mobutu-Zairisation	Mobutu Decline
Formal Political Institutions	Colonial rule	Parliamentary Democracy, Contested Statehood/ Secession	Military Putsch, Presidentialism	Single Party State	Re-emergence of multi-party politics, Continue Presidential Dominance
Formal Economic Institutions	Private market economy Rule of law	Continue Prevalence on	Mixed economy	Mixed Economy	Increasingly informal economy
Principal Elites	Belgian colonial/ economic interests	Emerging political class, Belgian colonial/ economic interests	Emerging political class, international interests	Political/ economic elites (Zairisation benefiaries)	"Mobutuists"
Principal Source of Rents	Mining/ Plantation Rents	Mining/ Plantation Rents	Aid Mining Rents (Gecamines)	Aid Mining Rents (Gecamines)	Mining, Seignorage/Black Markets

Kabila Father (1997–2001)	Kabila Son (2001–2003)	Kabila Transitional Government (2003–06)	Kabila AMP (2006 ff)	2011ff?
Military overthrow, single party state, no political activity	Succession of assassinated father, liberalization of multi-party politics, peace negotiations and internationally-mediated political dialogue	Post-war Power-Sharing Coalition (4 VPs)	Electoral Democracy	
Min of Finance, Economy, Congolese Central Bank	Min of Finance, Economy, Congolese Central Bank	Min of Finance, Economy, Congolese Central Bank	Min of Finance, Economy, Congolese Central Bank, various parliamentary economic and financial committees	
Kabila allies, Tutsis ONLY until 1998, Katangans, Senior military officers, Some businesspeople, Old Marxists	Some Kabila father allies, Katangans, Senior military officers, Some businesspeople	PPRD members, Kabila allies, former rebel leaders and their allies, Katangans, Senior officers, Some businesspeople	Senior AMP members, Kabila allies, former rebel leaders and their allies, Katangans, Senior officers, Some businesspeople	
Diamond Rents (MIBA), Copper, cobalt Mining rents, Parastatal rents, Military rents	Diamond, copper, cobalt mining rents, Parastatal rents, Military rents	Aid, Mining, Parastatals, Military, Infrastructure deals	Aid, Mining, Parastatals. Military, Infrastructure deals	*Forestry?* Resource of Infrastructure Deals

FOUR

Seeking the Elusive Developmental Knife Edge

Zambia and Mozambique – A Tale of Two Countries

Brian Levy

4.1 Introduction

This chapter aims to explore the practical and analytical usefulness for development policy of a new framework for interpreting the evolution and performance of political and economic institutions suggested by Douglass North, John Wallis, and Barry Weingast (NWW) in their recent book, *Violence and Social Orders*.[1]

A central distinction of the framework is between open access orders (OAOs) and limited access orders (LAOs). Most contemporary theorizing and prescription on the appropriate governance arrangements for low-income countries uses as its benchmark the institutions of OAOs: elections, and more broadly pluralistic, open and competitive political arrangements; and a free market economy underpinned by the impartial protection of property rights. The corollary prescription has been to advocate for the immediate, comprehensive construction of these institutions in less developed countries.

By contrast, NWW suggest that these institutions are the outcome of a long historical process, that the relevant dynamics are those of the LAO – and that the appropriate analytical and policy challenge is to understand how "doorstep conditions" that lead to OAOs can emerge out of LAOs. In LAOs, political stability depends on effective coordination among elites on

[1] Douglass C. North, John Joseph Wallis, and Barry R. Weingast, *Violence and Social Orders: A Conceptual Framework for Interpreting Recorded Human History* (New York: Cambridge University Press, 2009).

I am grateful to David Trichler for his helpful research assistance, to Scott Taylor for helping me to better understand contemporary Zambia, and to Douglass North, John Wallis, Barry Weingast, Steven Webb, Mushtaq Khan, Alan Hirsch, and others for helpful comments on an earlier draft.

access to, and allocation of, economic rents – with competition for rents carrying with it the threat of a violent disruption of the existing social order. Only in OAOs can competition – economic and political – and stability comfortably coexist. Moreover, OAOs emerge only as the culmination of a long (and by no means inevitable) historical process through which three necessary "doorstep conditions" have been institutionalized.[2]

As a way of exploring the usefulness of the approach, this chapter will examine and interpret through the lens of the AO framework the political and economic development over the past half century or so of two southern African countries: Zambia and Mozambique. Both former colonies – Zambia won independence from the United Kingdom in 1964 and Mozambique gained independence from Portugal a decade later – the two countries offer a rich basis for analysis and comparative assessment. Considered over time, both countries have undergone dizzying cycles of back-and-forth institutional changes in their political and economic orders since independence; the clear "periodization" in each offers a good vantage point for identifying the relevance of underlying continuities of the kind suggested by the LAO approach. Considered across countries, there are large, continuing, underlying variations between Zambia and Mozambique in their institutional orders, importantly (from an LAO perspective) in the role and management of elite conflict and violence in the two countries. These variations have the potential to offer analytical insight as to different types of LAOs, each with distinctive development opportunities and risks.

Sections 4.2 and 4.3 of the chapter present analytical narratives of the two countries using the LAO lens. The review will be organized around four sets of questions central to the LAO approach:

- What are the *formal political institutions* intended to govern interactions among elites, and in what ways (and with what relationship to informal political arrangements) do they serve this function?
- What are the *formal economic institutions* that govern relationships among producers, consumers, and factors of production?
- Who are the *principal domestic elite groups*, and what are their relationships with one another? What is their relationship to international actors? What threat do disaffected elites pose to the stability of the governing elite coalition?

---

[2] The "doorstep conditions" comprise the institutionalization of: (i) the rule of law for elites; (ii) perpetually lived organizations in the public and private spheres; and (iii) consolidated, civilian control of the military and other legally accepted organizations with violence potential (North, Wallis, and Weingast, *Violence and Social Orders*).

- What are the principal sources of *rent*, and how are they allocated? How does the allocation of rent correspond to the relative influence of elite groups and/or their ability to threaten the stability of the governing coalition?

The analytic narratives are organized around the interactions among the emphasized elements in each of the four questions at different points in time.[3]

The first two questions address what NWW hypothesize to be a "double balance" – the proposition that LAOs and OAOs are characterized by distinctive, and aligned, political and economic institutions, and that open economic institutions cannot be sustained with closed political institutions (and vice versa). The latter two questions extend the framework to include structural characteristics of the polity and economy. The natural extension to the double balance hypothesis – which will be explored for the Zambian and Mozambican cases – is that sustainability requires a balance among all four elements.

Section 4.4 of the chapter provides a comparative interpretation of the analytic narratives, organized around five propositions concerning the value added, and limitations of the LAO/OAO approach for analyzing and addressing the development challenges of low-income countries.

4.2 Zambia through an LAO Lens

4.2.1 Some Structural Features

Though Zambia and Mozambique are southern African neighbors, their patterns of integration into the global economy, and the institutional legacies that resulted, have been very different. Mozambique's sixteen hundred-mile north-to-south coastline made it irresistible to even the earliest ocean-going explorers. Traveling along the coast in 1498, Vasco da Gama came upon Arab trading settlements that had inhabited the coastline for several centuries. Over the course of the subsequent century, the Portuguese took control of the coastal towns. Chains of settlements were built along rivers that

---

[3]   The interrelationships among the emphasized elements can usefully be depicted (including graphically) as a "governance diamond." Brian Levy, "Governance and Economic Development in Africa," chapter 1 of Brian Levy and Sahr Kpundeh (eds.) *Building State Capacity in Africa* (Washington, DC: World Bank Institute Development Studies, 2004) used such a governance diamond – with four similar elements, but with each defined in a more schematic way – to assess the dynamics of governance change across a variety of African countries, including Zambia and Mozambique.

flowed from east to west into the African interior; these became conduits for trading – initially ivory, and then slaves (the slave trade continued into the mid-nineteenth century, with slavery abolished in Mozambique itself only in 1879, and forced labor practices continuing thereafter). In the latter nineteenth century, the Portuguese granted charters to three massive companies, one each for the southern, central and northern parts of the country. Though a Portuguese colonial government took direct control in the 1930s, the east–west bias of the country remained: the southern part of the country (including the capital, Lourenco Marques/Maputo) was a hub for South Africa; the central part (including the port of Beira) was a hub for Southern Rhodesia/Zimbabwe; and the northern part linked into the central African economies of Nyasaland/Malawi. Through to the present day, no trunk transport infrastructure links the country from north to south.

Zambia's origins as a national entity are even more haphazard. As the British empire pushed north from southern into central Africa in the latter nineteenth century, it found its imperial ambitions coming into conflict with those of Germany (seeking to move into central Africa from its colonies in the west – what is now Namibia – and the northeast – what is now Tanzania), those of Belgium (expanding its positions from the immediate north, in the Congo), and the Portuguese (to the west, from Angola, as well as Mozambique in the east). Zambia's borders were the residual result of successful diplomatic maneuvers by the British to halt the advances of their rivals on each of these fronts. The residual land area was vast, inhabited by multiple scattered indigenous populations that had little in common other than their colonial overlord.

While the twentieth-century, colonial-era patterns of growth were very different across the two countries, they were exceedingly unequal. Zambia's economic growth was driven by the discovery of huge, underground copper deposits. Mining took off, with the demand for labor transforming Zambia into one of the most urbanized economies in Africa; by the 1950s, about half of the population was urbanized. Mozambican growth was anchored in plantation agriculture, so the population remained principally rural. As Table 4.1 details, at the close of their colonial eras, the per capita incomes of both countries put them in lower-income to lower-middle-income range. But the benefits flowed disproportionately to settler populations: for the indigenous populations, the welfare indicators were little different from those of the world's least developed economies. Evidently, the end of colonial rule would witness a shift of political and economic power to the indigenous population. But what would be the resulting political, economic, and institutional order?

Table 4.1 *Development indicators at the end of colonial rule*

	Zambia (early 1960s)	Mozambique (early 1970s)
GDP per capita (2,000 US$)	$2,690	$840
GDP per capita (2008)	2008: $1150	2008: $465
Urban population as percentage of total	40%	20%
Life expectancy at birth	40 years	38.6 years
Adult literacy	33%	Under 10%
Child mortality (under-five deaths per 1,000)	230	280

4.2.2 Independent Zambia's Political and Institutional Trajectory

Viewed through a conventional lens, the history of Zambia's political economy in the forty-five years since independence is a by now familiar story of a country that became impatient with liberal politics and market economics, embarked on a top-down statist experiment, became disillusioned with that, and found its way back to markets and pluralism. Viewed through an LAO lens, however, the story becomes altogether more complex and interesting. Through this lens, the narrative becomes a quest to meet two (and perhaps three) distinct goals:

- To ensure political and social stability in a country created by colonialism, which, at independence, had no track record of governance outside the colonial umbrella.
- To meet and balance the aspirations for wealth and power of the country's elites.
- To respond to pressures from – and the aspirations of – non-elites, including for a reduction of poverty (although it should be noted up front that these non-elite pressures and aspirations have had remarkably little force in Zambia's modern history).

Zambia's quest to meet these goals played out in three acts. The first act (1964–72) opened with the bequest at independence of OAO institutional forms, followed in short order by their rapid unraveling in the face of their evident inadequacy to ensure stability and meet the aspirations of a newly politically empowered set of elites. The second act (1972–90) opened with the promulgation in 1972 of a new constitution that transformed Zambia into a basic LAO one-party participatory democracy with expanded state control of the economy. The subsequent eighteen years witnessed the gradual unraveling of this alternative order as it, too, proved incapable of meeting the priority objectives. The third act commenced in 1991 with a multiparty election, the defeat (and subsequent disintegration) of the formerly dominant party, followed in short order by rapid market liberalization. The third act continues into the present day. The mixed performance of this period raises some fascinating questions (which will be considered further in Section 4.4) as to the potential and limits for low-income countries of a soft pluralist institutional order. Table 4.2 summarizes the dominant institutional characteristics of each of these three periods. The subsections that follow explore the interactions among the four elements – highlighting the stress points during each of three periods.

A colonial bequest – and its unraveling. It is a commonplace that exiting colonial powers bequeath political and economic institutions that are more aspirational than a reflection of the newly independent country's political and economic realities. A principal reason, commonly noted, is that opposition to the colonial authority becomes the basis for a nationalist coalition that brings together disparate groups with divergent and conflicting underlying differences – but with these differences remaining latent until after independence has been won.

This, indeed, is largely what happened in Zambia though, of course, with some country-specific wrinkles. The nationalist struggle was not simply for independence from British rule, but to extricate Zambia (then Northern Rhodesia) from a federation with Southern Rhodesia and Nyasaland, which would have entrenched settler at the expense of indigenous interests. And the nationalist movement was quite early on subject to factionalization, with the initially dominant group (the African National Congress), eventually superseded by the United National Independence Party (UNIP) under Kenneth Kaunda. Constitutional negotiations that led to majority rule were begun in 1962; the federation was dissolved in 1963; and Zambia attained independence in October 1964, with a hybrid (parliamentary/presidential) democratic constitution, the full panoply of market institutions – and a dominant electoral majority for UNIP. However, this bequeathed institutional form emerged with little, if any, attention to how to address two fundamental disconnects.

The first disconnect was economic. Though political power had transferred to the African majority, in the years immediately following independence the patterns of ownership, control, and access to income opportunities continued to reflect those of the former colonial LAO order: The best paid

Table 4.2 *Zambia's governance diamond – key features*

	1964	1972–91	1991–
Formal political institutions	- multiparty democracy - parliament, with constituency elections - directly elected president	- one-party state - multicandidate constituency elections within UNIP - president nominated by UNIP	- multiparty democracy - parliament, with constituency elections - directly elected president, authority de facto centralized in presidency
Formal economic institutions	- private market economy - judicial protection of property rights - ease of entry/exit	- majority state control of industry and mining - ubiquitous price controls - generally unfavorable business environment	- private market economy (ongoing privatization in 1990s) - market-set prices - high-transactions-costs business environment
Principal elites	1. political elites (i) UNIP (ii) Other parties 2. economic elites (i) settlers of European and Asian origin; (ii) trade unions; (iii) Anglophone foreign investors	- fused political and economic elite under UNIP umbrella; parliament, parastatals, and businessmen (including trade unions and minorities, generally linked to UNIP) - some foreign investment joint venture partners	- fragmented political and economic elites (many within MMD coalition); multiple localized patronage networks; weakly organized; - foreign investors - emerging indigenous business
Principal sources of rent	- copper rents	- copper rents (especially including revenue stream) - parastatal revenues - 1980s: public spending (deficits and foreign aid)	- rents from privatization - copper revenues (until 2000) - public spending (aid - accounts for 18% – 27% of expenditure) - links to foreign investors

and most senior jobs in both the public and private sectors were almost all held by Europeans; sixty percent to seventy percent of all marketed agricultural goods were produced by white settler farmers on large commercial farms; the copper mines, which dominated the nonagricultural part of the economy, were wholly owned by South African, British, and American interests (colonial authorities had systematically located manufacturing within Southern Rhodesia).[4] Put differently, political institutions and the composition of political elites had shifted – however, rents remained principally in the hands of the preexisting elites, with their control over those rents supported by the bequeathed economic institutions.

The second disconnect was in how to address an underlying tendency toward fragmentation in a new country possessing no natural national identity of its own. At independence, Zambia had in place the full range of formal political institutions of an OAO order – including, seemingly, at least one political party organized around the pursuit of national collective interests. But, given the arbitrary way in which Zambia's national boundaries were set, this sense of any collective national interest was fragile. Once independence was won, entropy began to set in. One set of challenges came from organized labor, especially the influential mineworkers' union that had been a powerful ally of UNIP in the struggle for independence: between 1964 and 1966, the number of person hours lost due to labor disruptions rose five-fold. A second set of challenges was more territorially anchored: In the years immediately following independence, regional, sometimes ethnically based opposition – internal party dissension and electoral contestation, often accompanied by low-level violence – emerged from many of the regional factions that initially had come together under the UNIP umbrella.

Viewed through the lens of hindsight, the events of the next eight years seem inevitable. On the economic front, President Kaunda declared his intent in the 1968 Mulungushi Declaration to "Zambianize" the economy. That same year, twenty-six large foreign-owned commercial and industrial firms were required to sell a majority of their shares to the state. The year 1969 saw the beginning of a process (concluded in 1970) of transferring fifty-one percent of the two dominant copper companies (plus all mining rights) to state ownership. In 1971, insurance companies and building societies were nationalized, and a state-owned commercial bank was established to compete with the remaining private commercial banks. On the domestic

---

[4] The dominant mining company was the South African-based Anglo American Corporation; the second company was the Roan Selection Trust (forty-five percent of which was owned by American Metal Climax).

political front, in 1970 a breakaway faction threatened to pose a serious electoral threat to UNIP's hegemony in the next round of scheduled elections – including in its Copperbelt heartland; 100 members of the faction were detained, Meanwhile, a 1969 referendum weakened a series of constitutional protections included in the independence agreement. Regionally, too, geopolitics contributed to a sense of siege, with the settler population of Southern Rhodesia unilaterally declaring independence in 1965, the first act in a fifteen-year military conflict.

In 1972, all political parties except UNIP were banned. The following year, a new constitution was passed initiating a one-party participatory democracy. In less than a decade, Zambia had shed its bequest of OAO institutional forms and reconstituted itself firmly as a limited access order in both the political and economic dimensions.

A one-party LAO – and its discontents. Zambia's one-party LAO lasted for eighteen years – a brief surge of enthusiasm followed by a sustained period of ongoing crisis, response, backtracking, and deeper decline. The root cause of this failure is not the LAO logic itself. Indeed, according to the AO approach, all sustainable OAOs emerge out of successful LAOs. Rather, the root problem was an inability to tailor the political logic of Zambia's LAO elite bargains to the country's unexpectedly stringent economic realities – including the decline of copper prices, with associated limitations in the availability of rents.

The new one-party LAO rapidly took on a form that aligned, in a "triple balance," political and economic institutions, and a new elite bargain – fusing economic and political power under the umbrella of state control. The civil service (a key source of patronage and control) began growing rapidly immediately following independence – from under twenty-three thousand in 1964 to fifty-two thousand in 1967. Between 1968 and 1976, over two and a half times as many jobs were created in the public sector as in the rest of the formal economy. By 1975, the central civil service had overtaken the copper industry to become the largest employer in Zambia. The patronage-driven creation of civil service jobs continued into the 1980s, until it was rendered infeasible (except at modest margins)[5] by economic crisis and subsequent political change.

---

[5]   The announced intention of the MMD government that came to power in 1991 was to cut the civil service by twenty-five percent. In actuality, civil service employment rose by nineteen percent in the initial years of MMD rule, with no significant cuts materializing subsequently.

- Price control became ubiquitous with major restrictions on the purchase and sale of food crops and extensive controls on other products.
- State control was consolidated, with parastatals dominating mining, industry, and commerce – and with all state participation managed under the umbrella of the giant supra-holding company, the Zambia Industrial and Mining Corporation.
- The 1971 Industrial Relations Act mandated that all worker organizations affiliate with the Zambia Congress of Trade Unions and ordered the payment of dues to the national unions. ZCTU's three hundred and fifty thousand workers comprised seventy percent of all formal sector employment.[6]

The management of this entire apparatus was centralized in the office of the charismatic president, Kenneth Kaunda. Kaunda told ministers that "loyalty to the ruling [UNIP] party would be the prime criterion for senior appointments within the civil service."[7]

In the very short term, UNIP's aggressive spending brought a surge of growth, with real GDP rising by almost seven percent in 1974. But this initial burst of economic activity soon gave way to a prolonged period of economic decline. Zambia's 1991 per capita income was $390, down from $540 in 1964. The powerful labor movement turned decisively against government; 1989 witnessed food riots and a coup attempt. A 1990 referendum demonstrated widespread support for multiparty democracy. Presidential elections in 1991 were won by the opposition party, whose leader was the head of the trade union movement, and signaled the end of Zambia's single-party LAO.

Three sets of reasons – external, economic, and political – accounted for the failure of the LAO. The key external influence was the price of copper – as of the early 1970s, copper accounted for ninety-five percent of the country's foreign exchange receipts and forty-five percent of government revenues. Throughout the 1960s and early 1970s copper prices had been buoyant. The Zambian authorities had projected this forward, and borrowed on that basis. But between 1974 and 1975, copper prices fell from ninety-three dollars per pound to fifty-six dollars per pound – and did not recover on any sustained basis for almost three decades. From 1980–3, Zambian copper

6   Lisa Rakner, *Political and Economic Liberalisation in Zambia 1991–2001* (Stockholm: The Nordic Africa Institute, 2003), pp. 50–1.
7   Quoted from William Tordoff, *Administration in Zambia* (Manchester: Manchester University Press, 1980), p. 73.

averaged only fifty-one percent of its 1970–4 indexed purchasing power.[8] (Another noteworthy external political influence was the accelerating conflict in southern Africa: first, the Zimbabwean war that was resolved in 1980; then a brutal civil war in Mozambique; and, finally, rising opposition to apartheid in South Africa. All of this complicated political management and any effort to build positive economic momentum.)

Economic policy weaknesses at the macro and micro levels comprise the second set of reasons for the failure of the LAO. Zambia's economic policy makers were unwilling (and, as discussed further later in the chapter, unable politically) to adapt economic policy to the more stringent realities associated with the sharp fall in copper prices. Instead, they resorted to large-scale foreign borrowing. External debt ballooned from 61 percent of GDP in 1980 to 317 percent of GDP by 1986. Ever more desperate measures to find the requisite rents also undercut economic performance at the micro level – with the mining industry and other parastatals progressively bled dry of revenues that ought to have been set aside for operations, maintenance, and replacement investment.

The third, and most fundamental, set of reasons for the failure of the LAO was political. Only a few years into the one-party era, UNIP no longer was an institution capable of winning commitments for collective action from its members – let alone from society more broadly. On the one hand, the party lost its broad base of participation: membership in the Copperbelt declined from twenty-five percent of the voting population in 1968 to eight percent in 1974; by 1980, the party had no real presence in the countryside. As of 1982, only eighty-nine thousand of 3 million Zambian youths were members of UNIP.[9] On the other hand, with no outlets for ambition other than UNIP, pressures from elites multiplied for access to resources and authority, "affecting the ability to plan and enact policies in every conceivable area."[10]

The central tool available to political leadership to maintain stability and political authority was the distribution of patronage to key elite stakeholders. The beneficiaries of rents were powerful urban and ethnic constituencies, represented by key elites, who were awarded positions in the cabinet, carefully balanced ethnically. The economic dimensions of development policy making became increasingly subordinated to the imperatives of creating and allocating the rents necessary for political management.

---

[8] Burdette, p. 117.
[9] Burdette, p. 116.
[10] Data and quote are from Burdette, p. 116

In the face of increasingly stringent economic circumstances, the continued conferral of patronage resources to an expanding set of claimants was not a sustainable strategy. In the latter part of the 1980s, the UNIP regime finally sought reform – but found itself without the political tools to lock in a sustainable bargain. Between 1985 and 1990, Zambia went back and forth between supporting and opposing structural adjustment reforms, with major internal conflicts between technocratic and more politically oriented advisers. Disputes over economic policy also were the proximate cause of the powerful trade union movement turning decisively against the government. On two separate occasions (in 1986–7 and again in 1990) reductions in food subsidies resulted in riots in the capital, Lusaka, and the Copperbelt, with people killed, and reforms reversed. Following the collapse of the Berlin Wall in 1989, constituencies outside the one-party UNIP fold became increasingly emboldened in their calls for multiparty democracy. Eventually, Kaunda acceded to multiparty elections, held in October 1991, which he confidently expected to win. In the event, UNIP was decisively defeated, with the opposition Movement for Multi-party Democracy (MMD) winning 125 of a total of 150 seats. Frederick Chiluba, head of Zambia's trade union movement, became president.

From a dominant party to a competitive clientelistic LAO. The eighteen-plus years since the 1991 election have been among the most stable in Zambia's modern history. Moreover, accelerating economic growth since 2000 (between five percent and six percent per annum from 2003–9, including through the global economic crisis) suggests that the post-1991 institutional order has not been subject to the fundamental disconnects that characterized the earlier two postindependence periods. But, viewed from the perspective of the AO framework, what type of order is it?

At first glance, Zambia's post-1991 institutional order seems to be characterized by significant openness. On the political front, the dominance of UNIP was decisively ended. Though President Chiluba won reelection in 1996 with over two-thirds of the vote, subsequent elections were more closely contested; the MMD has remained in power, but its vote total has hovered at or below forty percent. Moreover, when President Chiluba sought to amend the constitution to run for a third term of office, he was rebuffed by sustained civic opposition. The country has a vibrant independent media. On the economic front, an equally far-reaching transformation was effected, with the MMD victory ushering in a period of economic reform. The new government, with strong, sustained support from the World Bank and International Monetary Fund, aggressively implemented the Washington Consensus package of macroeconomic stabilization, exchange rate and market liberalization, and privatization. Though this recipe had been perceived by UNIP as politically infeasible, President Chiluba gave it credibility – both because the policies represented a sought-for radical departure from UNIP's half-hearted commitment to policy implementation; and because people believed that, as a former leader of the miners' union, he would be more empathetic to problems of the poor and help bring about economic growth and development. Hitherto far-reaching price controls were eliminated entirely; hitherto radically overvalued exchange rates became market determined; privatization, especially of commercial enterprises, proceeded rapidly and, for the most part, transparently – accelerated by the establishment of the Zambia stock exchange. In support of these reforms, aid flows increased rapidly and have remained high. The vast majority of Zambia's debt obligations to international finance institutions and bilateral donors were forgiven. And ongoing aid flows still accounted in the latter 2000s for about eighteen percent of total government spending (down from a peak of twenty-seven percent in 2002).

But for all of its seeming openness, neither Zambia's political nor its economic institutions are characterized accurately as facilitating open access. Less than two years after it came to power, the MMD split, with some of the most committed reformers leaving office. Top-down presidentialism and political management via the allocation of rents reasserted itself in the more liberalized environment – but with important differences from the UNIP period in the specific patterns of rent seeking and corruption.

Instead of using rents to buy group loyalty in the mold of Kaunda, beneficiaries were less representatives of their groups than individual entrepreneurs, seeking individual gain and opportunities for patronage, which were almost always conditioned by their success in the never-ending game of winning access to the president's (revolving) inner circle through the continual forming, unforming, and reforming of political coalitions under the MMD umbrella.

With the ending post-UNIP of a leadership code during the Kaunda era that had (not always successfully) prohibited senior public officials from owning businesses, the opportunities for extracting rents were many.[11] Over time, insiders found ways of circumventing the rules governing privatizing and acquired former parastatals, including tourist lodges, manufacturing firms, and trade enterprises for little or no compensation. Procurement

[11] These examples are taken from Scott Taylor and Neo Simutanyi, "Governance and Political Economy Constraint to Development Priorities in Zambia: A Diagnostic," mimeo, July 2007.

contracts were directed to businesses owned by public officials (with many documented cases of overinvoicing and of payment for work not done). President Chiluba had direct control of the Presidential Discretionary Fund and the resources of the Presidential Housing Initiative. At a lower level, the red tape that continues to permeate Zambia's business environment provided abundant opportunities for petty corruption on the part of public officials.[12]

Three consequences for Zambian development of these individualized rentier institutions are noteworthy. First, Zambia's bureaucracy (which was functioning well in the immediate aftermath of independence) remains chronically weak and has been impervious to repeated efforts at reform. Second, Zambia has been chronically unable to provide public goods. At a macro level, public investment has languished below six percent, even in the face of major infrastructural constraints.[13] At a micro level, Zambia's major nontraditional export success over the past two decades has been cotton outgrowing, with inputs provided to small-scale peasant farmers by ginneries, who in turn purchase the seed cotton for ginning and export. Production rose ten-fold from twenty thousand metric tons in 1994 to two hundred thousand tons by 2005. But the industry has been bedeviled by repeated side selling to independent traders, which twice sent the institutional arrangements and industry performance into a severe tailspin. Repeated efforts to pass a new cotton law to put in place sustainable institutional arrangements have languished in the face of competing lobbying pressures by stakeholders.[14]

The third consequence is the high collective cost to Zambians of some of the individual "wins." The saga of the privatization of Zambia's largest copper mine offers an especially compelling example. Following pressure from donors, the government began the process in 1996; by the end of 1997 bidding had been completed, and negotiations with the winning bidder (a consortium comprising South Africa's Anglovaal Mining, Canada's Noranda company, Phelps Dodge, and the Commonwealth Development Corporation) were completed, with finalization of the agreement scheduled

---

[12] Even the formal rules of Zambia's business environment rates at the midpoint – ranking 90th of 183 countries – of the 2008 Doing Business indicators. Within that average, some activities rate especially low; dealing with construction permits rates 151st; trading across borders rates 157th (DB 200x?).

[13] See World Bank, *What are the Constraints to Inclusive Growth in Zambia? A Policy Note*, Report No. 44286-ZM, 2008.

[14] See David Tschirley and Stephen Kabwe, "The Cotton Sector of Zambia," World Bank Africa Region Working Paper Series No. 124, March 2009.

for March 1998. Independent observers considered the bid fair and good, but in a surprising move the government turned it down at the last minute. Two years later, the company was sold to the Anglo American Corporation (its original owner and long-standing participant via management contract) for a significantly lower price – $60 million up front (versus $150 million earlier), and a commitment to $300 million in follow-up investment (versus $1 billion earlier). Subsequently, though, Anglo American walked away from the deal, and the mines were threatened with closure. Rapid-fire negotiations produced a new agreement with the Vedanta Corporation, which purchased the mine for $25 million cash plus an additional $23 million over the subsequent three years. A right to carry forward all past losses against future tax obligations meant that Vedanta could clear over $1 billion in profit before having to pay a penny to the Zambian fiscus.[15] In 2006 alone, Vedanta earned $300 million from its Zambia venture. In April 2008 (after the end of the copper boom) the Zambian parliament passed a new mining taxation regime that introduced a new windfall tax and tightened up on write-off allowances. But in early 2009, the windfall tax was again eliminated and the capital allowance for tax purposes restored to 100 percent. The details of which local actors benefited personally from these various deals are (for obvious reasons) obscure, but surely relevant to the outcome.

One set of reasons for the more individualized approach to elite bargaining (relative to the immediate post-1964 period) has to do with the absence of nationalist fervor. Relevant here is the radical lowering of expectations (both hope and fear) as to what could be expected of the state – with citizens left exhausted from the turbulence and economic dysfunction of the latter Kaunda period, and with noninsider, traditional elites less fearful that an ambitiously modernizing state would threaten their privileged status. A short-term consequence was a generous honeymoon period that enabled MMD to shift substantial blame for rising hardships onto international financial institutions – who, in addition to the substantial financial support described earlier, also provided sustained, high-level technical advice on policy reform. Also relevant is the disintegration of the founding nationalist party, UNIP, and the entire party and state planning apparatus associated with it. This left significant gaps in domestic policy making capabilities.

---

[15] For details of the negotiation with the Anglo American Corporation, see Scott Taylor, *Business and the State in Southern Africa: The Politics of Economic Reform* (Boulder: Lynne Rienner Publishers, 2007), p. 78. For details of the deal with Vedanta, see Andrew Sardanis, *A Venture in Africa: The Challenges of African Business* (New York: Palgrave Macmillan, 2007).

There was no institutionalized capacity (within or outside the state) for advocating national rather than individual interests, heightening dependence on technical advice from the IFIs.

A second, perhaps more fundamental, set of reasons for individualized rather than group-oriented bargaining has to do with changes in the composition and interests of elites. The putative need to placate ethnic constituencies had diminished: ethnic factionalism had been successfully subdued under Kaunda, and MMD's initial genuinely pan-ethnic appeal diminished the urgency of such explicit patronage efforts. Further, there was a shift among indigenous elites from being outsiders to insiders. By contrast to the immediate aftermath of independence, as of 1991 indigenous Zambian bureaucrats and politicians – part of an urban middle class comprising government, professional, and business employees, with generally shared values and aspirations, and many with earlier roots in the parastatal industrial sector – were positioned as gatekeepers for all business interactions with the state (procurement, privatization, entry of new businesses, land deals, and so forth). Taken together with discretionary governance via the presidency and the absence of robust accountability institutions, this transformation of the bureaucracy provided a strong bargaining position to extract rents.

A final feature of Zambia's elite order – one that perhaps is as much continuity as it is change from the earlier orders – is that the boundary between which elites were insiders and which were outsiders has been permeable. Insiders in the inner circle of the president tended not to remain so indefinitely; those in outer circles of elite influence sometimes moved inward. The opportunity of proximity to power meant that even if, for the moment, one was not a direct beneficiary of this individualized patronage, this could readily change. The status quo was thus workable, while change was unpredictable, even potentially destabilizing.

In sum, to answer the question posed at the outset of this subsection as to how to characterize Zambia's access order: its entrenched clientelism organized around centralized presidential discretion is consistent with limited access. But the fluidity of the boundary between insiders and outsiders, and the fact that elections are closely contested, marks it as "competitively clientelist"[16] – that is, rather more open than the limited access nomenclature implies. So far, these competitive clientelist institutions have delivered fairly effectively on two of the three goals laid out at the outset of this section. They have provided a platform for stability and a framework for meeting

---

[16] I am indebted to Mushtaq Khan for this phrase, which he introduced in his LAO analysis of Bangladesh.

and balancing the aspirations for wealth and power of the country's elites. Indeed, the economic track record has improved – with growth accelerating to six percent throughout the 2006–9 period, and private investment as a share of GDP almost trebling from seven percent in 2000 to twenty percent in 2007. The robustness of these benefits – and the prospects for growth becoming more inclusive – will be considered further in Section 4.4, against the comparative benchmark of the very different LAO dynamics that have unfolded in Mozambique.

4.3 Mozambique Through an LAO Lens

4.3.1 Mozambique's Political and Institutional Trajectory

Over the past forty years, Mozambique like Zambia, has undergone vast institutional changes: from a tightly controlled colony, to a single-party Marxist-Leninist regime, to a multiparty democracy. Even so, as Table 4.3 overleaf summarizes, viewed through the prism of the AO framework, Mozambican institutions – unlike those of Zambia – consistently have exhibited the classic features of an LAO. Both the colonial and one-party Marxist-Leninist periods were organized around tightly controlled political and economic access managed by a robust and exclusionary elite bargain. Since the early 1990s, Mozambique formally has been a market democracy, but the actual operation of society parallels in a variety of ways the earlier LAOs, though exclusionary control is somewhat less rigid.

Also consistent with the LAO approach – and, again, unlike Zambia – the shadow of violence has been a consistent undercurrent and, between 1984 and 1992, a tragically vivid presence. The subsections that follow detail: first, the background to Mozambique's striking institutional continuity; second, the ways in which exclusionary LAO rule helped fuel a violent civil war in the 1980s; and, third, how the veneer of competitive electoral institutions – pasted on top of a continuing exclusionary LAO order – have provided a platform for stability and economic recovery for the past fifteen years.

From a colonial to a Marxist-Leninist LAO. Portuguese rule in Mozambique consistently was absolutist – from its early conquest in the sixteenth century of local ports, to its conferral in the nineteenth century of control to chartered companies, to the incorporation of Mozambique in 1951 as a province of authoritarian Portugal under the rule of a governor appointed directly from Lisbon. Immigration from Portugal was actively encouraged. Commercial as well as industrial businesses, small farms, and blue-collar industrial jobs all were in the hands of the hundreds of thousands of settlers

Table 4.3 *Mozambique's governance diamond – key features*

	The Colonial Order	Circa-1980–2	1994 => [current]
Formal political institutions	-province of Portugal -governor appointed by authoritarian Portuguese government	-single-party Marxist-Leninist state. -Frelimo top-down oligarchy, with fifteen-person political bureau (meets fortnightly), central committee (meets annually), and vanguard one hundred thousand members	-formal, multi-party democracy -1.4 million Frelimo membership in 2001, organized in cells; political bureau continues (renamed as Commissao Politica) -growing centralized authority of presidency since 2004 -Renamo dominated by personalized rule of ex-military leader; very weak party structures; declining support
Formal economic institutions	-mercantilist; -government-conferred corporate syndicates; -forced/contract labor	-planned economy; -state control; - small farmer marginalized	-market economy (1,000 of 1,250 parastatals privatized); -high-transactions-costs business environment, with preferential access available to some.
Principal elites	-colonial governors -settlers from Portugal -European and Asian traders, and *assimilados*	-Frelimo: political bureau, central committee, and vanguard members	-Elites linked to Frelimo; -Post-civil war: Renamo members linked to personalized leadership of Alfonso Dhlakama that share in cash payments to Renamo; declining relevance in recent years -foreign investors (generally in joint ventures with locals, including government equity).
Principal sources of rent	-plantation agriculture -forced labor; migrant workers on South African gold mines	-allocation of formerly colonial-owned property -foreign aid	-foreign investors seeking to develop natural resource-linked megaprojects. -foreign aid accounts for half of public sector activities -which locals get to participate is the key rent allocation mechanism

that had migrated from Portugal, most in the 1950s and 1960s – a time when other European powers were bringing their colonial ventures to an end.[17]

Colonial Mozambique was thus an exclusionary LAO par excellence. Specific policies aimed at extracting rent from the local territory and inhabitants and allocating it to chartered companies, settlers, and the colonial metropole included:

- The conferral of control over large swaths of the country's agricultural land (and administrative control over the territories) to the Zambezi, Niassa, and Mozambique chartered companies, a mode of control that continued into the 1940s.
- The mandatory production by peasant farmers of cotton for sale to Portugal through a state-controlled marketing board, which gave the Portuguese textile industry access to cotton at about half the world price.[18]
- Tight limitations on the development of industry in Mozambique, including a ban on domestic manufacture of textiles. As of 1961, the total value of Mozambican manufacturing was $14 million.
- The *chibalo* forced labor system that required African males to work under contract for six months of the year at a fixed salary of three dollars per month; local administrators used this system to provide labor upon request to plantation farmers.
- A labor policy that pressured males to work on the South African gold mines. The Mozambican authorities received twelve shillings per worker, plus six pence more for each month's service beyond an initial one-year contract. In addition, half of each worker's salary was paid (on behalf of the mineworker who received the difference in local currency) directly to the colonial government in gold at a price appreciably below the market price; the gold was then resold (at market prices) with the difference kept by colonial authorities. Mozambican workers accounted for upward of forty percent of mineworkers through 1926, and over a quarter (the largest supply source) even in 1969.

Portugal's authoritarian Estado Novo used its military might to maintain tight control of its African "provinces," giving no sign that it intended to follow the decolonization policies of other colonial powers. But change came

---

[17] Malyn Newitt, *A History of Mozambique* (Hong Kong: Indiana University Press), p. 467.

[18] This and other details in this paragraph are from Allen Isaacman and Barbara Isaacman, *Mozambique: From Colonialism to Revolution, 1900–1982* (Boulder: Westview Press), pp. 42–6.

from an unexpected quarter. Military and civilian opposition to the Estado Novo from within Portugal culminated in an April 1974 "carnation revolution" coup in Lisbon. Little more than a year later, the new democratizing Portuguese authorities granted sovereign independence to Mozambique and handed power directly to the umbrella nationalist organization, the Front for the Liberation of Mozambique, Frelimo (established in 1962 as a coalition of three nascent anti-Portuguese nationalist groups).[19]

When Frelimo took power, it moved rapidly to reconsolidate an LAO – one with radically different political and economic institutions than had prevailed before. The suddenness of the Portuguese exit meant that there was no realistic prospect of a Zambia-style OAO bequest. Instead, an institutional near vacuum was left behind. All the institutional arrangements of the Mozambican state had been Portuguese. It had been governed as a province of Portugal, with all public officials appointed by Portugal (and most coming directly from Portugal into their local posts). Further, the imminent arrival of independence and Frelimo rule, plus sporadic attacks on Portuguese and white settler property, terrified Mozambique's Portuguese settlers, who left the country en masse; by the end of 1975, barely fifteen thousand of the two hundred thousand settlers who had been in Mozambique as of late 1973 remained.[20] The resulting skills shortage was acute. Frelimo had no option but to improvise with a strong sense of urgency.

But Frelimo's institutional changes were driven by conviction as well as necessity. In the course of its exile and low-level guerrilla war, it had evolved from a coalition of nationalist organizations into a tightly controlled Marxist-Leninist party. The Soviet Union was its principal source of funding, weapons, military training, and beliefs about effective strategies for development. Through its military efforts, it had successfully taken control of the far northern part of Mozambique, and had (seemingly successfully) used agricultural cooperatives to support economic recovery. It was governed along classic Marxist-Leninist lines: membership was offered only to a carefully selected vanguard group; party congresses (generally every five years) set broad strategy; a central committee (which met annually) discussed and ratified all major decisions; day-to-day control was in the hands of a ten-to-fifteen-person political bureau (whose members remained almost identical for over two decades).[21]

---

[19] Newitt, *A History of Mozambique*, p. 538.
[20] Abrahamsson and Nilsson, p. 27.
[21] Giovanni M. Carbone, "Emerging Pluralist Politics in Mozambique: The Frelimo-Renamo System," *Crisis States Programme Development Research Centre*, Working Paper 23, Series No. 1 (London: London School of Economics, 2003) provides details.

Frelimo's Marxist-Leninist-inspired commitment to transform the lives of the mass of the population led to its placing a high priority on the provision of basic services. In the first six years, primary school enrollment doubled from 700,000 to 1,376,000 and secondary education moved from 20,000 to 135,000. By 1979, a national immunization campaign against smallpox, tetanus, and measles had reached an estimated ninety percent of the population and infant mortality had fallen by twenty percent. But it also led to the adoption of more draconian measures:[22]

- The nonagricultural economy shifted rapidly into state hands. At independence, all land was constitutionally made into national property. One month after independence, education, health, and legal services were nationalized. Eight years after independence, the state had direct control of over seventy percent of the nonagricultural economy.
- An aggressive program was initiated to reorganize peasant agriculture around rural communes, including the forcible removal of many peasants from their land and their resettlement into villages.
- Dynamizing groups were established shortly after independence as transitional institutions (and were phased out by the early 1980s). They were comprised of a dozen Frelimo supporters, elected at public meetings and responsible for promoting democracy and unity. The groups organized public campaigns, created grassroots groups to attack ethnic stereotypes, and emphasized the integration of women into society as equal citizens. They also took on political and administrative functions, at times operating as popular tribunals until new legal systems could be created, sometimes meting out harsh treatment.
- During the late 1970s, as many as ten thousand people were held in reeducation camps, including some considered politically unreliable and others accused of corruption.

Even under the best of circumstances, the centrally planned management of an economy is a nearly impossible task (although the track record in the USSR suggests that the most profound problems emerge more in the longer term than in the short term). But Mozambique's were hardly the best of circumstances. The government was extraordinarily lacking in the educated, skilled staff needed for a centrally planned system to function. Even more fundamental, Frelimo's roots were spread very unevenly across the

---

[22] The details in this paragraph are from Bertil Egero, *Mozambique: A Dream Undone* (Sweden: Motola Grafiska, 1988), p. 72, Isaacman and Isaacman, *Mozambique*, p. 113, Harold D. Nelson, *Mozambique: A Country Study* (Washington, DC: American University Press, 1984), p. 65, and Newitt, *A History of Mozambique*, pp. 543, 549.

country: strong in the north and south, but weak in the central heartland, home to over half of the population and the dominant source of agricultural wealth.[23] As with the Portuguese in an earlier era, the weak spot of Frelimo's governance diamond was that its elite bargain was narrowly exclusive. As Frelimo tightened its grip and extended the ideological ambitions of its agenda, this weakness increasingly came to the fore.

The undoing – and remaking – of an LAO. In Mozambique, much more than in Zambia, the shadow of repression and violence has been a constant backdrop to the political order. In the 1980s, the darkness of violent conflict overwhelmed the country, with nine hundred thousand people killed and 6 million (one-third of the country's population) displaced.[24] This violent civil war destroyed Frelimo's exclusive, one-party LAO. But between 1990 and 1994 things turned around in remarkable fashion: Just five years after one of the most brutal years of the civil war, the country had restabilized around a new institutional bargain, ushering in – as if the war had never happened – fifteen years of peace and accelerating economic development.

The precipitating events for the Mozambican civil war came from outside the country. The white minority regimes of Rhodesia and South Africa felt enormously threatened by the sudden, unexpected emergence of an African-majority-ruled, Marxist-Leninist Mozambique on their borders. Predictably, their response was violent. An anti-Frelimo insurgency (that eventually became Renamo) was initiated in 1975 by Southern Rhodesia's Central Intelligence Organization. When majority rule came to Rhodesia/ Zimbabwe in 1980, sponsorship of Renamo was taken up by South Africa.[25]

But there was more to Renamo's rise than its sponsorship by southern Africa's minority regimes. As noted earlier, Frelimo's support in Mozambique was spread unevenly in Mozambique, and was especially thin in the center of the country. Frelimo, rather than acknowledging its weakness and treading carefully, determined to extend its agenda of collectivization and state control relentlessly into the agriculturally rich center. Viewed through the lens of Frelimo ideology, the elites in this central region were irretrievably reactionary – *regulos*, tools of exploitative colonialism not worthy of engaging and certainly not likely to command the support of the exploited local population. But this is not how it was perceived locally. Renamo leveraged

---

[23] Abrahamsson, p. 189.

[24] William Finnegan, *A Complicated War: The Harrowing of Mozambique* (University of California Press, 1993).

[25] Ibid., pp. 31–3.

resentment against Frelimo to build in the center of the country a strong, indigenous home base for its guerrilla activities. Despite the brutality of the civil war and of Renamo's tactics, even after the end of violent conflict it maintained a strong base of support in the area. In every election from 1994 to 2004, it consistently won a large majority of the vote in the central provinces of Sofala, Manica, and Zambezia.

As with its beginning, the end of Mozambique's civil war involved a combination of domestic and international forces. Domestically, the horror and brutality of the war and the emergence of new leadership helped spur reforms within Frelimo, culminating in a new party constitution in 1990 in the direction of greater economic and political pluralism. This domestic momentum was buttressed by regional and global events: a 1986 agreement in which Mozambique agreed that South Africa's African National Congress could no longer use the country as a staging ground for guerrilla activities, with South Africa agreeing in turn to stop supporting Renamo; the death knell that the collapse of the Soviet Union and fall of the Berlin Wall sounded for Marxist-Leninist ideology; and the 1990 release of Nelson Mandela, unbanning of the ANC, and ending of apartheid rule in South Africa.

Negotiations between Frelimo and Renamo, facilitated by the Vatican, began in 1990. In 1992, the parties signed a peace agreement and a seventy-five hundred-strong United Nations peacekeeping force came to the country to oversee a two-year transition to a democratic election, won by Frelimo with fifty-three percent of the vote (with thirty-four percent of the vote going to Renamo). The UN troops left the following year. Since that time, sovereign Mozambique has successfully held elections in 1999, 2004, and 2009. The country has been an aid darling, with aid inflows rising to upward of ten percent of GDP. Foreign private investment began flowing in. Economic growth accelerated – for a while into the double digits, and remaining consistently above six percent through to 2009.

A new LAO equilibrium. Crucial to the new equilibrium was a shift by Frelimo to a more open approach to governance across four dimensions. First was support for multiparty elections. Second was a shift away from direct state control of the economy. Already by the late 1980s, Frelimo had abandoned its push to cooperatize agriculture. Subsequent to the 1994 elections, and accompanied by strong financial and technical support from the international financial institutions, it embraced both markets and privatization: over 1,000 small, medium, and large state enterprises were sold between 1992 and 2000; price controls were radically scaled back, from covering over seventy percent of GDP in 1986 to less than ten percent a decade later.[26] While as of 2009–10 the country ranked 135th out of 183 on the World Bank's Doing Business indicators (Zambia ranks ninetieth) – liberalization and privatization has created substantially more economic space than had existed previously. Third, Frelimo shifted its stance in relation to preexisting rural leaders from overt hostility to constructive engagement and an effort at cooptation via the establishment in 2003 of inclusive consultative councils in rural localities throughout the country.

The fourth shift was in the governance of Frelimo itself. Frelimo evolved from a vanguard party with tightly restricted membership (totaling about one hundred thousand) in the early 1980s to "a vast front congregating Mozambicans of all classes and strata"[27] in the 1990s; by 2001, membership had risen to 1.4 million. Though Frelimo's inner workings remain closed to the public eye (with a political committee apparently still dominant), there is a clear perception that, corresponding to the expansion of party membership at this inner level, too, the party became more diverse – with a continued social commitment (represented by a grouping around Graca Machel, the widow of the first president Samora Machel and today the wife of Nelson Mandela) counterbalanced by a variety of semi-rivalrous business groups organized around Joaquim Chissano (president from 1986–2005) and Armando Guebuza. But closely knit decision making within this inner core maintained party coherence for a decade or more beyond the 1994 election.

Social peace also required compromise on the part of Renamo. It ended its violent uprising and agreed to respect the results of elections and sit in parliament. Renamo's performance in the first two multiparty elections was surprisingly strong (especially to those who had perceived it solely as a creation of Rhodesia and South Africa). Its presidential candidate, Alfonso Dhlakama, won thirty-four percent of the vote in 1994 and forty-eight percent in 1999; and it won 112 of 250 parliamentary seats in 1994 (and 117 of 250 in 1999), with large majorities in the provinces in the center of the country. It achieved these strong electoral showings despite making almost no effort to institutionalize its party structure or to share among its members some of the financial benefits that came to the leadership from its participation in the multiparty structure.[28] At least for a while, its position as

---

[26] Anne M. Pitcher, *Transforming Mozambique: The Politics of Privatization, 1975–2000* (New York: Cambridge Press, 2002), p. 127; Abrahamsson, p. 114.

[27] Frelimo, *Estatutos de Partido*, 1997, *art. 2.2* quoted in Giovanni Carboni: "Emerging Pluralist Politics."

[28] The UN peacekeeping force, for example, explicitly earmarked $17 million to facilitate the participation of Renamo in the 1994 multiparty arrangements.

the not-Frelimo voice of more traditional interests, especially in the center of the country, was sufficient to secure support.

In sum, the governance equilibrium that prevailed in the aftermath of civil war and elections can be characterized as follows: First, an insider set of Frelimo elites that negotiated and renegotiated the terms of governance on an ongoing basis, balancing multiple constituencies. Second an economic policy regime that, with the support of the international financial institutions, seemingly took on board many of the policy principles of the Washington Consensus, and where business activity was not actively blocked – though doing business was not easy, and was dependent on the (at least passive) acquiescence of Frelimo political elites and government officials. Third, a set of outsider elites that, at least prior to 2009, were mostly aligned with Renamo, but for whom the combination of parliamentary representation, cash payment, and economic and political space from state control provided a sufficient basis for sustaining a commitment to social peace. As each of these characteristics underscore, discretionary negotiation rather than formal rule boundedness continued to be at the heart of governance.

What price success? The governance equilibrium since 1994 provided Mozambique with a spectacularly effective platform for economic recovery and development. As already noted, growth was very rapid, and had two drivers. The first comprised direct foreign investment (generally with politically well-connected local partners) into natural resource-linked megaprojects (with the largest of these investments, the Mozal aluminum smelter, backstopped by finance from neighboring South Africa's parastatal Industrial Development Corporation). The second driver comprised foreign aid, broadly targeted toward social expenditures, and annual flows that amounted in the latter 2000s to half of the country's public expenditures. The gains in some key social indicators were spectacular:

- The number of children enrolled in primary education more than tripled from 1.3 million in 1992 to 4.2 million in 2008, with the number of primary school teachers rising from thirty thousand to seventy-four thousand over the same period.
- The gross enrollment rate in lower secondary education increased from five percent in 1998 to twenty-eight percent a decade later.
- Under-five mortality rates decreased from 212 per 1,000 live births in 1996 to 138 in 2008; over the same period, infant mortality fell from 145 to 93 per 1,000 live births; and maternal mortality declined from an estimated 1,000 to 340 per 100,000 live births.

The combination of strong performance and the continuing institutional weakness of Renamo has translated into growing electoral success for Frelimo. Armando Guebuza won election as president in 2004 and was reelected five years later, with sixty-four percent and then seventy-five percent of the vote. Meanwhile, Frelimo consolidated its base, with its number of parliamentary seats rising to 191 – including, finally, winning electoral majorities in the central heartland of the country. By contrast Renamo – which remained a top-down dominant leader party even in the face of Frelimo's increasing efforts to draw away support from local rural leaders – imploded. Internal leadership struggles led the party to reject popular incumbent Daviz Simango as its candidate for reelection for mayor of the second largest city, a Renamo stronghold. Simango then ran, and was reelected, as an independent, with the Renamo candidate winning under five percent of the vote.

Mozambique's success and subsequent dynamism carries with it a risk: it could undermine the governance equilibrium that made it possible. For one thing, Frelimo no longer faces a credible electoral threat, making it less accountable to citizens for its performance. For another, President Guebuza's success has altered the dynamics in Frelimo. Among the party's core leadership, he has long been positioned as the results-focused, pro-business candidate. He has a business track record of his own – including direct and family participation in a group of holding companies that, during his term of office as president, have been important players in attracting foreign investors to Mozambique and partnering with them.

Only time can tell how large is the risk that personalized consolidation of power will weaken the policy balance that has prevailed in Frelimo. To reduce this risk, the crucial policy challenge is to identify and implement actions that support interelite transparency and continued bottom-up accountability for inclusive development – and thereby enable Mozambique to continue to traverse what has been, for the past fifteen years, an unusually effective developmental LAO knife edge.

4.4 A Comparative Assessment

A principal purpose of this chapter is to assess the value added of the AO approach for better understanding and addressing the governance and policy reform challenges in low-income countries. This final section offers that assessment in the form of five propositions. The first three propositions concern how well AO theory fits Zambia and Mozambique's institutional and political realities. The fourth proposition focuses on the extent to which an AO approach adds new value to the effort to identify governance and policy reforms that can move forward the development effort in the two countries – and in low-income settings more broadly. The final proposition suggests a possible focus of a next generation of theoretical development of the AO approach.

- *Proposition 1: The LAO focus on bargaining among elites offers a helpful entry point for better understanding the development challenges of low-income countries and why they are difficult to address.*

Contemporary Zambian and Mozambican economic history look very different when considered through an LAO lens than through the more standard technocratic or ideologically focused narratives. Interelite bargaining in both countries emerges as a knife edge. Both countries confront the risk that overreach could destabilize carefully constructed equilibria, although the forms that overreach might take differ widely across the two countries – and are not adequately captured by a narrow focus on the threat of violence.

In Zambia, the risk is that a political culture of buying in potential rivals could be economically destabilizing – whether directly, as during the Kaunda era, or more insidiously (post-Kaunda) through the corrosive effects of pervasive corruption. In Mozambique, the greater risk has come from the opposite direction – that a political culture that distinguishes sharply between insiders and outsiders might go too far, with insiders consolidating power and undercutting countervailing spheres of influence to the point that accountability is lost. In both countries – regardless of whether the political culture is inclusive or exclusionary – discretionary allocation of rent emerges as central to political management. Contra the standard economic prescriptions, it cannot simply be wished away, but needs to be engaged centrally as part of an agenda of political and economic reform.

- *Proposition 2: LAOs are not incompatible with the presence of significant areas of openness – indeed openness can be leveraged to enhance LAO stability.*

Recourse to increased openness was part of the way out of governance dead ends in both Zambia and Mozambique. Strikingly, both countries utilized multiparty elections as a key mechanism for renewing political legitimacy following the collapse of an earlier elite equilibrium – and in both countries the elections were genuinely contested affairs, with the incumbent President Kaunda unexpectedly defeated in Zambia in 1991, and (though Frelimo has consistently won) with unexpectedly close contests in

Mozambique in both 1994 and 1999. Moreover, both countries have utilized partial liberalization to create space and opportunity for potential rivals to thrive economically.

- *Proposition 3: LAOs come in distinctive varieties, with distinctive strengths and weaknesses. The fragile/basic/mature access order framework – especially the basic subcategory – needs additional disaggregation.*

North, Wallis, and Weingast (NWW) highlight two fundamental features of basic LAOs: "a durable and stable organizational structure for the state ... [and] only organizations with direct connections to the state possess durability."[29] These characteristics accurately describe Mozambique under both Portuguese and Frelimo rule, but fit less well with contemporary Zambia.

Three distinctive features of contemporary Mozambican history have the potential to enrich our understanding of basic LAOs. First, civil war between 1984 and 1992 brought Mozambique to the brink of being caught in a seemingly unending trap of fragility or worse – but, remarkably, despite weak institutions, huge human resource gaps, and brutal violence, that did not happen. Mozambique's success in avoiding the abyss stands in stark contrast to other disruptive decolonization episodes – with Zaire/Congo an especially apposite comparison. The reasons for Mozambique's success – around which further comparative inquiry could be useful – most likely have to do with the combination of distinctive regional/international roles and path dependence linked to the country's particular historical experience.

The second and third distinctive features of Mozambique's basic LAO follow from the fact that, since independence, it consistently has been governed by a dominant political party, Frelimo. An initial reading of the evidence suggests (this is the second feature) that since 1992, when party membership became more inclusive and more space and rent-creating opportunities were provided under the Frelimo umbrella – both for party members, and for elites that were not Frelimo members – this party structure has provided important layers of stability and accountability and hence a strong platform for economic growth and strengthened provision of basic services to the poor. Third, though, by 2009, potential risks to the sustainability of this dominant party LAO were becoming apparent. Frelimo's success threatened to weaken the balances upon which stability was built – with Frelimo becoming increasingly dominant electorally vis-à-vis Renamo and with President Guebuza becoming an increasingly dominant figure within Frelimo, perhaps consolidating rents around his inner circle. Put differently,

---

[29] North, Wallis, and Weingast, *Violence and Social Orders*, pp. 43, 45.

Mozambique points to one way in which a basic LAO can position itself successfully on the developmental knife edge – but also how easily (including as an unintended consequence of success) it could fall off.

In contrast to Mozambique, contemporary Zambia cannot be slotted as straightforwardly into the AO schema. Clearly, it is not an OAO – evident in the realities of presidential discretion and institutional weakness that lie behind OAO trappings. At the same time, as a haven of social peace for over forty-five years in a turbulent neighborhood, it also is far from being a fragile LAO – defined by NWW as a state that "can barely sustain itself in the face of internal and external violence ... capable of containing violence, but all politics is real politics: people risk death when they make political mistakes."[30] Nor, given the relative openness and weakness of Zambia's state institutions – and the fluidity of the boundaries that separate elite insiders from outsiders – can it usefully be characterized a basic LAO.

But neither does post-Kaunda Zambia fit with the third LAO type – the mature LAO. NWW characterize a mature LAO as consisting of "durable institutional structures for the state and the ability to support elite organizations outside the immediate framework of the state ... private law provides individuals with ... a framework to reach agreements within the law's bounds ... public law provides for methods of resolving conflicts within the state and, by extension, within the dominant coalition." This is not consistent with the competitive clientelism described earlier.

Taken together, the comparative experiences of Mozambique and Zambia thus potentially enrich AO analysis by pointing toward two distinct paths of institutional evolution among intermediate LAOs (i.e., those between fragile and mature) – one via a dominant party basic LAO, and the other with more recourse at an early stage to competition, albeit anchored in discretionary clientelism. Further, the experiences of the two countries suggest three hypotheses as to distinctive strengths and weaknesses of each path:

- H1: The host country benefits from direct foreign investment will be higher when deals are struck within a dominant party framework than when deal making is more individualized.
- H2: The organization of politics around a dominant, inclusive political party offers greater potential for equitable, poverty-reducing growth than more individualized (or personalized clientelistic) approaches to elite management.

[30] Ibid, p. 42.

- H3: The risks of destabilizing violence are higher when elite management is tightly organized (as can be the case in a dominant party framework) than when the boundaries between insiders and outsiders are more fluid.

One final layer of complexity, not adequately captured within the LAO framework and equally relevant for both Mozambique and Zambia, comprises the ways in which globalized engagement – with foreign investors and with donors, as well as via global and regional geopolitics – influences interactions among elites and between elites and non-elites. Even the brief summary of the historical record in Sections 4.2 and 4.3 confirm that for centuries these global influences have been overwhelming in their impact in both countries: the ravages of the slave trade in Mozambique; the economic transformation wrought by copper mining in Zambia; colonial domination; apartheid and its end in Southern Africa, and so forth. But a distinctive feature of the present period is that it is characterized not by subjection of domestic elites or by their determined assertions of independence, but by their proactive engagement with the global game.

As both Zambia and Mozambique illustrate vividly, in the globalized order that has prevailed in the two decades subsequent to the end of the Cold War, effective management by domestic elites of their relations with aid donors and with foreign investors provides access to major resource flows and to sophisticated organizational options only partially dependent on the domestic polity. An assessment of the net impact of this global window on development goes way beyond the scope of this chapter. But what can be said is that these opportunities give domestic elites seeking power and/or wealth an alternative to focusing narrowly on how to leverage domestic options (whether via predation or via the development of sustainable domestic institutions). This may perhaps be part of the explanation why, over the past quarter century, in both Mozambique and Zambia – in different ways and to different degrees – the focus of governmental as well as other domestic elites has moved away from the reorganization of domestic society toward more individualized modes of engagement.

- *Proposition 4: The LAO approach – expanded to incorporate the complexities highlighted previously – offers rich new insights as to what might be value adding governance and economic policy reforms across different country settings.*

The crucial contribution of the AO framework to the development reform discourse is to underscore how difficult it can be in institutionally weak settings to assure a stable bargain among elites, one also accepted by non-elites. In different ways, Mozambique's dominant party basic LAO and Zambia's competitive clientelist LAO have thus far been able to meet this challenge. While both fall well short of OAO good practice, as NWW make clear, the normative benchmark of OAO reforms is unhelpful, precisely because, with weak institutions, OAO openness is likely to be destabilizing. By contrast, the AO framework suggests that, for a reform agenda to be value adding, whatever is done to enhance policy making, public service provision, and private sector development needs also to sustain and strengthen the foundation of stability. This implies working with the grain of the existing institutional arrangements.

How, working with the grain of what has so far been achieved, can Mozambique and Zambia continue to move forward? Consistent with the differences in their prevailing AOs, the answers are very different for the two countries. For Mozambique, a principal challenge is to identify reforms that reduce poverty *and* assure continuing interelite stability. This dual focus highlights the opportunities – and the challenges – of three sets of priority reforms:

- Reforms that strengthen citizen participation in the provision of basic services (e.g., schools, committees, village-maintained infrastructure) potentially have the triple merit of (i) improving service provision directly; (ii) being consistent with Frelimo's bottom-up, participatory political platform; and (iii) strengthening the bonds of accountability that link citizens and the state, bonds that could be at risk in the face of possibly growing concentration of authority by, and within, Frelimo.
- Reforms to strengthen public administrative capability by fostering meritocracy within the civil service have a more mixed impact. On the one hand, they could strengthen state authority and capacity – and hence potentially the power and legitimacy of Frelimo. On the other hand, by limiting discretionary authority over appointments, they would constrain what has been an important tool of political management for the state (and Frelimo), especially in locales that had been strongholds of opposition during the civil war period. But note that Frelimo's growing electoral success in these areas, and the receding memory of the civil war, could over time increase the willingness of government to give up discretion in favor of meritocracy.
- Also mixed in their implications for development and stability are reforms that bring transparency to investment deals involving international companies and Mozambican interests. A key driver of

Mozambique's rapid growth has been foreign investment in its abundant natural resources and its economically valuable (for South Africa, as well as other countries in the subregion) infrastructure. As with most other countries the world over, Mozambican national interests seek to become part of these deals by offering political access. The difficult challenge is to assure that the process is sufficiently transparent and competitive that the results serve the country well. Creative intermediate approaches are needed that can achieve this result – in the context of a process that, as an LAO perspective underscores, will surely remain under tight Frelimo control.

Zambia's frontier institutional challenge is to strengthen capacity for collective action, else run the risk, not of a sudden spasm of violence but of a continuing, slow downward spiral in institutional capability. A central feature of the country's LAO is the individualized character of interelite bargaining. This has been accompanied by an almost complete absence of collective action – evident, as noted earlier, in exceptionally low rates of public investment, which averaged only six percent per annum even at the height of the country's 2005–8 boom. As long as the scope of ambition is modest (at least initially), a focus on enhancing collective action potentially offers win-win opportunities from the perspective of both development and stability.

A good place to begin could be to focus on infrastructural services to elites. Zambia's urban water supply, for example, has long been locked into a low-level equilibrium of disintegrating infrastructure, prices that are set too low to cover maintenance or investment costs – and disgruntled consumers who expect price increases to be pocketed by water utilities with no investment or service improvement. A feasible and low-risk way forward could be to work to build a coalition among urban residents, private firms, and water utilities organized around mutual commitments to higher prices in return for better services. Other examples that follow a similar logic might include electricity distribution and roads that link towns and commercialized agriculture – although note that the more attenuated are the linkages between service recipients and the source of finance the greater will be the challenge of forging a coalition for collective action.

- *Proposition 5: More theorizing on the intermediate stages of institutional evolution – that is, those between the looming shadow of violence of fragile LAOs, and the 'doorstep conditions' that characterize mature LAOs en route to becoming OAOs – will enhance the usefulness of the AO approach in addressing governance and policy challenges in low-income countries.*

Table 4.4 *Strengths and weaknesses in the quality of state institutions in low-income countries*

	Bureaucratic Capability (A)	Quality of Checks and Balances (B)	Difference (A-B)
Group 1: Stronger Bureaucratic Capability			
Tanzania	+0.75	+0.10	+0.60
Indonesia	+0.55	+0.25	+0.30
Vietnam	+0.35	−0.25	+0.60
Ethiopia	+0.35	−0.25	+0.60
Pakistan	+0.35	−0.35	+0.70
Uganda	+0.30	−0.05	+0.35
Group 2: Stronger Checks and Balances			
India	+0.55	+0.75	−0.20
Ghana	+0.35	+0.70	−0.35
Senegal	+0.35	+0.65	−0.30
Nicaragua	+0.35	+0.55	−0.20
Albania	+0.10	+0.40	−0.30
Zambia	−0.10	+0.30	−0.40

Note: **Countries** (selected countries 2004; minus 1 = weakest; plus 1 = strongest).
Source: Adapted from Brian Levy, *Governance Reform: Bridging Monitoring and Action*, (Washington DC: World Bank, 2007), appendix 1, pp. 121–5.

Isaiah Berlin once famously remarked that "the fox knows many things, the hedgehog knows one big thing." NWW offer us two important hedgehogs. The first is the insight that OAOs emerge only as the culmination of a long historical process – one that passes through the mature LAO and requires the institutionalization of three 'doorstep conditions.' Their second hedgehog is the insight that LAO elites bargain with one another for advantage against a backdrop of the shadow of violence, that institutional weakness carries with it the risk of regression into a fragile LAO or even a Hobbesian state of nature.

Viewed from the perspective of low-income countries, the dilemma is that these hedgehogs address principally the early and late acts of the development saga. The richness and variety of the middle acts go way beyond what is captured by the conceptual schema of the intermediate stage basic LAO. To underscore this point, consider Table 4.4. The table uses composite indicators of institutional quality to distinguish among two selected groups of countries – one with a comparative advantage in the capability of their public bureaucracies, and another with relatively stronger checks and balances institutions.[31] The measurement of institutional quality is, at best, an imperfect science, so margins of error are large. However, the overall patterns evident in the table generally are consistent with intuition, and the magnitude of the differences between the two groups in the table – and between the stronger and weaker performers within each group – are sufficiently large to suggest that the broad distinctions between them are empirically robust.

The first group, with its relatively strong bureaucracies and weak checks and balances institutions, aligns well with the definition of a basic LAO. But the fit is less apparent for the second group – in which checks and balances institutions rate as relatively stronger than their bureaucracies. This diversity in the relative strength of bureaucracies and checks and balances institutions underscores the potential benefits of further theorizing as to what might be a different route to a mature LAO from one that passes through the Group 1-like basic stage. Three interconnected sets of theoretical exploration seem worth pursuing:

- First, a comparison of the stability properties of two different types of elite bargain. Both would involve insiders and outsiders – and in both outsiders would confront a choice between acquiescing in the arrangements or taking up arms (with uncertain result). The first type of bargain (a la Mozambique and perhaps Group 1) would be characterized by sharp boundaries between insiders and outsiders, and certainty as to the expected payoffs of each, with high payoffs for insiders and low payoffs for outsiders. By contrast, in the second type of bargain (a la Zambia and other countries in Group 2),[32] the boundaries

---

[31] The data are for 2004. The measure of bureaucratic quality is an average of the quality of (i) a country's budgetary and financial management, and (ii) its public administration, both measured using the World Bank's Country Policy and Institutional Assessment database. The measure of the quality of checks and balances institutions is an average of two measures from the Kaufmann-Kraay Worldwide Governance Indicators – voice and accountability, and the rule of law – and the Polity IV measure of executive restraints. To facilitate comparison, all measures are linearly transformed to range between minimum −1 and maximum +1. For details, see Brian Levy, *Governance Reform: Bridging Monitoring and Action* (Washington, DC: World Bank, 2007), appendix 1, pp. 121–5 provides the data for a more complete set of sixty-two low-income aid-recipient countries.

[32] It must be noted that using the quantitative approach of table 4.4 to distinguish among countries yields only a small difference between Zambia and Mozambique: all scores are very similar other than for the Polity IV executive constraints variable, for which Zambia's

between insiders and outsiders would be more diffuse: payoffs would be distributed along a continuum, and ex ante individuals would be less certain what would be their position along that continuum.

- Second, for each of the two types of elite bargain, an assessment of the incentives and risks to insiders of investing in strengthening the public bureaucracy and/or checks and balances institutions – on the presumption that stability and prospects for further progress are higher the larger are the net incentives to strengthen one or both of these institutions. (Intuitively, at low levels of income insiders will have a greater incentive to consolidate their authority by building bureaucratic capability than to invest in checks and balances institutions of restraint.[33])

- Third, an assessment of the extent to which each of the two types of elite bargain (i) supports accelerated private investment and growth by enhancing credibility – with (ii) accelerating growth leading in turn to enhanced incentives to invest in bureaucratic or checks and balances institutions.[34]

The NWW framework is highly suggestive as to how a virtuous spiral might unfold for basic LAOs anchored in a dominant leader or a dominant political party – with the stability provided by a dominant insider group providing incentives both for private investment and for continued strengthening of bureaucratic capability. The recent historical record suggests multiple examples – from Korea to China to the countries in Group 1 and numerous others (e.g., Tunisia).

But might there be another virtuous spiral? Might the less certain, but less exclusionary pattern of payoffs of competitive clientelism, exemplified by Zambia and the other Group 2 countries, provide a platform that offers enough opportunity to outsiders that they choose to abide within the institutional status quo? On a day-to-day basis, the result would seem quite chaotic, as elites vie with one another to improve their payoff matrix by getting

---

2004 score was a five, and Mozambique's a three. But this points only to the bluntness of the measures and the importance of complementing them with qualitative historical assessments – where the differences between the two countries emerge starkly.

[33] It is noteworthy that in the sixty-two-country data set there are multiple instances (including the four shown in table X) of countries with a positive bureaucratic capability score and a negative checks and balances institutions score – but very few with the reverse (and most of them are very small countries). Zambia (and Mozambique) aside, the others are Moldova, Comoros, Lesotho, and the Solomons Islands.

[34] See Brian Levy and Francis Fukuyama, "Development Strategies: Integrating Governance and Growth," World Bank Research Working Paper Series #x, January 2010 for an analysis of the potentially cumulative character of these interdependencies.

closer to the throne. But there might nonetheless be sufficient stability in this second route to attract private investment with, in a muddling through sort of way, gradual strengthening of institutional capability. As an intermediate option, countries might oscillate, Albert Hirschman style[35], between more exclusionary and more inclusive arrangements for assuring stability – with each oscillation moving them forward via an incremental accretion of institutional capability. Either way, further work could enrich the range of institutional options for developing countries, pointing to ways forward that are less starkly antithetical to the values that underpin liberal democracy – and the potential viability of institutional choices for low-income developing countries that follow from them – than are the dominant leader or dominant party variants of a basic LAO.

References

Abrahamsson, Hans and Anders Nilsson. 1997. *Mozambique: The Troubled Transition*. London: Zed Books.

African Elections Database. *Elections in Mozambique*. Available at http://africanelections.tripod.com/mz.html. Accessed December 21, 2009.

African Elections Project. Mozambique. Available at http://www.africanelections.org/mozambique/news/page.php?news=4629. Accessed December 21, 2009.

All Africa. Mozambique: Frelimo Coasts to Victory in Maputo. Available at http://allafrica.com/stories/200811210565.html. Accessed December 21, 2009.

Burdetter, Marcia M. 1988. *Zambia: Between Two Worlds*. London: Westview Press.

Carbone, Giovanni M. 2003. "Emerging Pluralist Politics in Mozambique: The Frelimo-Renamo System," *Crisis States Programme Development Research Centre*, Working Paper 23, Series No. 1, London: London School of Economics.

Chingono, Mark F. 1996. *The State, Violence and Development*. Vermont: Ashgate Publishing Company.

A família Guebuza. Available at http://doismaisdoisigualacinco.blogspot.com/2008/10/famlia-guebuza.html. Accessed December 21, 2009.

Egero, Bertil. 1988. *Mozambique: A Dream Undone*. Sweden: Motola Grafiska.

Finnegan, William. 1992. *A Complicated War*. Oxford: University of California Press.

Hall, Richard. 1965. *Zambia*. London: Pall Mall Press.

1976. *Zambia: 1890–1964*. Hong Kong: Longman Group Limited.

Hamalengwa, Munyonzwe. 1992. *Class Struggles in Zambia: 1889–1989 and The Fall of Kenneth Kaunda: 1990–1991*. Ontario: University Press of America.

Henriksen, Thomas H. 1980. *Mozambique: A History*. Southampton: The Camelot Press.

---

[35] See Albert Hirschman, "The Turn to Authoritarianism in Latin America and the Search for its Economic Determinants," in David Collier (ed.) *The New Authoritarianism in Latin America* (Princeton: Princeton University Press, 1979); also Albert Hirschman, *Shifting Involvements* (Princeton: Princeton University Press, 1982).

Hirschman, Albert. 1982. *Shifting Involvements*. Princeton: Princeton University Press.

Hirschman, Albert. 1979. "The Turn to Authoritarianism in Latin America and the Search for its Economic Determinants." in David Collier (ed.) *The New Authoritarianism in Latin America*. Princeton: Princeton University Press.

Isaacman, Allen and Barbara Isaacman. 1984. *Mozambique: From Colonialism to Revolution, 1900–1982*. Boulder: Westview Press.

Kaplan, Irving (ed.) 1979. *Zambia: A Country Study*. Washington, DC: The American University.

Levy, Brian. 2007. *Governance Reform: Bridging Monitoring and Action*. Washington DC: World Bank.

Levy, Brian and Francis Fukuyama. 2010. "Development Strategies: Integrating Governance and Growth," World Bank Policy Research Working Paper number 5196, January.

Levy, Brian and Sahr Kpundeh (eds.) 2004. *Building State Capacity in Africa*. Washington, DC: World Bank Institute.

Manning, Carrie L. 2002. *The Politics of Peace in Mozambique*. London: Praeger.

Nelson, Harold D. 1984. *Mozambique: A Country Study*. Washington, DC: American University Press.

Newitt, Malyn. 1995. *A History of Mozambique*. Hong Kong: Indiana University Press.

Pitcher, M. Anne. 2002. *Transforming Mozambique: The Politics of Privatization, 1975–2000*. New York: Cambridge Press.

Olukoshi, Adebayo O. 1998. *The Politics of Opposition in Contemporary Africa*. Stockholm: Elanders Gotab.

Rakner, Lisa. 2003. *Political and Economic Liberalisation in Zambia 1991–2001*. Stockholm: The Nordic Africa Institute.

Roberts, Andrew. 1976. *A History of Zambia*. New York: Africana Publishing Company.

Sardanis, Andrew. 2007. *A Venture in Africa: The Challenges of African Business*. New York: Palgrave Macmillan.

Sichone, Owen and Bornwell Chikulo. 1996. *Democracy in Zambia: Challenges for the Third Republic*. Zimbabwe: Southern Africa and Publishing House.

Taylor, Scott D. 2007. *Business and the State in Southern Africa: The Politics of Economic Reform*. Boulder: Lynne Rienner Publishers.

Tordoff, William (ed.) Robert Molteno, Anirudha Gupta, Thomas Rasmussen, Ian Scot, and Richard L. Sklar. 1974. *Politics in Zambia*. Berkeley: University of California Press.

Tordoff, William (ed.) 1980. *Administration in Zambia*. Manchester: Manchester University Press.

Tschirley David and Stephen Kabwe. "The Cotton Sector of Zambia," World Bank Africa Region Working Paper Series No. 124, March 2009.

FIVE

Change and Continuity in a
Limited Access Order

The Philippines

Gabriella R. Montinola

The Philippines has exhibited characteristics of both a fragile and basic limited access order since independence in 1946, but the nature of the Philippine state has not been static. The country has experienced two critical junctures since independence, resulting in three distinct historical periods. Democratically elected representatives ruled the country from 1946 to 1972. The democratic experiment ended in 1972 when then incumbent president Ferdinand Marcos executed a coup against the system and began his rule as dictator. A nonviolent revolution ended Marcos's authoritarian rule in 1986, and the country is once again ruled by democratically elected representatives.

These significant political changes were accompanied by changes in the nature of the country's ruling coalition as well as the rents used to sustain the coalition (see Table 5.1). From 1946 to 1972, the country was dominated by a coalition of elite families and foreign capitalists who controlled access to economic and political power. The major source of wealth at independence was agricultural land, but this source was soon augmented by industrial policy-induced rents. The ruling coalition used these rents to secure loyalty and to defuse periodic violence from non-elite groups. The strategy was unsustainable, however, because the rent-creating policies did not produce enough resources to satisfy the increasingly restive non-elite groups.

I would like to thank Toti Chikiamco, Jaime Faustino, Chito Gascon, Bong Montesa, Joel Rocamora, and Cesar Virata, who graciously granted me interviews that provided the basis for some parts of this chapter. I would also like to thank Emil Bolongaita for his assistance in the research and drafting of the segments on the tensions in Mindanao and civil–military relations. I am grateful to Ed Campos and the editors and other contributors to this volume, particularly John Wallis and Barry Weingast, for helpful comments on earlier drafts. This work was supported in part by the Hoover Institution. Any errors and inconsistencies remain my own.

Table 5.1 *Change and continuity in a limited access order:*
The Philippines, 1946–Present

1946–1972	• Two-party democracy
	• Ruling coalition of elite families and foreign capitalists
	• Rents from import and foreign exchange controls
	• Threats to system from landless farmers and labor
1972–1986	• Autocratic rule
	• Ruling coalition of elite families and the military
	• Rents from credit subsidies and monopoly control
	• Threats to system from communist insurgents and Muslim separatists
1986–present	• Multiparty democracy
	• Ruling coalition of elite families and the military with civil society organizations as junior partners
	• Rents from monopoly control and government contracts
	• Threats to system from communist insurgents, Muslim separatists, and disgruntled military factions

The threat of disorder and violence enabled Ferdinand Marcos to install himself as dictator in 1972.

The ruling coalition under Marcos included a much smaller core of elite families as well as the military. Non-elites were marginalized further, giving rise to armed movements against the state. Rents, which were more concentrated, were sustained by favorable international agricultural prices and credit conditions. When this conditions turned around, and it became clear that rents could no longer be sustained, the coalition began to fall apart. Not long thereafter, Marcos was forced to flee the country in the wake of a nonviolent revolution that restored the democratic regime.

The restoration of democracy in 1986 moved the country closer to the threshold between limited and open access orders, but most of the ground lost during the authoritarian period under Marcos has yet to be recovered. The current order is once again dominated by elite families – those who opposed Marcos as well as many who supported him. Today, however, the dominant coalition also includes the military because its members have refused to return quietly to their barracks. Most of the rents that sustained the Marcos regime's coalition are no longer available, but new forms have emerged. The government has not been able to control the actors with violence potential who emerged during the authoritarian period. It continues to move back and forth between peace talks and all out war with communist insurgents and Muslim separatists. The democratic regime is unlikely to be overthrown in the near future, but institutions within and outside of the state tend to be short-lived. Rule of law – if only for elites – is still lacking.

This chapter begins with a description of the dominant coalition in the Philippines at independence in 1946 and a brief history of the coalition's origins. It provides a coalition-based explanation for the weakness of the democratic institutions adopted at independence and describes how Marcos was able to take advantage of this weakness and declare martial rule in 1972. It then explains why the Marcos regime eventually collapsed and describes the new political-economic equilibrium that emerged. It ends with an assessment of the country's prospects for transition from a limited access order to an open access order.

5.1 Conditions at Independence

5.1.1 The Postcolonial Ruling Coalition

The Philippine economy in the 1940s was based primarily on agriculture, which constituted around thirty-seven percent of GDP (Hooley 2005: 469). The country's principal crops included rice, corn, coconut products, tobacco, and sugar. Three-fourths of the total work force was employed in the agricultural sector. Agricultural land was highly skewed in its distribution. The vast majority of those employed in agriculture – 65.5 percent – were landless. A substantial minority – 26.6 percent – owned plots of less than five hectares. A small minority – less than two percent – owned large tracts of land of over twenty hectares. A 1955 study paints a clear picture of the unequal distribution of agricultural land. It shows that 41.5 percent of total farm area in the country was owned by 0.36 percent of the population, and that those with more than 1,000 hectares – 221 families or 0.01 percent of the population – owned over five hundred thousand hectares or nine percent of total farm area (Simbulan 2005).

The unequal distribution of agricultural land allowed families with large landholdings to capture substantial economic rents with little capital investment and little risk. Large agricultural estates were often fragmented into holdings of between two to three hectares and farmed by tenants. Roughly forty percent of the farm population lived on farms under full tenancy, and an additional fifteen percent worked as tenants for large landowners as well as cultivating their own small plots (Simbulan 2005). In the dominant form of tenancy – the *kasama* system – the landowner typically provided land, seed, and animals and implements if necessary. The harvest was divided between landowner and tenant according to how much the landlord furnished as well as the fertility of the land.

Landownership conferred not only economic wealth, but also political power. As Lande (1967: 25) notes:

[T]enants depend upon members of the landed gentry not only for access to arable land, but also for ... loans or gifts of grain or money at times of distress, free medical and other professional services, and the patron's intercession to help protect them against the rigorous enforcement of the law. Such benefits, going beyond the terms of the tenancy contract, are regarded as favors which must be repaid. Because of the tenant's poverty, repayment usually takes the non-material form of service. One type of service is ... voting and campaigning for the benefactor, should he choose to run for public office, or for whatever candidates he designates.

Thus, owners of large landholdings dominated the economy as well as the halls of political power. They composed the major part of the ruling coalition at independence in 1946.

Land ownership, however, was not a necessary condition to entrench oneself in power. The ruling coalition also included individuals of more modest means who managed to monopolize control of coercive resources in their localities, and who subsequently enriched themselves. These individuals, referred to by scholars as *caciques* or local "bosses," emerged where control over economic resources hinged on local government power, for example, transportation chokepoints or public lands with natural resources (Sidel 1997). They were often engaged in illegal activities, such as illegal logging and mining, smuggling, and gambling.

Finally, the dominant coalition in the 1940s also included foreign capitalists. Before independence in 1946, the country's most lucrative economic sector – agricultural exports – was dominated by foreign capital. Fifty-five percent of investment in sugar centrals came from Americans and Spaniards.[1] Of the eight large plants involved in coconut oil production, only one plant was Filipino-owned; Americans, British, and Chinese owned the rest. Of the thirty tobacco manufacturing companies, sixty percent of capital invested was Spanish with the rest coming from Americans, Swiss, Chinese, and Filipinos (Hartendorp 1958).

---

[1]   Due to economies of scale and the need for sugar cane to be processed shortly after it is harvested, sugar centrals have local monopsony power. This gave owners of sugar centrals the advantage when negotiating with planters. Thus, as Larkin (1982) notes, owners of sugar centrals were at the top of the socioeconomic pyramid.

When the Americans relinquished political sovereignty over the Philippines in 1946, they secured their continued economic dominance in the country by requiring the Philippine Congress to approve the Philippine Trade Act, also known as the Bell Trade Act. The act required reciprocal free trade between the Philippines and the United States for eight years, to be followed by a twenty-year period of gradually diminishing privileges. The act established an exchange rate policy favorable to the United States. Finally, the act called for parity or equal rights for United States citizens in the development of natural resources, operation of public utilities, and ownership of business enterprises in the Philippines (Jenkins 1954).

5.1.2 The Origins of the Postcolonial Ruling Coalition

The composition of the dominant coalition at independence in 1946 was the product of over 300 years of colonial rule under the Spanish and over 40 years under the Americans, superimposed on pre-Hispanic social structures. Before the Spanish arrived, Philippine society was organized in villages or *barangays*, which consisted of 30 to 100 families related to each other by blood or marriage. Within each *barangay*, society was divided into at least three major classes. At the top of the hierarchy stood the nobility, who served as the ruling class. Each *barangay* was headed by a chief or *datu* who came from the ranks of the nobility. Below the nobility were freemen who swore allegiance to particular *datus* in exchange for security. At the bottom of the hierarchy were "dependents." Most dependents were debt peons who paid tribute to *datus*, nobility, or freemen. They served their masters in their homes and fields, and could not be bought or sold. Other dependents, especially those captured in battle, could be disposed of as their masters saw fit.

When the Spanish established control over the Philippines in 1571, they reinforced this social structure by ruling with the assistance of the previous nobility, then referred to as the *principales*, and by their institutionalization of private ownership of land. Spanish law recognized the ownership of all who held and cultivated land at the time of conquest as well as the communal ownership of grazing or forest lands in the *barangay*. All other lands were considered property of the Spanish crown. Royal decrees were passed granting all landholders the opportunity to obtain title to their lands free of charge. Since, however, the majority of small landowners were illiterate and unaccustomed to written rules of land tenure, they failed to avail of the policy. In fact, the decrees simply enabled the fraternal orders and *principales* to extend the boundaries of their estates at the expense of small landowners or to incorporate previously communal land in their estates (Pelzer 1945: 109). Spanish law on land tenure thus facilitated the concentration of land in the hands of the *principales*.

Finally, the *principales* also accumulated land through a moneylending practice called the *pacto de retro*. The practice was outlawed as early as 1768, however, the colonial government seems to have turned a blind eye to the *pacto*'s continued use (Schumacher 2001). The practice was employed not only by the traditional nobility of pre-Hispanic times but also by Chinese *mestizos* – the descendants of Chinese who had come to the Philippines as traders and married Filipinos. The *pacto* was the principal means by which wealthy but landless Chinese *mestizos* acquired land and the prestige that came with it.

The transfer of Philippine sovereignty to the United States after the Spanish-American War in 1898 did little to change the socioeconomic structure of the Philippines. The U.S. government in the Philippines, that is, the insular government, recognized that land distribution was a serious problem. The friar estates in particular had been the focal point of many peasant revolts. Hoping to avoid future rebellion, the insular government launched major land reforms. The government purchased the friar estates with the intention of distributing the land to the approximately sixty thousand tenants cultivating it before 1898. The government also passed a homestead act that allowed farmers to apply for frontier land in plots of up to sixteen hectares and granted families living on public land without title since 1898 the opportunity to free patent over their land.

Two decades later, however, land distribution had changed little. By 1913, sixty-one percent of friar land had been disposed of by the U.S. government, but most land ended up in the hands of wealthy landowners and American firms (Saulo-Adriano 1991). By 1918, only 2.2 percent of public land had been settled through homesteads or free patenting, and the incidence of squatting on public land had increased (Iyer and Maurer 2008: 20). Moreover, the tenancy rate had increased from eighteen percent in 1903 to thirty-five percent in 1933 (Simbulan 2005).

Why were the agrarian reforms ineffective in reducing land concentration? The proximate causes center on the insular government's policy decisions. First, because the insular government paid a relatively high price for the friar lands and wanted to recoup its costs, the land was sold at a price that poor farmers could not afford (Iyer and Maurer 2008: 17).[2]

---

[2] Iyer and Maurer estimate that the purchase price for the friar estates was twenty-six times the annual income that could be generated from the land (2008: 12).

Second, because the insular government did not have sufficient funds to conduct land surveys, only wealthy farmers could comply with the homestead act's land survey requirement by hiring private surveyors. Poor farmers had no choice but to continue cultivating land they did not own (Corpuz 1997: 278).

The deeper cause of the failure of agrarian measures was the American government's lack of political will. The U.S. Congress had no interest in subsidizing Philippine land reform. Moreover, limits on land ownership in the Philippines, which would have reduced land concentration, went against U.S. business interests in the archipelago. In fact, many American corporations were exempted from the size limitations imposed on sales of public lands (McCoy 2009: 255, Putzel 1992: 55).

Land reform measures were also ineffective because the Americans, like the Spanish before them, found it expedient to govern the country with the cooperation of the traditional ruling elite (Hutchcroft and Rocamora 2003). Almost as soon as they established their control over the Philippines, the Americans began to introduce institutions of self-government. The way in which the Americans devolved political authority to Filipinos allowed the landed elite to further consolidate their dominance. The franchise for elective office was effectively limited to men with large landholdings. Limiting the franchise "had the effect of reaffirming the historic role of the principalia as the intermediary between the native lower classes and their colonial rulers" (Doronila 1985). It also ensured that those in power would be sympathetic to the interests of landowners.

During the second and third decades of American rule, the franchise was gradually liberalized. For example, in 1916, the property ownership qualification for the vote was eliminated. Nonetheless, the characteristics of those elected remained the same. Political parties emerged to contest elections, but their members were almost all from the same socioeconomic group. By the time the electorate included non-elites, the landed elite had consolidated its control over the country's political institutions (Doronila 1985, Hutchcroft and Rocamora 2003). "New" parties were usually the product of personal rivalry for dominance within established parties.

In 1934, the U.S. government passed the Tydings-McDuffie Act, also known as the Philippine Independence Act. The act provided for a ten-year "transitional period" before independence and guidelines for the drafting of a constitution. The 1935 constitution drafted under the terms of the Tydings-McDuffie Act created the Commonwealth of the Philippines and provided the basis for the country's postcolonial political institutions. The constitution featured an extremely powerful executive and a unicameral legislature.

In 1940, the constitution was amended to provide for a bicameral legislature. Although all laws enacted by the Commonwealth government were still subject to the authority of the U.S. Congress, in practice, the former enjoyed substantial autonomy.

In 1935, Manuel L. Quezon was elected president of the Commonwealth, and candidates from his political party – the Nacionalista Party – took all seats in the legislature. The Nacionalista Party was a "patronage-oriented party that was to become the prototype for most subsequent twentieth century Philippine political parties" (Hutchcroft and Rocamora 2003: 269). Broad control over appointments and budgets of the bureaucracy helped Quezon secure the loyalty of his party mates.

The 1930s were a period of increasing agrarian unrest in the Philippines. While uprisings were quickly crushed, they clearly indicated peasants' frustration with the land tenancy situation. To defuse the situation, Quezon adopted a "social justice" program shortly after assuming office. The impact of Quezon's social justice program is unclear, however, because it was soon interrupted by the Japanese occupation of the Philippines during the Second World War. Given that the Commonwealth government was dominated by the landed elite, it is likely that the measures would have been rendered ineffective as previous measures under the Americans.

5.2 The Postwar Period of Democratic Government (1946–1972)

The United States transferred full sovereignty to the Philippines on July 4, 1946. The new Republic started at the threshold between a fragile and basic limited access order. The ruling coalition, composed mainly of the landed elite and foreign capitalists at independence, were soon joined by industrialists who emerged as a result of policy-induced rents. The democratic political institutions that elites designed while under American tutelage were capable of moderating conflict between members of the ruling coalition, but they failed to respond to the needs of landless farmers and industrial workers. Decreasing real wages in the industrial sector and increasing land alienation in the rural areas resulted in strikes, demonstrations, and armed rebellions. The government managed to defuse threats from marginalized groups with promises of reform, but reforms were never fully implemented, if at all. Unrest would resume as soon as marginalized groups realized that reform was not forthcoming. Reforms did not occur because of resistance from ruling coalition members and because the economic policies that created rents for the ruling coalition were not promoting sufficient growth. It gradually became clear that the government would not have enough resources to sustain the current ruling coalition. It is thus unsurprising that a sitting president, Ferdinand Marcos, was able to take advantage of this weakness and install himself as dictator in 1972.

5.2.1 Politics

Elections for the first government of the Republic were dominated by two political parties: the prewar Nacionalista Party and a newly founded Liberal Party. Competition between the two parties was vigorous. They alternated in power from 1946 to 1972, cycling approximately every eight years. The appearance of competitive two-party politics in the Philippines, however, was an illusion. Politics was extremely personalistic. The parties were merely shifting coalitions held together by patron–client relationships extending from prominent families in each province through lesser gentry in towns, petty leaders in villages, and down to the common person (Lande 1966: 156).

The two political parties were virtually identical in ideological stance. During any given election campaign or under any particular administration, one might discern slight differences between the parties on some social, economic, or foreign policy issue, but party positions and corresponding reputations were highly fluid. For example, in the mid-1950s under President Ramon Magsaysay, the Nacionalista Party passed legislation on agrarian reform that was, by the standards of the time, quite progressive. Yet, by 1961, the Liberals, under Diosdado Macapagal were considered by most Filipinos as the party more sympathetic to poor farmers. Transposition of reputations on this particular matter over such a short period of time was remarkable given that agrarian reform was one of the most hotly contested socioeconomic issues of the time.

The two parties were also constantly subject to mass defections of legislators. For example, immediately after the 1961 elections, twenty-four of seventy-four Nacionalistas in what was then a 106-member house of representatives switched to the Liberal Party. After the 1965 elections, fifteen of sixty-two Liberal representatives switched to the Nacionalista Party. In both instances, the defectors switched to the incoming president's party to increase their chances of sharing in the spoils. In each case the switching handed a majority to a president elected with initially only minority support in Congress. The parties' lack of political consistency and the unbridled party switching by politicians was due to their clientelistic structure.

5.2.2 Import Subsidies, Credit Controls, and Rents

Given the nature of political parties, politics in the period from 1946 to 1972 was basically about creating and dividing rents among the ruling elite. Under the Spanish, rents from land ownership were the main source of wealth. As the Americans introduced institutions of self-government, elites learned to use government as a source of rents. Not long after independence, policies adopted as emergency measures to resolve a balance of payments crisis became the new source of rents.

In the first two years of the Republic, demand for imports necessary for economic rehabilitation far outstripped exports. Heavy fighting on Philippine soil during the Second World War had resulted in severe casualties and destruction of the country's productive assets. Three years of Japanese occupation disrupted production in the country's prewar agricultural export industries. The import surplus was paid for by war damages payments from the United States and uncharacteristically high prices for one of the country's traditional exports – copra.

In 1948, decreasing war damages payments, a drop in copra prices, and the continued failure of domestic industry to meet demands for consumer goods resulted in a trade imbalance so severe that the government was compelled to adopt import and exchange controls. The Central Bank of the Philippines was authorized to license all transactions in gold and foreign exchange. The policy was intended to secure sufficient foreign exchange for the importation of essential goods. In addition, the government created an Import Control Board whose task was to regulate all imports through licenses. The granting of an import license automatically entitled an importer to a foreign exchange license.

The foreign exchange and import control policy, which began as an emergency measure, soon became an explicit part of the country's industrialization strategy until 1962 when controls were lifted. The strategy promoted industrial growth because it made investment in industry highly profitable. When foreign exchange and imports are rationed, excess demand for these goods is met in parallel or black markets. The higher prices paid in parallel markets allow those with access to foreign exchange and imports at official prices to capture excess profits, or rents. Following Gallagher (1991), I assume that the difference between the value of foreign exchange allocated at the official rate and the value of the same amount of foreign exchange at black market rates provides a rough measure of these rents. I thus estimate rents associated with foreign exchange controls in the Philippines using the following formula: $FXR_t = (1-(OER_t/BMR_t)) * (FX_t)$, where FXR is the

Table 5.2 *Estimated rents from foreign exchange controls*
(period averages, 1954–1972)

	Official/ Black Market Rate	FXR[a] (Millions U.S.$)	FXR[b] (Millions of pesos)	FXR/Government Consumption (%)[c]
1954–57	0.64	217.3	439.0	57.4
1958–61	0.54	292.7	591.3	55.1
1962–65	0.98	4.9	18.8	1.1
1966–69	0.91	30.9	121.5	4.1
1970–72[d]	0.91	42.2	265.1	6.4

[a] FXR = Rents from foreign exchange controls estimated with the following formula: $FXR_t = (1-(OER_t/BMR_t)) * (FX_t)$; where FXR is the value of estimated rents from foreign exchange controls in U.S. dollars, OER is the official Philippine peso to the U.S. dollar exchange rate, BMR is the corresponding black market rate, FX is the amount of foreign exchange sales by the Central Bank of the Philippines, and $_t$ refers to year. Rents were estimated by year and averaged over the four-year periods.

[b] The value of estimated rents in pesos is calculated at the official exchange rate.

[c] FXR/Government consumption is calculated in peso terms.

[d] Three-year period refers to the second term of democratically elected Ferdinand Marcos. Marcos cut short his second term by declaring martial law on September 21, 1972. The data for 1972 refer to the whole year.

Sources: For black market peso-dollar rates: *Picks World Currency Yearbook* (New York, various years); for foreign exchange sales used to estimate rents: Central Bank of the Philippines, *Statistical Bulletin* (Manila, various years); for official (market) peso-dollar rates and government consumption: IMF *International Financial Statistics* (CD-ROM).

value of estimated rents from foreign exchange controls in U.S. dollars, OER is the official Philippine peso to the U.S. dollar exchange rate, BMR is the corresponding black market rate, FX is the amount of foreign exchange sales by the Central Bank of the Philippines, and *t* refers to year.

Table 5.2 provides a breakdown of the ratio of official to black market exchange rates averaged over each four-year congressional term from 1950 to 1972. It also shows the annual average rents from foreign exchange controls by four-year congressional terms. The formula estimates rents in U.S. dollars. The table presents the value of rents in U.S. dollars and in pesos calculated at the official exchange rate. As the table shows, official exchange rates were thirty-five percent to forty-five percent lower than black market rates from 1954 to 1961. Annual average policy-induced rents reached a high of over $292 million or over 591 million pesos for the years from 1958 to 1961. These rents were sizable. They amounted to over fifty percent of government consumption from 1954 to 1961.

These substantial rents induced many of the landed elite to invest in commercial and manufacturing industries, and the economic elements within the dominant coalition were diversified. The nature of political institutions ensured that benefits would be further divided among elites. Firm owners were clearly willing to share a part of their extra-normal profits with public officials. Shortly after import and exchange controls were established in 1949, the term "ten percenter" became popular. The term referred to congressmen who acted as brokers for firm owners applying for import and foreign exchange licenses. The total amount of foreign exchange allocated from 1953 to 1961 was $5.53 billion (U.S. billion). At the rate of ten percent, this implies that congressmen received $553 million due to the de facto rationing of import and exchange licenses brought on by controls.

Import and foreign exchange controls were abolished in 1962, and rents from foreign exchange controls declined thereafter (see Table 5.2). The dominant coalition gradually began to rely on a new source of rents – loans from the Central Bank. As early as the mid-1950s, real discount rates (the rate at which the Central Bank made loans to commercial and government-owned banks) were sometimes negative. Government-owned banks often passed on the benefits of negative real lending rates to clients with influence in government. Commercial banks, a majority of which were family owned, extended similar benefits to companies whose directors and controlling stockholders sat on the boards of the banks. When real lending rates are negative, lenders incur losses – rather than receive interest payments, they effectively provide subsidies to credit recipients. Negative real discount rates in the Philippines thus suggested that the Central Bank was subsidizing credit recipients – government-owned banks, commercial banks, and their borrowers – through its rediscount facility.

To estimate the size of subsidies that those with access to credit at negative lending rates secured, following Gallagher (1991), I first calculated real discount rates by subtracting the rate of inflation – the annual percentage change in the Philippine consumer price index – from the Central Bank's nominal discount rates. I then calculated rents for those years when the real discount rate was negative with the formula: $CR_t = (-(I_{r,t}) * (CBcredit_t))$ where CR is the value of estimated rents from credit allocated at negative lending rates, I_r is the real discount rate, CBcredit is end-of-period credit from the Central Bank of the Philippines in pesos, and t refers to year. Observe that rents from credit allocation are likely to be underestimated because they are calculated only for years when the real discount rate was negative. Data necessary to calculate subsidies from credit allocation at rates that are positive but lower than market rates were not available.

Table 5.3 *Estimated rents from the Central Bank's credit allocation
(period averages, 1950–1972)*

	Real Discount Rate[a]	Rents from CB Credit(CR)[b] (Millions of pesos)	CR/Government Consumption (%)
1950–53	2.57	0.65	0.23
1954–57	0.22	0.26	0.13
1958–61	0.95	–	–
1962–65	0.77	2.56	0.53
1966–69	−0.58	1.83	0.15
1970–72[2]	−7.47	63.50	2.36

[a] Real discount rate is the nominal discount rate minus the percent change in the consumer price index.

[b] Rents from Central Bank credit were estimated with the following formula: $CR_t = (-(I_{r,t}) * (CBcredit_t))$ where CR is the value of estimated rents in millions of Philippine pesos from credit allocated at negative lending rates, I_t is the real discount rate, CBcredit is end-of-period credit from the Central Bank of the Philippines in pesos, and $_t$ refers to year. Rents were calculated only for years when the real discount rate was negative and averaged across the four-year periods.

Sources: For discount rates, the consumer price index used to calculate real discount rates, credit from the Central Bank used to estimate rents, and government consumption: IMF *International Financial Statistics* (CD-ROM).

Table 5.3 presents real discount rates for Central Bank loans averaged over four-year congressional terms from 1950 to 1972. It also shows the annual average subsidies, or rents, that those with access to credit at negative lending rates would have secured by congressional term between 1950 and 1972. As the table shows, average real discount rates were above zero for most congressional terms between 1950 and 1972. However, rates were negative in five years between 1950 and 1968, and they remained negative from 1969 to 1972. Estimated subsidies or rents from these negative discount rates added up to 211.7 million pesos for the period from 1950 to 1972, almost all of which were secured in the last three years. The annual average amount of rents from Central Bank credit reached a high of 63.50 million pesos in the period from 1970 to 1972. This amounted to an average of 2.36 percent of government consumption in the same years.

Import and exchange controls as well as credit subsidies were thus major sources of rents for the dominant coalition in the postwar period. They transformed the dominant coalition from a landed elite to a more complex coalition based on commerce and industry as well as land. Conflict of interest between the new and old elites did emerge but was muted, in part, because many of the new elite came from the old elite, and in part, because many new elites continued to have kinship or marriage ties to families with agricultural interests. But the fluid political system also ensured sufficient distribution of rents among elites. The politically powerful sugar exporters, for example, lobbied hard against foreign exchange controls, and the latter were gradually eliminated in 1962. But as Crowther (1986: 344) observes:

Given the bargaining inherent in the Philippine political process . . . currency deval-uation to aid exporters was . . . coupled with measures intended to offset its neg-ative impact. Tariffs protecting domestic manufacturers were increased, as were the already substantial tax incentives that they enjoyed, and monetary policy was relaxed in order to sustain economic activity.

Finally, while the landed elite had to compromise with the commercial and industrial elite, they remained powerful enough to undermine legislation that would require redistribution of wealth in favor of tenants and landless agricultural workers.

5.2.3 Strategies to Coopt or Suppress Non-elites with Violence Potential

While the political system was fluid enough to moderate conflict between members of the dominant coalition, it was incapable of addressing the needs of the majority of the population. Industrialization spurred by import and foreign exchange controls increased the size of the working class in the urban industrial centers. But the gains from import and foreign exchange controls did not benefit labor in the manufacturing sector. As shown in Table 5.4, real wages for skilled labor barely kept up with inflation through the 1950s and had dropped slightly by 1961. Wages for unskilled workers increased slightly in the first half of the 1950s but then dropped to their 1949 level in the second half of the decade.

Stagnant wages resulted in increasing labor unrest. To address the issue the Philippine Congress passed an Industrial Peace Act (R.A. 875) in 1953. The act emphasized collective bargaining and arbitration to resolve labor–man-agement disputes and promote workers' interests. During the period that the act was effectively operative (1953 to 1971), labor unions increased in number. Before the act, approximately 180 new unions were registered per year; after the act, the annual rate increased to approximately 570.

The Industrial Peace Act's effect on wages was limited, however. As Table 5.4 shows, real wages for both skilled and unskilled workers increased shortly after the law's passage in 1953 but started declining again after 1955.

Table 5.4 *Manufacturing real wages and strike activity, 1949–1971*

	Real Wages Skilled Sector	Real Wages Unskilled Sector	Strikes	Workers on Strike (WOS)	WOS/Paid Employees In Manufacturing (%)
1949	100.7	93.1	77	14,796	–
1950	97.6	79.1	42	8,111	–
1951	84.5	78.8	28	4,943	–
1952	91.8	90.1	14	2,293	–
1953	97.1	95.9	13	9,683	–
1954	99.0	96.1	53	18,417	–
1955	100.0	100.0	47	14,574	–
1956	97.7	98.8	77	21,165	10.8
1957	95.7	96.1	–	–	–
1958	95.8	93.5	–	–	–
1959	98.4	95.1	–	–	–
1960	94.3	91.4	–	–	–
1961	92.6	92.2	–	–	–
1962	88.6	89.7	–	–	–
1963	86.4	89.6	88	47,520	16.5
1964	81.2	83.6	101	64,624	21.2
1965	81.5	87.3	109	55,229	17.6
1966	80.6	88.2	108	61,496	19.4
1967	79.8	87.3	88	47,524	–
1968	86.0	96.9	121	48,445	12.7
1969	89.2	100.0	122	62,803	16.3
1970	80.9	94.5	104	36,852	9.5
1971	71.5	85.1	157	62,138	15.2

Sources: For wages: Robert Baldwin, *Foreign Trade Regimes and Economic Development: The Philippines* (New York: Columbia University Press, 1975), pp. 147–8. For strike activity: Leopoldo J. Dejillas, *Trade Union Behavior in the Philippines 1946–1990* (Manila, Philippines: Ateneo de Manila University Press), p. 34. For paid employees in manufacturing: National Economic and Development Authority, *Philippine Statistical Yearbook*. (Manila: Philippines, various years).

Not surprising, the average number of strikes per year and the number of workers involved increased after the act was adopted. Although data on the number of strikes, workers involved in strikes, and labor in the manufacturing sector is spotty, a rough trend is apparent. Between 1948 and 1953, the industrial sector faced an average of forty-four strikes per year, and the average number of workers involved in these strikes was approximately ten thousand four hundred. Between 1963 and 1971, the average number of strikes increased to 111 and the average number of workers involved in strikes increased to fifty-four thousand (Dejillas 1994: 32–4). In 1956, the workers involved in strikes constituted under eleven percent of paid employees in manufacturing establishments employing five or more workers. The average number of workers involved in strikes as a percent of paid employees in manufacturing establishments increased to sixteen percent in the sixties.

Meanwhile, in the countryside, violent conflict between landlords and tenant farmers, which had been interrupted by the Japanese invasion, resumed. Those referred to as Huks, members of the Hukbo ng Bayan Laban sa mga Hapon, were a group of poor farmers who organized in 1942 to resist the Japanese. During the Japanese occupation, the Huks organized self-governing communities, undertook land reform, and ensured food production and distribution when many large landholders had fled to safer areas of the country.

With the return of U.S. forces at the end of the Second World War, the prewar political status was revived. Large landowners returned and in many cases set up private armies to reestablish their right to the land taken over by the Huks in their absence. With the help of the Communist Party of the Philippines (PKP), the Huks regrouped, renamed their army the Hukbong Mapagpalaya ng Bayan (HMB), and turned their attention to fighting for agrarian reform (Fifield 1951).

The PKP and HMB initially attempted political means to reach their goal. In the elections for the first government of the Republic, they backed members of the Democratic Alliance (DA), a political party of progressive candidates. Six DA candidates won congressional seats, but they were prevented from taking their seats nominally on grounds of electoral fraud and violence, but more plausibly because they were likely to oppose the Philippine Trade Act (e.g., Hutchcroft and Rocamora 2003, Lara and Morales 1990). With the unseating of the DA congressmen, the two organizations turned to armed struggle. In 1950, they were reported to be active in twenty-two provinces and Manila (Saulo 1990).

The U.S. government, initially concerned about the agrarian situation in the Philippines, sent a land reform expert, Robert S. Hardie, to survey the situation in 1951. Hardie proposed a comprehensive program that would have resulted in substantial land redistribution, but his program was never implemented. It was vehemently opposed by landlords and their representatives in government. Moreover, by 1953, the tide had turned against liberal reform advocates like Hardie in the United States. Future U.S. representatives suggested that peasant revolt could be prevented with only minor reforms.

The push for comprehensive land reform was also mitigated by the collapse of the HMB rebellion in the late 1950s. The movement collapsed because of the two-pronged strategy of Ramon Magsaysay, who was appointed defense secretary in 1950 and then won the presidency in 1953. In 1950, Magsaysay coopted HMB members with liberal cash incentives and amnesty in exchange for assistance in capturing other militants. He also provided land to former HMB members in less populated provinces on the southern island of Mindanao (Saulo 1990, Shalom 1977). In 1954, the government launched a massive military operation sponsored by the United States that resulted in the capture or death of many remaining HMB and PKP leaders (Saulo 1990).

Although the HMB movement was eliminated, Magsaysay recognized that ongoing tension between landlords and tenants could generate future rebellions. Thus, he initiated legislation intended to reduce these tensions: The Agricultural Tenancy Act of 1954, The Act Creating a Court of Agrarian Relations, and the Land Reform Act of 1955. Since, however, it was clear that peasant unrest had been defused at least temporarily, the landed elite felt confident in hamstringing Magsaysay's reform efforts. Congress allocated too few funds for the Agrarian Court and land reform program. The retention limits for land reform left few estates eligible for redistribution. Finally, land could be redistributed "only when a majority of tenants therein petition for such purchase." As Putzel (1992: 92) argues, "a tenant would have to be irrational to make such demands given the economic and political power of the landlord." Ultimately, less than twenty thousand hectares – less than one-fourth of one percent of total cultivated land – was acquired by the government for redistribution (Saulo-Adriano 1991).

With the collapse of the HMB, the Federation of Free Farmers (FFF), an anticommunist organization, took up the cause of farmers. In 1963, the FFF's founder, Jeremias Montemayor, was appointed by President Diosdado Macapagal to help draft the Agricultural Land Reform Code of 1963. Disillusionment with the results of the reformist approach, however, and the shooting of an FFF leader at a demonstration in front of the office of the president in January 1971 eventually radicalized some of the organization's younger leaders. By the end of 1971, the FFF's membership had grown to approximately one hundred and twenty thousand in forty-five provinces, and its mass actions were supported by radical youth groups (Kimura 2006).

Table 5.5 *Internal and external debt of the government and monetary institutions (period averages, 1950–1971)*

	Internal Debt (Millions of pesos)	Internal Debt/ GDP (%)	External Debt (Millions U.S.$)	External Debt/ GDP (%)
1950–53	666	8.4	111	2.8
1954–57	1,266	12.5	89	2.0
1958–61	2,136	15.7	175	2.6
1962–65	2,904	14.2	324	6.1
1966–69	4,522	14.8	2,686	8.8
1970–71	6,635	13.4	1,058	13.6

Sources: For internal and external debt: Central Bank of the Philippines, *Statistical Bulletin*, December, 1970; and Central Bank of the Philippines, *Annual Report*, 1971, cited in Robert Baldwin, *Foreign Trade Regimes and Economic Development: The Philippines* (New York: Columbia University Press, 1975), p. 69. For GDP used to calculate debt as a percentage of GDP: IMF *International Financial Statistics* (CD-ROM).

Meanwhile, in 1968, the Communist Party of the Philippines (CPP) was reestablished under the leadership of "Amado Guerrero," later identified as Jose Ma. Sison. Sison was most inspired by Mao Zedong's strategy of protracted people's war and ultimately launched a new type of revolution with the creation of a new military arm – the National People's Army (NPA). The NPA was headed by Bernabe Buscayno, a former HMB commander, who assumed the name Commander Dante.

5.2.4 Implications

While the Philippine state managed to defuse serious threats to its survival during its first twenty-five years, by 1971 its survival was tenuous. As mentioned previously, non-elite organizations, including trade unions, the FFF, and the CPP, were turning to more radical means to promote the welfare of the lower classes. It was increasingly obvious that the implicit rent-sharing agreement among the elites was becoming unsustainable. The economy, which had been limping along at per capita growth rates averaging around two percent per year since the mid-1950s, faced another serious balance of payments crisis in 1969. The crisis was due to high import levels stimulated by the government's easy credit policies. The country's internal and external debts were clearly unsustainable (see Table 5.5). By the early 1970s, the government's internal and external debt both amounted to around thirteen percent of GDP.

Moreover, in the political arena, the cost of election campaigns had increased over time. Traditional patron–client ties were eroding, and voters – especially those in the urban areas – expected more and more benefits in exchange for their support. In 1946, private expenditures of national parties and presidential candidates amounted to 3 million pesos, and the incumbent had access to another 3.5 million pesos in relief and public works funds. In 1969, incumbent president Ferdinand Marcos was estimated to have spent between 800 million and 900 million pesos, around half from government funds (Doronila 1985: 114). Electoral violence was increasing as well. The 1969 election was the most violent to date. Perhaps it is unsurprising that a political entrepreneur such as Ferdinand Marcos was able to use the specter of disorder to install himself as a dictator.

5.3 The Authoritarian Period Under Marcos (1972–1986)

On September 22, 1972, President Marcos declared martial law in order to "eliminate the threat of a violent overthrow of [the] Republic ... [to] clean up government ... [and to encourage] systematic development of the economy."[3] Closer examination of events leading up to the declaration of martial law, however, suggests that the president's desire to maintain power indefinitely was a stronger motivating force. First, Marcos had been filling the military's higher ranks with men from his home province, personally loyal to him. Second, he was serving his second term as president and was prohibited by the constitution from serving a third term. Third, he declared martial law in the midst of a constitutional convention that among other issues was considering a provision to ban immediate family members of an incumbent from running for the presidency. The provision was clearly aimed at banning the president's wife from seeking office. Finally, declining rents and rising violence increased support for martial law.

5.3.1 The Marcos Coalition

To consolidate his position, Marcos quickly formed a new coalition that included a smaller core of trusted elites, who came to be known as Marcos's cronies, as well as the military. By discriminating among elite families, Marcos disorganized the once powerful elite who could have served as the most viable opposition. Elite families that openly opposed Marcos suffered imprisonment and/or confiscation of wealth, but those that acquiesced maintained most of

---

[3] "Statement of the President on the Proclamation of Martial Law in the Philippines," in I. T. Crisostomo, *Marcos the Revolutionary* (Quezon City: J. Kriz Publishing, 1973).

their assets although they did not profit from the dictatorship's policies. In keeping with the logic of the limited access order, he maintained his coalition's loyalty through a system of selective rewards and punishments.

Although the structure of the economy under the martial law regime was not unlike that under the democratic regime with its large private conglomerates, a distinctive feature was the number of new conglomerates that emerged as well as their phenomenal growth rates. Herminio Disini, for example, started a company called Herdis Management & Investment Corp., in 1969 with a loan of thirty-five hundred dollars. Ten years later, Disini headed a conglomerate with more than fifty companies involved in diverse sectors such as tobacco filters, logging, petroleum, cellophane, nuclear power, real estate, insurance, and banking, with estimated assets totaling over $200 million (Manapat 1991: 316–43).

Like many business empires created under the prior democratic government, these conglomerates were built primarily on preferential treatment in economic controls and government contracts in exchange for a part of future rents. Unlike the period of democratic rule, however, the power to confer preferential treatment during the martial law period rested primarily on a single public official – Marcos. For example, Disini's Philippine Tobacco Filters Corporation received a special exemption from the 100 percent tax on cigarette filters at the personal behest of Marcos. The exemption gave Disini's firm an advantage that allowed it to crowd out rivals.

The most widely used instrument for inducing rents, however, was credit allocation. Preferential treatment in credit allocation occurred mainly through the Central Bank's (CB) rediscount facility as well as through "behest loans" from government financial institutions. A central bank's rediscount facility can be employed as a tool for liquidity management, as it is used by most central banks, or as a tool for fiscal policy through the allocation of credit to priority activities. Under the first Marcos administration in 1966, the allocative features of the facility were institutionalized. A comprehensive credit priority classification system was adopted. By the 1970s, credit was extended at ten different rates for various special programs and government-sponsored projects.[4]

Special rediscount rates were all well below the rate of inflation in five out of seven years from 1973 to 1979, effectively providing subsidies to recipient banks and/or their clients. Examination of the amount of Central Bank credits that commercial banks received suggests that not all banks had equal access to rediscount credits. In a study on the Philippine commercial

---

[4]   "Notes on Central Bank Rediscount Rate" (Central Bank Circular, September 30, 1986), Manila (mimeo).

banking system, Patrick and Moreno found that out of twenty-six banks, three – Republic Planters Bank,[5] Philippine Banking Corporation, and International Corporate Bank – secured credits from 1978 to 1980 that amounted to more than double their net worth in the three years. Four other banks had loans more than double their net worth in one or two years. Various factors affected the amount of credit that banks received from the Central Bank, but it is unclear what objective economic criteria could have led to the substantial differences in debt to equity ratios among banks. Instead, it appears that political connections were critical.[6]

Table 5.6 presents real discount rates, estimated rents from the allocation of Central Bank credit at negative real discount rates, and rents as a proportion of government consumption from 1973 to 1980.[7] Real discount rates and rents were estimated with the formulae used for values presented in Table 5.3. As shown in Table 5.6, real discount rates were negative from 1973 to 1980, and estimated gains from nonmarket allocation of credit added up to 3.495 billion pesos for the period. These rents were more than ten times as much as the credit subsidies allocated during the prior twenty years under democratic rule. As a proportion of government consumption, rents from negative discount rates were never as high as rents from foreign exchange controls in the 1950s, however, they were still substantial. In 1974 and 1980, they were over seven percent of government consumption.

Political connections were also often critical in securing loans from government financial institutions (GFIs). The extent of preferential treatment in financing through GFIs was gradually exposed by the Commission on Audit and the Presidential Commission for Good Government. The latter body was created by executive order in 1986 to recover "ill-gotten wealth accumulated by former President Ferdinand E. Marcos, his immediate family, relatives, subordinates and close associates."[8] Both agencies investigated the

---

[5] As Patrick and Moreno note, the figures for RPB are extremely high because the bank's primary clients are sugar farmers, and agricultural exports are on the Central Bank's priority list. Hugh Patrick and Honorata A. Moreno, "Philippine Private Domestic Commercial Banking, 1946–80, in Light of Japanese Historical Experience," *The Philippine Economic Journal*, Number 56, Vol. 23, Nos. 2 & 3, 1984.

[6] Interview with bank official, Development Bank of the Philippines, August 17, 1993 (name withheld); See also Patrick and Moreno; Mario B. Lamberte, "Assessments of the Problems of the Financial System: The Philippine Case," Philippine Institute for Development Studies, Working Paper Series No. 89–18; Paul D. Hutchcroft, *Predatory Oligarchy, Patrimonial State: The Politics of Private Domestic Commercial Banking in the Philippines* (Doctoral dissertation, Yale University, 1993).

[7] See pp. 15–16 and Table 5.3 notes for how rents from Central Bank credit were estimated.

[8] Online PCGG report accessed on May 1, 2010 at http://www.dbm.gov.ph/opif2009/doj-pcgg.pdf.

Table 5.6 *Estimated rents from the Central Bank's credit allocation* (1973–80)

	Real Discount Rate[a]	Rents from CB Credit(CBR)[b] (Millions of pesos)	CBR/Government Consumption (%)
1973	−6.58	82.25	1.32
1974	−28.16	639.23	7.16
1975	−0.76	48.64	0.43
1976	−3.20	175.04	1.32
1977	−3.90	173.94	1.21
1978	−3.33	185.81	1.15
1979	−6.53	570.06	3.12
1980	−13.66	1,620.07	7.33

[a] Real discount rate is the nominal discount rate minus the percent change in the consumer price index.
[b] See Table 5.3 notes for how rents from Central Bank credit were estimated.
Sources: For discount rates, the consumer price index used to calculate real discount rates, credit from the Central Bank used to estimate rents, and government consumption: IMF *International Financial Statistics* (CD-ROM).

circumstances surrounding loans extended by the government-controlled Philippine National Bank and other GFIs during the Marcos regime. These loans were assumed by the national government in 1986 due to their recipients' inability to remit further payments. In 1989, the Commission on Audit revealed that out of 70 billion pesos granted by one government financial institution – the Development Bank of the Philippines – 59 billion pesos went to Marcos's cronies. In August 1993, the PCGG announced that thirty-five percent of over 200 loans under investigation were "behest" loans,[9] that is, substantially undercapitalized, undercollateralized loans; loans to proponents close to the Marcos family; and/or loan applications accompanied by marginal notes from Marcos urging bank officers to approve them.

The PCGG's findings also point to the extreme concentration of rent beneficiaries. By August 1993, the PCGG had filed charges in the Sandiganbayan, a court specifically for graft and corruption cases, against 383 individuals for illegal acquisition of assets. Forty-two of the individuals charged were also alleged in a U.S. court case to be fronts for Marcos in 195 financial

[9] "Memorandum for the chairman of the PCGG, Magtanggol C. Gunigundo, from Virgilio Hermosura, 'Summary of Accounts,'" August 4, 1993, Manila (mimeo); *Philippine Star*, August 30, 1989.

institutions and enterprises. Sixty-seven of the enterprises named in the U.S. case were among the top 300 corporations in the Philippines.[10] Many of them were in the most lucrative sectors of the economy, such as banking, mining, logging, and telecommunications.

While the Marcoses were acquitted by the U.S. courts in 1991,[11] there is good reason to believe that the PCGG's information was correct. For example, as early as 1986, one businessman under investigation for benefiting from substantial government contracts at the behest of Marcos admitted that he held a major part of Marcos's assets in trust. The businessman admitted to organizing and operating twenty-seven corporations for the Marcos family with funds that the PCGG believed were illegally extracted from the public treasury. He agreed to turn over all properties he claimed to be holding for Marcos in exchange for the lifting of writs of sequestration on his family corporations.

A second distinct feature of the rent-sharing system during the dictatorship was the distribution of monopoly rights over key agricultural markets by way of quasi-state marketing boards (Hawes 1987). In 1974, Marcos issued a decree giving the Philippine Exchange Company (Philex), monopoly control over the export of sugar. Philex was controlled by Roberto Benedicto, a long-time friend of Marcos's (Manapat 1991: 100). Monopsony power allowed Philex to dictate the price it paid planters for their sugar. Invariably, the company purchased sugar at prices significantly lower than international prices, raising substantial profits for Benedicto, Marcos, and their close supporters on the board of directors.

In the coconut sector, Marcos created the Philippine Coconut Authority (PCA), whose governing board initially included government and private sector representatives. The agency's task was to collect levies from farmers and use the funds to conduct regional and national conventions, promote new technology, and finance new coconut mills. Instead of ameliorating the lives of the 2 million landowners, tenant farmers, and landless farmers who worked in the coconut industry, the PCA's proceeds were appropriated by the president and one particularly powerful crony, Eduardo Cojuangco. Levies collected from farmers were used to prop up Cojuangco's United Coconut Planters Bank (UCPB), and UCPB was given the right to establish a monopoly in coconut oil milling. Cojuangco's monopoly guaranteed his

---

[10] Supporting document from PCGG for criminal case filed under the U.S. Racketeering Influenced and Corrupt Organizations Act (RICO) against the Marcoses, Adnan Kashoggi, and others, October 21, 1988 (mimeo).

[11] Ferdinand Marcos died shortly before the trial, thus, it was actually his wife Imelda that was acquitted.

coconut oil mills substantial profits. But the president is believed to have appropriated millions, if not billions, of pesos as well. Nearly ten percent of UCPB bank shares were held in trust for "beneficiaries unknown," assumed by PCGG investigators to be the Marcos family (Wurfel 1988: 259).

Agricultural monopsonies thus generated substantial extra-normal profits for favored individuals. I estimate the rents from these monopsonies using the following formulae: [12] For rents in the sugar industry: $R_{s,t} = (1-(P_{f,s,t}/P_{w,s,t}))*(X_{s,t})$, where R_s is the value of estimated rents from sugar exports, $P_{f,s}$ is the price received by farmers for their sugarcane, $P_{w,s}$ is the world price of sugar, X_s is the value of sugar exported from the Philippines to the rest of the world, and $_t$ refers to year. For rents in the coconut industry: $R_{c,t} = (1-(P_{f,c,t}/P_{w,c,t}))*(X_{c,t})$, where R_c is the value of estimated rents from coconut oil exports, $P_{f,c}$ is the price received by farmers for copra, the dried meat of coconuts from which coconut oil is extracted, $P_{w,c}$ is the world price of coconut oil, X_c is the value of coconut oil exported from the Philippines to the rest of the world, and $_t$ refers to year.

Estimation of rents from monopsony power in the sugar and coconut industries using these formulae leads to inflated figures because the ratio of farm to world prices was not adjusted for processing, transport, and marketing costs due to lack of data. Nonetheless, the results of the analysis are suggestive.

Table 5.7 presents the rough estimates for rents in the sugar and coconut industries. As the table suggests, the creation of marketing boards for agricultural exports during the authoritarian regime generated substantial extra-normal profits for their boards of directors. Rents for Philex, the sugar monopsony, increased from $8.40 million in 1972 to $82.58 million in 1974. This amounted to twenty-seven percent of the value of sugar exported in 1972 to as high as seventy-six percent of the value of sugar exported in 1974. Although rents from sugar exports began to decrease after 1974 as world prices declined, they were still substantial in 1976, amounting to $18.59 million, or 32.4 percent of the value of sugar exports.

Monopoly control of coconut oil milling generated even greater extra-normal profits. Rents ranged from $165.65 million in 1975 to over $486 million in 1979. They amounted to an average of seventy-one percent of the value of coconut oil exports from 1975 to 1982. When these rents from agricultural monopolies are added to the rents generated by nonmarket

[12] Due to incomplete data, rents from agricultural monopolies were measured only for a few selected years. The formulae used to measure these rents are based on work by Gallagher (1991).

Table 5.7 *Rents from agricultural monopolies in sugar and coconut industries[a]*

	Sugar Industry Rents (R_s) (U.S.$ Millions)	R_s/Sugar Exports (%)	Coconut Industry Rents (R_c) (U.S.$ Millions)	R_c/Coconut Oil Exports (%)
1972	8.40	26.6	–	–
1973	15.78	38.9	–	–
1974	82.58	76.0	–	–
1975	–	–	165.65	71.93
1976	18.59	32.4	213.13	71.35
1977	1.07	1.5	285.23	69.19
1978	–	–	436.86	67.15
1979	–	–	486.86	65.57
1980	–	–	432.92	76.37
1981	–	–	398.89	74.77
1982	–	–	293.17	73.10

[a] Rents from agricultural monopolies were estimated using the following formulae: For rents in the sugar industry: $R_{s,t} = (1-(P_{f,s,t}/P_{w,s,t}))^*(X_{s,t})$, where R_s is the value of estimated rents from sugar exports, $P_{f,s}$ is the price received by farmers for their sugarcane, $P_{w,s}$ is the world price of sugar, X_s is the value of sugar exported from the Philippines to the rest of the world, and $_t$ refers to year. For rents in the coconut industry: $R_{c,t} = (1-(P_{f,c,t}/P_{w,c,t}))^*(X_{c,t})$, where R_c is the value of estimated rents from coconut oil exports, $P_{f,c}$ is the price received by farmers for copra – the dried meat of coconuts from which coconut oil is extracted, $P_{w,c}$ is the world price of coconut oil, X_c is the value of coconut oil exported from the Philippines to the rest of the world, and $_t$ refers to year.
Source: For sugarcane farm prices and sugar export values: Philippine Council for Agriculture and Resources Research. *Data Series on Sugar Cane Statistics in the Philippines*. Manila, 1980. For world price of sugar: Philippine Sugar Millers Association: http://www.psma.com.ph/index. php?option=com_content&view=article&id=1&Itemid=2. For copra farm prices: Bureau of Agricultural Science, *Statistical Compendium on Agriculture, Fishery, and Forestry* (Quezon City, 1988). For world price of coconut oil: UNCTAD, *Commodity Yearbook 1988* (New York: United Nations, 1989). For coconut oil export values: United Nations Commodity Trade Statistics Database (http://comtrade.un.org/db/default.aspx).

allocation of credit, one can see that the Marcos coalition continued to generate rents that were at least as high, and probably much greater, than those during the democratic period.

5.3.2 Strategies to Coopt or Suppress Non-elites with Violence Potential

In keeping with the logic of the limited access order, Marcos also used a system of selective rewards and punishments to disorganize non-elite opposition forces. Segments of the CPP/NPA support bases were coopted by

Marcos's land reform program. Shortly after declaring martial law, Marcos passed a decree (PD 27) declaring tenants in rice and corn lands "owners" of the land they were tilling. The government then established a system whereby tenants could begin to purchase their land in installments. Notably, the regions most affected by PD 27 were areas where the NPA was initially concentrated. The remaining dissenters were dealt with by the military. Military intelligence units infiltrated NPA ranks and spread disinformation regarding their penetration of the organization. In the late 1970s, this led to the capture of CPP founder Sison and a number of NPA commanders. The strategy also led to massive purges by the NPA of suspected individuals, which initially frightened potential recruits (McCoy 1989: 37).

Despite these setbacks, the ranks of the organization continued to increase for at least two reasons. First, the land reform program was never fully implemented. PD 27 was expected to affect approximately three hundred ninety-six thousand farmers on seven hundred thirty-one thousand hectares of land. By 1982, only 2,352 peasants had received title to 1,903 hectares of land (Lara and Morales 1990). Second, economic conditions continued to deteriorate, providing fertile ground for the CPP/NPA.

Tensions over land and resources in the southern island of Mindanao also turned into armed conflict between the government and Muslim separatists during the Marcos dictatorship. In the late 1940s, the Muslim or Moro population of Mindanao did not pose a threat to the stability of the nascent independent state. The American colonial regime had pacified different Moro groups through brutal military campaigns and "the judicious use of 'divide-and-rule' tactics among the disunified Muslim communities" (Abinales 2000: 19–20; see also McKenna 1998). The Muslims, then as now, fell into ten major groups, with the three biggest being the Tausugs, the Maranaos, and the Maguindanaos.[13] Their differences are sharp, each speaking different languages and each having distinct social and political practices. Beyond religion, the groups did not have anything in common (Madale 1986).

Together with its military might, the American colonial regime applied a political approach to win over Moro elites and maintain stability. The Americans were aided by Filipino politicians who were starting to participate in government. These politicians recognized the electoral advantages of

---

[13] The Tausugs are mainly from the island of Jolo; the Maranaos are in present-day Lanao del Sur and Lanao del Norte; while the Maguindanaos are in North Cotabato, Sultan Kudarat, and Maguindanao provinces. The Samals and Bajaus are in the Sulu Archipelago; the Yakans are in Zamboanga del Sur Province; the Ilanons and Sangirs in various parts of southern Mindanao, the Melabugnans in southern Palawan; and the Jama Mapuns in the Cagayan Islands (see Dolan 1991).

being supported by Muslim blocs that could support candidates as a group (see Abinales 2000: 36). Conversely, Moro elites found political engagement with the capital to be rewarding, providing them with positions and resources that reinforced their titles and status.

The fabric of stability in Mindanao started to fray after the Philippines gained its independence and the new government embarked on a policy of in-migration to Mindanao in response to agrarian unrest in the more densely populated area around Manila. The regime reduced the prewar Muslim majority in the Moro provinces in the first two decades of the postwar period by resettling Christian Filipinos in Mindanao. For example, in central Mindanao, the Christian population in 1948 was only 0.7 million; by 1970, it had grown to 2.3 million (McKenna 1998). Muslims in Mindanao in the postwar period were, thus, peripheralized, increasingly becoming a minority in a land they once dominated.

The influx of Christians in Mindanao resulted in conflicts over land and claims of dispossession (Gowing 1979). Conflict over land ownership became a driver of violence, and the stability in Mindanao started to unravel (Costello 1984). Growing economic disparities between Christians and Muslims were increasingly evident, and efforts by the Muslims to seek redress from the capital were rebuffed (McKenna 1998).

From 1946 to 1970, these tensions were moderated by the participation of Moro elites in the elections for national and subnational local government positions. Elections became a new arena for expanding political and economic power among Moro elites. However, the rewards of electoral politics were limited only to the ruling elites who were focused in their pursuit of political power during elections, but neglectful of their responsibility to provide public goods during the intervening period.

Growing resentment over economic and social problems led a group of educated Muslims to resist the state. In 1971, Nur Misuari founded the Moro National Liberation Front (MNLF), seeking a separate Moro homeland governed by a Moro state focused on Moro needs. From 1971 to 1976, the MNLF waged a violent secessionist campaign with support from different Muslim countries. In 1976, the organization forced the Marcos government to the negotiation table to reduce the spiraling economic and political costs of the conflict. Hosted by the Libyan government, the negotiations between the Philippine government and the MNLF led to the Tripoli Agreement, which provided a roadmap for autonomy in the regions of Mindanao where most Muslims resided.

The MNLF's victory was short-lived. Disputes arose between the Philippine government and the MNLF over the implementation of the agreement. The government required that the agreement be ratified by plebiscite in Mindanao. The call for a plebiscite raised concerns in the MNLF about the government's commitment to the agreement because by then Christians were a majority in the region. Some factions within the MNLF advocated a return to armed struggle and formed the Moro Islamic Liberation Front (MILF). The Marcos government's strategy of accommodation weakened the MNLF, however, it did not result in peace. The MILF continued to promote armed struggle long after Marcos's downfall.

5.3.3 The Collapse of the Marcos Coalition

Ultimately, the political system that Marcos devised collapsed in 1986. What led to its demise? The Philippines' primary sources of revenue were export agriculture and foreign loans, and as mentioned in the previous section, most of these resources were used by the president to maintain political support. In the early 1980s, however, the rise in global interest rates and the drop in the prices of the Philippines' major commodities undermined this equilibrium. From 1972 to 1982, commodity prices fell by more than fifty percent (Lindsey 1984: 1192). Moreover, in 1983, net inflows of medium- and long-term capital dropped 22.8 percent below inflows of the previous year, while short-term capital registered a net outflow – \$607 million – for the first time since the declaration of martial law. These external shocks led to a contraction in state revenues, and the government was forced to withdraw some of the benefits it had been providing cronies. Import restrictions on various products were relaxed. The coconut levy, one of the major sources of rents for Marcos and his cronies, was suspended in January 1981. In an attempt to accommodate his cronies, Marcos reinstated the coconut levy one month later. But under pressure from IMF officials pushing for economic liberalization, the government again suspended the levy in August 1982 (Montes 1985: 112–13). Marcos was clearly trying to maintain the collusive relationship he had with cronies, but the latter, recognizing their vulnerability, began to withdraw their support.

A major blow to the system was dealt by Dewey Dee, who headed four joint venture textile companies and sat on the boards of three banks. On January 9, 1981, Dee fled the country, leaving approximately \$67 million in debt (Haggard 1990: 235). Dee's actions provoked a run on a number of investment houses and banks. The government was compelled to offer assistance to failed banks, investment houses, and crony firms severely affected by the financial uncertainty in order to stabilize the economy. Real growth rates declined from 3.4 percent in 1982 to 1.9 percent the following year (Dohner and Intal 1989: 173).

Attempting to take advantage of the economic crisis in his quest to oust Marcos, Benigno (Ninoy) Aquino, Marcos's long-time nemesis and leader of the old Liberal Party, returned to the Philippines in 1983 after three years in exile in the United States. Aquino was assassinated at the Manila airport before he could set foot on Philippine soil. Aquino's assassination led to demonstrations against the regime and increased opposition activity. This turn of events prompted Marcos, who was then trying to legitimate his rule, to call for parliamentary elections in 1984. Marcos and his close supporters won a substantial majority of the available seats, primarily due to a boycott of elections by opposition groups, electoral fraud, and massive public works expenditures.

The increase in government spending during the campaign period resulted in an annual rate of inflation of 50.3 percent. While this figure is well below the rates of hyperinflation experienced by many Latin American countries, it was substantial when compared to the average rate of 10.9 percent over the previous three years (Dohner and Intal 1989: 173). More crony firms found themselves unable to repay their massive debts, and the government eventually took over the firms and put them up for sale. Marcos was in search of new supporters. But with the economy deteriorating so rapidly, he could not credibly commit to a specific allocation of wealth and had little compensation to offer. Thus, elites were less willing to compete for his favors. The final blow to the Marcos regime came when Defense Minister Juan Ponce Enrile, General Fidel Ramos, and factions within the military joined non-cronies in a four-day nonviolent revolution that brought Corazon Aquino to power.

The division within the military that contributed to Marcos's downfall was ironically a product of his own making. In the period immediately following independence, the Philippine military was effectively controlled by the civilian government. At no time between 1946 and 1972 did the military openly challenge the civilian government, much less attempt to overturn the democratic regime (McCoy 1999: 28). By 1986, however, his policy of promoting family, co-ethnics, and fellow ROTC graduates politicized the military and led to tensions among the officer corps (McCoy 1999: 28).

The tensions among officers who did not benefit from Marcos's patronage and those who did became particularly acute after the assassination of opposition leader Benigno Aquino in 1983. With mass protests swelling following the Aquino murder, the divisions in the military prompted a group of officers to openly organize a group called the Reform the Armed Force Movement

(RAM). The military division led to an attempted military coup by RAM in February 1986. The coup collapsed because the cover of the plotters was blown beforehand. Fortunately, supporters of Corazon Aquino intervened to protect the coup plotters and together they toppled the Marcos regime in an event now remembered as the 1986 People Power Revolution.

5.3.4 Implications

Some have argued that the assassination of Ninoy Aquino was the beginning of the end for Marcos. I suggest, however, that the beginning of the end for Marcos was the economic crisis triggered by changes in the international economic system. The economic crisis exposed the delicate nature of the commitment between Marcos and his cronies. The nature of that commitment is one reason the Marcos regime collapsed while other authoritarian regimes in the region, South Korea and Taiwan, were able to weather the changes in the international system.

In effect, Marcos had been caught in a vicious cycle. Substantial rents made agreements between Marcos and his cronies credible. As rents declined due to changes in the international economy, the number of credible agreements possible declined, inducing cronies to withdraw their support. As cronies defected, Marcos's political control waned, further reducing potential rents. Thus, the fall of the Marcos regime was due in part to his failure to devise an institution that could credibly guarantee cronies some schedule of rewards should the economy take a downturn.

5.4 The Post-Marcos Democratic Period (1986–present)

On February 25, 1986, Ferdinand Marcos, who was in power for twenty-five years, was forced into exile, and Corazon Aquino was sworn in as president. Aquino was swept into power in the wake of mass demonstrations now referred to as the 1986 People Power Revolution. She was supported by a broad-based coalition that included progressive organizations, the urban middle class, economic elites who opposed Marcos, the church, and factions of the military. Not surprising, each group expected to be part of the ruling coalition in the new social order.

5.4.1 The Post-Marcos Coalition

In the early years of the regime, it did appear as though the ruling coalition would be broader than ever before. Aquino's transitional cabinet included leaders of progressive social movements, representatives of elite interests, and leaders of the military factions that opposed Marcos. The composition of the commission that she created to rewrite the constitution reflected the broad base of her support. The new constitution, which was ratified in 1987, maintained many features of the pre-martial law constitution that had allowed traditional politicians representing elite families to dominate politics. However, the new constitution also included a provision expected to promote broader representation in the legislature. In particular, the constitution stipulated that twenty percent of seats for the House of Representatives be filled by a party-list system. It was believed that non-elite sectoral organizations would have a better chance of being represented in the legislature if voters were given the chance to vote for parties rather than individual candidates in single-member districts. The constitution also called for decentralization of fiscal policy to the subnational governments and the inclusion of nongovernmental organizations (NGOs) in local councils to be created later. Finally, the constitution expressly prohibited the establishment of political dynasties,[14] however, as will be discussed in the following section, Congress was left with the responsibility for defining the term *political dynasties* and specifying procedures to enforce the provision. The provision's aim was to prevent families that had dominated politics in the pre-martial law period from dominating during the post-Marcos period.

Aquino even reached out to the communist insurgents who had not participated in the revolution – the latter chose to sit on the sidelines because they viewed the conflict between Marcos and Aquino "as nothing more than intramural politics within the elite" (David 1996: 10). Aquino negotiated a cease fire with the communists and released hundreds of political detainees, including Jose Ma. Sison, head of the Communist Party of the Philippines (CPP), and Bernabe Buscayno, commander of the New People's Army, the CPP's military wing. She created a Presidential Committee on Human Rights to investigate complaints by individuals who suffered in the hands of the police and military during the Marcos dictatorship. She also at least partially addressed the issue most pressing to supporters of the communists: land reform. In particular, she issued an executive order declaring all agricultural land subject to land reform regardless of crop planted.

Given the conflicting interests of the diverse groups in her coalition, it soon became clear, however, that Aquino would have to narrow her support base to consolidate the new regime. Ultimately, Aquino chose to favor

---

[14] Article II, Section 26 of the 1987 Constitution of the Republic of the Philippines reads: "The State shall … prohibit political dynasties as may be defined by law."

economic elites, and to a certain extent the military. Successive governments since then have sustained this coalition. While progressive organizations representing the poor and previously marginalized sectors of society are not completely devoid of influence in the current regime, their role in the policy process is limited.

Aquino was compelled to include the military in her ruling coalition because it refused to remain quietly in its barracks. In her first three years in office, Aquino faced several coup attempts from various factions within the military. Some were pro-Marcos; others had been part of the revolution against Marcos. They had in common their increasing dissatisfaction with conditions within the military and Aquino's policy toward communist insurgents (Abinales 1987). Some members of the rebellious military factions were also concerned that they would be implicated in the investigations into military abuses under martial law by the newly created commission on human rights. The coup makers were emboldened by a growing rift between Aquino and Defense Minister Enrile, who was in fact one of the prime enforcers of the martial law regime before he led military rebels against Marcos in 1986.

To avoid the overthrow of the newly restored democracy, the Aquino government adopted institutional reforms to increase civilian control over the military. The police were separated from the military, and the military's role was restricted to external defense. The oversight powers of the Congress over the defense budget and military promotions and appointments were restored (Hernandez 2007). However, the government also took steps to appease the military with each coup. By the end of her term in office, Aquino had raised military salaries, broken off peace talks with the communists, and agreed to the deployment of paramilitary groups who assisted the military in the war against the communists.

While military factions used violence (and the threat thereof) to ensure their position in the ruling coalition, elites used constitutional means to entrench their position. Congressional and local elections were held in 1987 and 1988 respectively, and many families that had dominated during the pre-martial law period once again dominated politics. Of the candidates elected to the House of Representatives, eighty-two percent had previously held public office or had relatives who previously held office. New faces were more likely at the local level, but candidates from previously powerful political families still constituted fifty-six percent of those elected to local government positions (Gutierrez et al. 1992). Even politicians who held office under Marcos were elected to the first post-Marcos legislature as members of the Kilusang Bagong Lipunan (KBL), the political party Marcos created during his dictatorship (Putzel 1999).

Elites have also ensured their dominant position in the system by diluting the provisions in the 1987 constitution that might have increased the power of progressive social movements. First, the legislation passed by Congress translating popular votes into seats for the party-list component of the legislature make it difficult for non-elites to gain enough seats to influence the policy process. The rules provide that parties are allotted one representative for every two percent of all votes cast, up to a maximum of three seats. The three-seat maximum means that any votes that parties receive over six percent are wasted. It prevents the emergence of a strong progressive party that might eventually be able to win twenty percent of the seats in the legislature.

Second, enabling legislation to implement the constitutional provision banning political dynasties was never passed. After very little discussion, it was tabled in committee by both the Senate and the House. Today, over sixty percent of members in the House of Representatives serve concurrently with relatives in other elective office (Coronel 2004). Elective office is once again a means of enriching one's family and protecting the family's economic interests.

Third, the Local Government Code (LGC) that Congress passed in accordance with the guidelines of the 1987 constitution provides for participation of NGOs in several local councils and committees. It also stipulates that a system similar to the party-list system at the national level be adopted at the local level so that non-elite sectors of society would be represented in local legislatures. Compliance with the LGC across the country, however, has been uneven and less than full (Capuno 2005).[15]

Elites have also managed to evade agrarian reform efforts. In 1988, the Congress passed the most progressive agrarian reform law to date. The goal of the Comprehensive Agrarian Reform Programme (CARP) was to redistribute 10 million hectares of farmland to 4 million poor farmers, comprising eighty percent of the agricultural population (Borras 2005). Much to the surprise of critics, the program achieved significant success in its first ten years. By 1999, the government had redistributed around sixty percent of its target, resulting in higher per capita incomes for farmer beneficiaries (Borras 2001, Reyes 2002).

---

[15] First, NGOs have to be accredited by local legislatures to participate in local councils. In many cases, this has led to the accreditation of NGOs that are not autonomous from local governments (Eaton 2003: 485). Second, even after accreditation, many NGO representatives are not invited to meetings regularly. Third, Congress has not passed the legislation necessary to implement sectoral representation at the local level.

The program was relatively successful in its early years, however, because most of the lands redistributed were settlement areas, landed estates, and government-owned lands, which were less contentious to acquire and required less funding. Since then, the process of redistribution has slowed significantly due to legal disputes relating to coverage and land valuation, landowners' resistance, and government budget constraints (Balisacan 2007). As Borras (2005: 101) notes, "Congress has consistently cut annual budget allocations for CARP's land acquisition component."

5.4.2 Rents in the Post-Marcos Era

The Philippines has witnessed substantial economic reforms since the restoration of democracy. In fact, some reforms actually began under Marcos when it became clear that the country's debt-led development strategy could no longer be sustained. Reforms have met with some success; however, new types of rents have emerged to maintain the new ruling coalition.

Today, tariffs range between three percent and ten percent from highs of over 100 percent (Medalla 2002). Effective protection rates have declined from twenty-nine percent in 1990 to six percent in 2004 (Aldaba 2005). The government has employed a more flexible exchange rate regime since 1984. The black market premium on foreign exchange dropped from an average of ten percent during the authoritarian period under Marcos to four percent for the years from 1984 to 1999.[16]

Restrictions on new bank entry and branching have been eased.[17] Interest rates on all deposits and loans are now essentially market determined (Milo 2002). Loans to directors, officers, stakeholders, and other related interests (i.e., DOSRI loans) must now be approved by a majority of banks' directors. The new general banking law (RA 8791) requires that banks include on their boards two directors who are not officers or employees of the bank or other related interests. RA 8791 also requires that DOSRI loans be reported to the Central Bank.

Since the early 1990s, many economic sectors have also been deregulated. Before deregulation, domestic airways were monopolized by one carrier, Philippine Airlines (PAL). Today six carriers compete for domestic passenger traffic, airfares are lower, and the quality of service and efficiency

---

[16] Calculated using data from Banks' Cross National Time Series Database.

[17] The number of commercial banks increased significantly from thirty-two in 1980 to a high of fifty-four in 1997. Most of the new entrants were foreign banks. The ownership structure of domestic banks has also changed due to liberalization. Most domestic banks are now partially foreign owned (Milo 2002).

Table 5.8 *Selected economic indicators (1960–2008)*

	1960–1971	1971–1985	1986–2008
GDP growth (annual %)	4.97	3.44	4.05
GDP per capita growth (annual %)	1.87	0.67	1.84
Gross fixed capital formation (annual % growth)	6.30	4.55	4.74
Agriculture, value added (% of GDP)	27.93	27.15	18.71
Manufacturing, value added (% of GDP)	24.39	25.48	23.38
Services, etc., value added (% of GDP)	40.79	36.17	48.68

Source: World Bank World Development Indicators (Accessed online May 1, 2010 http://data. worldbank.org/).

has improved.[18] In the water transport sector, the capacity of the domestic passenger and cargo fleet has grown significantly, and the average age of the passenger cargo fleet has dropped (Austria 2002). In the telecommunications sector, "at least two operators [are] allowed to compete in the same geographic market" (Serafica 2002: 161), and consumers have better access to, and better quality of, service.

These reforms have eliminated most of the rents that sustained Marcos's coalition; however, as shown in Table 5.8, the economy's overall performance and structure has changed little. Gross domestic product has grown at an average rate of four percent per year since democracy was restored in 1986. The corresponding figures for the democratic episode immediately after independence and the authoritarian interregnum are 5 percent and 3.4 percent respectively. Agricultural output as a percent of GDP has declined from 27.9 percent to 18.7 percent, but manufacturing output has not increased.

One reason for the economy's subpar performance may be the persistence of rent seeking for monopoly rents. Despite substantial trade liberalization, the domestic manufacturing sector remains highly concentrated, resulting in high price-cost margins. The four-firm concentration ratio for the whole industry actually increased from approximately seventy in 1988 to eighty in 1998 (Aldaba 2005). Concentration of ownership in the financial industry also continues to be of concern. Mergers between domestic commercial

[18] Although PAL remains the dominant carrier, the degree of competition among the six carriers has intensified since deregulation, especially over major routes. The Herfindahl-Hirschman Index for the domestic air industry based on market share declined from. 92 in 1995 to. 34 in 1999 (Austria 2002).

banks have recently increased asset concentration. Before 1994, the five largest domestic banks in the country accounted for around fifty percent of the sector's total assets. This share declined to thirty-seven percent with the reduction of limits on bank entry, but increased again to around fifty percent after recent mergers in the industry (Pasadilla and Milo 2005).

International air services remain effectively restricted to one carrier – Philippine Airlines. This is in part because the government is reluctant to liberalize international air traffic rights (Austria 2002). In the shipping industry, price-cost margins remain high despite deregulation in large part because the industry today is dominated by one firm formed out of a merger between the three top shipping firms. As Austria (2002) states "major players [seem] to have divided the market among themselves." About fifty percent of the primary routes have only one operator, and almost fifty-nine percent of secondary routes and seventy-eight percent of tertiary routes have been monopolized.

5.4.3. The "Doorstep Conditions"

Substantial political and economic liberalization has occurred in the Philippines since 1986. Is the country closer to the threshold between a limited and open access order? North, Wallis, and Weingast (2009) argue that three conditions must obtain before limited access orders are likely to transition into open access orders. These "doorstep conditions" are: (1) state control over actors with violence potential; (2) the presence of perpetually lived organizations, including the state itself; and (3) the rule of law for elites. The Philippines today appears closer to attaining these doorstep conditions when compared to the authoritarian period under Marcos, however, the country may actually be further from the threshold today than it was immediately after independence in 1946.

5.4.3.1. Control over Actors with Violence Potential

The government has less control over actors with violence potential today than in the period from 1946 to 1972. Civilian control of the military is still tenuous. On-and-off armed conflict with communist insurgents and Muslim separatists continues. Vigilante groups have emerged in response to raids by insurgents and increasing crime. Election-related violence continues to occur.

As mentioned earlier, the Philippine military shortly after independence was effectively "indoctrinated into an ideal of civilian supremacy and generally avoided political entanglements" (McCoy 1999: 28). Marcos politicized the military, employing troops to conduct political arrests, to torture and assassinate dissidents, to quell demonstrations, and to prop up the dictatorship. In exchange, loyal officers were allowed to engage in rent-seeking activities in the form of smuggling and illegal concessions (Karnow 1989).

Although democracy was restored in 1986, parts of the military refused to submit to civilian control. During Aquino's term in office, the military attempted at least six coups. While none were successful, they established the threat potential of the military toward the regime. While the subsequent administrations of Ramos and Estrada did not experience any coup attempts, the succeeding administration of President Arroyo faced two serious military revolts and several smaller coup attempts.

The coups against Aquino did not continue into the Ramos era in part because Ramos himself was a military man. He also extended unconditional amnesty to the coup plotters and military rebels (Hernandez 2007). A deeper reason for the lack of military restlessness during the Ramos administration was lack of public support for a military solution to the country's problems. Surveys during that period "showed the people rallying to support President Aquino and to oppose the coup plotters" (Mangahas 2009). Equally important, a majority of the military sided with the civilian government to effectively put down coup attempts by fellow soldiers in their ranks.

At present, no imminent danger of military intervention exists. The public may be dissatisfied with democracy, but they distrust the military's ability to do a better job than the civilians. However, the coup attempts against Aquino and Arroyo have created a civilian government highly sensitive to military needs. All administrations to date have accommodated at least some of the coup makers' demands, and this has set an unhealthy precedent. Presidents since Ramos have sought to give military officers a stake in civilian rule by appointing retired generals to their cabinets as well as to top diplomatic, bureaucratic, and state corporate positions. President Arroyo has at least six former generals in her current cabinet. Many other retired generals were appointed as heads of other agencies and statutory bodies as well as given key ambassadorial postings (Boehringer 2009).[19]

Other challenges in the area of civil–military relations also render civilian control of the military tenuous. First, politicians and economic elites

---

[19] While retirement legally turns military officers into civilians, the practice of appointing retired generals to civilian office is a double-edged sword. Retired officers are likely to maintain strong ties with active officers due to their common training and combat experience. High-level civilian positions provide retired officers with a platform from which to call on junior colleagues in active service to join in plots against the government.

continue to enlist military support for their private purposes (Hernandez 2007: 93). For example, local strongmen use policemen as private armies to further their private interests (Kreuzer 2009). Second, the ongoing armed conflict against the communist insurgents and Muslim separatists has set back the separation of police and military functions. The military remains involved in these domestic conflicts, and in the field, there is very little consultation among local commanders and civilian officials. Third, due to limited resources, the government has turned to the use of paramilitary units – Civilian Armed Forces Geographical Units (CAFGU) – in the fight against communist insurgents. Local strongmen and private interests have taken advantage of the legislation allowing for the creation of CAFGU to legitimize their private armies. De Leon and Escobido (2004: 72–3) report, for example, that many commercial plantations in the banana industry finance CAFGU to act as security guards and to ensure that company unions are endorsed by workers.

A second indication of the government's weakness vis-à-vis actors with violence potential is the ongoing armed conflict with communist insurgents. Over the years, the government has started many peace talks with the Communist Party of the Philippines (CPP) and its legal organization, the National Democratic Front (NDF), but none have resulted in a final peace agreement. The most recent talks stalled in August 2009 and guerrillas of the CPP continue to stage raids against isolated military units in the countryside (Abinales 2010).

A rift in the revolutionary movement has reduced the numerical strength of the insurgents. The CPP-NPA continues to advocate armed revolution, but the breakaway units have accepted collaboration with progressive political parties as a valid strategy (Arcala 2007). On one hand, the turn to electoralism of at least part of the communist movement is a positive development. Bayan Muna, the party associated with the CPP and the NDF, has been relatively successful since it started contesting seats in the party-list component of the legislature. In 2001, Bayan Muna won three seats – the maximum allowed in the party-list competition. In 2007, the party won two seats. Somewhat troubling, however, are reports of how Bayan Muna's campaigns are conducted. Campaigners of other party-list entries, especially the left-leaning but noncommunist Akbayan, report having experienced harassment and violence from CPP activists and NPA guerrillas (Arcala Hall 2007). As Patino and Velasco (2004: 9) state, "The communist insurgency ... has established credence in elections by assassinating candidates who have participated in the military's counter-insurgency operations.

Extorting fees for safe access to rebel territory ... has also become a practice in many parts of the country. Conversely, there have been allegations that NPA guerrillas have snatched ballot boxes to ensure the victory of their allies."

As discussed earlier, armed conflict with Muslim separatists is another indication of the government's inability to control actors with violence potential. After Marcos was ousted, the government under Corazon Aquino revived peace talks with the MNLF, the organization that had signed the Tripoli Agreement calling for autonomy in Muslim Mindanao. The government held another referendum in 1989 (the first was held under Marcos) asking the people of the eighteen Mindanao provinces covered by the Tripoli Agreement whether they would agree to be part of an Autonomous Region of Muslim Mindanao (ARMM). Majorities agreed in only four provinces (another plebiscite in 2001 added a fifth province to the ARMM). Although far short of what the MNLF envisioned, the creation of the ARMM helped end the conflict between the government and the MNLF. The autonomous region was officially inaugurated in 1990, and MNLF leader Misuari was subsequently elected its governor.

By then, however, the MNLF was not the only organization claiming to represent Muslim interests. As mentioned earlier, a breakaway faction of the MNLF – the MILF – continued to wage war against the government. The costs of this conflict have been substantial. By one estimate, the total economic cost during the high-conflict period from 1997 to 2001 was about $200 million. The human and social costs include an estimated one hundred twenty thousand deaths, undetermined numbers of wounded and disabled, and more than 2 million people displaced (Schiavo-Campo and Judd 2005). Recognizing that a military solution may be too costly, the government is currently attempting to negotiate a peace agreement with the MILF with the help of third parties such as the Organization of the Islamic Conference (OIC) and the European Union (EU) as well as accredited international nongovernmental organizations. As of this writing, it is unclear whether a final solution will be reached.

Since 1991, another Muslim group – the Abu Sayyaf – has also engaged in armed conflict with the government. It has provoked the harshest government response because of its ruthless kidnap-for-ransom strategy, the most recent kidnapping being that of International Red Cross members early in 2009. The group is on the United States' list of terrorist organizations, and its members are suspected of having received training and funds from Al-Qaeda. The organization appears much weaker today due to "improved counterinsurgency tactics by the Philippine Marines assisted by U.S. special forces" (Abinales 2010: 223), but the group may continue to be a thorn in the side of the government for years to come.

The government's inability to control actors with violence potential is also suggested by the emergence of vigilante groups in response to what the groups consider indiscriminate violence of insurgents and rising crime (Kreuzer 2009). By one estimate, there were as many as 640 vigilante groups scattered around the country in 1989 (Hedman 2000: 130). They are an indication of the inability of the state to perform the vital function of ensuring law and order.

Finally, election-related violence continues to be a problem. According to Patino and Velasco (2004), over twelve hundred violent incidents occurred surrounding elections from 1988 to 2001, resulting in 500 deaths. Estimates of election-related violent incidents during the 2004 presidential polls range from 192 to 249 while casualties, which include wounded and dead, range from 329 to 468 (Linantud 2005; Quimpo 2009). It is difficult to determine whether elections are more dangerous today than in the previous democratic episode because many factors have changed between the two periods, including the number of candidates running in any given election as well as the number of organizations reporting on election-related violence. What is clear, however, is that "Philippine elections are still unsafe" (Linantud 2005).

5.4.3.2 Perpetually lived Organizations

While there is little chance that the democratic regime will collapse, many institutions within and outside the state are short-lived. The major political parties that have contested elections since 1986 are once again merely shifting coalitions of patron–client relationships. Government agencies and policy programs are not expected to persist beyond the administration that creates them. Policy programs are often delayed or reversed within the same administration.

The two political parties that dominated politics in the pre-martial law period have been replaced by many more parties, however, the nature of parties has changed little. Most continue to be temporary alliances designed to maximize the election chances of representatives of elite families. Many are simply personal vehicles set up by major contenders for the presidency. For example, Fidel Ramos, president from 1992 to 1998, formed the Partido Lakas Tao (aka Lakas) after losing the nomination for presidential candidate for the dominant party Laban ng Demokratikong Pilipino

(LDP). Party switching has also returned as the standard operating procedure of politicians. In 1992, the LDP won forty-three percent of the seats in the House, while Lakas, the party of incoming president Fidel Ramos, won only eighteen percent. The LDP could have played the role of a constructive opposition in a divided government, but sixty-two percent of LDP House members switched to Lakas. The switches were clearly just a means to securing the good graces of the incoming president (Montinola 1999). Politics is once again mainly about creating and dividing rents among the ruling coalition.

Like political parties, some institutions within the state as well as policy programs are short-lived. In 1986 the Aquino administration established the Asset Privatization Trust (APT) to dispose of government-owned and government-controlled properties. In 2001, the Arroyo administration replaced the APT with a new agency – the Privatization and Management Office (PMO) – with a similar mandate. Not long after the PMO's creation, however, Arroyo lost faith in the agency that she established. Claiming that the PMO was working too slowly, Arroyo ordered her cabinet to bypass the agency in the disposal of government properties (Carino 2008).

Policy programs are also often delayed or reversed. The tariff reform program provides one example (Aldaba 2005). For example, in June 1998, President Estrada signed a comprehensive tariff reform package. Six months later, he signed another executive order *increasing* tariff rates on some industries. Tariff liberalization was restarted in 2001 but soon reversed by the succeeding administration (Aldaba 2005). Commenting on the failure of government programs, Carino (2008: 80) states that agencies and initiatives "have not borne much fruit ... because programs have not been institutionalized. With the constitutional ban on presidential reelection, programs are conceived with a shelf life of six years and are expected to be changed by the next president."

5.4.3.3 Rule of Law for Elites

Confidence in the rule of law appears stronger today than during the authoritarian period, however, it seems weaker than during the country's previous democratic episode. This is most evident when comparing perceptions of the Philippine Supreme Court over time. While there are no surveys of the population's perceptions of the Supreme Court before the 1980s, the following statements from contemporary American and Filipino observers indicate Filipinos' respect for the high court during the pre-martial law period. "[The Supreme Court] is the most important legitimizing institution in the

Philippines." "[The Supreme Court] is a special repository of the Filipino's faith in legitimacy and legality. "We are a nation that has ... grown skeptical of anyone who occupies a public office, but there remains somehow that curious faith in the high Court."[20] The Supreme Court apparently elicited this praise for its decisions upholding the rule of law even "against the 'pleasure' of the President" (Locsin 1964).

The autonomy of the Supreme Court was seriously eroded during the authoritarian period. Although Marcos did not abolish the courts as he did the Congress, "the [Supreme] Court ... openly defaulted on its ability to consider allegations of human rights failures ... or to challenge the president in any other significant way" (Tate 1992: 117). When Aquino replaced Marcos in 1986, she quickly moved to strengthen the powers of the judicial branch, hoping to prevent any future chief executive from manipulating the Court as Marcos did. The damage to the Supreme Court's reputation from politicization during the authoritarian period, however, could not be so easily undone.

Surveys performed by a nonprofit organization, Social Weather Stations (SWS), suggest that the post-Marcos Supreme Court does not evoke the same sentiments as its pre-martial law counterpart.[21] When a random sample of the population was asked in 2003 how satisfied they were with the performance of the Supreme Court, only forty-five percent responded positively. Twenty-nine percent expressed dissatisfaction, and twenty-six percent were undecided. The Supreme Court did not fare as badly in surveys of lawyers and trial court judges. Around eighty percent of lawyers and judges responded that they were satisfied with the high court's performance. Yet when asked "at what level do you find corruption among judges," a significant minority – twenty-seven percent of lawyers – named the Supreme Court.[22]

---

[20] Quotations are by American scholar of Philippine politics Jean Grossholtz, Jesuit sociologists Francisco Araneta and John J. Carroll, and Filipino journalist Yan Makabenta, respectively, cited in Tate (1997) and Tate and Haynie (1993).

[21] SWS performs periodic surveys on the issue of confidence in government institutions. Responses to the items on confidence in government change little over time. For more details on the results of these surveys, see www.sws.org.ph.

[22] Top-level enterprise managers do not provide a rosier picture. When asked in 2000 to rate the Supreme Court in terms of its sincerity in fighting public sector corruption, only eleven percent of respondents rated the Supreme Court as "very sincere." Forty-seven percent rated the high court as "somewhat sincere," but twenty-two percent were "undecided." It is unsurprising then that a senior partner in the country's largest law firm would state in a letter to one chief justice: "In my 37 years of practice I have never seen the image of the Supreme Court ... sink to such levels in the eyes of the business community" (Coronel 2000).

Perceptions of the lower courts are even less sanguine. When asked how much trust or confidence they had in trial courts, only forty-three percent of respondents from the general population expressed high trust in the lower courts. Moreover, when asked whether they agreed that "rich or poor, people … receive equal treatment in court," less than forty percent agreed.[23] Perceptions regarding equal treatment differed from those *before* democratization, and the changes vary according to socioeconomic status. The number of upper- and middle-class respondents who perceive courts to be dispensing equal treatment *increased* from forty percent in 1985 to forty-eight percent in 1993, while the number of lower-class respondents *dropped* by eight percent. Democratization has not led to the perception of more equal treatment in courts.

Negative perceptions of the judicial system are not confined to the lower classes. Sixty-seven percent of lawyers surveyed in 2003 felt that court decisions were unpredictable. Twenty-four percent felt that many judges were corrupt. Substantial majorities perceived that judges' decisions were influenced by their fraternity and sorority connections, pressure from politicians, public attention, the professional reputation of lawyers before them, and ties to relatives and friends. These perceptions have led not only to loss of confidence in the judicial system, but also to distrust among citizens whose interests are on the line. As an aide to one litigant before the Supreme Court stated, "when [the governor] thought the other side was maneuvering, he wanted to move also.… If we didn't maneuver, we would have lost.… [The opposing litigant] was outbidded [*sic*]" (Coronel 2000). It thus appears that even elites perceive the rule of law to be lacking.

5.5 Conclusion

The Philippines has undergone two critical junctures since independence in 1946: (1) a transition to authoritarian rule in 1972 and (2) restoration of democracy in 1986. These significant political changes were accompanied by changes in the nature of the country's ruling coalition and the rents used to sustain the coalition. From 1946 to 1972, the country was dominated by a coalition of elite families sustained by rents from land and industrial policy. With the transition to authoritarian rule, the ruling coalition was reduced to a smaller core of elite families as well as the military. Credit subsidies, agricultural monopsonies, and illegal activities such as smuggling and extortion generated the rents that sustained this smaller coalition. In

---

[23] Data are from a national survey performed by SWS in 1999.

1986, democracy was restored and access to political power was extended once again to all elite families. Most of the rents that sustained the previous regime's coalition were eliminated through reform. Monopoly rents sustain the current ruling coalition.

Given the restoration of democracy and substantial economic reform, is the country closer today to the threshold between limited and open access orders? I argue that the country may be even further from the threshold than it was at independence. First, the government appears to have less control today over actors with violence potential. The military was politicized during the authoritarian period, and factions of the military continue to periodically rise up against the civilian government. The government continues to move back and forth between all-out war and peace talks on two fronts – against communist insurgents and Muslim separatists. Second, while it is unlikely that the democratic regime will be overthrown in the near future, few institutions within and outside the state are perpetually lived. Political parties are merely shifting coalitions of patron–client relationships that come together and fall apart with electoral fortunes. Bureaucratic agencies and policy programs are expected to last only as long as the administration that conceived of them. Finally, confidence in the rule of law appears weaker today than during the democratic episode immediately following independence. The Supreme Court that was highly respected in the earlier democratic period evokes more negative views today. Negative perceptions of the Supreme Court, and the judicial system more generally, are not confined to non-elites, suggesting that the rule of law – if even only among elites – is still lacking. In sum, despite substantial political and economic liberalization, the Philippines has not yet achieved the doorstep conditions that increase a country's likelihood of moving from a limited to an open access order.

References

Abinales, Patricio N. 1987. "The August 28 Coup: The Possibilities and Limits of the Military Imagination." *Kasarinlan: Philippine Journal of Third World Studies* 3(2): 11–18.

Abinales, Patricio. 2000. *Making Mindanao: Cotabato and Davao in the Formation of the Philippine Nation-State* . Manila: Ateneo de Manila University Press.

Abinales, Patricio N. 2010. "The Philippines in 2009: The Blustery Days of August." *Asian Survey* 50(1): 218–27.

Aldaba, Rafaelita M. 2005. "The Impact of Market Reforms on Competition, Structure and Performance of the Philippine Economy." Philippine Institute for Development Studies Discussion Paper Series No. 2005–24.

Arcala Hall, Rosalie. 2007. "Living in the Shadow of Violence: Local Civil-Military Engagement during Anti-Communist Insurgency Operations in the Philippines." *Asian Security* 3(3): 228–50.

Austria, Myrna S. 2002. "Philippine Domestic Shipping Industry: State of Competition and Market Structure." PASCN Discussion Paper No. 2002–04.

———. 2002. "The State of Competition and Market Structure of the Philippine Air Transport Industry." Pp. 189–252 in Erlinda M. Medalla (ed). *Toward a National Competition Policy for the Philippines.* Makati, Philippines: Philippine Institute for Development Studies.

Baldwin, Robert E. 1975. *Foreign Trade Regimes and Economic Development: The Philippines.* New York: National Bureau of Economic Research.

Balisacan, Arsenio M. 2007. "Agrarian Reform and Poverty Reduction in the Philippines." Paper presented at the Policy Dialogue on Agrarian Reform Issues in Rural Development and Poverty Alleviation. Manila, Philippines.

Boehringer, Gill H. 2009. "Arroyo's Generals: Militarization and Patronage" at http://www.bulatlat.com/main/2009/02/28/arroyo%e2%80%99s-generals-militarization-and-patronage/.

Borras, Saturnino M. 2001. State-Society Relations in Land Reform Implementation in the Philippines. *Development and Change* 32: 545–75.

———. 2005. "Can Redistributive Reform be Achieved via Market-Based Voluntary Land Transfer Schemes? Evidence and Lessons from the Philippines." *The Journal of Development Studies* 41(1): 90–134.

Burton, Sandra. 1986. "Aquino's Philippines: The Center Holds." *Foreign Affairs* 65(3): 524–37.

Capuno, Joseph J. 2005. "The Quality of Local Governance and Development under Decentralization in the Philippines." UPSE Discussion Paper No. 0506.

Carino, Ledivina V. 2008. "Towards a Strong Republic: Enhancing the Accountability of the Philippine State." *Public Administration Quarterly* 32(1): 59–92.

Coronel, Sheila. 2000. "Justice to the Highest Bidder." In Sheila S. Coronel (ed.). *Betrayals of the Public Trust: Investigative Reports on Corruption.* Quezon City, Philippines: Philippine Center for Investigative Journalism.

Coronel, Sheila S. 2004. "Born to Rule." Pp. 44–117 in Sheila S. Coronel, Yvonne T. Chua, Luz Rimban, and Booma B. Cruz (eds.). *The Rulemakers: How the Wealthy and Well-Born Dominate Congress.* Quezon City, Philippines: Philippine Center for Investigative Journalism.

Corpuz, O. D. 1997. *An Economic History of the Philippines.* Quezon City, Philippines: University of the Philippines Press.

Costello, Michael. 1984. "Social change in Mindanao: A review of the research of a decade." *Kinadman: A Journal of the Southern Philippines,* 6: 1–41

Crowther, William. 1986. "Philippine Authoritarianism and the International Economy." *Comparative Politics* 18(3): 339–56.

David, Randolf S. 1996. "Re-democratization in the Wake of the 1986 People Power Revolution: Errors and Dilemmas." *Kasarinlan: Philippine Journal of Third World Studies* 11(3): 5–20.

Dejillas, Leopoldo J. 1994. *Trade Union Behavior in the Philippines 1946–1990.* Quezon City, Philippines: Ateneo de Manila University Press.

De Leon, Teresita O. and Gema Maria O. Escobido. 2004. "The Banana Export Industry and Agrarian Reform." Alternative Research Forum in Mindanao.

Dohner, Robert S. and Ponciano Intal, Jr. 1989. "Debt Crisis and Adjustment in the Philippines." In Jeffrey D. Sachs (ed.). *Developing Country Debt and the World Economy.* Chicago: The University of Chicago Press.

Dolan, Ronald E. (ed.) 1991. *Philippines: A Country Study.* Washington, DC: GPO for the Library of Congress.

Doronila, Amando. 1985. "The Transformation of Patron-Client Relations and Its Political Consequences in Postwar Philippines." *Journal of Southeast Asian Studies* **16**(1): 99–116.

Eaton, Kent. 2003. "Restoration or Transformation? "Trapos" versus NGOs in the Democratization of the Philippines." *The Journal of Asian Studies* **62**(2): 469–96.

Fifield, Russell H. 1951. "The Hukbalahap Today." *Far Eastern Survey* **20**(2): 13–18.

Gallagher, Mark. 1991. *Rent-Seeking and Economic Growth in Africa.* Boulder, CO: Westview.

Golay, Frank. 1955. "Economic Consequences of the Philippine Trade Act." *Pacific Affairs* **28**(1): 53–70.

Gowing, Peter. 1979. *Muslim Filipinos: Heritage and Horizon.* Quezon City: New Day Publishers.

Gutierrez, Eric U., Ildefonso C. Torrente, and Noli G. Narca. 1992. *All in the Family: A Study of Elites and Power Relations in the Philippines.* Quezon City, Philippines: Institute for Popular Democracy.

Haggard, Stephan. 1990. "The Political Economy of the Philippine Debt Crisis." In Joan M. Nelson (ed.). *Economic Crisis and Policy Choice: The Politics of Adjustment in the Third World.* Princeton: Princeton University Press.

Hartendorp, A. V. H. 1958. *History of Industry and Trade of the Philippines.* Manila: American Chamber of Commerce of the Philippines.

Hawes, Gary. 1987. *The Philippine State and the Marcos Regime: The Politics of Export.* Cornell, NY: Cornell University Press.

Hedman, Eva Lotta E. 2000. "State of Siege: Political Violence and Vigilante Mobilization in the Philippines." Pp. 125–51 in Campbell, B. B. and Brenner A. D. (eds.). *Death Squads in Global Perspective: Murder with Deniability.* New York: Palgrave Macmillan.

Hernandez, Carolina G. 2007. "The Military in Philippine Politics: Retrospect and Prospects." Pp. 78–99 in Rodolfo C. Severino and Lorraine Carlos Salazar (eds.). *Whither the Philippines in the 21st Century?* Singapore: Institute of Southeast Asian Studies.

Hooley, Richard. 2005. "American Economic Policy in the Philippines, 1902–1940: Exploring a Dark Age in Colonial Statistics." *Journal of Asian Economics* **16**: 464–88.

Hutchcroft, Paul D. and Joel Rocamora. 2003. "Strong Demands and Weak Institutions: The Origins and Evolution of the Democratic Deficit in the Philippines." *Journal of East Asian Studies* **3**: 259–92.

Iyer, Lakshmi and Noel Maurer. 2008. "The Cost of Property Rights: Establishing Institutions on the Philippine Frontier Under American Rule, 1898–1918." Harvard Business School Working Paper 09–023.

Jenkins, Shirley. 1954. *American Economic Policy Toward the Philippines*. Stanford, CA: Stanford University Press.

Karnow, Stanley. 1989. *In Our Image: America's Empire in the Philippines*. Random House.

Kimura, Masataka. 2006. The Federation of Free Farmers and Its Significance in the History of the Philippine Peasant Movement. *Southeast Asian Studies*, **44**(1): 3–30.

Kowalewski, D. 1992. "Counterinsurgent Paramilitarism: A Philippine Case Study." *Journal of Peace Research* **29**(1): 71–84.

Kreuzer, Peter. 2009. "Private Political Violence and Boss-Rule in the Philippines." *Behemoth: A Journal on Civilisation* **1**: 47–63.

Lamberte, Mario B. 1999. "Some Issues on the Liberalization of the Entry and Scope of Operations of Foreign Banks (RA 7721)." Working paper.

Lande. Carl H. 1966. *Leaders, Factions, and Parties: The Structure of Philippine Politics*. Monograph Series No. 6. New Haven: Yale University Southeast Asia Studies.

Lande, Carl H. 1967. "The Philippine Political Party System." *Journal of Southeast Asian History* **8**(1): 19–39.

Landé, Carl H. and Allan J. Cigler. 1979. "Competition and Turnover in Philippine Congressional Elections, 1907–1969." *Asian Survey* **19**(10): 977–1007.

Lara Jr., Francisco and Horacio R. Morales, Jr. 1990. "The Peasant Movement and the Challenge of Rural Democratisation in the Philippines." *Journal of Development Studies* **26**(4): 143–62.

Larkin, John A. 1982. "Philippine History Reconsidered: A Socioeconomic Perspective." *The American Historical Review* **87**(3): 595–628.

Linantud, John L. 2005. "The 2004 Philippine Elections: Political Change in an Illiberal Democracy." *Contemporary Southeast Asia* **27**(1): 80–101.

Lindsey, Charles W. 1984. "Economic Crisis in the Philippines." *Asian Survey* **24**(2): 1185–1208.

Locsin, Teodoro. 1964. "Men of the Year: The Rule of Law" *Philippines Free Press* **4** (January).

Madale, Nagasura T., 1986, "The Future of the Moro National Liberation Front (MNLF) as a Separatist Movement in the Southern Philippines." Pp.180–1 in Lim Joo-Jock and S. Vani (eds.). *Armed Separatism in Southeast Asia*. Singapore: Institute of Southeast Asian Studies.

Manapat, Ricardo. 1991. *Some Are Smarter Than Others: The History of Marcos' Crony Capitalism*. New York: Aletheia Publications.

Mangahas, Mahar. 2009. "The Popularity of Cory Aquino," *Philippine Daily Inquirer*, July 11, 2009, online version at http://opinion.inquirer.net/inquireropinion/columns/view/20090711-214896/The-popularity-of-Cory-Aquino.

McCoy, Alfred W. 1989. "Quezon's Commonwealth: The Emergence of Philippine Authoritarianism." In Ruby R. Paredes (ed.). *Philippine Colonial Democracy*. New Haven: Yale University Southeast Asia Studies Monograph No. 32.

1999. *Closer than Brothers: Manhood at the Philippine Military Academy*. New Haven: Yale University Press.

2009. *Policing America's Empire: The United States, the Philippines, and the Rise of the Surveillance State*. Madison, WI: University of Wisconsin Press.

McKenna, Thomas. 1998. *Muslim Rulers and Rebels: Everyday Politics and Armed Separatism in the Southern Philippines*. Berkeley: University of California Press.

Medalla, Erlinda M. 2002. "Government Policies and Regulations: Interface with Competition Policy." Pp. 307–26 in Erlinda M. Medalla (ed.). *Toward a National Competition Policy for the Philippines*. Makati, Philippines: Philippine Institute for Development Studies.

Milo, Melanie S. 2002. "Analysis of the State of Competition and Market Structure of the Banking and Insurance Sectors." Pp 254–306 in Erlinda M. Medalla (ed.). *Toward a National Competition Policy for the Philippines*. Makati, Philippines: Philippine Institute for Development Studies.

Montes, Manuel F. 1985. "Financing Development: The Political Economy of Fiscal Policy in the Philippines." Philippine Institute for Development Studies Situational Report.

Montinola, Gabriella R. 1999. "Parties and Accountability in the Philippines." *Journal of Democracy* 10(1): 126–40.

North, Douglass C., John J. Wallis, and Barry R. Weingast. 2009. *Violence and Social Orders: A Conceptual Framework for Interpreting Recorded Human History*. New York: Cambridge University Press.

Pasadilla, Gloria and Melanie S. Milo. 2005. "Effect of Liberalization on Banking Competition." Philippine Institute for Development Studies Discussion Paper Series No. 2005-03.

Patino, Patrick and Djorina Velasco. 2004. "Election Violence in the Philippines." Online Papers: Friedrich Ebert Stiftung Philippine Office.

Patrick, Hugh and Honorata A. Moreno. 1984. "Philippine Private Domestic Commercial Banking, 1946–80, in Light of Japanese Historical Experience." In Kazushi Ohkawa and Gustav Ranis (eds.). *Japan and the Developing Countries: A Comparative Analysis*. New York: Basil Blackwell.

Pelzer, Karl J. 1945. *Pioneer Settlement in the Asiatic Tropics: Studies in Land Utilization and Agricultural Colonization in Southeastern Asia*. New York: International Secretariat Institute of Pacific Relations.

Putzel, James. 1992. *A Captive Land: The Politics of Agrarian Reform in the Philippines*. Quezon City, Philippines: Ateneo de Manila University Press.

1999. "Survival of an Imperfect Democracy in the Philippines." *Democratization* 6(1): 198–223.

Quimpo, Nathan Gilbert. 2009. "The Philippines: Predatory Regime, Growing Authoritarian Features." *The Pacific Review* 22(3): 335–53.

Reyes, Celia M. 2002. "Impact of Agrarian Reform on Poverty." Philippine Institute for Development Studies Discussion Paper Series No. 2002-02.

Rivera, Temario C. 2002. "Transition Pathways and Democratic Consolidation in Post-Marcos Philippines." *Contemporary Southeast Asia* 24(3): 466–83.

Saulo, Alfredo B. 1990. *Communism in the Philippines: An Introduction*. Quezon City, Philippines: Ateneo de Manila University Press.

Saulo-Adriano, Lourdes. 1991. "A General Assessment of the Comprehensive Agrarian Reform Program." Philippine Institute for Development Studies Working Paper No. 91-13.

Schiavo-Campo, Salvatore and Mary Judd. 2005. "The Mindanao Conflict in the Philippines: Roots, Costs, and Potential Peace Dividend." Conflict Prevention and Reconstruction Working Paper No. 24.

Schumacher S. J., John N. 2001. "Eighteenth- and Nineteenth-Century Agrarian Developments in Central Luzon." Pp. 168–202 in Jesus T. Peralta (ed.). *Reflections* on *Philippine Culture and Society: Festschrift in Honor of William Henry Scott.* Quezon City, Philippines: Ateneo de Manila University Press.

Scott, William Henry. 1982. *Cracks in the Parchment Curtain and Other Essays in Philippine History.* Quezon City: New Day Publishers.

Serafica, Ramonette B. 2002. "Competition in Philippine Telecommunications: A Survey of the Critical Issues." Pp. 157–87 in Erlinda M. Medalla (ed.). *Toward a National Competition Policy for the Philippines.* Makati, Philippines: Philippine Institute for Development Studies.

Shalom, Stephen R. 1977. "Counter-Insurgency in the Philippines." *Journal of Contemporary Asia* 7(2): 153–77.

Sidel, John T. 1997. "Philippine Politics in Town, District, and Province: Bossism in Cavite and Cebu." *The Journal of Asian Studies* 56(4): 947–66.

Simbulan, Dante C. 2005. *The Modern Principalia: The Historical Evolution of the Philippine Ruling Oligarchy.* Quezon City, Philippines: The University of the Philippines Press.

Tate, C. Neal. 1997. "Courts and the Breakdown and Recreation of Philippine Democracy: Evidence from the Supreme Court's Agenda." *International Social Science Journal* 49(2) (June): 279–91.

————— 1992. "Temerity and Timidity in the Exercise of Judicial Review in the Philippine Supreme Court." Pp. 107–28 in Donald W. Jackson and C. Neal Tate (eds.). *Comparative Judicial Review and Public Policy.* Westport, CT: Greenwood Press.

Tate, C. Neal and Stacia Haynie. 1993. "Authoritarianism and the Function of Courts: A Time Series Analysis of the Philippine Supreme Court, 1961–87." *Law & Society* 27(4): 707–39.

Wurfel, David. 1988. *Filipino Politics: Development and Decay.* Quezon City, Philippines: Ateneo de Manila University Press.

SIX

India's Vulnerable Maturity

Experiences of Maharashtra and West Bengal

Pallavi Roy

Limiting violence in India with its population of more than a billion people and its many languages, religions, castes, and regional diversities involves a complex web of economic and political compromises. The distribution of rents to powerful groups is jointly determined by institutions and politics at the national level and political arrangements within each state. While the national institutional and political system sets an overall architecture for the distribution of rents, individual states have their own distinct political and economic arrangements. This diversity creates tensions between the center and the different states, but the diversity at the level of states also explains how such a big country stays together at all. By contrasting the construction of the social order in two Indian states, Maharashtra and West Bengal, we explore how dominant coalitions can be constructed in very different ways within the overall architecture set at the national level. These differences in the ways in which rents are used to construct social orders at the level of each state also help to explain differences in economic policies and performance across Indian states.

In terms of the LAO framework, India after its independence in 1947 had many features of a basic LAO but gradually acquired significant characteristics of a mature LAO. This is true at the national level and in most states. But the transition conceals significant regional differences and many parts of the country have characteristics of a fragile LAO, often at the brink of intense insurgencies that sometimes break out. The Congress Party as an inclusive ruling coalition dominated Indian politics for the first three decades after independence from Britain in 1947. Its dominance came to an end by the late 1970s with a host of other parties, including regional parties, emerging that could construct alternative governing coalitions at the center. The significant increase in the effective mobilization of political organizations outside the Congress Party can be described as a gradual move in the direction of a mature LAO. At the same time, strategies of national economic management also went through changes after the 1980s as older variants of industrial policy were abandoned and the types of rents in the economy changed as a result.

The hold of the Congress Party and its ability to deliver stability in the early years was based on its inclusion of the most significant political coalitions within its fold and its control of significant rents as part of its industrialization and modernization strategy. As part of that industrialization strategy, rents were created through import protection, licensing, and other policies to provide incentives to domestic entrepreneurs to invest in industry. Policy-based rents were also available to further a range of other objectives such as reducing regional economic differences, assisting small firms, or reducing poverty. These multiple objectives allowed the center to have considerable flexibility to allocate rents in ways demanded by powerful constituencies. Effectively, rent distribution achieved political stability and created incentives for powerful constituencies to compete for these rents using the political structures within the Congress Party. However, the achievement of political stability had negative implications for the economic outcomes associated with these rents in India in the 1960s and 1970s. The significant political constraints on rent allocation meant that India could not achieve the same successes with industrial policy as the East Asian tigers.

By the mid-1960s, the exponential growth in the numbers of aspiring political organizers joining the competition for rents meant that the Congress Party could no longer define the dominant coalition using the old methods. The number of political factions competing for rents within the Congress Party was growing rapidly and the failure to accommodate all of them to their satisfaction led to the coalition gradually falling apart. As a result the political system lost its ability to control violence at its fringes. The declining ability of the center to allocate economic rents also made economic reforms necessary. The growing internal crisis of rent allocation was possibly a much more important determinant of the direction of reform in India from the 1980s onward than the emerging international consensus on the need for liberalization. Sectors and firms that had already achieved global competitiveness did very well subsequently, but the reduction in centralized rent allocation was also associated with an increase in violence and instability at the fringes.

We focus on two of India's biggest states, Maharashtra and West Bengal, to look at some of the different ways in which LAOs evolved across India during this period. The LAO in each state has distinct features in terms of how the local dominant coalition distributes rents to stay in power.

Maharashtra follows more closely the trends at the national level in India, with a growing fragmentation of state-level political parties and growth increasingly driven by business organizations that have already achieved high levels of sophistication. While this state is an industrial success story, a third of its population of close to 100 million fall below India's official poverty line. The dominant coalition in the state was led by large and medium capitalists and rich farmers who were part of the sugar lobby. With the fragmentation of politics, public policies that could assist broad-based development have become even more difficult to organize. In contrast, West Bengal bucked the trends toward political fragmentation for a long time with its well-organized and more inclusive Communist Party of India Marxist (CPM) government. But the accommodation of elites from a large rural constituency led to the neglect of industry and built up problems for the party as aspirations for jobs and growth became harder to meet. Industry and business were not part of this dominant coalition, though they could operate by buying support for their organizations. Nevertheless, the unfavorable position of industrial capitalists in West Bengal meant that the state did not become a destination of choice for major industrial investments.

The chapter is structured as follows. The next section outlines the economic and political development of India from independence in 1947 in terms of the LAO framework. The contours of the national story set the scene for looking at significant regional differences. The second section is the case study of Maharashtra. This section explores the organization of its dominant coalition and how it gradually unraveled. The third section focuses on West Bengal. Unlike Maharashtra, the very different construction of the dominant coalition here led to an agrarian focus for economic strategies. When this agrarian strategy began to run out of steam, this again led to a gradual unraveling of the dominant political coalition. The final section concludes. The variations in how the social order was constructed in the two Indian states are related to differences in their political organizations and also to differences in the organization of their economies and societies. The differences in the rent strategies underlying the LAO in turn had implications for strategies of development that the regional states followed.

6.1 From Independence to the present

The evolution of the LAO in India can be divided into three phases summarized in Table 6.1. The *Nehruvian period* lasted from independence in 1947 until the mid-1960s. The dominant political coalition was well-defined

Table 6.1 *Characteristics of the Indian LAO*

Fragile/Basic LAO (1947–8)	• Violence marred transfer of power from the British leading to the partition of British India into India and Pakistan
Basic LAO- Nehruvian Period (1948–mid-1960s)	• First parliamentary election held in 1952 established Congress Party dominance
	• De facto basic order with well-defined dominant coalition but other independent organizations could exist.
	• Central control of critical rents through centralized planning and licensing by the Congress Party defined the basic order: trappings of a developmental state
	• Helped develop industrial capabilities that India built on in the 1980s and 1990s
Transition period: Crisis of the Basic Order (mid-1960s to late 1970s)	• Increasing redistributive pressures as economy grows
	• Failure to discipline infant industries, breakdown of developmental model
	• Indira Gandhi comes to power on a populist agenda and nationalizes banks and coal mining to strengthen basic order
	• Increasing authoritarianism as Congress Party dominance is challenged by other political contenders in competition for rents
	• Culminates in the Emergency of 1975
Evolution of an LAO with Characteristics of Maturity but also Vulnerability (Vulnerable Maturity) (Late 1970s onward)	• Establishment of first non-Congress Party government at the center in 1977, evolution of coalition politics at the center and growing influence of regional parties
	• Declining ability of the state to allocate rents from above, associated with increasing political fragmentation
	• Mobilizations based on caste and communalism with right-wing Hindu political movements for the first time in independent India
	• Secessionist movements in Assam, Punjab and Jammu and Kashmir
	• Balance of payments crisis in 1991
	• Economic liberalization formally begins in 1992
	• New types of rent creation after liberalization driven by alliances of business and politicians
	• Increasing communal and political violence (secessionist movements, Maoist insurgencies)
	• Acceleration of economic growth but with increasing inequality

during this period and India had many of the characteristics of a basic LAO. A *transition period* took place from the late 1960s to the mid-1970s when the basic LAO began to fall apart. *Vulnerable maturity* emerged from the late 1970s onward, when characteristics of a mature LAO can be identified, but with qualities of growing fragility at the fringes. Significant regional variations exist within India and our two case studies, Maharashtra and West Bengal, show why it is important to examine the LAO in India at both the state and federal levels. The movement from features of the basic LAO to the mature LAO does not correspond neatly with an increase in the sophistication and complexity of underlying political and economic organizations. Some organizations have become more complex and sophisticated, but other complex organizations have become more difficult to sustain and some have retrogressed.

6.1.1 The Nehruvian Period: 1947 to Mid-1960s

The Nehruvian period was characterized by an attempt to plan the economy using tools like the licensing of investment, protecting the economy from imports, and controlling the use of foreign exchange. The political system was based on the dominance of the Congress Party as an inclusive organization. In the first parliamentary elections in 1952, the Congress Party established its dominance. Led by India's first prime minister, Jawaharlal Nehru, it won 364 of the 380 seats in parliament. This was not a basic LAO in the sense that the dominant coalition did not actually control the establishment of all organizations, but the electoral dominance of the Congress Party and its control of rents meant for a time that organizations that did not toe the line were relatively easy to isolate and effectively weaken or destroy. This was therefore a de facto basic order under which the ruling coalition was well-defined and had effective control over significant rents. But Congress Party hegemony in this sense was gradually declining from the very outset.

The basic LAO at this stage was based on the effective central control of a number of critical rents necessary for setting up sophisticated organizations in the productive sector. India's dirigiste policies included favoring several large sectors like engineering, chemicals, power, and automobiles (Chatterjee 1997). Instruments including direct state ownership and the granting of industrial permits or licenses to investors created rents used to direct industrial development. In addition, a number of other rents were used for redistributive purposes. For instance, a growing share of public sector jobs was reserved for particular castes, the small-scale sector was protected, privileges were provided for employees in the modern sector, and so on. The Congress Party initially dominated the central and most state legislatures. Its control over the allocation of this wide range of rents allowed it to sustain its dominance because it could ensure that powerful organizations supporting the party got a share of the rents, and those falling out of favor had a hard time.

This situation did not, however, last for very long. India's social structure threw up successive layers of new organizers and political movements that persistently challenged the distribution of rents at any particular time. The redistributive rents had to keep growing or the center had to punish organizations demanding an excessive share of rents. Both became progressively more difficult as the numbers of organizations grew and the center's relative power declined. This also affected the management of the potentially growth-enhancing rents created as part of the state's industrial policy to counter market failures. Infant industries did get set up, but those that failed to grow could not be disciplined and their rents could not be withdrawn because any firm could always buy the support of some political faction or other to protect their rents (Khan 2009). Growth began to slow down by the mid-1960s.

Despite being unsustainable, this period of relative political stability also saw the growth of complex organizations like centers of research and development, educational establishments, and large industrial organizations using modern technologies. These included the Indian Institutes of Technology, set up by Nehru and now recognized as one of the main contributors to India's eventual success in information technology, and early pioneering companies like Hindustan Antibiotics Ltd and Indian Drugs and Pharmaceuticals Ltd, which laid the basis for India's leading position in the generics market later. The first phase also helped to lay the foundations for future Indian multinationals like Tata.

6.1.2 The Transition: Mid-1960s to Late 1970s

The unraveling of the basic LAO in India was not a smooth process. Indira Gandhi, elected prime minister in 1966, tried to clamp down on the political interests that were mushrooming, many of which could not be accommodated within the Congress Party. On the one hand she sought to exert control within the Congress Party by tightening the system of internal patronage. On the other hand, where patronage failed, she increasingly used harsh measures to exercise authority. Paradoxically, as she became more authoritarian in order to preserve her position (and to sustain the Congress Party's control over the country), the stronger her opposition grew.

A number of Indira Gandhi's agendas can be better understood from this perspective. For instance, the drive toward nationalization was partly motivated by the need to make more rents available for distribution through patronage. In particular, the nationalized banking sector became the only conduit for large-scale borrowing and lending activities. The monopoly of Coal India Ltd, formed after nationalization, was another example of a nationalized entity providing significant rents for political patrons to distribute. The populist logic for nationalization was very likely window dressing for a policy driven by hard political calculations of generating rents for a growing number of organizations.

These strategies were not enough to stave off the collapse of the basic LAO. India's slow descent into chaos was marked by Mrs. Gandhi's increasingly "jealous populism" (Selbourne 1977) and her attempts at snuffing any opposition by using all the state machinery at her disposal. In 1975, Indira declared an emergency, which was effectively a suspension of electoral democracy. This was an attempt at enforcing the basic LAO by an exercise of authoritarian restrictions on organization, and has strong parallels with similar populist-authoritarian experiments in Bangladesh and Pakistan at that time. Power was centralized in New Delhi and opposition state governments were dismissed. A significant number of rents were now allocated not just by the Congress Party but by the Gandhi family through its control of the party's finances (Chatterjee 1997). Planning and financing of campaigns by local Congress Party organizations was discouraged. The attempt to institutionalize a basic LAO thus happened at the very time that it was becoming unsustainable as a result of changes in the number and capabilities of organizations.

Mrs. Gandhi called fresh elections in 1977 in a move to legitimize the new populist-authoritarian version of the basic LAO. She believed that electoral support for her populist policies would override the opposition she faced from organizations of competing elites and that the voters below would keep her in power on the grounds that they had nothing much to gain from the organizations challenging central authority. For the first time the Congress Party reached out directly to voters without attempting to construct a coalition of elite interests backing the party. The result was a resounding electoral defeat and the replacement of the Congress Party by the Janata Party, a coalition of four opposition parties. There is a remarkable parallel in the turn to populist authoritarianism in the mid-1970s and its failure across India, Pakistan, and Bangladesh. Indira Gandhi, Bhutto, and Mujib would all be remembered for their failed attempts to institutionalize authoritarian versions of socialism based on controls over the organizational freedoms of critical and powerful organizations (Khan 2008). All three leaders paid a heavy political and personal price for their brand of politics: all three were eventually assassinated or executed.

6.1.3 Vulnerable Maturity: Late 1970s Onward

The failure of the authoritarian attempt at institutionalizing a basic LAO gradually led to a much greater openness for new economic and political organizations to form outside the Congress Party. This had always been possible and was increasingly uncontested by the ruling coalition. By the 1980s, India's LAO began to acquire significant characteristics that resembled a mature LAO. The ability of the ruling coalition to control the political organizations it had created declined dramatically. Indeed, to challenge and balance political organizations in confrontation with the Congress Party and other parties at the center, the latter increasingly resorted to a strategy of patronizing new political organizations to "divide and rule." The new organizations in turn could no longer be as tightly controlled by the Congress Party as they may have been during the days of the basic LAO. This period also saw the beginning of coalition politics at the center, as no party, including the Congress Party, could rule on its own. Since 1989, barring one instance in 1991, no single party has been able to rule for the term of five years on its own. Nor have the two principal national parties – the Congress and the BJP – been able to form a government on their own without the support of smaller regional parties.

India's transition from a basic LAO to one with characteristics of a mature LAO has many similarities with its subcontinental neighbors, Bangladesh and Pakistan. The turn toward authoritarianism in the 1970s was a common feature in all three countries, and their trajectories since then have in many ways been similar, though the higher economic growth in India has tended to overshadow the very dynamic and evolving economies of the two other countries in the region. In fact, there were growth accelerations in all three countries in the 1980s (Khan 2008). The general consensus in the economic literature is to link the growth takeoff, particularly in India, to the onset of liberalization (Basu 2003, Panagariya 2005). While some aspects of liberalization were undoubtedly important, our analysis suggests that the years of protection in all three countries were critical in building entrepreneurial and technical capabilities as well as organizational capabilities that enabled businessmen to break free from the state and establish their own productive enterprises. This allowed pockets of global competitiveness to emerge across the subcontinent. India's auto, information technology, and software industries are part of a spectrum that includes, for instance, garments and textiles and ship building in Bangladesh, and the power loom textile sector and small consumer durables in Pakistan (Khan 2008).

Politics, on the other hand, has become more competitive and redistributive rents appear to be growing. Just as economic organizations have become more sophisticated, so have political organizations. But the central states have fewer rents to allocate through formal mechanisms of managing the economy. Redistributive rents have therefore become even less productive as they are no longer part of operating industrial policy or regional policy but are directly captured by emerging political organizations in an increasingly fractious competitive environment. This reflects the earlier basic LAO breaking down in all three countries. As the competition for rents became more intense, violence has also increased. The paradox of the LAO in India has therefore been the simultaneous emergence of aspects of maturity and fragility, a combination that we describe as *vulnerable maturity*. The increasingly competitive organization of politics and the growing weakness of a central arbiter have allowed the structural exclusion of marginal groups in these polities to be transformed into violent confrontations. The current Maoist and Taliban-led insurgencies in India and Pakistan respectively can be better understood in this context. In both cases, central elites have been unable to create rents for these segments of society and their exclusion has resulted in the formation of new organizations even more difficult to satisfy with the rents that are available. The result has been endemic violence at the margins of the Indian LAO, and even more so in Pakistan.

In this context of increasing political fragmentation, two other political strategies emerged during this period that contributed to the volatility of Indian politics. One was the movement to extend reservations of public sector jobs to a wider range of defined castes. This began with the move by the National Front coalition of 1990 to reserve twenty-seven percent of jobs in the government for India's Other Backward Classes (OBCs), who make up about forty percent of India's population. In the caste hierarchy, they come between the upper castes and the "untouchables," who are part of the Scheduled Castes and Tribes. This led to an increase in caste mobilizations and caste politics, as new groups demanded protection. This further deepened the characteristics of maturity as political organizations proliferated but also increased the levels of conflict and fragility. The second was the emergence of ideological politics that attempted to create mass support for the ruling coalition without offering any significant rents by appealing to the need for national unity against internal and external enemies. Over eighty percent of India's population is Hindu, and the Congress Party realized that appealing to Hindu sentiments could attract electoral support that was cheap in terms of the rents involved. But in doing so it laid the basis for right-wing Hindu or "Hindutva" politics that was aggressive against India's minorities and in particular its Muslims, as a strategy of constructing support for a ruling coalition. This too contributed to making politics more divisive and increased violence in many parts of India.

An important consequence of the decline of inclusive parties at the center was that states became important theaters for local elites to create organizations and demand rents. The importance of controlling political power at the level of a state meant that excluded groups in many states often agitated for a smaller state to be carved out for them from the larger state. Thus, new states emerged out of bigger states, driven by the political demands of excluded groups. The overall level of political violence has increased dramatically in India since the 1980s. The current Maoist insurgency in the central and eastern areas of the country is only one indicator of the significant fragility that exists in pockets within an otherwise increasingly mature LAO.

The first decade of the twenty-first century saw a continuation of these trends. The system of coalition governments at the center has become an enduring feature of India's governance. The ability and freedom to set up new political organizations and mobilize new constituencies has become well established. It was always a formal entitlement but now it is effectively exercised by many aspiring political organizers with the money and muscle to make the necessary investments. The most sophisticated organizations within Indian business have continued to grow and enhance their global competitiveness. The most aggressive Indian multinationals have not only penetrated markets in the West, they have also begun to acquire and operate corporate entities in advanced countries like the United Kingdom and Germany as well as in developing areas like Africa, demonstrating the growing sophistication of India's corporate organizations. It is in this overall context of transition and maturity that we locate the differences in the construction of the LAO in our two states.

6.2 Maharashtra

Maharashtra is one of India's leading industrial states, and its capital, Mumbai (previously Bombay), is India's premier financial and commercial hub. Its key sectors include automobiles, pharmaceuticals, financial services, and IT services. Apart from a relatively successful economy, the state has for long been characterized by high levels of political mobilization.

The Congress Party ruled the state almost uninterrupted from 1960 (when the state was created by partitioning Bombay Presidency into Gujarat and Maharashtra) to 1995. But in line with developments at the national level, the state's politics has become fragmented and faction-ridden through the 1980s with continuous horse trading among parties to form and operate a ruling coalition at the state level.

The dominant coalition in the early years in Maharashtra (corresponding to the period of the basic LAO in India) was constructed in a way that allowed the creation of significant growth-enhancing rents as part of the political arrangements underpinning the LAO. These rents could be created for business leaders who were part of the dominant coalition and some of these rents helped to overcome market failures that had limited investments in the past. At the same time, political stability was achieved by rent allocation to other powerful constituencies. As the composition of this coalition changed over the years, so did the balance between growth-enhancing rents and other types of rents. Until the 1980s, two types of rents played an important function in keeping the dominant coalition together while also supporting growth. A major part of the rents required for political stabilization were generated by politicians who controlled the state's sugar lobby in rural northwest Maharashtra. The generation of a significant part of the rents required for political stabilization in agriculture indirectly protected the capitalist sector in manufacturing as politicians did not need to extract rents from them. As the immediate rents required for running politics came from agriculture, politicians could look to industry for longer-term relationships and rents, and this too helped the capitalist sector in manufacturing. These relationships worked through patron–client networks where politicians would grant businesses favors like land or subsidies for industrial projects in exchange for relatively small immediate payoffs but with the understanding that those businesses would stand behind particular politicians. As politicians were not heavily dependent on rents from business to finance their survival, the terms of these bargains were business friendly and helped the rapid industrialization of the state.

These arrangements became vulnerable with the political fragmentation that affected Indian politics from the 1980s onward. Maharashtrian state politics became equally fragmented and ruling coalitions were less able to take a long-term view in developing relationships with business interests. The key players in the state now include the mainline Congress Party; the right wing but mainstream Bharatiya Janata Party (BJP), a key breakaway faction of the Congress Party; the Nationalist Congress Party (NCP); the nativist/communal Shiv Sena (SS); and a subsequent splinter group of the

Shiv Sena that is a swing player in elections. Smaller parties based on caste affiliations also exist. These divisions have made the state's political landscape volatile and unstable, especially over the last fifteen years.

This was also the period when the Bombay underworld and crime syndicates became more assertive and conflicts between syndicates began to have an impact on violence in the city. Different communal organizations also came to the fore, using religious politics, among other things, to engage in slum clearance and land grabbing. Bombay began to suffer more than its share of riots, bombs, and religious violence. This was partly driven by wars between underworld gangs. It was also partly driven by the growing strength of communal organizations like the Shiv Sena that sought to mobilize poor Hindus against outsiders to create new power bases at a time when the collapse of the old politics left spaces to be filled (Katzenstein et al. 1997, Lele 1995). These processes contributed to the decline of industrial and manufacturing growth rates in Maharashtra after 2000 and the growth of service sectors like finance and software with lower sunk costs that did not require the same level of trust in the long-term stability of political arrangements.

6.2.1 The Alliance of Industry and Sugar

Maharashtra was formed in 1960 after demands for a separate Marathi-language state were accepted by the central government. The state was earlier part of the Bombay Presidency that also included the current state of Gujarat. While the capital had been controlled mostly by non-Marathi-speaking industrialists, political power in the state resided with Marathi-speaking leaders, who first came to prominence in the last decades of India's independence movement. The early mobilization for a separate state in the erstwhile Bombay Presidency was based on the mobilization of Maratha peasants (a particular caste within the broader Marathi-speaking population). Thus, the tension between a Marathi political elite and a largely non-Marathi business elite was an incipient problem from the founding of the state.

For most of the next fifty years, political stability and economic growth in Maharashtra was based on balancing the significant rents generated by the sugar cane lobby for political entrepreneurs while leaving enough rents for the industrial sector in Mumbai. The sugar lobby consisted of powerful Maratha leaders who kept out most other castes and political groupings from the state's politics for a long time. The Maratha caste is an intermediate caste and has significant power as a provider of political organizers.

The name should not be confused with the Marathi language, which is spoken by two-thirds of the state's inhabitants and is the native language of the region. Maratha politicians created rents for sugar cane growers (and indirectly for themselves) in regions that voted for the Congress Party by setting higher prices at which sugar cooperatives would buy cane from growers. Maharashtra accounts for close to thirty percent of India's sugar production and about ninety-nine percent of this comes from the state's sugar cooperatives (Bavadam 2005). This makes the control of the sugar cooperatives a key part of the redistributive politics of the state. The losses for the cooperative's processing activities due to higher cane prices were in turn covered by complex public subsidies and debt write-offs as these Congress Party politicians also had power at the center (Kumar 2004, Lalvani 2008).

As Congress Party politicians distributed their patronage in the areas devoted to growing and processing sugar, these parts of Maharashtra (the Nasik and Pune Belts) become more developed. Ironically, this was one reason why the Bharatiya Janata Party and the Shiv Sena eventually gained a firm footing in the impoverished eastern regions of Maharashtra called Vidharbha and Marathawada that did not benefit from this redistributive politics. Each sugar cooperative is governed by a board of directors headed by a chairman. For instance, the Malegaon Sugar Factory, owned by one of the foremost Maratha politicians in India, Sharad Pawar, has ten thousand member families. On a crude but plausible calculation, if there are just two members of voting age in each family, one of Pawar's cooperatives alone would provide at least twenty thousand voters for his party, the Nationalist Congress Party, an ally of the Congress Party at the state and central levels. In fact, the cooperative would likely gain many more votes because a broader economy is indirectly dependent on sugar rents. Moreover, politicians like Pawar would often own several factories. A large number of Maratha politicians were involved in running sugar cooperatives and collectively the swing votes they controlled gave them a substantial hold on power over several decades (Jenkins 1999). The numbers explain why the sugar cooperatives were important simply from a numerical electoral logic.

The price of sugar cane has been an important part of the Congress Party electoral equation, a way of rewarding its farmers for their electoral support. In eastern Maharashtra, where the Congress Party had a very weak base, factories could not offer the higher cane prices that prevailed in the West (Lalvani 2008). The price support policies are justified in terms of protection for poorer cane farmers but the differences between prices that cooperatives close to the ruling coalition could offer compared to other cooperatives shows that these were rents generated by powerful politicians

Table 6.2 *Differences in Cane Prices among Regions*

YEAR	REGION	CANE PRICE (Rs/metric ton)
1999–2000	West	679.0
	East	542.6
	Difference (W-E)	136.4
2000–2001	West	782.6
	East	621.8
	Difference (W-E)	160.9
2001–2002	West	736.2
	East	611.8
	Difference (W-E)	124.4
2002–2003	West	730.0
	East	601.9
	Difference (W-E)	128.1
2003–2004	West	715.8
	East	681.4
	Difference (W-E)	34.5
Average	West	782.72
	East	611.9

Source: Lalvani 2008.

to reward their supporters (Banerjee et al. 2001, Kulkarni 2007). Part of the price differential also benefited the politicians directly because many of them owned the factories that served as the conduits through which government subsidies were allocated to sugar farmers. It must be noted though that higher cane prices did not necessarily mean prosperity for sugar farmers. Prices were generally low and what mattered for political support was the difference in price between cooperatives.

Table 6.2 shows that cane prices in the Nationalist Congress Party (NCP)-Congress Party strongholds of western Maharashtra were consistently higher than in the east, where the combination was not very successful electorally. Procuring the cane at consistently high prices would ordinarily mean putting pressure on the cooperatives' cash flows, but anecdotal evidence suggests this did not happen. Finances are usually controlled by the cooperative's chairman and his or her family members. The payout is usually made from medium-term working capital loans given by the

Maharashtra State Cooperative Bank, which also lends to various District Central Cooperative Banks. In fact, according to Lalvani (2008), the state government indirectly shoulders the costs of these subsidies. Government-run financial institutions have extended close to a further Rs 21 billion as medium-term loans to the factories. Loans to powerful politicians that were not paid back not only allowed them to pass on some of the rents to their electoral supporters in the form of high prices, but may also have allowed them to skim some of the rents for themselves. While very successful for a long time, this was clearly not a viable permanent strategy. Toward the end of the 2000s, close to 71 factories out of around 200 were declared sick (Kaur 2007). The private sector entered in a small way and began to buy sugar cooperatives. The likelihood is that the system of manipulating rents in the sugar lobby is coming to a close.

This complex circuit of funds created a significant part of the rents that sustained the dominant coalition in the state, particularly during the period of the basic LAO. The sugar lobby was led by ministers and policy makers who also served as senior functionaries in the state's district cooperative banks that extended the loans. They were also the politicians who ran the sugar cooperatives in the areas offering higher prices. For instance, in 2004, the chairman of the Pune District Cooperative Bank owned several large sugar cooperatives. And this pattern was replicated for most of the sugar cooperatives in western Maharashtra (Kumar 2004). Most of Maharashtra's key political leaders of the 1980s and 1990s associated with the sugar industry come from western Maharashtra – sixty-eight out of a total of ninety-three key political personalities (Lalvani 2008). The sugar rents gave the Congress Party a firm base in western Maharashtra until the late 1970s, which we described as the basic LAO period, and the sugar rents persisted well beyond that period (Palshikar and Deshpande 1999).

This rural support base was never in conflict with the capitalists in Bombay. In fact, this apparently wasteful rent creation created a temporary swathe of rural prosperity and provided enough political stability to give politicians a longer time horizon important for their relationships with industry. The Congress Party politicians running the basic LAO had both the incentives and the political space to organize land and other resources for businesses in manufacturing at a reasonable price in terms of the rent-sharing arrangements with industry. Thus, industrial capitalists indirectly benefited greatly from the stability as they too got rents from this political order through land grants, financial subsidies, and prioritized infrastructure provision. This in turn enabled them to take a long-term view on their investments. The rapid growth of the industrial sector testifies to this. Maharashtra, with around ten percent of India's population, contributed twenty-two percent of the net value added in India's organized industrial sector in 2007. This balance of interests between two very disparate groupings sustained the dominant coalition in Maharashtra for close to two decades.

The relationships between businessmen and politicians in the early years of industrial policy could therefore work on a long-term basis rather than on a deal-by-deal basis. Favors did not have to be traded over particular projects because politicians were not desperate and could themselves take a long-term view with their business partners. If, for example, a minister was asked for an industrial license by a businessman with whom he had a long-term relationship, it was likely granted without an upfront payment on the basis of the favor being returned over time. Thus, industry in Maharashtra had the leeway to make long-term investments and spread risks across projects without having to pay for each decision. These long-term arrangements were also helped by the fact that the stability and staying power of Maharashtra's Congress Party politicians gave them considerable say at the center, and the state was the largest beneficiary of the license regime, getting one of the largest numbers of industrial licenses over time. But as Table 6.3 shows, manufacturing growth rates declined after 2000, coinciding with the ongoing reconstruction of the LAO in the state.

The benefits for the industrial sector can be understood by looking at how it in turn benefited from the rent regime during the basic LAO. An important source of rents for industry during this period was the Maharashtra Industrial Development Corporation, or MIDC. MIDC was the largest Public Sector Unit (PSU) owned by the state government in Maharashtra. It facilitated industrial investment in the state by operating a simple rent-creation model. It purchased land cheaply using the support of local Congress Party politicians when necessary, which it then sold or leased at a higher price to emerging industry. But this price was still significantly lower than the market price if investors had to acquire land using their own devices. The strategy therefore provided rents to the MIDC, its political masters, and to the industrialists who benefited from the land allocation. The MIDC became an effective political tool in the hands of ministers and bureaucrats in charge and they used it to buy and bestow favors. But overall, these rents ensured high industrial growth for the state. It was in any politician's interest to have an MIDC estate in his or her constituency. It provided jobs and raised the value of the lands belonging to the large landowners. The downside is that it decimated small landowners through eminent domain purchases or purchases using subtle political pressure and converted many marginal farmers into landless drifters.

Table 6.3 *Growth Rates: GDP, Industry, Agriculture, Services*

Growth Rates %	India	Maharashtra	West Bengal	World
GDP				
1980–85	5.2	3.9	4.6	2.5
1985–90	6.3	7.4	4.4	3.7
1990–95	5.2	8.5	5.8	2.3
1995–2000	5.7	11.6	7.0	3.2
2000–05	6.7	9.1	6.8	2.8
1980–2005	5.6	8.9	5.8	2.9
Per Capita GDP				
1980–85	3.0	1.8	2.4	0.8
1985–90	4.2	5.0	2.2	2.0
1990–95	3.4	6.4	3.9	0.8
1995–2000	3.9	9.6	5.4	1.8
2000–05	5.2	7.5	5.5	1.5
1980–2005	3.7	6.8	4.0	1.4
Agriculture				
1980–85	3.4	0.8	6.2	1.5
1985–90	4.2	7.9	4.8	0.8
1990–95	3.1	3.6	5.8	0.6
1995–2000	2.3	2.5	3.4	2.2
2000–05	2.4	-1.8	2.6	1.6
1980–2005	2.9	3.4	4.6	1.2
Industry				
1980–85	5.9	3.4	2.2	1.4
1985–90	8.0	7.4	4.4	3.9
1990–95	5.9	5.5	5.1	1.5
1995–2000	4.8	5.8	6.8	2.7
2000–05	7.2	4.1	4.4	2.0
1980–2005	6.2	5.6	5.2	2.5
Manufacturing				
1980–85	7.1	2.9	1.9	na

Growth Rates %	India	Maharashtra	West Bengal	World
1985–90	8.1	8.1	4.6	na
1990–95	7.1	5.8	3.2	na
1995–2000	4.3	6.0	7.3	na
2000–05	6.7	3.5	3.8	na
1980–2005	6.4	5.8	4.5	na
Services				
1980–85	6.1	6.6	5.3	2.8
1985–90	6.9	7.1	4.3	3.6
1990–95	6.7	9.3	6.8	2.6
1995–2000	8.2	7.8	9.1	3.4
2000–05	8.1	9.0	9.9	2.7
1980–2005	7.1	8.0	7.1	3.1

Na = not available.
Source: Khan (2008: table 2).

The Congress Party was able to follow these policies because Maharashtra is essentially a nonagricultural state with a relatively impoverished and therefore politically weak peasantry. Only sixteen percent of its farmland is irrigated and the monsoon typically fails in more than sixty percent of the state. Irrigated land gravitated toward cash crops like sugar. The only effect of a conscious focus on industry was that inequality in the state remained high. Poor farmers outside the dominant coalition could not initially organize themselves and political organizers from elite groups were initially not interested in organizing this group for their political advantage. It is possible that the easy availability of sugar rents made the Maratha elite in the Congress Party and the NCP ignore other political constituencies (Vora and Palshikar 1996). Other types of redistributive policies, like the state government's Employment Guarantee Scheme that formally operated in Maharashtra long before the central government introduced it across India, were not properly implemented. But the sugar lobby could not accommodate a big enough section of the elites and in the absence of populist redistributive policies, the Congress Party coalitions began to lose their electoral grip on power. By 1995, a BJP-Shiv Sena coalition won power and formed its first government in Maharashtra (Jadhav 2006).

6.2.2 Congress Party Fragmentation and the Rise of the Shiv Sena

In the 1980s, Maharashtra's politics witnessed dramatic changes with the advent of a nativist movement spearheaded by the Shiv Sena (SS), a party whose name means "the army of Shiva," a Hindu god. The party later became openly and militantly communal and anti-Muslim and gained ground in the state. It was especially strong in Mumbai and in the more impoverished regions in the east of the state. It mobilized groups, particularly the poor and the urban unemployed left out of the Congress Party coalition. The Congress Party itself became more factionalized and the other opposition party, the Bharatiya Janata Party (BJP), aligned with the SS due to its ideological moorings in Hindu fundamentalism.

The rise of the BJP-SS coalition reflected a combination of four factors. First, there was a growing dissatisfaction with the Congress Party' rigid, access-restricting politics. The opposition parties were successful in cobbling together coalitions of castes that the Congress Party had overlooked. In India's political lexicon, these included Other Backward Classes (OBCs) and a section of the Marathas, both of which were seeing rising levels of economic prosperity thanks to industrialization but had limited access to political rents. But the new BJP-SS coalitions left out the Muslims and the Dalits (the lower castes). Table 6.4 shows how the SS made inroads into the upper intermediate caste base of the Congress Party, into its Maratha, Kunbi, and OBC base. Second, the Congress Party's strategy gave it access to a limited stream of rents and other parties began to access much greater potential sources of rents. Businesses with long-term investment plans could only provide limited immediate kickbacks to their Congress Party patrons. The rents from sugar and the kickbacks from productive investors could only accommodate a limited number of the potential groups demanding a share of political rents. New parties that could mobilize rents from criminals, speculators, and a host of new quick-return investors in real estate and other sectors could provide significant kickbacks immediately and could organize new groups previously excluded. Third, the opposition took advantage of a growing "vernacularisation" based on the rising identification of Marathis of all castes with Marathi linguistic nationalism (Hansen 1996). Finally, local issues, both social and economic, gave rise to a specific Hindutva agenda that led to the popularity of the Shiv Sena. The communally charged social and political environment in India during the late 1980s and early 1990s helped parties with a right-wing communal agenda in Maharashtra.

Table 6.4 *Caste Composition of Voters for Major Parties in Maharashtra*

CASTE GROUP	CONG 1996	CONG 1999	SS 1996	SS 1999	BJP 1996	BJP 1999	NCP 1999
Maratha	20.5	19.6	30.4	30.5	6.3	19.0	31.5
Kunbi	10.6	7.1	21.6	20.0	15.3	13.7	16.0
OBC (Non-Kunbi)	28.4	21.4	30.4	34.0	32.4	32.7	20.0
Scheduled Castes	6.6	15.4	3.0	3.0	5.4	2.0	8.2
Scheduled Tribes	6.6	7.5	1.0	2.0	9.0	5.2	4.1
Others	27.7	28.9	13.4	10.5	31.5	27.5	20.2

Note: Figures in percentages.
Source: Palshikar (2004).

The traditional business–government relationships in Maharashtra came under severe stresses as a result of these changes. Apart from its new caste coalitions, the SS typified the criminal–politician nexus thanks to its involvement in Mumbai's underworld. The very tradition of business buying into political power was subverted when the criminal underworld began to play the same game. This period was an inflexion point for Maharashtra's patron–client politics. As the Indian economy liberalized, Maharashtra's advantage in getting industrial licenses grew irrelevant. Maharashtra had to compete with other states for industrial investments based on what its state government could offer in terms of infrastructure and hidden subsidies. By the late 1970s, the industrial licensing system had practically broken down, and by the 1990s, the formal procedures of licensing had largely disappeared. With the seismic changes brought about by the fragmentation of the Congress Party and a new more fluid ruling coalition based on allocating rents from a variety of sources to a broader coalition of castes, Maharashtra found it difficult to offer investors significant, stable rents over time. The services sector saw a spurt in this period that has continued, particularly services related to construction and real estate as the new politics facilitated land grabs from slums and squatters in a city with one of the highest urban population densities in the world: 27,715 persons per square kilometer in 2001 according to the government of Maharashtra.

Mumbai's real estate prices rival those found in New York and London, the high prices reflecting a combination of demand and intense speculation. This has encouraged an increasing involvement of Mumbai's underworld in real estate. Deregulation meant smuggling operations had become less lucrative, hence attention turned toward real estate speculation. Businessmen and politicians were forced to take sides with different underworld gangs engaged in slum clearance and the city went through a violent phase that ended in a series of bomb blasts and communal riots. According to observers, the riots of 1993 were an expression of the fight to control Mumbai between two underworld groupings, one Muslim and the other Hindu. Anecdotal evidence suggests that the Hindu grouping was linked to the Shiv Sena while the Muslim grouping remained without any apparent mainstream political links in the state. This violence does not mean Maharashtra was a fragile LAO during this period. It was a mature order under which openness was not based on a rule of law but on contestations for dominance that could turn violent.

The underworld's links with business date back at least to the economic troubles of Bombay's famous textile mills, which started closing down in the 1980s. Realizing that they were sitting on very lucrative real estate, many mill owners simply refused to invest in modernization. The government of Maharashtra and sections of the underworld wanted a piece of that real estate pie. The labor conflicts that were the ostensible cause of the mills shutting down were often engineered by gangland hoodlums to make it easier for the mills to shut down, which they ultimately did. In 1961, the mills employed more than two hundred fifty thousand people. Today, fifty-eight working mills employ a mere twenty thousand people. While this deindustrialization and the shift to services had similarities with transitions in advanced economies, this was happening in a labor-surplus developing economy.

The much closer involvement of the underworld in politics proved an important inflexion point for Maharashtra's patron–client politics. Even though the SS-BJP coalition was voted out in the assembly election in 1999, the NCP-Congress Party coalition that succeeded had to recognize the new model of rent creation and coalition building. The more fluid and opportunistic set of rent opportunities and alliances that defines post-1980s politics in Maharashtra has many features of a mature LAO with much greater formal and real opportunities for setting up new political organizations and with its economic organizations targeting new types of rents. The NCP and the Congress Party in the 2000s did not and could not go back to the old LAO. They have instead developed their own links with the underworld – an easier, faster way to gain access to the significant rents required for binding together restive coalitions than the long-term model of business–government relationships and sugar lobby rents. It is not surprising that media reports of extortion and 'protection money' being collected by underworld groups and their links with political bosses have grown.

6.2.3 Summary

Maharashtra remains a leading industrial state in India and a politically sophisticated state with keenly contested local elections and significant mass movements. Yet its political evolution has come at a cost as the polity has become more fragile and fractured since the 1980s, and industrial growth is no longer providing the necessary growth in employment. The state also has one of the most impoverished regions in India, Vidharbha, which gradually became a base for a violent Maoist movement spreading across central and eastern India. In the 1960s and 1970s, when Maharashtra had features of a basic LAO, the distribution of rents achieved political stability but also ensured politicians had a longer time horizon that helped growth in the industrial sector. The changes in the construction of the LAO that began in the 1980s contributed to a decline in the manufacturing growth rate by the 1990s. The growth in the service sector compensated for some of the slowdown in industrial growth, but the aggregate growth of the state was dragged down by the continuing poor performance of its agriculture.

The emergence of features of maturity in the LAO in Maharashtra thus had complex features. While political competition had adverse effects on the time horizon of politicians and the deals that business could expect, this also coincided with the liberalization that forced business organizations, already sufficiently sophisticated, to further enhance their competitiveness through global links and acquisitions. Nevertheless, Maharashtra began to lose ground to states like Tamil Nadu and Gujarat when allocations of industrial licenses were no longer decided by the central government and investors were free to choose locations. Other states were providing more incentives to attract investment and Maharashtra failed to provide a sufficiently attractive competing package. Given the significant industrial base the state had already achieved, initiatives like its comprehensive industrial policy package of 2001 did keep a flow of industrial investments going. Nevertheless, the political base underpinning these policies had become much more vulnerable.

The important point in the evolution of the LAO in Maharashtra is that the transition from a basic LAO to an LAO with significant characteristics of maturity does not necessarily mean that there has been a simultaneous improvement in economic and political prospects across the board. Maturity was characterized by easier entry for both political and economic organizations. Some of these organizations were sophisticated economic organizations like the Indian automobile companies with production facilities in Maharashtra. Other entrants, particularly new parties in the political arena or shady construction companies, were far less sophisticated and sometimes generated significant negative externalities and occasionally induced violence. The dominant coalition was now based on the outcomes of intense political contestations that verged on the violent at the margins. Compared to the basic LAO that preceded it, Maharashtra's politics is likely to remain more volatile and more violent given the rent allocation system that underpins the new LAO with characteristics of maturity and greater vulnerability.

6.3 West Bengal

At the time of independence, West Bengal, along with the Bombay Presidency, was one of the most industrially advanced states in the country. Today, while Maharashtra and Gujarat, the two states emerging out of the Bombay Presidency, have retained their rankings as India's top industrial states, West Bengal has slipped close to the bottom of the list of major states. The partition of India affected the state of West Bengal very significantly, as Bengal was split into Indian West Bengal and East Pakistan, later to become Bangladesh. Bengal had closely linked markets, and the partition sundered them in a manner that took West Bengal (and Bangladesh) years to recover, and never fully. Even though West Bengal was the industrial part of Bengal, East Bengal (Bangladesh) was its hinterland, providing markets and agricultural raw materials, in particular raw jute for the jute industry centered in West Bengal.

West Bengal differed significantly from Maharashtra in the way in which the dominant coalition was constructed. The dominant coalition in Maharashtra was based on a combination of business interests and the sugar lobby. In contrast, the Left Front coalition that emerged as the dominant coalition in West Bengal issued redistributive rents to a more dispersed set of elites in the state's impoverished agrarian community, who created an unassailable electoral constituency for the Left Front led by the Communist Party of India, Marxist (CPM). Even though this rent distribution system ignored industrialization and industrial capitalists, it provided political stability for three decades. The basic LAO was thus constructed differently and lasted longer in West Bengal.

But as agricultural growth started petering out in the 1990s, the electoral constituency that underpinned the rent allocation strategy of the CPM grew increasingly restive. While the Left Front did read the warning signs, it read them a little too late and ended up trying to force through an industrial agenda to make up for lost time. The change in strategy was responding to the demands for jobs and prosperity coming from its core constituency, but the support for industry required land acquisition for industry and other policies that alienated critical parts of this constituency and strengthened the hand of an opportunistic opposition. In the 2000s, the state witnessed mass mobilizations against land acquisition for industrialization and this resulted in the loss of a potential auto project in the state despite the project being strongly supported by the Left Front government. In this case, the success of the Left Front in constructing a stable dominant coalition ultimately turned out to be inimical for the long-term growth prospects for industry in the state.

6.3.1 A Congress Party Government that Never Struck Roots

The basic LAO in West Bengal was untypical because the Congress Party was weak in the state and the strong version of the basic LAO in the state was constructed by the CPM. During the Nehruvian phase, when India as a whole had characteristics of a basic LAO, a Congress Party government held power in West Bengal, but it was weak and the state was never a significant recipient of industrial licenses despite being one of the two most industrialized states in the country. Some analysts have suggested that Nehru had a poor political relationship with the first chief minister of West Bengal and as a result the state effectively got punished. Except for a break in this pattern in 1969, Maharashtra always got at least double the industrial licenses of West Bengal. This partly reflected the better organization of Maharashtrian capitalists and their ability to buy influence from politicians, a feature discussed in our section on Maharashtra. When the new Left Front government took over in 1977, the already neglected capitalist sector found it even more difficult to get a voice in the state government as the new coalition focused on rent allocation to and electoral support from a rural constituency (Banerjee et al. 2002). Moreover, the access of the Left Front government to the center was even worse than the preceding West Bengal Congress Party, as the central Congress Party and other coalition governments did not share a comfortable relationship with the Left Front. And while the basic LAO at the center fell into crisis in the mid-1960s, West Bengal bucked the national trend as the Left Front consolidated a stronger version of a basic LAO at the state level in the late 1970s. This created a single dominant party with a rent distribution strategy sufficiently effective to make it electorally unassailable for three decades before it too faced growing crises by 2010.

During the early Congress Party years, the state did get some public sector investments such as an integrated steel plant and a few mega hydroelectric power projects, but these were insufficient to sustain a drive toward industrialization. With India still a basic LAO, the poor relationship of the state Congress Party with the central Congress Party meant that despite

Table 6.5 *Industrial licences issued to different states in India, 1965 to 1976*

	1965	1966	1967	1968	1969	1970	1971	1972	1973	1974	1975	1976
AP	24	19	11	4	6	13	37	30	29	61	61	51
GJ	39	33	29	23	16	39	66	57	78	89	97	83
TN	59	29	18	7	12	36	51	36	64	99	141	61
MH	134	109	100	66	80	112	162	131	183	265	255	143
P&H	24	31	16	14	7	39	45	52	44	107	109	52
WB	64	42	48	34	62	46	81	54	47	107	74	56

Note: The abbreviations for the states are as follows- AP = Andhra Pradesh, GJ = Gujarat, TN = Tamil Nadu, MH = Maharashtra, P&H = Punjab & Haryana, WB = West Bengal.
Source: Raychaudhuri and Basu (2007).

being one of the industrial leaders in 1947, the state got significantly fewer industrial licenses compared to Maharashtra (Table 6.5). Nor did capitalists in West Bengal have close relationships with leaders in the national Congress Party. This too was different from capitalists in Bombay. The most important difference was that the West Bengal Congress Party did not have a state-based rent strategy that allowed them to consolidate a basic LAO. There was no equivalent of the sugar lobby in West Bengal and the Congress Party there found it much more difficult to construct a stable coalition compared to the Maharashtra Congress Party.

The Congress Party-based dominant coalition collapsed earlier in West Bengal, by the late 1960s. It fragmented enough for the first non-Congress Party coalition, a communist one, to come to power. The first coalition did not last long but the stage was set for a Left Front-oriented coalition in the state. The Congress Party government that came to power after this short-lived coalition brutally put down a popular leftist movement. The movement, called Naxalite, was the result of a peasant uprising in 1967 that struck not just at the Congress Party coalition but also divided the communist movement in West Bengal. The emergence of the Naxalite movement was itself in part a manifestation of the unraveling of the Nehruvian basic LAO in West Bengal and the inability of the Congress Party to offer rents to potential organizers of violence in the state.

6.3.2 The Left Front: Prioritizing Agrarian over Industrial Interests

The Left Front won a landslide victory in 1977 and was quick to consolidate its position among its rural constituents by focusing on land reforms and the establishment of the Panchayati system of local self-government. The Panchayat level is the lowest level of elected government in India and operates through the devolution of administrative power to the level of a village unit. These actions helped the Left Front mobilize a large section of the rural and largely agricultural support base that it was to draw on for the next three decades (Mukherjee 2007). The Panchayati system came into force in the state almost a decade before it was adopted at the national level and proved to be the Left Front's political master stroke. Once the Left Front won Panchayat elections in a village, it could appoint its cadres to run the administration on party lines, ignoring the bureaucratic district administration authorities that were more difficult to command. This gave Panchayat members significant powers over rent allocation at the village level, for instance in the allocation of public funds. The land reforms, on the other hand, gave the Left Front the greatly needed perception of using state power for a progressive social transformation (Yadav 2006).

Land reform in West Bengal distributed very little land to the poor, but it did strengthen the rights of sharecroppers and landless workers. The most substantial effect was to enable a shift in the state's rent distribution strategy toward subsidies for fertilizers, tube wells, and other investments for the small and medium peasants who made up the bulk of the peasantry (Rogaly et al. 1999). The shift in rent distribution priorities was both politically successful in creating a constituency for a stable ruling coalition and developmental in driving strong growth in West Bengal's agriculture (Table 6.3). The source of stability was that the allocation of small rents to a broad population of small and medium peasants gave the party an unassailable electoral constituency while also helping peasants to drive high rates of agricultural growth. The way in which the dominant coalition was constructed, however, meant that the coalition could ignore the importance and necessity of allocating rents to develop industry. On the contrary, the Left Front at this time actively encouraged militant trade unionism in the cities to keep potential industrialists and their Congress Party supporters in check, while basing its own power on a stable coalition based in the rural economy.

The Left Front, therefore, created a second, apparently more successful, basic LAO compared to the one the Congress Party had constructed in West Bengal. However, this strategy had its limitations. First, agricultural growth based on the middle peasantry had its shortcomings in terms of political stability. The really poor and landless were left out, as were the growing intermediate classes in the urban areas, except for those incorporated as party activists and organizers. Second and perhaps more important, agricultural growth in a land-scarce economy had its economic limits. When in the 1990s agricultural growth started petering out, the Left Front faced very serious problems in reorienting its strategy toward industry.

The Left Front's ability to use the Panchayati system effectively through the 1980s and most of the 1990s to direct rents to its constituents was an important part of its rent allocation system. Most local developmental activities were funded through this system and bypassed the bureaucracy of the district administration. This allowed the Left Front to gain a head start over other Indian states in streamlining the process of funds disbursal through the Panchayati system. Channeling funds for local development projects through the Panchayats helped the Left Front to decide allocation politically, bypassing the bureaucracy of the district administration. This was a vital part of the mechanism through which it consolidated its cadre base at the grassroots level. Party members were members of the Gram (village) Panchayat and so at the grassroots level, the party and government structure coalesced. The allocation of development funds not only provided rents to the core organizers of the party, but to a significant extent were also developmental rents as they provided subsidies for investment in agriculture that otherwise might not have happened. Money disbursed went to villagers who had organizational capabilities or to win over those hesitating in their support for the Left Front. Winning a majority in every Panchayat election helped to consolidate the Left Front's base, which translated into money and muscle during state and national elections (Bhattacharya 2002, Mitra 2001).

The developmental aspect of this rent allocation strategy resulted in significant growth in agricultural productivity. Between 1980 and 2005, the average agricultural growth rate in West Bengal was 4.6 percent as opposed to 2.9 percent for India and 3.4 percent for Maharashtra (Table 6.3). As Rogaly et al. (1999) show, a large part of the subsidies resulted in increased investments in tube wells, fertilizers, and other agricultural inputs. Bardhan and Mookherjee (2006) also argue that the distribution of agricultural kits and credit to poor farmers contributed to higher productivity. In Khan's terminology, these were developmental rents (Khan 2008). Given that not much land was redistributed and tenancy reforms were limited, these developmental rents are likely to have been an important contributor to West Bengal's higher than average agricultural growth over this period.

The Flight of Industry
The Left Front-organized basic LAO in West Bengal coincided with, and possibly partly caused, a flight of organized industry from West Bengal to Maharashtra and other states. It began with the shifting of a number of

corporate headquarters from Kolkata to Mumbai. The basic LAO created by the Left Front left no space for industrial or capitalist interests. Industrial corporations offered no opposition to these proagrarian policies; they clearly felt there would be little point in fighting such a well-organized political order. The corporate interests that stayed behind were typically family-owned organizations in commodity businesses like tea and jute, unlike the blue chips whose bottom lines were hit by industrial unrest and limited policy and incentive support from the state.

For industrial companies, the lack of support for investment translated into low firm-level productivity growth and ultimately adverse effects for shareholders. In contrast, owner-capitalists in commodity businesses required less support and were also much more adept at maintaining cozy relations with the CPI-M's top leaders. Yet, until the early 1990s, the Left Front blamed West Bengal's industrial decline on New Delhi's antagonistic policy toward states ruled by opposition parties. This argument became weaker after the liberalization or economic deregulation policies that the Congress Party and later governments at the center implemented beginning in 1991 (Sinha 2004). As the allocative decisions of the center became less important, the Left Front government found it more difficult to explain why industrial performance in West Bengal continued to lag in the new economic regime. To make matters worse, agricultural growth in the state also began to taper off at around the same time.

6.3.3 The Limits of the Left Front

While the Left Front's prorural, anticapitalist rent-creation strategies paid political dividends for two and a half decades, toward the end of the 2000s came signs that the strategy had reached its limits. As late as the 2003 elections, the CPI-M won 2,303 out of a total of 3,220 panchayat seats. But this fell to 1,597 in 2008, while the opposition, which won 744 seats in 2003, increased its position to 1,479 seats in 2008. The CPM also suffered serious electoral reverses in the 2009 general elections. At the heart of its difficulty was a significant slowdown in agricultural growth in the state and the challenge of shifting to an industrial strategy at a late stage.

The limits to agricultural growth in West Bengal stem from an adverse person to land ratio and small farm sizes that make mechanization impractical. The average cropping intensity (the number of crops grown every year) is one way of raising output, but this is already 1.78 in West Bengal, second only to Haryana. The person to land ratio is three times the Indian average. The growth that could be achieved initially with these small peasant farms by pumping in more inputs clearly had its limits. Even this growth did not really make a significant dent on poverty at the bottom (Sarkar 2007). The dominant coalition began to realize that further rapid growth would require addressing much more difficult issues like significantly improving rural infrastructure and land consolidation to enable mechanization. At the same time, the dominant coalition ran into problems with its own constituency in trying to promote industrialization.

Beginning in 2007, West Bengal witnessed massive protests and violence directed at the Left Front against its land acquisition strategy to assist industry, especially after fatal police firings in Nandigram, South Bengal. When the Left Front belatedly realized that it had to promote industry, its strategy of trying to provide cheap land for industrial investors failed because it could not acquire this land without significant violence. Plans for building a car manufacturing plant in the state by the leading Indian auto maker, Tata Motors, had to be dropped because of the ferocity of the protests, spearheaded by a resurgent opposition taking advantage of the pent-up frustration against the CPI-M. The frustration is partly of the CPI-M's own making. The party's tight control of allocative decisions down to the village level is a feature of this basic LAO. But party control that is so intrusive means that there is no choice of schools, villagers cannot make their own decisions about where to take cooperative loans, and so on. The single-party LAO in a context where a challenge by the opposition cannot be formally blocked by administrative methods can only work if the benefit from higher growth and material welfare is perceived by the electorate to compensate for the more extensive control over choices and rents. When agricultural growth was rapid, these conditions were met, and for well over two decades the Left Front was unassailable at the polls. But this dramatically changed with the decline of agricultural performance, particularly after the mid-2000s. The Left Front suddenly faced the unexpected specter of losing in the rural areas where electoral battles are really won and lost in West Bengal. Nor was the Left Front equipped to create a new pattern of rents that could support broad-based small and medium-scale industrial capitalism that could satisfy the dual goals of industrial employment generation and moderate equity consistent with its support base.

An ever hopeful and watchful opposition caught on to the dissent and sought to turn it to its advantage. The opposition campaigned successfully to block the Left Front strategy of acquiring agricultural land for industry. These mobilizations are likely to have a lasting negative effect for whoever wins power in West Bengal because the challenge of supporting industrialization is not going to disappear. Greater openness in political access is likely to make it even more difficult to address these issues. At the same time, the unraveling of the Left Front LAO has led to many of the poor and displaced being mobilized by violent insurgency movements like the Maoists. A dormant Maoist movement has been rejuvenated in the state and was following a path of considerable violence by 2010. While drawing support from the Maoist insurgency in the rest of the country, the movement in West Bengal also draws support from the vast section of the state's tribal population largely overlooked by the Left Front. Finally, the unraveling of this basic LAO has further harmed the state's industrial performance to a greater extent than Maharashtra because the size of the manufacturing sector was smaller to begin with and the challenge in West Bengal was to attract new investments, not just to enable existing clusters to grow.

6.3.4 Summary

West Bengal appears to be a case of missed opportunities. The Left Front had thirty years of uninterrupted rule, a feat not seen before and very unlikely to be repeated in India's current political environment. It succeeded in building up a loyal constituency and a committed cadre base that worked hard at the rural grassroots. The conventional explanation of the Left Front's failure is that it neglected social investment in education and primary healthcare and squandered its goodwill. More important perhaps was its failure to formulate a strategy beyond agricultural growth. Agriculture could not in any case absorb a younger generation who no longer wanted to be involved in the sector. But it also took its constituency for granted and failed to develop support for difficult decisions. When the Left Front attempted to forcibly acquire land for industry, it paid the price by losing heavily in the general elections of 2009.

Behind all these explanations is a broader problem: the strategy of rent creation and allocation that underpinned the Left Front's basic LAO did not allow the growing intermediate classes avenues for rapid integration into the dominant coalition and access was severely limited to loyal supporters. It ignored the really poor and left them to be organized by disenchanted intermediate class political entrepreneurs. And its rent allocation strategy did not provide industrial interests with growth-generating rents until it was too late. By the end of the 2000s, the Left Front found itself in the unenviable position of losing the confidence of its traditional constituency and with no other support base to fall back on (Khan 2008).

6.4 A Comparison and Conclusion

The evolution of the LAO in Maharashtra and West Bengal has to be understood in the context of changes happening across India, but they also exhibit critical regional differences that are just as important. In both cases, the state-level differences in the construction of their dominant coalitions implied significant differences in the types of rents and their allocation. These differences help us to make sense of differences in economic and political strategies, as well as the challenges the states faced.

As North, Wallis, and Weingast (2009) point out, institutions and organizations have a path-dependent history. Some of the most important institutions and organizations in Maharashtra revolved around industry. The state's dominant coalition was built to accommodate the urban industrialists and the rural rich. After independence, the dominant coalition was kept together by two distinct types of rents. Long-term rents for industry assisted investment and technology acquisition, initially through the licensing system, and also through land acquisition through the MIDC, the prioritization of infrastructure, and other interventions. In return, the industrialists were expected to provide kickbacks to politicians. But the most important rents that kept the dominant coalition in political business were damaging in a narrow economic sense but nevertheless provided political stability. These rents included the rents created by the pricing policies of the sugar lobby that provided the rents for a patron–client politics focused on Maratha political organizers and their electoral clients. As this basic LAO evolved, the long-term rents to industry became more difficult to sustain, and political competition became more fragmented and violent. The growth of communal politics and the criminalization of politics in Maharashtra during the 1990s tracked the changes at the national level toward greater maturity in the characteristics of the LAO. Long-term investment in industry suffered, but industry already had a deep enough base to carry on investing on its own.

In West Bengal, the Congress Party-led LAO ended much earlier, followed by a new Left Front-led LAO with significantly different characteristics. Unlike the Congress Party-led basic LAO of the Nehru period, the Left Front-led basic LAO was organized through a mass party. It incorporated many but not all potential organizers, and as a result open competitive violence was much less in evidence in West Bengal during this period compared to other states. However, the nature of this dominant coalition ruled out rents that attracted productive investments in industry. The coalition's productive rent allocation focused on small and medium peasants, and for a time greater investments by middle peasants in particular drove significant agricultural growth. However, when agrarian growth hit a ceiling due to land fragmentation and population density, the dominant coalition could not shift rent allocation strategies sufficiently to attract a significant increase in industrial investment. The growing violence and insurgency in the late 2000s in West Bengal reflects the gradual breakdown of this basic LAO. As West Bengal moves toward maturity, it faces uncertainty in terms of the nature of the coalitions that will emerge and their rent allocation strategies.

Both states are at different stages of moving from more stable basic LAOs to much more volatile mature LAOs. In Maharashtra, this has already progressed in the form of the emergence of new coalitions, such as the BJP-SS-led coalition of excluded elites, with an attendant increase in political instability. In West Bengal, the electoral defeats of the Left Front in 2008 and 2009 probably signal the beginning of a transition to a more mature LAO in the sense that the space for establishing new organizations, particularly political organizations, is likely to significantly increase as a result. It has also resulted in an upsurge in insurgent violence led by Maoists. The emerging maturity in the LAO in both West Bengal and Maharashtra has therefore been associated with greater violence and political fragmentation.

West Bengal comes off poorly when compared to Maharashtra in terms of industrial growth but leads if we compare agricultural performance. West Bengal also enjoyed uninterrupted political stability for thirty years and did more to target poverty, while Maharashtra suffered from more fractious politics and serious communal strife and did less to fight poverty even during the basic LAO phase. But West Bengal used its political organizations to create rents that supported agricultural growth in a context of pressing land scarcity where sustaining growth required an industrialization strategy. In Maharashtra, industry and commerce flourished, even if the breakdown of the basic LAO resulted in a slowdown in industrial and particularly manufacturing growth in the late 1990s.

Taken together, our examination of the LAOs in West Bengal and Maharashtra demonstrates a few principles and raises many questions. First, the transition to maturity in India according to the NWW definition appears to have very strong political determinants. In particular, the basic LAO of the Nehruvian period failed because the ruling coalition could not accommodate all the potential organizers and violence specialists who emerged. The LAO with greater characteristics of openness and maturity was simply a response to these pressures, rather than being driven by the growing sophistication of productive organizations. Fortunately for India, small sectors of the economy were also growing in organizational sophistication, particularly the organized industrial and service sectors that were globally competitive. But these were still sectors that employed tiny numbers of people as a share of the total population.

Second, while our case studies corroborate the important role of violence and the need to distribute rents to maintain political stability in LAOs, the role of the violence specialist needs closer scrutiny. Receiving rents does not necessarily make a violence specialist stop violence. They may instead ask for more rents. The perpetual splitting of parties sometimes happens because political organizers are unhappy with the rents they are getting, not because they are not getting any. Similarly, exclusion from rents does not necessarily induce an organizer to engage in violence. We do not know ex ante what the rent allocation should be to stop violence or whether the current allocation is excessive or insufficient. This is a weakness in terms of policy advice to developing country leaders. But the framework can describe the evolutionary process through which stability is achieved in developing countries.

Finally, in developing countries like India where the mobilization of the intermediate classes for rent capture is an ongoing and expanding process, the transition to aspects of a mature LAO can and does result in greater volatility and perhaps vulnerability. India has evolved toward a political and economic system under which many types of organizations can be set up and function successfully outside the ambit of the dominant coalition. However, the very ease with which organizations can be set up can destabilize the rents of the dominant coalition and threaten its viability. If the dominant coalition hits back with restrictions, it reverts to having more characteristics of a basic LAO. If it gives in, it can create incentives for more organizers to try and capture rents and result in an outbreak of violence and fragility. Until an extensive and productive capitalist class is created that can pay for the protection of basic property rights, as well as pay significant taxes to allow stability to be achieved through fiscal redistribution, reaching the doorstep conditions for establishing an extensive rule of law for elites in both political and economic organizations is not going to be easy.

References

Banerjee, Abhijit, Pranab Bardhan, Kaushik Basu, Mrinal K. Datta-Chaudhuri, Maitreesh Ghatak, Ashok Sanjay Guha, Mukul Majumdar, Dilip Mookherjee, and Debraj Ray. 2002. Strategy for Economic Reform in West Bengal. *Economic and Political Weekly* 37 (41): 4203–18.

Banerjee, Abhijit, Dilip Mookherjee, Kaivan Munshi, Kaivan, and Debraj Ray. 2001. Inequality, Control Rights and Rent Seeking: Sugar Cooperatives in Maharashtra. *Journal of Political Economy* **109** (1): 138–90.

Bardhan, Pranab and Dilip Mookherjee. 2006. *Land Reform, Decentralized Governance and Rural Development in West Bengal*. Paper prepared for the Stanford Center for International Development Conference on Challenges of Economic Policy Reform in Asia, May 31–June 3.

Basu, Kaushik. 2003. *The Indian Economy: Up to 1991 and Since*. BREAD Working Paper No. 052. Bureau for Research in Economic Analysis of Development. Cambridge, MA: Kennedy School of Development, Harvard University.

Bavadam, Lyla. 2005. A Movement in Decline. *Frontline* Vol. 22, Issue 8. http://www.thehindu.com/fline/fl2208/stories/20050422000804300.htm.

Bhattacharya, Moitree. 2002. *Panchayati Raj in West Bengal: Democratic Decentralisation or Democratic Centralism*. New Delhi: Manak Publications.

Chatterjee, Partha. 1997. Introduction: A Political History of Independent India, in Chatterjee, Partha (ed.). *State and Politics in India*. Calcutta, Chennai, Mumbai: Oxford University Press.

Hansen, Thomas Blom. 1996. The vernacularisation of Hindutva: The BJP and Shiv Sena in rural Maharashtra, *Contributions to Indian Sociology* **30** (2): 177–214.

Jadhav, Vishal. 2006. Role of Elite Politics in the Employment Guarantee Scheme. *Samaj Prabodhan Patrika*. http://www2.ids.ac.uk/gdr/cfs/pdfs/vishalmarathiart.pdf.

Jenkins, Robert. 1999. *Democratic Politics and Economic Reform in India*. Cambridge: Cambridge University Press.

Katzenstein, Mary Fainsod, Uday Singh Mehta, and Usha Thakkar. 1997. The Rebirth of Shiv Sena: The Symbiosis of Discursive and Organizational Power. *The Journal of Asian Studies* **56** (2): 371–90.

Kaur, Gagandeep. 2007. Sugar Co-Ops face a Downturn. http://www.indiatogether.org/2007/apr/agr-sugarcoop.htm#continue.

Khan, Mushtaq H. 2008. *Vulnerabilities in Market-Led Growth Strategies and Challenges for Governance*. DFID Research Paper Series on Governance for Growth. London: School of Oriental and African Studies, University of London. Available at http://eprints.soas.ac.uk/9963/1/Vulnerabilities_internet.pdf.

———. 2009. *Learning, Technology Acquisition and Governance Challenges in Developing Countries*. DFID Research Paper Series on Governance for Growth. London: School of Oriental and African Studies, University of London. Available at https://eprints.soas.ac.uk/9967/1/Learning_and_Technology_Acquisition_internet.pdf.

Kulkarni, Dhaval. 2007. Bumper Sugar Cane Crop in Maharashtra. Bitterness for Many. *Indian Express*, May 10.

Kumar, Salil. 2004. *The Pawar Game*. Available at http://insports.rediff.com/election/2004/oct/08spec.htm.

Lalvani, Mala. 2008. Sugar Co-operatives in Maharashtra: A Political Economy Approach. *The Journal of Development Studies* **44** (10): 1474–1505.

Lele, Jayant. 1995. Saffronisation of Shiv Sena: Political Economy of City, State and Nation. *Economic and Political Weekly* **30** (25): 1520–8.

Mitra, Subrata K. 2001. Making Local Governments: Local Elites, Panchayati Raj and Governance in India, in Atul Kohli, (ed.). *The Success of India's Democracy*, Cambridge: Cambridge University Press.

Mukherjee, Sanjeeb. 2007. The Use and Abuse of Democracy. *Economic and Political Weekly* **42** (44): 101–8.

North, Douglass, John Wallis, and Barry Weingast. 2009. *Violence and Social Orders: A Conceptual Framework for Interpreting Recorded Human History.* Cambridge: Cambridge University Press.

Palshikar, Suhas and Rajeshwari Deshpande. 1999. Electoral Competition and Structures of Domination in Maharashtra. *Economic and Political Weekly* **34** (34/35): 2409–22.

Palshikar, Suhas. 2004. Shiv Sena: A Tiger with many Faces, *Economic and Political Weekly,* **39** (14/15): 1497–1507.

Panagariya, Arvind. 2005. *The Triumph of India's Market Reforms, the Record of the 1980s and 1990s.* Policy Analysis No. 554. Washington, DC: CATO Institute.

Raychaudhuri, Ajitava and Gautam Kumar Basu. 2007. *The Decline and Recent Resurgence of the Manufacturing Sector of West Bengal: Implications for Pro-Poor Growth from an Institutional Point of View.* Discussion paper series number ten for the Institutions and Pro Poor Growth research programme, University of Manchester.

Rogaly, Ben, Barbara Harriss-White, and Sugata Bose (eds.). 1999. *Sonar Bangla? Agricultural Growth and Agrarian Change in West Bengal and Bangladesh.* New Delhi: Sage Publications.

Sarkar, Abhirup. 2007. Development and Displacement: Land Acquisition in West Bengal. *Economic and Political Weekly* **42** (16): 1435–42.

Selbourne, David. 1977. *An Eye to India.* London: Penguin.

Sinha, Aseema. 2004. Ideas, Interests, and Institutions in Policy Change: A Comparison of West Bengal and Gujarat, in Rob Jenkins (ed.). *Regional Reflections: Comparing Politics across India's States.* New Delhi: Oxford University Press.

Vora, Rajendra and Suhas Palshikar. 1996. Maharashtratil Sattantar (Marathi – Power Transfer in Maharashtra) *Granthali.* Mumbai.

Yadav, Yogendra. 2006. "The Opportunities and the Challenges," *The Hindu,* May 16. Available at http://www.hindu.com/2006/05/16/stories/2006051611501200.htm.

SEVEN

Entrenched Insiders

Limited Access Order in Mexico

Alberto Díaz-Cayeros

7.1 Introduction

Despite advances in social development and the presence of a very stable political order, during much of the twentieth century Mexico was unable to produce rapid economic growth. Even after dramatic economic transformations at the close of the century, including trade liberalization, privatization, and deregulation, economic performance has remained mediocre at best (Levy and Walton 2009). Democratization was a long and protracted process that only became a reality after a long delay, compared to political openings in Latin America and the rest of the world (Magaloni 2006). At the beginning of the twenty-first century the economy is stagnant; young men and women are unable or unwilling to find jobs in the modern formal economy (Levy 2008); and the state is unable to provide the most basic public good of controlling its territory and protecting its citizens from extortion and violence.

This chapter applies the theoretical framework developed by Douglass North, John Wallis, and Barry Weingast in their book *Violence and Social Orders* (2009) to the study of the social, political, and economic development of Mexico. In the context of this analytic lens, Mexico has already fulfilled what the authors call the "doorstep conditions" (rule of law for elites, perpetually lived organizations in the public and private spheres, and consolidated control of the military) that could enable it to transform into an open access order (OAO) society. But I argue that the prevailing political arrangement and the organization of economic interests have produced entrenched insiders who are preventing such transition.

The chapter highlights four aspects of Mexico's political economy that can shed light on the social arrangement that awards insiders huge advantages that prevent mobility, economic dynamism, and political accountability.

The nature of this arrangement is the following. The main opportunities for capital accumulation are reserved for a narrow group of powerful citizens. Those citizens have privileged access to policy makers and political players and true violence potential they can call upon when needed. In sharp contrast, the vast majority of Mexican citizens enjoy few opportunities to build assets and engage in productive investments. Furthermore, citizens are often disempowered from influencing political processes. The lack of access to opportunity and disempowerment of the masses has sometimes led to expressions of violence.

In order to illustrate the nature of the socioeconomic and political equilibrium prevailing in Mexico, I analyze: 1) the failure of land reform as a strategy allowing for the formation of assets among poor peasants; 2) the limited role played by stock markets in the formation of capital for the vast majority of firms; 3) the regulatory framework that has assured the dominance of a small number of economic organizations, including monopolistic firms and unions; and 4) the role played by oil rents in the preservation of a ruling coalition insulated from societal pressures.

1. *Land reform and assets.* In the aftermath of the Mexican Revolution (1910–17), the threat of violence among elites and the imperative of pacifying the countryside led to the establishment of a hegemonic political party, the Partido Revolucionario Institucional (PRI). This party prevented the development of rural markets and the accumulation of capital for the poorest Mexicans living off the land. Land was a tool used to garner electoral support, and never became an asset that could allow for development. The country was pacified as civilian rule emerged, but the peasants under whose name the social revolution had been fought were unable to use land as a mechanism to escape poverty.

2. *Access to stock markets.* The process of capital formation in the industrial and commercial sectors of the economy was limited to few individuals and families: financial institutions, particularly stock markets, did not allow for the expansion of opportunities to a wide population. The stock market entrenched the advantages of dominant industrial groups and family firms. Stock market financial mobilization was therefore not the trigger for sustained economic growth. While private and public markets for capital became increasingly sophisticated and transactions became impersonal, only a minority of potential entrepreneurs could access financial markets. These entrepreneurs had potential for violence to the extent that they concentrated a disproportionate share of the national economy and influence.

3. *Monopolistic regulation of firms and labor.* In addition, the regulatory framework in both public and private sector enterprises ensured the redistribution of rents among the dominant actors, limiting opportunities for the vast majority of the population. Unions expressed themselves through threats and the mobilization of workers by coercive corporatist mechanisms. The truncated welfare state that Mexico generated was not a mechanism to share risks, but rather a protection for the privileged modern sector of the economy shifting the burdens and vulnerability of the economy to the so-called informal sector.

4. *Oil rents and low public revenue yield.* Private privileges remained because the Mexican political system was extremely successful at redistributing rents, particularly those coming from natural resources. Public finances relied on oil revenue as the main source to redistribute rents from commodities to both sector interests and unions. Those oil windfalls paid for ambitious social programs for which citizens and the private sector were not asked to bear a burden in the form of direct or indirect taxation. Therefore, a link of accountability between citizens and governments through the benefit principle of connecting taxation to the provision of public goods was mostly missing.

The failure of the country in moving toward an open access order is reflected in the prevalence of a highly stratified and unequal social structure in which political and economic elites still undertake transactions on the basis of their personal connections, privileged access to capital, and lopsided government regulation and policy making. The arrangement has excluded rural dwellers, small businesses, and informal entrepreneurs. In this divided social context, sporadic violence sometimes flares up among socially disadvantaged groups, while the rich have retained the threat of using violence through their potential control of police corporations or their private security guards.

The framework provided by North, Wallis, and Weingast (2009) can offer some insights into the Mexican case that would not be available using other perspectives. Scholars have emphasized many features discussed in this chapter: the use of patronage and vote buying as a source of political hegemony (Cornelius 1975); the manipulation of land property rights leading to the impoverishment of peasants (Warman 1980); the rent-seeking character of Import Substitution Industrialization (ISI); or the pernicious effects of the monopolistic market structure (Levy 2008). But the prevailing theoretical frameworks usually privilege either the political arrangement or the forms of economic organization without shedding light on how one relates to the other. In economic models, politics is often portrayed as the friction or distortion that prevents markets from functioning smoothly. In political accounts, the underlying economic structure is usually treated as an exogenous constraint.

The LAO perspective emphasizes that the stability of the ruling coalition is always under threat of violence generated either from external challengers or from within the coalition itself. Economic performance depends on how those threats are dealt with. The solutions the ruling coalition formulates to prevent violence are usually not optimal from the point of view of the organization of economic activity, but without those suboptimal arrangements, there would be no economic accumulation at all. Hence LAOs are stable arrangements that keep violence in check, but are only second best in terms of productivity and growth.

An additional important insight of the framework is to suggest that there is no necessary progression or end point or a teleology that justifies the means to a particular end in the construction of social orders. Ideological parties and leaders often use metaphors of progress or evolution toward a greater goal as a way in which they can justify their rule and the closed nature of the ruling coalition. But the LAO framework asserts that these arrangements are not gradually moving toward a desirable end state, but rather that they are an equilibrium in themselves, and therefore relatively stable. Their permanence does not imply, however, that there are no shifts in the political and economic fortunes of the rulers, but rather that social orders are able to successfully keep violence in check, generating enough rents to keep the arrangement acceptable to the main stakeholders.

The chapter is organized as follows. The next section presents a narrative of Mexico's development in which a certain balance has been kept between the development of private and public organizations. That section ends with a discussion of the nature of rents and its distribution in the Mexican social arrangement. The section after that delves into the four selected issues that will be explored in more detail, seeking to shed light on the nature of exclusion and the mechanisms through which the arrangement has been preserved through time. The final section discusses the shadow of violence and the way in which many of the unresolved tensions discussed in the chapter may come back to haunt the development prospects of Mexico.

7.2 The Balance between Private and Public Organizations

Mexico has reached what can be characterized as a mature limited access order (LAO) at various points in its history. Under the long *Pax Hispanica* of the colonial order (1521–1810), which was disrupted 200 years ago with the War of Independence, one could argue that the economic reforms brought about by the Bourbon kings at the end of the eighteenth century initiated a process that created autonomous corporate bodies, an opening of trade flows with the metropolis, and the development of perpetual political organizations to structure social life. In the context of the time, these reforms brought the New Spain to the doorstep conditions of what could have become an open access order (OAO). The ruling coalition was dominated by so-called *Peninsulares*, Spaniards living overseas, to the exclusion of indigenous peoples, *mestizos*, and white Creoles born in the colonies. Although Spain as a colonial power did not keep a large standing army, the potential for violence was kept in check by a powerful bureaucracy that forbade the vast majority from bearing arms and kept tight control of ports, mining towns, and the main Spanish cities. In Indian towns, a system of indirect rule empowered local bosses (*caciques*) to dispense justice and monopolize violence.

The War of Independence (1810–21) brought about a great transformation that created vast opportunities for political participation through the enfranchisement of most male adults and vigorous forms of municipal republicanism. Despite periods of political instability and social turmoil, with frequent outbursts of violence in the form of indigenous rebellions, the first century of independent statehood culminated with a *Pax Porfiriana* (1874–1910) at the end of the nineteenth century, which seemed again to set the stage for a move toward an OAO. The ruling coalition was kept in place through what Haber el al. (2003) refer to as Vertical Political Integration, in which a narrow elite, linked by close networks and cemented through family ties and joint membership in corporate boards, dominated access to political office and economic opportunities. A highly professionalized army and repressive police forces in the states kept social unrest at bay.

The Mexican Revolution starting in 1910 interrupted the liberal model of development, to be replaced by a more progressive project based on ideas of social justice and redistribution. A highly promising start transformed the regime and included land reform, universal education, workers' rights, and social protection. These reforms could have moved the country to an OAO. But the revolutionary regime was only stabilized with the establishment of a highly entrenched hegemonic party regime starting in 1929. While maintaining peace and stability, the Partido Revolucionario Institucional (PRI) ruled Mexico uninterruptedly from 1929 to 2000. The party failed to deliver sustained economic growth. The ruling coalition in the era of PRI dominance was more inclusive than those of previous periods, incorporating labor unions and peasant organizations. Political and business elites shared an interest in keeping access to political power limited to competition within one hegemonic political party. Violence potential was mostly embodied in police forces that, although frequently corrupt and willing to sell their services to the highest bidder, tended to keep crime in check. However, as the economic crisis of the 1980s deepened, the coercive apparatus of the state increasingly became incapable of providing public safety. Table 7.1 provides a summary overview of some of the key features and events characterizing social order in Mexico during the twentieth century.

After 2000, Mexico lived through a transition to democracy that once again seemed to place it at the doorstep conditions of a radical break with the past. However, the conditions most Mexicans encounter in their daily life are not characterized by open access: rural dwellers depend on the state in order to survive; regulatory frameworks limit competition and benefit entrenched firms that dominate markets; labor unions capture rents without enhancing worker productivity; financial institutions and the stock market do not open up opportunities for capital formation but reinforce the advantages of firms already with access to capital; and local governments do not unleash local entrepreneurship or compete to offer the best conditions of public goods that may improve well-being. The ruling coalition after 2000 did not change dramatically as compared with the groups dominating economic and political life before the transition. Violence has been unleashed as drug traffickers have increasingly disrupted the everyday life of citizens through extortion; they resist government efforts to fight them and compete over trade routes and territories with other criminal organizations.

When characterizing mature LAOs, North, Wallis, and Weingast (2009) note that these social arrangements are in no way static. There are continuous tensions between political and economic organizations that shift their relative balance and generate various crises and accommodations within the ruling elite. A well-known peculiarity of Mexican development is that during the twentieth century it created a remarkably successful political organization (Hansen 1974). The conventional wisdom notes that political elites in Mexico established in 1929 a party that limited competition by establishing clear career paths for ambitious politicians who saw their fortunes better served by belonging to the hegemonic organization (Camp 1982, Smith 1979). The party was remarkable in that by prohibiting reelection at all levels of government it allowed for the circulation of cliques and shifts in the ideological priorities of various presidential administrations. At the apex of the political arrangement was the president, who could decide almost single-handedly how to allocate the federal budget, whom to nominate for high political office, and how to manage his own

Table 7.1 *From fragile LAO to mature LAO and back: Mexico, 1917–present*

Mature LAO (1874–1910)	• Pax Porfiriana, personal dictatorship, limited participation • Federal control of army and public finances • Development of mining, railroads, banking, and retail • Civil code for private corporations
Fragile LAO (1910–1917)	• Mexican Revolution (1910–17) • First oil boom (1914–29)
Basic LAO (1918–1928)	• First wave of land reform (1917–24) • Reconstruction of monetary authority and banking • Cristero Rebellion (regional civil war) • Assassinations of political contenders
Basic LAO (1929–69)	• Foundation of hegemonic party (1929) • Electoral autocracy with regular government turnover • Civilian control over the military • Accelerated land reform • Import substitution industrialization • Stabilizing development (1954–69) • Repression of student movement (1968)
Mature LAO (1970–89)	• State-owned enterprises in oil, telecom, railroads, steel, utilities, sugar mills, paper, airlines • Debt crisis (1982) • Guerrilla unrest and social movements
Doorstep Conditions LAO (1990–2006)	• Gradual democratization and expansion of civil society • Improvements in the rule of law • Privatization with monopolistic market power • Economic liberalization and NAFTA (1994) • Financial crisis (1995) • Alternation in presidential power (2000)
Basic LAO ? (2006–present)	• War on drugs and trafficker insurgency • Violence and increase in size and role of the military • Fragile party competition

succession by naming the next candidate for the official party, the PRI, to the highest office (Brandenburg 1964).

This was achieved in an environment where other political parties marginally competed in regularly held elections at all levels of government. In this sense, the system was very far from an exclusionary military dictatorship, but resembled more a communist party organization using corporatist forms of social organization to incorporate workers, peasants, and the so-called popular sector organizations. But although there was a very active role for the state in a model of mixed economy, Mexico was in no way a command economy. Business groups and firms were clearly autonomous and often at odds with the government over various policy issues. The party leadership and the federal bureaucrats had direct links with business groups and interests in a relationship of mutual dependence that worked relatively well from the 1930s to the 1970s.

In regards to private corporations, Mexico had firmly established since the nineteenth century a clear set of laws and regulations copied from Spanish, French, and American models for the organization of modern firms. Decentralized private corporations have been in existence in the country since its independence in 1821. Some of the great debates and conflicts of the nineteenth century involved the destruction of premodern economic institutional arrangements such as the dominance of the Catholic Church in its tenure of vast expanses of land and its role as banker for the government and the elimination of privileges enjoyed by Indian communities as corporate bodies. After the end of the nineteenth century, powerful industrial groups were developed, often connecting banking, mining, retail, and railroads. This private sector was regulated through mercantile and civil laws mostly passed during the relatively stable years of the Porfiriato – named after Porfirio Diaz, "reelected" president for almost thirty years.

It is possible to show in a schematic manner how the double balance between decentralized private corporations and public organizations shifted in Mexico throughout the course of the twentieth century. Figure 7.1 shows a two-dimensional diagram of the double balance, where the scales do not have an exact quantitative meaning, but are meant to provide a ranking of the degree of complexity and sophistication developed by each of these two realms of the social order: the coherence of political organizations on the vertical axis and the decentralization of economic organizations on the horizontal one.

At the starting point in the nineteenth century, the diagram suggests that, with the liberal model of export-oriented growth of the Porfiriato, the country had relatively developed institutions in the private sector. This was, however, a personalist dictatorship in which political organizations were thwarted. Although liberal political clubs were increasingly frequent and there was much political ferment surrounding the possibilities of an opening of the political system to competition as the dictator aged, the ruling group was reduced to a number of regional strongmen in the states who often controlled local economies through their *haciendas*, where sometimes one family would control virtually all the land in a given state; and the closely knit group of the *científicos*, close advisers and collaborators of Don Porfirio.

This stable arrangement changed drastically with the social forces unleashed by the Mexican Revolution in 1910. Economic organizations became seriously disrupted as the *haciendas*, which had been the main economic institution for the export-oriented boom in agriculture, were disassembled as productive units. In their place, indigenous communities were allowed to recover lost land to the *haciendas* in the form of *ejidos*, collective land holding arrangements that allowed peasants to have their own land, in principle protecting them from opportunistic land grabbing by powerful economic interests through the prohibition of the sale or transfer of those property rights.

The bloody civil war also meant that institutions of public finance and banking were seriously disrupted. Sound public finances were only reconstructed in the 1920s with the establishment of an income tax, the creation of an independent central bank, and the signing of an agreement between the federal government and international bankers to restructure the public debt. In the political realm, the country lived through a disintegration of the established political organizations and the successive murder of revolutionary leaders. The Revolution officially ended in 1917 with the passing of a new constitution that established the *ejido* as the main form of organization of property rights in the countryside (article 27); universal, state-provided education (article 3); the guarantee of workers' rights through progressive labor legislation (article 123); and the firm control of all natural resources including mining and oil in the hands of the federal government as the embodiment of the nation (art 23). But in terms of a stable political agreement, the victorious revolutionaries did not solve the problem of violence: virtually every revolutionary leader died an unnatural death. Thus the diagram shows the 1910s as a situation of extreme fragility in both the private and the public realms, almost lapsing into a fragile limited access order.

After 1918, a balance was reached in which private and public institutions become far more stable and predictable. Despite a regional civil war (the *Cristiada*) in the western highlands of the country, military uprisings, and mass mobilizations of workers and peasants that sometimes took a violent turn, the 1920s were an era of reconstruction. The period witnessed an export-oriented economic reactivation in mining, oil, and agriculture that was cut short by the Great Depression. A steady process of consolidation

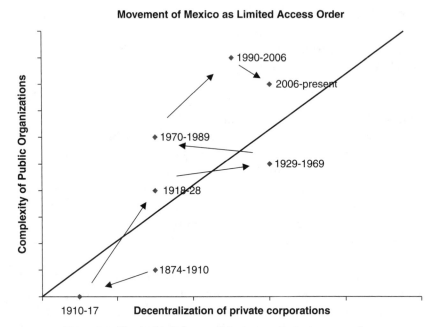

Figure 7.1 The double balance of Mexico as a limited access order.

of decentralized private corporations became the basis of the economic growth of the country during the 1950s. Private firms set the stage for the so-called stabilizing development, enjoying protection from international competition through a strategy of Import Substituting Industrialization (ISI) while sources or finance were made available to them through publicly funded development banks. Although agricultural production stagnated, the impetus of industrial growth and the development of service sectors created an era of urban migration, social mobility, and a general increase in well-being. Politically the country was marred, however, by a hegemonic party that curtailed independent representation, controlled unions and peasant organizations, and when faced with discontent or opposition did not hesitate to resort to electoral fraud.

Not much changed in the political arrangement established in 1929 until the 1990s, but in the 1970s, the complexity and decentralization of private corporations was reduced as the federal government took a greater role in the economy and industrial groups came to dominate several sectors, wielding monopolistic power while enjoying protection from international competition through high tariffs and nontariff barriers. By 1976, the federal government's State-Owned Enterprises controlled many sectors in the economy, including oil extraction, refining, and most petrochemical production; telecommunications; utilities; railroads; marketing and distribution of milk, corn, and many agricultural products; steel; sugar mills; paper distribution; airlines; among many others. By the 1980s, the relative weight of the public sector was further enhanced with the expropriation of the banking sector. Accordingly, the figure suggests that economic organizations had become highly centralized and lacked autonomy from the state after 1970.

The 1982 peso crisis was a profound economic debacle triggered by foreign debt and the collapse in the international price of oil, the most important export commodity and source of most public finances. The crisis led to a haphazard opening of political spaces that gradually eroded the hegemony of the PRI, despite massive electoral fraud undertaken in the 1988 presidential election. On the economic front, stabilization of the economy required a radical break with the past protectionist policies leading to trade liberalization, privatization, and deregulation of the economy, which culminated in 1994 with the enactment of the North American Free Trade Agreement (NAFTA).

The graph suggests that a high degree of complexity, sophistication, and openness was achieved in the political realm after 1989; but in the economic sphere, despite greater decentralization of private economic activity, companies were able to reap monopolistic advantages from the processes of privatization, the most exemplar of which was the case of Telefonos de Mexico, the telecommunications giant owned by Carlos Slim. In the years after the transition to democracy in 2000, the figure suggests, there has been an increase in the development of decentralized private corporations but a slight decrease in the political realm. This is based on the impression that the transition to democracy has allowed many entrepreneurs to have new points of access to public officials as states and municipal governments have become more important in creating the overall environment for business.

To some extent regions have had to compete to provide better conditions for foreign and domestic investment, and this competition has created some true "islands" of efficiency in mid-sized cities where a virtuous cycle has been generated: local governments enable firms by providing a relatively flexible regulatory framework and infrastructure that allows them to reap the benefits of open trade, including the provision of technical schools and job retraining, while firms are generating high productivity jobs in relatively sophisticated sectors such as microchips, pharmaceuticals, or software.

However the figure also suggest a certain retrenchment on the political front as the multiparty system of political competition has become more insulated from citizen demands: although Mexico is still a democratic system, most observers suggest that parties have become too indifferent to citizen demands, enjoying public financing, free access to media for their campaigns, and little accountability, since the decentralized political setting allows them to shift blame for policy failures to other levels of government. Although it is too early to tell, the challenge to the state and economic activity posed by drug violence might quickly undermine the advances made on both the political and the economic fronts.

In the sections that follow, I argue that the main failure of the Mexican political-economic arrangement to produce a qualitative leap leading to sustained economic growth is related to a social arrangement that in equilibrium has allowed elites to successfully create mechanisms to produce and preserve many types of rents. Some of these rents are directly derived from the control of natural resources such as oil in the public sector. Oil revenue has not only allowed the Mexican government to finance its activities, but has meant that the tax burden on the private sector of the economy, particularly the large firms and the wealthiest families and individuals, has been relatively low. An additional source of rents has been found in the form of public sector employment, contract awards, and access to permits for economic opportunities. Many of those rents have involved outright corruption by public officials at all levels of the bureaucratic structure. A third source of rents has been generated by the protection of monopolistic privileges for firms, unions, and political and social organizations that have been granted by the state dominant positions in their realm of action. Finally, one must acknowledge that there have been Schumpeterian rents in some sectors of the economy and individual firms that have become players in global markets since the liberalization of trade in the 1990s. But in the overall composition of rents, these "good rents" have not been a driving force of increased productivity and dynamism in the Mexican economy.

7.3 The Persistence of Limited Access

This section seeks to provide further evidence on selected aspects of Mexican development where the persistence of limited access to power and income can be understood as a social equilibrium. Sometimes this is a perverse arrangement, as in the case of land, because it hinders the accumulation of wealth among peasants and perhaps impoverishes them further by making them dependent on the state. Such intentionality is less clear in the way stock markets have functioned, allowing only a small set of entrepreneurs to tap those sources of capital, or regulatory capture that has entrenched monopolies in both factors of production, labor and capital. Unions have taken advantage of the regulatory framework to generate rents for their members and leaders without contributing to the increase in firm productivity. Large firms have thrived by extracting consumer surplus, particularly in nontradable sectors of the economy.

7.3.1 Land Reform

The political success of the PRI was rooted to a large extent in its capacity to deliver goods to its clienteles within its patronage networks. Nowhere was this more pervasive than in the case of land reform. As argued by Díaz-Cayeros, Magaloni, and Weingast (2008), the postrevolutionary regime failed to grant land to Mexican peasants in a way that made it an income-generating asset that empowered peasants and allowed them to escape poverty. Instead, the state created a system of dependence, designing land reform so that peasants needed the flow of federal financial resources and subsidies to survive (i.e., credit, insurance, seeds, and fertilizers). In this way, the regime locked peasants into supporting it: receiving subsidies required that the new landholders support those in power.

Perhaps the most notable trait of land reform in Mexico is the long period over which it was undertaken: it became a permanent fixture of the regime's policies. The Mexican government redistributed land for seventy-five years, from the last years of the Mexican Revolution to 1991. The early land reform process involved redistribution: land was taken from large landowners and granted to peasants, typically those already living on the land. Later land reform tended to involve federal lands, so in this sense it was not strictly redistributive. In the 1970s, land reform became again redistributive: land was taken away from medium-scale farmers and constituted into *ejidos*, and previously distributed land was distributed again, creating more than one legal claimant (see Sanderson 1984).

Figure 7.2 shows land distributed by definitive presidential decrees in Mexico from 1916 to 1976. The graph uses Sanderson's (1984) data on land reform, which is the most reliable statistical reconstruction of land reform in Mexico. Although there was some land distribution in the 1980s, the graph shows that the most intense episodes of land grants occurred in the 1930s and the late 1960s and early 1970s. The Lázaro Cárdenas (1934–40) administration distributed around 9.6 percent of the total land area in the country; the Díaz Ordaz (1964–70) administration distributed 12.6 percent; and Echeverría (1970–6) distributed around 5.5 percent. One should note that the graph shows the evolution of land distribution in Mexico according

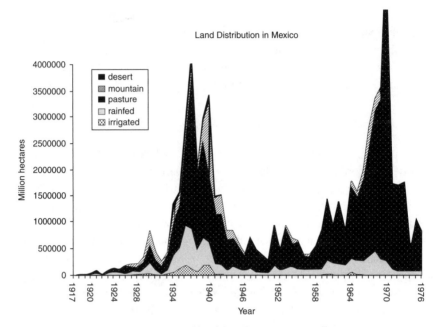

Figure 7.2 Quality of land distribution through time.

to the quality of land. Irrigated and rain-fed land at the bottom constitutes only a fraction of distributed land, while most years the darker shaded land (mountain or pasture, and even deserts!) constituted the majority of land area distributed.

By 1990 when land reform officially ended, more than half of the national territory had been distributed in land grants, even though Mexico's territory only has a small percentage of land suitable for agriculture. This is more clearly seen in Figure 7.3, which compares a map of all the *ejido* landholdings in the country on the left panel, and the land suitable for agriculture on the right panel. Clearly land was distributed despite its marginal quality.

Since high-quality land is scarce and its supply fixed, as land distribution continued it became increasingly common to distribute very marginal, low-quality land or for the same plot of land to be distributed more than once, with two or more communities claiming presidential resolutions entitling them to the land. According to Zepeda (2000,66), by the time the land reform came to an end in 1991, around 17 million hectares (out of perhaps 80 million distributed) were in dispute.

From 1916 to 1976, the Mexican government distributed, on average, 1.3 million hectares of land each year. Scholars have explained this trend

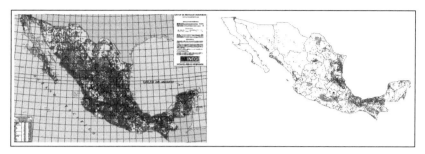

Figure 7.3 Ejido distribution and land suitable for agriculture.

in total land distribution as attributable to bureaucratic inertia (see Grindle 1977) or to presidential ideological commitments to land distribution (Wilkie 1978). To a large extent, the focus of much scholarship was geared toward understanding why land reform was reactivated in the 1960s and 1970s, with an underlying assumption that distributing land was the natural thing for the revolutionary state, or at least for populist leaders, to do.

It is well documented that the Cárdenas administration used land reform as a crucial mechanism to reconstruct its reformist political coalition (Cornelius 1975). However, the literature on land reform in Mexico is never too clear as to why the Díaz Ordaz administration carried out such massive land reform. The ideological commitment to land distribution is not a good explanation, since by virtually every account Díaz Ordaz was as an example of a heavy-handed "law and order" conservative politician. His successor, Luis Echeverría, who by all accounts was a leftist, populist leader, did not distribute land more intensely than other presidents. Our theoretical discussion suggests why Díaz Ordaz accelerated land reform. Land redistribution was pursued as a political strategy to reduce the erosion of PRI support and to avert the risk of violence.

The 1960s were a time of electoral and social challenges for the hegemonic party. By the late 1960s, the PRI faced increasing opposition to its hegemony, including the loss of one gubernatorial election (Nayarit), and most likely fraudulent victories in several state elections (Chihuahua, San Luis Potosi, and Sonora) and municipal races (Lujambio, 2001). The erosion of the PRI's electoral support was accompanied by more social unrest, culminating with the violent repression of the student movement in 1968, which revealed the authoritarian side of the regime. The hegemonic party rarely resorted to violence if it could achieve political support through other means. But the 1960s and early 1970s were characterized by social unrest, guerrilla activity, and frequent rebellions in the countryside.

But perhaps the most crucial aspect of land reform is that it created dependence of peasants on the state: first while they waited to get land; and later as they received subsidized credit and fertilizer from the state, which was the only way to make their marginal land viable. They became the most reliable supporters of the hegemonic party. Díaz-Cayeros, Magaloni, and Weingast (2008) calculate that, controlling for the effects of economic modernization on political support, the distribution of land slowed the decline of PRI support in the states. In an estimation carried out in first differences, the PRI's distribution of land had a positive and significant effect on changes of PRI support in a state. The size of the effect is meaningful: if ten percent of the land in any given state was distributed, PRI votes increased from one presidential election to the next by three percentage points.

7.3.2 Privileged Access to Stock Markets

One of the core aspects of development is accumulation of capital. Access to capital in Mexico during the nineteenth century depended mostly on the Catholic Church and foreign sources of finance. In the twentieth century, the state created development banks and a private financial system was developed to intermediate private savings and credits. Mexico also developed a stock exchange after the nineteenth century. Scholars have noted that there are typically two models of financial development, one based on stock markets (as in the United States), and another based on banks (as in Germany). Mexican financial development in the nineteenth century followed a route similar to the American one. The story of banks in Mexico has been well documented by Haber (2009). But the stock market failed to develop as a major source of financing for entrepreneurs in the twentieth century. The roots of this failure lie in the closed access that has characterized the stock market.

The beginnings of the Mexican stock market were related to mining companies' trading stocks in 1850s. A law was put in place in 1867 by the liberal governments of the time to regulate the financial operations taking place mostly among those companies. But the stock exchange was finally established in Mexico City only in 1886. That was a time of openness to international trade and inflows of foreign capital in the development of railroads and incipient industry. It is noteworthy that the transactions of this market were made in the street of Plateros in the city, where all the silversmith retailers had their shops, and where jewelry shops remain to this day, indicating that the original purpose was to provide a market to a tight group of merchants and businessmen already engaged in activities surrounding mining. This first stock exchange was highly vulnerable to international price shocks given that the fluctuations of mineral commodities determined much of the value and operations in the market. This vulnerability became reduced as the stock exchange expanded its listing of domestic companies in 1908. However, the revolution and the instability in the country in its aftermath meant that steady operations to raise capital in stock markets were not in place until 1933.

The 1930s correspond with an era of important activity in the reconstruction of financial institutions in Mexico, including the Central Bank and the creation of modern tax systems. A clear regulatory framework was put in place in 1933 for the operations in the Bolsas de Valores, plural because this included stock markets in Mexico City, Monterrey, and Guadalajara. This was perhaps the moment in which the regional character of two stock markets outside the center of power in Mexico City signaled the incorporation of entrepreneurs from various areas in the country: Monterrey was gradually becoming an industrial powerhouse and Guadalajara was the hub of retail and commercial activity in the central highlands. But the regional stock markets did not last, and by 1975 they were integrated into Bolsa Mexicana de Valores (BMV). The centralization of the stock market is probably a reasonable move in terms of the size of the market and allowing all transactions to happen under the same floor, but it signals the peak of restriction in access of this institution to outsiders. A few dozen companies were listed in a moment of financial repression, when capital was not easily obtainable from either public development or private commercial banks.

The regulatory requirements for a firm to become listed in the stock market were daunting. Firms that already were insiders could spin off subsidiaries or other firms that became listed. The barriers were not just internal to the stock market, but involved the financial regulators and the Central Bank. Financial repression was also prevalent in the banking system, while the central government successfully raised funds in money markets only accessible to large investors. The stock market was hence a club of big industrialists, bankers, and government financial institutions. Big firms financed political campaigns for PRI officials and obtained regulatory provisions, tax breaks, and other conditions that enhanced their market power.

In the last three decades, the stock exchange has developed into a sophisticated source of capital with electronic trading, futures markets, a building located in the core of Mexico City, and all the characteristics of a modern exchange. But it has not been a source of capital for new entrepreneurs. In keeping with its origin, it is a closed institution where the entry of companies is highly restricted. One can measure the degree of closed access

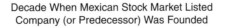

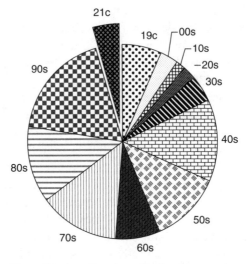

Figure 7.4 Age of stock market listed companies.

in the Mexican stock exchange by analyzing the listed companies and the original date in which those companies were founded. In 1966, there were 66 actively traded companies; around 120 in the 1990s (including financial institutions), and 132 in 1997. Although the stock market has grown in size and listings since 1997, few new companies outside of the financial sector (brokers and banks) have managed to tap into this source of finance. Outside of financial intermediaries, the firms listed remained the same throughout most of the twentieth century. In 2009, the median year of founding of listed companies in the Mexican stock market was 1961. Twenty-five years earlier, the mean year of founding was still in the same decade, at 1963. Figure 7.4 shows the decade in which a listed company was founded. As can be seen in the graph, most companies were founded in the 1980s and 1990s. However, those companies are not truly new listings, but rather a reflection of the changes in financial intermediaries including privatized banks and brokerage firms (*casas de bolsa*). If one considers primarily companies in the industrial, mining, or service sectors, the overwhelming majority of them were founded in the 1940s and 1950s. Finally, it is quite telling to note that seven of the listed companies in the stock market, specifically the one with the largest market capitalization, Telmex, are owned by Mexico's richest man, Carlos Slim, and his family.

Stock markets in Mexico have never become a source of capital for medium-sized companies that cannot fulfill all the requirements to be listed. Commercial banks do not provide great access to credit either, due to the profitability of holding other types of financial instruments instead of risky loans to business. This means that for most of the retail and manufacturing activity, the main sources of capital are often family savings and working capital lent by large firms to their chains of suppliers. Only the largest firms can offer bonds in the open market or stock series with very limited rights for minority stockholders. In such an environment it is very hard to imagine how stock markets might unleash the Schumpeterian creative destruction they are meant to produce. But perhaps the most serious issue that limited access to capital raises is that the power to buy protection and policing is not distributed equally. Access to justice is often limited to firms protected by the modern institutional framework, while the majority of firms resort to webs of informal subcontracting or moneylenders as sources of capital, and the enforcement for compliance with those contractual obligations of the firms that raise capital outside banks and stock markets is often achieved through intimidation. When the threat of violence surfaces among subcontractors, this is usually linked to protection bought from the political establishment, particularly local police forces and municipal regulators of commercial activity. In towns and small cities (but even in Monterrey), small firms are extorted payments by policemen and government inspectors in exchange for protection or issuing permits to remain in compliance with multiple laws and regulations.

7.3.3 Regulatory Capture and Labor

Scholars of Mexican corporatism have argued that the Mexican state successfully linked its policy initiatives with special interests by using peak-level organizations that disciplined and constrained labor and peasant groups as well as organized business interests. During the classic era of PRI hegemony, these interest groups organized pressures from the peasant communities that were granted land or were waiting to receive land distribution and support from the government into the Confederación Nacional Campesina (CNC), which claimed the monopoly of representation of interests in the countryside. It is important to note that the CNC was conceived from the beginning as one of the three sectors of the PRI, and its organizational abilities were intrinsically linked with the governance of agrarian communities through *ejido* structures. Disputes emergent from land tenure arrangements or the expropriation of farms were reserved to special courts and the possibility of appeals was severely limited, ensuring that state and federal governments through the agrarian bureaucracies would settle most conflicts over limits between communities or the management of common pool resources such as water.

In the labor movement, the process was somewhat more complex, since independent union movements were less likely to coalesce around the official party. Initially a deal was struck between the labor confederation (the CROM) and President Calles, which brought stability to the revolutionary regime in the cities. Haber et al. (2003) interpret the deal as one in which the CROM was to provide violent intimidation on behalf of Calles in exchange for legal privileges that gave them rents from employers. Employers abided by such an arrangement because the state let them have monopoly rents. However, this arrangement was not to last, as the CROM itself became a threat to the ruling coalition.

Moreover, the ruling coalition shifted somewhat after 1934 with the reactivation of land reform. A realignment of the state with organized labor led to the emergence of the Confederación de Trabajadores de México (CTM), which, sanctioned by the state, became after the 1960s the undisputed peak organization that represented workers vis-à-vis employers and the Mexican state. Negotiations around working conditions, minimum wage increases, and even the timing and sequence of strikes, were determined by the peak leadership of the labor unions. The power of the organization was reinforced by the particular way labor disputes were mediated by the state. Rather than having strikes be solved or negotiated by firms and individual labor unions, the federal government became the arbiter of labor conflicts through the so-called Juntas de Conciliación y Arbitraje, sanctioning whether a strike was declared legal and conducting the process of negotiation between those involved.

CTM and CNC leaders became entrenched in their political positions by holding leadership positions in the PRI and political office through party nominations to congressional and Senate seats. In fact, a large share of the congressional seats were earmarked to the sectors of the party, and even state governorships were traditionally reserved to either of these organizations. Additional labor organizations operated in a somewhat autonomous manner from the CTM, which were also granted privileged spaces in the legislature, such as the teachers' union (SNTE), the oil workers' union, and the telephone and electricity utilities' unions. Leaders in these organizations were members of the PRI and handsomely rewarded with nominations from the party, which at the time of party hegemony were practically equivalent to winning the elections.

It is important to note that many public policies were structured in such a way that the worker and peasant organizations would have privileged access to goods and services, so that it made sense for peasants and workers to join them and abide by their authority. For example, crop insurance and access to seeds, fertilizers, or granaries often was controlled by the CNC. Unionized workers were the most likely to have access to social security benefits and pensions through the Instituto Mexicano del Seguro Social (IMSS). In the case of the main program that provided low-cost housing in the cities, based on payroll contributions, the Instituto Nacional de Fomento de la Vivienda para los Trabajadores (INFONAVIT) allowed unions within the CTM to control the allocation of credits and the selection of beneficiaries among their rank and file.

Santiago Levy (2008) has recently argued, much in line with this literature, that labor regimes in Mexico have generated low levels of competition and entrenched interests in critical sectors of the economy. The unions have become sources of rents to their members, creating important bottlenecks for the competitiveness of the Mexican economy. But an additional insight in this work is that the policy changes of the last two decades have increased the role of the state in the compensation of uninsured workers (Seguro Popular) and the nonorganized poor through a Conditional Cash Transfer Program (Oportunidades). Those workers who have previously enjoyed the benefits of the truncated welfare state through the IMSS or farmers who enjoy agricultural subsidies through various programs including Procampo and Alianza para el Campo are facing a certain dilemma in their memberships in the traditional organizations.

It is no longer obvious, for example, whether a worker in a firm is better off in the formal sector of the economy, belonging to the labor organizations, when insurance and other benefits can be obtained outside the formal channels. But at the same time, it is clear that neither traditional social security nor new systems of coverage in health or pensions can ensure universal access or reach the poorest workers. This means that Mexico is somewhat caught in a dilemma regarding whether to expand the supports that are not occupationally based, and hence not financed through payroll taxes, or seek to improve the coverage of state welfare institutions.

The prominent role played by labor unions in key sectors of the economy raises an additional issue. Those workers have been able to capture rents generated in their economic activities, but those rents have also extended to the firms that concentrate monopolistic market power (as in the case of PEMEX and the utility companies), and a large share of the market (in sectors such as telecommunications). Although Mexico has set up an antitrust body (Comisión Nacional de Competencia), in critical cases it has failed to be particularly effective, with its rulings often challenged in courts or sidestepped by the dominant stakeholders. The creation of vested interests in the capture of rents is particularly obvious in the case of the oil sector.

7.3.4 Oil Revenue

Mexico has been able to escape, for the most part, the "Dutch disease." Even when oil became a dominant export, this did not mean that the whole economy depended exclusively on this specific sector. In fact, when the export booms of 1914–25 and 1976–82 ended, there were important adjustments, as oil-financed investment in non-oil sectors was sharply reduced (Tornell and Lane, 1999), but the economy was diversified enough to withstand those adjustments. The same is true about the adjustment to be expected after the recent boom (2001–7). On the political front, Mexico's political regime does not seem particularly cursed by oil as a natural resource: although oil revenue has surely allowed politicians to buy political support through patronage and pork-barrel projects, there is no one-to-one relationship between the authoritarian or democratic nature of the regime and its reliance for public finances on oil wealth. But the Mexican state – comprised of the federal, state, and municipal governments – has been extremely dependent on oil revenues, regardless of the system of government in place.

As noted by Lajous (2009), one of the remarkable features of the Mexican oil sector is the shift away from a situation before 1994 with the signing of NAFTA and a shift in the developmental strategy toward foreign trade, in which the overwhelming majority of exports had been comprised by oil, to the current situation in which oil plays only a marginal role in Mexico's foreign trade, even during the commodity boom after 2002. The oil industry has only represented around six percent of GDP during the last twenty-five years, which reveals the high degree of diversification of the Mexican economy, in contrast to other oil-producing nations. But as Figure 7.5 shows, the evolution of oil revenue over the last two decades both as a percent of federal revenue and of GDP implies a very large dependence of the budget on oil.

The evolution of oil revenue collected by the federal government is not just a consequence of the international price of this commodity or its extraction from extremely rich wells (particularly the Cantarell field) but of the bilateral bargaining situation between the finance ministry and the oil company. PEMEX has insider information regarding the true cost of

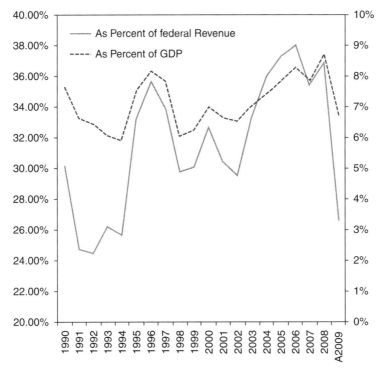

Figure 7.5 Evolution of oil revenue in Mexico.

oil extraction, and its management exercises discretion in the distribution of rents between management, a web of private contractors, the powerful union, and the national treasury; the finance ministry seeks to establish a tax regime that can curtail as much as possible the independent decisions of the company while extracting for the federal treasury as much of the oil rents as possible. Although both the federal government and the firm would want to see much delayed investment in exploration, in order to ensure the viability of the firm over the long run, the short-term competition over rent extraction has prevented this investment from materializing. A solution to this temporal inconsistency problem could be, of course, to have the firm raise capital from domestic or foreign partners or shareholders who may have a longer-term view, but this option is barred by a political commitment to keep the firm as a public monopoly. Thus, the bargain between PEMEX management and the federal government is more easily understood when compared with the situation of communist firms during the era of central planning in the Soviet Union or Eastern Europe: as Kornai (1992) has noted, planning ministries sought to control management through the establishment of targets and ratcheting the amount of funds extracted from the firms; management tried to escape those controls by creating coalitions that would capture rents and keep the production process as obscure as possible while enjoying soft budget constraints.

Federal policy responses of the last few years that have reshaped the fiscal regime of PEMEX and have modified the role oil rents play in the fiscal balance of the Mexican government should be understood in the context of a larger political economy of the relationship between state governors and the federal executive, and the redistributive role of federal expenditure. Governors have played a key role in the process, coaxing the federal government to redistributive oil resources, thus enhancing decentralization, rather than using oil rents to make federal expenditure and investment more redistributive in favor of the poor or more efficient in enhancing the overall productivity of the nation's economy. The deal struck between the federal government and the governors allowed for the creation of an oil stabilization fund, while also giving governors a larger share of oil revenue windfalls. Efforts to capitalize PEMEX, particularly seeking mechanisms to allow foreign companies to establish joint ventures in exploration. or the reclassification of secondary petrochemicals to enhance the role of the private sector, may indeed improve the overall performance of the oil industry. The new PEMEX law passed in 2008 would seem to allow this, but it remains to be implemented.

Such reforms in the energy sector will not sidestep the overriding logic of oil in Mexico, however, it is the main source of fiscal transfer to finance pork-barrel projects and patronage networks. In this respect, the Mexican case suggests that whether oil – or natural resources in general – is a hindrance or a facilitating condition to democratic development and economic growth depends, as Dunning (2008) has argued, on the combination of low taxation effects coupled with the redistributive potential of oil rents. Oil has allowed both democratically elected and authoritarian governors, as well as the federal governments from both the PRI (ruling as an hegemonic autocrat from 1929 to 2000) and the Partido Acción Nacional (PAN, in power since 2000), to redistribute resources to their constituencies while keeping taxes low.

7.4. Mexico in the Shadow of Violence

The theoretical framework offered by North, Wallis, and Weingast (2009) highlights the importance of limited access orders (LAOs) as the most pervasive forms of social organization in human history. According to this framework, mature LAOs are in a condition of opportunity, because they may make the shift away from an organizational and institutional equilibrium where access to power and wealth is limited to the elite, to one in which it is possible for members of society to openly access those opportunities. A critical aspect in understanding the stumbling blocks for a move away from a limited access order to an open one is that a double balance is struck between perpetual public organizations, in which there is a correspondence between power and the distribution of violence potential; and decentralized private corporations, where the formal organization of economic power corresponds with its actual distribution.

In the case of Mexico, the preservation of this double balance proves critical to understand the restrictions to access. Land was distributed to cement the PRI as a perpetual political organization solving challenges of violence and the articulation of political authority, not to generate a shift in economic power. Stock markets were developed to ensure that the private corporations organized around family firms could retain dominance in their economic sectors. The organization and recognition of labor unions by the state and the regulation of economic activity was geared toward the cementing of corporatist representation of interests, not the creation of an environment that would simultaneously promote competition among firms and increase labor productivity while protecting workers' rights. Rents from oil hindered the establishment of a clear link between citizens and firms as taxpayers and public officials as their agents, so that political actors were more attuned to addressing the challenges from potential violence holders and not the threats emerging from the unequal distribution of economic power.

While much of the chapter has concentrated on understanding the ruling coalition bargains that have preserved limited access, the issue of the violence potential needs a final reflection. Throughout the twentieth century and the beginnings of the twenty-first, the problem of violence has not been solved in Mexico in a satisfactory manner. In the early 1900s, the hardline dictatorship of Porfirio Diaz provided a relatively stable economic environment for economic activity and the expansion of Mexico's role in international markets. Haber et al. (2003) and Razo (2008) have noted that such an arrangement was not based on the universal protection of property rights but rather on the connections of families in the economic and political elites that shared power and wealth. The era was peaceful because Diaz did not hesitate to use violence to crush rebellions, forcibly displace indigenous communities, and even send them in a form of quasi-slavery to work in the *Henequen* plantations. That was the Barbarous Mexico portrayed by John Kenneth Turner (1912) that led to the Mexican Revolution.

The Revolution was a major upheaval, probably costing 2 million lives (McCaa 2001). This places the Revolution as the ninth deadliest conflict of the twentieth century. Most of the excess deaths and missing births were truly the consequence of the disruptions created by political violence (while the Spanish influenza surely played some role, the highest mortality occurred precisely in the areas where food supply was most disrupted by the fighting). The aftermath of the Revolution did not end violence, since the Cristero War raged in the central highlands throughout the 1920s and early 1930s. Thus violence was not really curbed in Mexico until the period of relative economic prosperity triggered by the Second World War and the so-called Stabilizing Development period from 1958 to 1970. That era of peace and stability was punctuated, however, by mass mobilizations that often signaled the level of citizens' dissatisfaction and the potential for violence, which the state countered with its own displays of force. The repression of railroad workers in 1959, medical doctors in 1964, and most prominently the student movement in the Tlatelolco massacre of 1968 clearly displayed the willingness of political elites to selectively use violence when they deemed it necessary. In addition, Mexico had relatively localized guerrilla movements that were effectively repressed or coopted by the state, particularly in the poor southern states of Guerrero, Oaxaca, and most prominent due to the international attention it generated, the Zapatista movement in Chiapas. Political purges and assassinations among the elite were relatively rare during the decades of PRI dominance because the party was able to pacify processes of political succession through a very effective mechanism of circulation of elites, namely the prohibition of reelection for all offices and at all levels of government. But political actors always felt at risk, as the display of their well-armed security details made obvious, and the series of political killings in the 1990s, including that of the PRI presidential candidate, made patently clear.

But another form of violence that did not quite disappear in Mexico, and in fact witnessed an upsurge during the 1980s and 1990s, was simple banditry, in the form of robbery, burglary, kidnappings, and murders. The concern over public safety in the last few years has uncovered the violent character of Mexican social interaction over the course of the twentieth century. While most observers have noted that crime and murder rates in Mexico are relatively high by international standards, it turns out that they have been declining over the course of the last two decades (Escalante 2009). Nevertheless, the Mexican political system did not solve the problem of violence as it related to the everyday life of citizens who are not provided the basic public good of safety.

Put into this perspective, the recent upsurge of violence related to drug trafficking since 2007 is not necessarily new. Mexico has not solved the challenge of violence because the arrangement that curtails it from surfacing is a deal among entrenched insiders who have protected their political and economic privileges, not a set of rules and organizations in a society characterized by equal opportunity and the universal protection of civil and political rights, that is, an open access order.

References

Brandenburg, Frank. 1964. *The Making of Modern Mexico*. Englewood Cliffs, NJ: Prentice-Hall.

Camp, Roderic. 1982. *Mexico's Leaders: Their Education and Recruitment*. Tucson: University of New Mexico Press.

Cornelius, Wayne. 1975. *Politics and the Migrant Poor in Mexico City*. Stanford: Stanford University Press.

Díaz-Cayeros, Alberto, Magaloni, Beatriz, and Weingast, Barry. 2003. "Tragic Brilliance: Equilibrium Hegemony and Democratization in Mexico" (typescript) Stanford University, 2003.

Dunning, Thad. 2008. *Crude Democracy: Natural Resource Wealth and Political Regimes*. Cambridge Studies in Comparative Politics, Cambridge University Press.

Escalante, Fernando. 2009. "La Muerte Tiene Permiso." Homicidios 1990–2007. *Nexos*.

Giugale, Marcelo and Steve Webb. 2000. (eds.) *Achievements and Challenges of Fiscal Decentralization. Lessons from Mexico*. Washington: World Bank.

Giugale, Marcelo, Lafourcade, Olivier, and Nguyen, Vinh H. 2001. *Mexico. A Comprehensive Development Agenda for the New Era*. Washington: World Bank.

Grindle, Merilee S. 1977. *Bureaucrats, Politicians, and Peasants in Mexico: A Case Study in Public Policy*. Berkeley: University of California Press.

Haber, Stephen, Armando Razo, and Noel Maurer. 2003. *The Politics of Property Rights: Political Instability, Credible Commitments, and Economic Growth in Mexico, 1876–1929* (Economy of Institutions and Decisions.) New York: Cambridge University Press.

Hansen, Roger. 1974. *The Politics of Mexican Development*. Baltimore: Johns Hopkins University Press.

Kornai, Janos. 1992. "The Postsocialist Transition and the State: Reflections in the Light of Hungarian Fiscal Problems," *American Economic Review*, American Economic Association, vol. **82**(2), pages 1–21, May.

Lajous, Adrian. 2009. "The Governance of Mexico's Oil Industry" In Levy, Santiago and Walton, Michael (eds.). *No Growth Without Equity? Inequality, Interests and Competition in Mexico*. New York; Palgrave MacMillan.

Levy, Santiago **and** Walton, Michael (eds.). 2009. *No Growth Without Equity?: Inequality, Interests, And Competition In Mexico*. New York: Palgrave MacMillan

Levy, Santiago. 2008. *Good Intentions, Bad Outcomes: Social Policy, Informality, and Economic Growth in Mexico*. Washington: Brookings Institution.

Lujambio, Alonso. 2001. "Democratization through Federalism? The National Action Party Strategy, 1939–2000" In Kevin Middlebrook (ed.). *Party Politics and the*

Struggle for Democratization in Mexico. National and State-Level Analysis of the Partido Acción Nacional. San Diego: University of California in San Diego.

Magaloni, Beatriz. 2006. *Voting for Autocracy: Hegemonic Party Survival and Its Demise in Mexico*. Cambridge: Cambridge University Press.

Magaloni, Beatriz, Weingast, Barry and Díaz-Cayeros, Alberto. 2008. *Why Developing Countries Sabotage Economic Growth: Land Reform in Mexico*. Typescript. Stanford University.

McCaa, Robert. 2001. Missing Millions: The human cost of the Mexican Revolution. University of Minnesota Population Center http://www.hist.umn.edu/~rmccaa/missmill/abstract.htm.

North, Douglass, Wallis, John, and Weingast, Barry. 2009. *Violence and Social Orders: A Conceptual Framework for Interpreting Recorded Human History*. Cambridge: Cambridge University Press.

Razo, Armando. 2008. *Social Foundations of Limited Dictatorship Networks and Private Protection During Mexico's Early Industrialization*. Stanford: Stanford University Press.

Sanderson, Susan Walsh. 1984. *Land Reform in Mexico, 1910 – 1980*. New York: Academic Press.

Smith, Peter. 1979. *Labyrinths of Power: Political Recruitment in Twentieth Century Mexico*. Princeton, NJ: Princeton University Press.

Tornell, Aaron and Lane, Philip. 1999. "Are Windfalls a Curse? A Non-Representative Agent Model of the Current Account and Fiscal Policy," NBER Working Papers 4839, National Bureau of Economic Research.

Turner, John Kenneth. 1912. *Barbarous Mexico. An Indictment of a Cruel and Corrupt System*. London: Cassell and Company.

Warman, Arturo. 1980. *"We Come to Object": The Peasants of Morelos and the National State*. Baltimore, MD: The Johns Hopkins University Press.

Wilkie, James. 1978. *La Revolución Mexicana (1910–1976): Gasto Federal y Cambio Social*. México, DF: Fondo de Cultura Económica.

Zepeda, Guillermo. 2000. *Transformación Agraria. Los Derechos de Propiedad en el Campo Mexicano Bajo el Nuevo Marco Institucional*. Mexico: M.A. Porrúa.

EIGHT

From Limited Access to Open Access Order in Chile, Take Two

Patricio Navia

8.1 Introduction

After having failed at transitioning from a limited access order (LAO) to an open access order (OAO) in the 1970s, Chile embarked on a second transition starting in 1990. If the democratic breakdown of 1973 dramatically proved the failure of the first transition, the consolidation of democracy and sustained economic growth experienced since the end of the Pinochet regime are symptoms of the presence of the three doorstep conditions necessary for an OAO to exist. The institutional structure that fosters gradualism and pragmatism and that guarantees private property rights – and that evolved out of the authoritarian enclaves left in place by the outgoing dictatorship – have allowed the doorstep conditions to become relatively permanent features of the social, economic, and political order in Chile. The solid economic growth in the 1990–2010 period, due to market-friendly policies, has allowed the government to adopt ambitious poverty reduction initiatives and other socially inclusive policies and has helped consolidate and legitimize the political and economic model. If Chile continues on this path, the nation will become the first Latin American country to complete a transition to an OAO. In what follows, I first discuss the previous failed experience of transitioning from an LAO to an OAO (1925–73) and, drawing lessons from those failed experiences, I then discuss the successful experience of economic growth and democratic consolidation since the end of the dictatorship in 1990.

Figure 8.1 summarizes the different time periods of the LAO order and its evolution since the early twentieth century. Between the adoption of the 1925 constitution – and the implementation of universal suffrage and competitive elections – and the breakdown of 1973, Chile had an LAO unable to cope with demands for social and economic inclusion. Rents were distributed

Table 8.1 *Summary of LAO moments in Chile*

Time Periods	Dominant Coalition	Rents	Assessment
1925–1973	Urban elites (including labor unions and political parties), rural landed elites, mining elites	Mining exports, Import-Substituting Industrialization and domestic markets	Insufficient inclusion. Urbanization as a result of high social, economic, and political exclusion in rural areas.
1973–1990	Military rule, landed oligarchy and urban elites (excluding labor unions and political parties)	Mining exports, increasing adoption of export-oriented and free market policies	System based on social and political exclusion. Repression allowed for the adoption of economic reforms that adversely affected labor unions and public sector workers
1990–2009	Urban elites, export sector, mining elites, and political parties	Mining exports, free market, export-oriented economy, slow but sustained growth of domestic middle-class markets	Rapid economic growth and increased earmarked government social spending have produced more inclusion.

Source: Author

among the elites – which included urban labor unions – but large segments of the population were excluded and forced into poverty and destitution, particularly in rural areas. During the military dictatorship, organized labor and political parties were excluded from the dominant coalition. The nature of rents varied as market-friendly, export-oriented policies replaced import-substituting industrialization. Under military rule, rapid urbanization continued, but a large urban poor class was destitute and marginalized, without access to political or social rights. Finally, since the restoration of democracy, the dominant coalition has extended to political parties, the middle-class urban sectors, and the export sector. The landed rural elites have reinvented themselves into export elites and the mining sector has expanded beyond state-owned mining enterprises into foreign and domestic privately owned companies. Earmarked policies have also achieved a drastic reduction in poverty. But inequality remains high. Though the country is headed in a good direction and the roadmap to reduce inequality and produce social and economic inclusion appears to be sustainable in the long term, the threat of growing demands for immediate social and economic inclusion has not disappeared. Thus, though Chile seems well positioned to advance from an LAO to an OAO in the next decades, the main cause of the previous failure at making that transition has not fully disappeared.

8.2 Limited Access Order in Pre-Pinochet Democratic Chile

Although by regional standards, Chile's democracy in the second half of the twentieth century was among the most developed and institutionalized, the LAO that emerged in that country met only two of the three doorstep conditions. Though Chile had rule of law for elites and perpetually lived organizations in the public and private spheres, as the bloody coup showed, there was no consolidated control of the military by the democratic government. As political demands for social and economic inclusion eventually resulted in the election of a socialist government that actively sought to redistribute income and wealth, the absence of that third doorstep condition facilitated the military reaction pushed for by some of the sectors threatened by the growing power and influence of the newcomers.

True, the system shattered by the 1973 coup was not an inclusive or sufficiently institutionalized democracy. The election of Salvador Allende, who promised a *Chilean road to Socialism*, and the previous sweeping victory by Christian Democratic (PDC) Eduardo Frei, who advocated a *Revolution in Liberty*, reflect that the old democratic system was not functioning very well (Drake 1978; Garretón 1989; Gil, E. et al. 1979; Kaufman 1972; Loveman 1976; Loveman 1988; Stallings 1978; Stallings and Zimbalist 1975; Valenzuela 1977; Valenzuela and Valenzuela 1976). The average annual growth between 1960 and 1970 was 4.1 percent, but only 1.7 percent when measured in per capita terms. According to World Bank figures, inflation averaged twenty-seven percent in the 1960s. Chile was a profoundly unequal society; the poorest twenty percent received 3.7 percent of national income in 1967, while the richest twenty percent received 56.5 percent (Beyer 1997).

To be sure, political inclusion grew in the second half of the twentieth century. After women's enfranchisement in 1949, 29.1 percent of voting-aged Chileans cast ballots in 1952. When Frei was elected in 1964, 61.6 percent of eligible voters went to the polls. In the last election before the coup, held in March of 1973, 69.1 percent of voting-aged citizens cast a ballot in that highly polarized contest (Navia 2004). The growing political polarization was caused by the efforts to promote social and economic inclusion. However, the inability of the state apparatus to make education, healthcare, and other public services more inclusive rendered the democratic system incapable of accommodating newcomers. The newly enfranchised population wanted in, but the structure of the state could not survive unaltered with the additional pressure to distribute resources (Jocelyn-Holt 1998). Although the military dictatorship was not inevitable (Garretón and Moulián 1983; Valenzuela 1978), nor was the legacy of human rights violations, Chile's old democracy, built around the premise of limited social inclusion, could not survive because of its own limitations to bring about sufficient social and economic inclusion. In what follows, I discuss the two failed moments of LAO experienced by the country in the twentieth century and then discuss its third and successful attempt.

8.2.1 The Deepening of LAO, 1925–1973

The history of Chile since its independence in 1810 has been characterized by inequality and restrictive access to decision making and limited political rights. Landed elites – and increasingly mining interests since the late nineteenth century – based their economic and political power on low wages and restricted political rights for the large majority of the landless population, including indigenous persons and rural *mestizo* dwellers. Political institutions were designed to strengthen and maintain that exclusionary structure. Although there were limited democratic practices to elect the president and members of the legislature after the mid-nineteenth century, restrictions on enfranchisement rights made it very difficult for the disposed to vote and have institutional influence over the political system. As Table 8.1 shows, the percentage of those who voted in Chile remained low well into the twentieth century, reaching more than ten percent of the voting-aged population only after 1920.

Although there had been considerable labor union organizing in the early twentieth century (DeShazo 1983; Drake 1978; Loveman 2001) and a competitive – though elitist – political party system emerged in the late nineteenth century (Valenzuela 1995), the nation was characterized by social, economic, and political exclusion. The election of President Arturo Alessandri in 1920, after a campaign on a platform that catered to labor union and middle-class voters, brought a political sea change resulting in an end to the old two-party oligarchy.

Table 8.2 *Electoral participation in Chile, 1870–1973*

Year	Total Population ('000)	Voting Age Population ('000)	Voters ('000)	Voters as % Total Population	Voters as % Voting-aged Population
	(a)	(b)	(c)	(d)=(c)/(a)	(e)=(c)/(b)
1870	1,943	919	31	1.6	3.3
1876	2,116	1,026	80	3.8	7.8
1885	2,507	1,180	79	3.1	6.7
1894	2,676	1,304	114	4.3	8.7
1915	3,530	1,738	150	4.2	8.6
1920	3,730	1,839	167	4.5	9.1
1932	4,425	2,287	343	7.8	15.0
1942	5,219	2,666	465	8.9	17.4
1952*	5,933	3,278	954	16.1	29.1
1958	7,851	3,654	1,236	15.7	33.8
1964	8,387	4,088	2,512	30.0	61.6
1970	9,504	5,202	2,923	30.8	56.2
1973	9,850	5,238	3,620	36.8	69.1

*Women gained the right to vote in 1948.
Source: Navia (2004).

Under Alessandri (1920–5 and 1932–8), a new political system emerged. A new constitution was adopted in 1925 and, after a few years of turmoil, it became the basis on which the first democratic order was established. The political party system included at least two working-class parties – socialist and communist. Enfranchisement rights were significantly expanded, as shown in Table 8.2, and political stability lasted from 1932 to 1970. Eight consecutive presidents were democratically elected. The percentage of those who voted expanded to include women and those in rural areas.

Yet, because the old order was structured around a landed oligarchy, the inclusion of the rural poor in the political system provoked such tensions that the system eventually could not cope with them. In addition, the political organization of the urban working class challenged the existing rent distribution system – based on an import-substituting industrialization scheme tilted toward factory owners rather than workers. Urban dwellers were also consumers. Because the economic system was focused on creating and protecting jobs through price controls and subsidizing industries, the interests of consumers stood in direct opposition to the interests of workers and factory owners. Factory owners demanded higher prices to meet workers' salary hike demands and the government gave in to the demands of the organized labor and industrial class to the detriment of the unorganized – but increasingly electorally active – urban poor.

Between 1925 and 1973, social and political rights expanded continuously but insufficiently. Women achieved the right to vote in 1935 for municipal elections and, in 1949, for presidential elections. An electoral reform in 1958 made it more difficult for landowners to coerce peasants into voting for the traditional oligarchic parties. As democracy expanded and consolidated, demands for inclusion produced tensions and ultimately led to instability.

The economic and political dimensions of the period were characterized by the implementation and expansion of import-substitution industrialization (ISI) policies. First adopted after the 1929 crisis – which heavily hit globalized Chile – ISI policies led to the consolidation of an urban entrepreneurial class and, later, an urban working class as well. The 1929 crisis also brought the end of nitrate exploitation in northern Chile. Eventually, copper would replace nitrate as Chile's most important export commodity. The growth of the copper industry also resulted in the formation of a strong working class in northern mining towns.

Yet, as Table 8.2 shows, most of the population remained marginalized, economically and politically. Less than seventy percent of the voting-aged population was registered to vote in 1970, a higher percentage than in the rest of Latin America but lower than in industrialized countries at the time. Fortunately, for those who sought to organize the disposed, since the mid-1960s, rapid urbanization had facilitated the growth of left-wing parties beyond their traditional organized working-class base. Additionally, political developments within conservative parties – associated to a reform within Catholicism – also led to the growth of reformist parties in rural areas. In fact, an agrarian reform was first adopted in the early 1960s. Later, with the election of reformist Eduardo Frei in 1964, a more comprehensive agrarian reform initiative was implemented. Rapid political incorporation and demands for economic and political rights, which had also led to Frei's election in 1964, helped Salvador Allende win the presidential election in 1970. However, as Allende sought to dramatically alter the distribution of political power – and ultimately rents – the landed oligarchy reacted by promoting a military coup that marked the end of the first attempt at establishing a limited access order in Chile.

The rents structure in the 1925–73 period was similar to that traditionally associated with landed oligarchies. The landed elite had had ample supply of cheap labor and a captive urban market for its goods. Those elites associated with conservative parties. They exercised quasi-monopoly control over the political system. The growth of an industrial class in urban areas, induced by the adoption of import-substituting industrialization policies, did not directly challenge the old oligarchy as many industrialists were also associated with the traditional landed oligarchies. Links and connections avoided tensions between two otherwise seemingly competing groups. Because the central government protected the agricultural sector with high tariffs and subsidized the industrial sector, the two new elites were protected by ISI policies. A limited organized working class – industrial, mining, and public sector – allowed for limited social and economic inclusion. Rents were extracted mostly by the agricultural oligarchy, ISI industrial class, public sector middle class (public education, health, services) and organized industrial and mining working class. The rural population (forty percent in 1960) and urban poor not in formal employment remained marginalized, without access.

The rents structure was also significantly shaped by the development of the mining industry, first salt pepper and, since the second half of the twentieth century, copper. Between 1901 and 1905, nitrates accounted for seventy-one percent of all exports. Their export share increased to 76.3 percent in 1906–10 (Meller 1996), but decreased considerably thereafter. Between 1901 and 1920, nitrate exploitation taxes accounted for half of fiscal revenue. In the 1921–35 period, nitrate-related taxes constituted 36.3 percent of total fiscal revenue (Meller 1996). As nitrates exports decreased and their contribution to fiscal revenues diminished, copper exports increased. Copper mining was mostly done by United States companies. The rapid growth of exports triggered a debate on the role of mining in fostering economic development. As opposed to nitrates, copper production did not generate sizable government revenues.

Before 1950, copper mining remained mostly free from government intervention. Advocates of a laissez-faire approach to mining claimed that the government should let mining enterprises do the exploitation and the government could just collect tax revenues. Excessive taxation would dissuade private companies from additional investments. Because Chile had an almost unlimited supply of copper, the higher the production by private companies, the higher the tax revenues. The experience with nitrate showed that taxing mining did not guarantee development elsewhere in the country. When the nitrate boom ended, poverty was still widespread. Even worse, governments had grown accustomed to relying excessively on nitrate export taxes. In the 1950s, the growth of left-wing parties and the expansion of the electorate – with the inclusion of lower-class voters – strengthened the argument in favor of increasing taxes on foreign mining companies. Nationalization of oil in Mexico and the larger role played by the state in Chile's economy since the 1930s, with the adoption of import-substituting industrialization policies, strengthened nationalization demands. Although most political actors agreed that mining should contribute more to fiscal revenues (in part because other sectors would be taxed less), there were disagreements on how to increase fiscal revenues. Some argued in favor of increasing taxes on mining to level that sector's rate of return with other areas of the economy. Others claimed that fiscal revenues would increase with more investments and increased production.

In the 1960s, the debate evolved from taxing private mining to nationalization. The election in 1964 of reformist Christian Democratic President Eduardo Frei (father of the homonymous president who held office in the 1990s) paved the way for partial nationalization. The "Chilenization" of copper production between 1966 and 1969, championed by Frei, was supported by all political sectors. Chilenization actually meant acquiring ownership of big private mining companies. In 1967, the state bought fifty-one percent of El Teniente from Kennecott, and twenty-five percent of Andina and Exótica. Because the price of copper rose shortly after, the government faced pressure to expand its participation in mining companies. So, in 1969, the state bought fifty-one percent of Chuquicamata and El Salvador, thus acquiring control of the most important copper mines in the country. The origin of the National Copper Corporation, CODELCO, can be traced back to the Chilenization process in 1966, though it was formally created under Pinochet in 1976.

In 1971, under the government of socialist Salvador Allende (1970–3), Congress unanimously voted for the total nationalization of copper production. Left-wing legislators also advocated for an increased state role in other areas of the economy, but right-wing parties supported only the nationalization of copper. Public opinion also overwhelmingly favored it. Nationalization made the state the sole owner of mining deposits. Existing contracts for partial nationalization with American companies Anaconda and Kennecot were cancelled. The state established means of compensating the former owners, though the details of such compensation were contentious, especially under Allende. Finally, due compensation was paid under the dictatorship.

Later, under Pinochet's regime, copper continued to play an important role in the economy. State copper giant CODELCO experienced consecutive growth in the 1970s (Meller 2000). A new constitution, enacted by the dictatorship in 1980, made the state the sole proprietor of mineral deposits.

But the Mining Law of 1982 introduced the concept of full concession by the proprietary of mineral deposits (Meller 2000). Thus, the state remained the sole owner of mineral deposits, but private investors retained permanent concession rights. This law represented an important departure from previous mining policies. If the Allende government wanted to control mining through nationalization, the military regime preferred to grant access to new investors. Thus, there was a shift in focus from the state being the owner and sole producer of copper to encouraging investment by private foreign – and eventually national – companies.

In 1977, the dictatorship enacted Decree Law 600, known as the FDI Statute. This law established special conditions and incentives for new foreign investors. Among them, a system of accelerated depreciation was introduced designed specifically to attract FDI for mining projects. The growth of private mining, however, did not occur until the late 1980s, when a democratic transition was in sight and the economy had recovered from the 1973–5 and 1982–3 recessions. Thus, rents from mining followed a similar trajectory as rents elsewhere. After a period when rents were produced for a mining elite – mostly in the hands of foreign-owned companies – and a limited mining working-class sector, the process of nationalization sought to distribute mining rents to the excluded population via government spending. The military coup of 1973 did not undo the nationalization of minerals until the late 1980s, when democracy was restored and private production once again boomed. Rents have since been distributed among the mining companies (both private and publicly owned) and the state (through taxes on mineral production, on companies' revenues, and through the production of state giant Codelco).

Despite this heavily uneven distribution of rents, the opportunities for violence potential were not widely expanded during the 1925–73 period. The landed oligarchy and the industrial sector kept close relations with the military. Left-wing reformist and revolutionary political parties were included in the system as long as they did not push their reforms too far (Allende was an exception in 1973, and a coup ensued). Labor unions protected organized labor, not the larger informal sector or rural areas (when parties and unions moved to rural areas in the mid-1960s, the political equilibrium collapsed). In fact, it can be argued, it was precisely the increase of violence potential, expressed in the political organizing of the working class and the marginalized urban poor who supported Allende, that triggered the violent reaction by the military that brought about the 1973 Pinochet coup. As the marginalized sectors came to control the central government – or at least political parties that sought to represent the "have-nots" – came to

power and sought to change the distribution of rents, the political equilibrium could no longer be sustained and the pre-1973 democratic experiment
came to an end.

As Figure 8.1 shows, Chile's journey of economic development and progress was a frustrating experience. Plagued by endemic high inflation and
particularly sensitive to the economic cycle with years of rapid growth followed by stagnation, Chile's economy underperformed Latin America in
the 1960–73 period. However, as I discuss in the next section, history began
to change during the dictatorship, specifically after the deep 1982 recession. After Chile performed below the Latin American average before 1984,
the next twenty-four years have seen Chile outperform its Latin American
neighbors in economic growth. Starting in 1984 – under military rule – the
economy began to expand robustly. Under the four Concertación administrations of Aylwin (1990–4), PDC Eduardo Frei (1994–2000), PPD Ricardo
Lagos (2000–6), and socialist Michelle Bachelet (2006–10), Chile experienced its longest run of economic growth and poverty reduction. As such,
economic growth has strengthened democracy. Moreover, at least the
Concertación would argue, it has also fostered it.

8.3 Dictatorship and the Foundations of the New LAO, 1973–1990

The 1973 democratic breakdown gave way to a fifteen-year military dictatorship led by General Augusto Pinochet. Political rights were constrained.
Rents were redistributed away from workers and political parties into the
landed oligarchy and a growing business sector. A new constitution was
adopted in 1980. Private property was protected and individual rights were
favored over collective rights.

Although the military government was initially triggered by the reaction
of landed elites against the efforts to promote redistribution, the dictatorship undertook the ambitious goal of redefining the economic model. Under
the leadership of a team of economists trained at the neoliberal economics
school of the University of Chicago, the so-called Chicago Boys pushed
replacing ISI with market-friendly neoliberal policies. State enterprises
were privatized, regulations and oversight structures were eliminated, and
government spending was drastically reduced – especially after the 1982
economic crisis. The involvement of the state in social spending was rede-
fined as well. Pensions were privatized in the early 1980s and vouchers were
introduced to elementary and secondary education to allow for the entry of
private providers and foster competition. A similar scheme was adopted in
health provision policies and public housing.

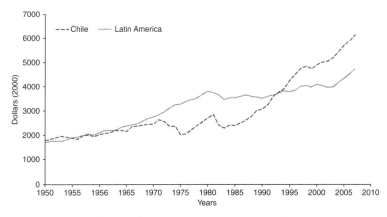

Figure 8.1 The Chilean and Latin American economic performance, 1950–2010.
Source: Compiled by author with data from World Bank Development Indicators.

Although the Chilean economy suffered badly from the crisis triggered by the Allende regime and the 1973 coup and the country paid a heavy toll after the 1982 economic crisis, Figure 8.1 shows that the Chilean economic miracle took off during the latter part of the Pinochet dictatorship. Starting in 1985, Chile's GDP grew more steadily than that of the rest of Latin America. A few years after democracy was restored in 1990, Chile's GDP surpassed that of the rest of the region and it has continued its fast growth ever since.

The Pinochet regime did not embrace neoliberalism from the start (Barros 2002; Cavallo, Salazar et al. 1997; Cristi 2000; Huneeus 2007; Vial Correa 2002). More preoccupied with eliminating the Marxist threat, the regime began to talk about "goals, not deadlines" (*metas, no plazos*) after it gained political control and stabilized the economy. The 1980 constitution, approved in a plebiscite held under undemocratic conditions, entrenched a political system full of deadlock provisions. Authoritarian enclaves hindered the emergence of full-flown democracy. A carefully designed institutional system of checks and balances made it clear that, even if the military were not to remain in power, the constitutional order would protect private property and consolidate a neoliberal economic model (Cavallo, Salazar et al. 1997; Huneeus 2007).

Yet, because even custom-made shoes bind (Barros 2002), the constitutional order masterminded to perpetuate the military in power provided an opportunity for the opposition to bring about democracy (Aylwin 1998; Boeninger 1997; Zaldívar Larraín 1995). After an economic crisis in 1982, the government opened political room for the opposition and social protests threatened the stability of the regime; democratic political parties seized the opportunity provided for in the constitution and agreed to hold a plebiscite to decide on a new eight-year presidential period for Pinochet.

Although the plebiscite was held under conditions that favored him, on October 5, 1988, Chileans rejected Pinochet. Democratic elections were held in 1989 and democracy returned in March 1990. Yet, because Pinochet was defeated within a constitutional framework of his choosing, the cost of forcing him to step down was to acquiesce to the institutional order entrenched in the constitution (Ensalaco 1994; Ensalaco 1995; Heiss and Navia 2007; Loveman 1991; Loveman 1994). A plebiscite approved constitutional reforms proposed by the dictatorship in mid-1989. True, the Concertación asked for more comprehensive reforms (Andrade Geywitz 1991; Aylwin, Briones et al. 1985; Geisse and Ramírez 1989). Acquiescence to the reforms and the overwhelming majority support in the plebiscite made it easier for the new democratic regime to take power peacefully, but also legitimated the constitution (Heiss and Navia 2007; Loveman and Lira 2000; Portales 2000).

The economic model initially implemented by the dictatorship and its economic team (Fontaine Aldunate 1988; Valdés 1995; Vergara 1985) has been the basis of the economic policies adopted since the return of democracy. Although several reforms – aimed at increasing social spending, reducing poverty, and creating a safety net for the needy – have been championed by successive Concertación governments (Boeninger 2007; Larraín and Vergara 2000; Martínez and Díaz 1996; Meller 2005; Ottone and Vergara 2006), the fact that the Concertación itself identifies its economic model as *neoliberalism with a human face* and *social market economy* reflects the extent to which Pinochet's legacy remains a defining factor.

When PDC Patricio Aylwin became president, the Concertación government began to eliminate other authoritarian enclaves and adopted reforms to reduce rampant poverty levels. With 38.7 percent of Chileans living in poverty, and one in every three of those in extreme poverty (Ministerio de Planificación 2006), the new government was hard pressed to show tangible results. Widespread poverty and social and economic exclusion could trigger an authoritarian regression or democratic instability (Aylwin 1998; Meller 2005). Thus, "democracy to the extent possible" – though never formally stated – became the guiding principle for the transition under Aylwin and democratic consolidation under his successors.

A number of authoritarian enclaves that survived the 1989 reforms made it difficult for the Concertación to carry out its policies (Drake and Jaksic 1995; Garretón 1999; Portales 2000). Although the Concertación enjoyed majority support in all parliamentary elections, non-elected senators, appointed by the outgoing military regime, stripped the Concertación of its electoral majority in the upper chamber. The non-elected senators gave the right-wing opposition an effective veto power that constrained the Concertación beyond the already strict limits imposed by the 1980 constitution.

Other scholars also pointed to the electoral system as an additional anti-majoritarian constraint (Angell 2003; Siavelis 2002; Siavelis and Valenzuela 1997; Valenzuela 2005). Designed as an insurance mechanism against an electoral defeat, the across-the-board two-seat proportional representation system makes it difficult to transform an electoral majority into a majority in Congress (Navia 2005). The electoral system tends to favor large coalitions at the expense of smaller ones (particularly the Communist Party). As Table 8.3 shows, the Alianza has systematically obtained a larger share of seats than its share of votes, but the electoral system has not severely underrepresented the Concertación's vote share (Zucco 2007). Critics of the system point to the fact that smaller parties are left without representation (Huneeus 2006). Yet that cannot be considered antidemocratic. Single-member majoritarian systems punish minority parties but are not antidemocratic.

The electoral system does have clearly negative features, but they have more to do with the structure of incentives on the political system. Because the two large coalitions tend to equally split the two seats in more than ninety-five percent of the districts, voters end up having little to say on the seat distribution in Congress. In every district, voters can only decide which candidate from each coalition will get the seat, but a sixty percent to forty percent vote advantage for one coalition will produce exactly the same one to one seat divide as a forty percent to sixty percent vote distribution. The lack of competition embedded in the system undermines one of the essential components of democracy, competitive elections.

The presence of designated senators certainly distorted seat allocation in the Senate until a constitutional reform eliminated them in 2005. Nonetheless, because it was imposed by the outgoing regime, the electoral system remains the most symbolic pending authoritarian enclave. A set of constitutional reforms passed under President Lagos in 2005 eliminated most remaining authoritarian enclaves. But there was a lack of agreement on how to replace the binominal system. The Concertación favored a more proportional representation system that would allow the Communist Party to gain seats in Congress, but the Alianza defended the binominal system. The binominal system should be considered an authoritarian enclave because of its origin, not because of its effects.

After the 2005 reforms, the constitution regained democratic legitimacy. Although some criticize the fact that it was first adopted under military

Table 8.3 *Vote and seat distribution in congress in Chile for the Concertación and Alianza coalitions, 1989–2005*

Election year	Alianza				Concertación			
	Chamber of Deputies		Senate		Chamber of Deputies		Senate	
	% Votes	% Seats	% Votes	% Seats (*)	% Votes	% Seats	% Votes	% Seats (*)
1989	34.2	40.0	34.9	42.1 (52.3)	51.5	57.5	54.6	57.9 (46,8)
1993	36.7	41.7	37.3	50.0 (54.3)	55.4	58.3	55.5	50.0 (45.7)
1997	36.3	39.2	36.6	47.4 (51.1)	50.5	57.5	49.9	52.6 (48.9)
2001	44.3	47.5	44.0	50.0 (50.0)	47.9	51.2	51.3	50.0 (50.0)
2005	38.7	45.0	37.2	44.7**	51.8	51.7	55.7	52.6
2009	43.5	48.3	45.2	50.0	43.5	47.5	43.2	50.0

*Including non-elected senators.
** it does not include one senator elected as an independent.
Source: Compiled by author with data from http://www.elecciones.gov.cl and (Engel and Navia 2006).

rule, the 1980 constitution has acquired democratic legitimacy during the twenty years of democratic rule. True, there are areas where more democratic reforms could be implemented – such as the direct election of regional Intendentes or voting rights for those residing abroad – but all remaining authoritarian enclaves were eliminated in 2005. For sure, Chile has pending issues in dealing with a complex human rights legacy (Aguilar 2002; Bacic 2002; Baxter 2005; Roth-Arriaza and Mariezcurrena 2006). New human rights concerns have emerged as well (Espejo 2008). But all democracies have such issues. The fact that they are part of public debate signals the health of the democratic process.

Other issues associated with democratic institutional design, such as the influence, scope, and powers of the constitutional tribunal, political party system reform (Fontaine, Larroulet et al. 2008), campaign finance reform (Valdés Prieto 2000), and balance of powers between the executive and the legislative (Burgos and Walker 2003; Linz 1990; Linz, Lijphart et al. 1990) also pertain to normal democratic consolidation debates. True, some have questioned the legitimacy of a democracy built upon a constitution designed by an authoritarian government (Cristi and Ruiz-Tagle 2006), but even those critics acknowledge that Chile today has a full-fledged democracy.

8.4 Transition from LAO to OAO in Democratic Chile, 1990–2010

The defeat of Pinochet in 1988 opened the road toward democracy. When President Bachelet completed her mandate in 2010 and turned power over to Sebastián Piñera, the moderate candidate of the right-wing Alianza, the Concertación completed twenty years in power, the longest rule for any coalition since universal suffrage was adopted. The Concertación's initial goal was to secure a smooth transition to democracy. The Concertación's first president, Patricio Aylwin, sought to deal with pending issues (such as human rights abuses) and launched an aggressive drive to build democratic institutions and overpower the institutional constraint left by Pinochet (Cavallo 1998; Ensalaco 1994; Ensalaco 1995; Heiss and Navia 2007; Loveman 1991; Loveman 1994; Otano 1995; Rojo 1995). Because unemployment was widespread, the Aylwin government prioritized a growth-inducing, poverty-reducing economic policy. For democracy to flourish, the government had to better distribute economic growth. Thus, though the Concertación realized that, by not taking on authoritarian legacies and enclaves right on, the new institutions of democracy would consolidate and gain legitimacy – including nonappointed senators, a powerful National Security Council, and a tutelary role for the military – the Aylwin administration favored economic development and poverty reduction rather than institutional change (Aylwin 1998; Boeninger 1997; Boeninger 2007). Figure 8.2 shows that the strategy proved successful. Unemployment went down, the economy grew rapidly, and inflation was brought under control after a spike provoked by increased government spending by the dictatorship in 1988 and 1989.

Because of Aylwin's success, the Concertación easily won the 1993 presidential elections. Frei continued the same *social market economic policies* during his six-year tenure. By the time Lagos became the third Concertación president in 2000, the center-left coalition had become inseparable from a market-friendly economic model. The Concertación proved that democracy would not inevitably lead to polarization and social upheaval. As Figure 8.2 shows, in its twenty years in power, the Concertación did exceptionally well in bringing about economic growth, reducing inflation, and producing the conditions for more and better employment. Chileans living

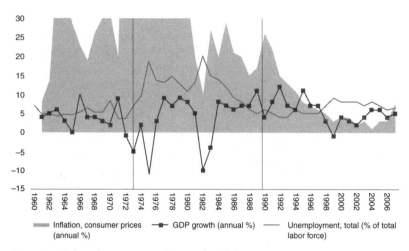

Figure 8.2 Selected economic indicators for Chile, 1960–2007.
Source: World Banks's World Development Indicators and selected data from CEPAL
and (Bardón M, Carrasco A. et al. 1985) Inflation for 1973–9 was 362 percent, 505 per-
cent, 375 percent, 212 percent, 92 percent, 40 percent, 33 percent, respectively.

in poverty decreased from 38.6 percent in 1990 to 27.7 percent in 1994.
Though part of that reduction is explained by the economic growth experienced since 1985, a tax reform brokered with the Alianza in the opposi-
tion-controlled Senate allowed Aylwin access to fresh resources to combat
poverty. Because the 1980 constitution provided for the outgoing regime
to directly and indirectly appoint nine non-elected senators – who transformed the Concertación's 22–16-seat majority among elected seats into a
25–22-seat majority for the opposition – the Concertación could not transform its commanding electoral majority into a majority in Congress. Thus,
all reforms had to be bargained with the overrepresented conservative
opposition. Poverty reduction continued during the Frei and Lagos administrations. Though economic growth was less robust – as Figure 8.2 shows –
under Lagos and Bachelet than under Frei or Aylwin, the Concertación
succeeded in reducing poverty.

Not surprising, Chileans rewarded the Concertación with electoral
majorities in all contests held since 1989. Until the Alianza won the 2009
presidential election, four presidential elections, five legislative elections,
and five municipal elections held between 1989 and 2008 had been won by
the Concertación. Democracy under the Concertación resulted in increased
welfare, better living conditions for all, less poverty, more social and political inclusion, growing levels of participation, and better indicators of civil

and political liberties (Lagos Escobar 2005; Stein, Tommasi et al. 2006; UNDP 2005; Walker 2006).

8.5 The Post-Pinochet Democratic Institutional System

The institutional system is based on the 1980 constitution adopted by the Pinochet dictatorship. Thus, democracy in Chile flourished within the constraints imposed by the dictatorship. Despite the fact that it was designed to limit and prevent democracy, the 1980 constitution became the tool used by the democratic opposition to bring an end to the Pinochet dictatorship. For the constitutionally mandated plebiscite in 1988, the opposition organized to campaign actively against Pinochet – who was nominated as the candidate by the Junta. Pinochet lost the plebiscite and elections were indeed held in December 1989. The center-left opposition coalition known as the Concertación won those elections.

Yet, after the Pinochet defeat in the plebiscite of October 1988 and before the elections were held in December 1989, the outgoing Pinochet regime and the Concertación opposition began discussing reforms to the constitution that would eliminate some of the most outrageous authoritarian provisions and, in turn, would also legitimize it by having the democratic opposition acquiesce to a number of constitutional reforms. Those reforms, correctly deemed as insufficient by the democratic opposition, were approved in a new plebiscite in mid-1989. The Concertación benefited by having a more democratic constitution to establish the framework for the transition to democracy, and in exchange the outgoing regime could claim a democratic legitimacy to its authoritarian constitution.

The 1989 reforms were not the only constitutional reforms adopted. Several other reforms were adopted in the 1990–2005 period to strip the constitution of other authoritarian enclaves. The 2005 reforms – championed by President Ricardo Lagos – were the most comprehensive reform package adopted since 1989. With the 2005 reforms, the constitution was left without any remaining authoritarian enclave. Issues remain with regards to the electoral system and the powers and attributions of non-elected bodies – like the constitutional tribunal – but those are issues common to other democracies as well and cannot be considered authoritarian enclaves.

Chile has one of the strongest presidential systems in Latin America, with a bicameral congress, a proportional electoral system with a district magnitude of two, an independent judiciary, and other enforcement mechanisms. Checks and balances are designed to allow for slow but incremental change, preventing policy instability as a result of changes in the balance of political power (Aninat et al. 2010).

The executive has exclusive legislative initiative on several policy areas, has a highly hierarchical control of the budget process, and has an array of urgency and veto options, which make it a de facto agenda setter. Yet capable law makers and a long legislative process with supermajorities for most economic policies impose on the executive the need to negotiate its legislative agenda with Congress. Presidents are elected for four-year terms and are prevented from running for immediate reelection. The constitutionally mandated agenda-setting powers enjoyed by the president are substantial. The executive has the sole legislative initiative over legislation concerning the political and administrative divisions of the state, its financial administration, the budget process, and the selling of state assets. Also, the executive has sole initiative in areas such as taxation, labor regulation, social security, and legislation related to the armed forces. In addition, the executive controls the flow of legislation through the use of "urgencies" – a constitutional mechanism designed to give the executive the power to force a rapid legislature vote on an initiative (Aninat et al. 2010).

Although, given the powers of the president, it is weak by comparison to the U.S. Congress, the Chilean legislature is unusually professional and technically competent by Latin American standards. The lack of term limits and high entry barriers for challengers allow Congress members to develop long legislative careers.

Constitutionally mandated supermajority thresholds for special legislation help offset the executive's substantial agenda-setting power. They range from an absolute majority of the total membership (as opposed to a majority of those present) up to two-thirds of the members. Those provisions permit a minority in one legislative chamber to block legislation. With the exception of the weakest threshold (a majority of total membership), when in power, the Concertación always faced the need to negotiate changes to legislation that require supermajority approval with the conservative opposition in at least one legislative chamber. These high thresholds, together with the repeated interaction of the president with Congress for long-time horizons, have led to tit-for-tat equilibrium legislative strategy. "Consensus politics" has emerged as the president does not only negotiate with the opposition bills requiring qualified majorities, but most legislative initiatives (Aninat et al. 2010).

Socioeconomic actors participate in the policy making process at a high level of aggregation, either through business organizations, labor unions, or influential think tanks and NGOs. The corporate sector is well organized in multilayered business federations that represent all areas of economic activity. They have high media standing and interact repeatedly with the executive and political parties in legislative negotiations that affect their interests. Moreover, the lack of transparent, well-designed campaign financing mechanisms allows these interest groups to exert unobservable influence in the political parties and think tanks' legislative agendas (Aninat et al. 2010).

Other social actors are business associations and economic conglomerates. Since the mid-twentieth century, a number of business associations have emerged as strong advocates of their particularistic interests. Thus, the Sociedad Nacional de Agricultura (SNA) brings together most large and mid-sized agro-industrial entrepreneurs. The Cámara Chilena de la Construcción (CChC) brings together the construction and infrastructure sectors. Altogether, six of such business associations form the Confederación de la Producción y el Comercio (CPC), the leading association that defends the interests of the entrepreneurial class. After having actively participated in shaping government policies in the 1940–60 period, as a result of governments that promoted import-substituting industrialization, these business sector organizations entered the political arena in the 1970s. By first opposing the socialist Allende government (1970–3) and then supporting the Pinochet dictatorship – but also opposing liberalizing, market-friendly policies adopted during military rule, these organizations slowly withdrew from an open political role after democracy was restored. In the late 1990s, the CPC made a conscious effort to renew its leadership so that it could present a less political face. In part because the policies championed by Concertación governments had produced positive results and also because it was in the best interest of their organizations to develop and maintain good relations with the government – regardless of the political color of the party in power – the business organizations made their own transition away from authoritarian rule. Most recently, the CPC has elected a former Allende supporter turned businessman as its leader in 2008 (Aninat et al. 2010).

Regarding informal networks between business associations and political parties, this can be of special importance for a small country like Chile with a very unequal income distribution, where economic power is highly concentrated. If we consider that sixty percent of the political elite of Chile (particularly deputies) come from private schools, maybe a social network between business people and political actors who share the same origin is developed (Espinoza 2010).

Labor unions also play an important role. Historical episodes added to specific economic conditions have led to more organized and strong public sector federations. Teachers, public health sector employees, and public employees in general – are well organized and play an important role in the electoral base of the Concertación coalition. Some of these labor unions are: CUT (National Association of Unions), ANEF (National Federation of Public Sector Workers), Teachers Union, Health Workers Union, Municipal Employees Union, and the CODELCO workers' union. The preferences of these socioeconomic players are related mainly to the maximization of job stability and salary increases based on seniority rather than performance (Aninat et al. 2010).

The Concertación parties – most notably the PDC and PS – have strong ties to labor unions. Public sector unions are among the strongest in Chile, including the powerful CODELCO state copper company union. Most unions are controlled by militants of the Socialist and Christian Democratic Parties. The Communist Party, to the left of the Concertación, also has a strong presence in labor unions. In fact, Communist Party militants led the national association of unions CUT for several years during the 1990s. Other powerful labor unions include the Teachers Union (Colegio de Profesores) where the Communist Party has commanding support, and the Health Professionals and Health Workers Unions (CONFUSAM) where the Socialist Party commands strongest support. Most unions represent formal sector workers and many union members are public sector workers, thus they have incentives to work within the system to obtain higher wages and more benefits.

The influence of unions within the party apparatus is far larger than their membership numbers would seem to indicate. Unions can mobilize organized voters and become crucial in manning campaigns and providing avenues to disseminate information to politically sophisticated unionized workers. This is mainly due to ideological features. Public workers (from the education, mining, health, and state sectors, among others) lean to the left, so they are more prone to support organized left-wing associations that defend, or seem to defend, public workers' rights from a leftist point of view. Thus, even though they are not formal members of these associations, they feel represented by them. This situation put these socioeconomic players in a privileged arena for exerting influence over specific actors in the policy making process. The limited understanding of public workers about complex problems and solutions, added to their leftist ideological leaning, gives unions enough space to act under opacity, promoting actions related to vested interests at the expense of more technical solutions. Given the strong influence of unions over the citizens they represent – formally or informally – and the power they have to threaten political stability through demonstrations, political parties – especially the PS and PDC – find it difficult to adopt policy positions that will alienate their strong union base support. Unions have incentives to exert pressure within the political process, as they largely represent public sector workers. Because a large majority of Chileans are not union members but depend on public sector services – such as health and education – unions have disincentives to become violent in their protests. Public opinion polls show that people prefer delivered public services to solidarity with public sector workers on strike (Aninat et al. 2010).

Think tanks and NGOs play an active role in the policy making process, both technical and political. Think tanks are independent and privately financed, but most of them are close to one or more political parties. There is a two-way relationship between the parties and think tanks. The latter offers legislative assistance in exchange for advancing their ideological agendas. The lack of congressional staffers to support the legislative work of congressmembers reinforces this relationship (Aninat et al. 2010).

Other social organizations like NGOs (Paz Ciudadana, the Chilean Chapter of Transparency International) and the churches (traditionally Catholic but increasingly others) play an important role in the aggregation and representation of social preferences in Chile's policy making process (Aninat et al. 2010).

Political parties are highly disciplined and organized, but they mostly lack technical expertise. Parties are much more concerned with organizing militants to run and win elections than with preparing technocrats who can design and analyze public policies. Thus, think tanks have emerged as the policy arm of the two coalitions. Given that the executive controls the legislative agenda, opposition parties can only react to government-sponsored legislation. Because bargaining is often necessary for the government to achieve majority and super majority support in Congress to advance its legislative initiatives, opposition think tanks advise opposition legislators on what issues they should compromise and what items they should stick to their initial positions. In fact, it is often the case that the government ministers negotiate directly with representatives from policy experts from opposition think tanks who also formally serve as legislative assistants for opposition senators and deputies.

In the Alianza coalition, the Instituto de Libertad y Desarrollo (LyD) has evolved into the think tank that provides the UDI with policy recommendations and with advice on how to vote on government's proposed legislation. For RN, Instituto Libertad (a different think tank) serves the same purpose. Because it is better funded and staffed, and because it has had a more constant leadership, the Instituto de Libertad y Desarrollo has emerged as the most influential think tank within the Alianza. Also, because the UDI is a much more disciplined, top-down party, the Instituto deLibertad y Desarrollo can better influence the positions of UDI legislators than Instituto Libertad can the position of RN congresspersons (Aninat et al. 2010).

As nonprofit corporations, these think tanks can receive non-tax deductable private funding from companies and interested parties. But as private entities, the think tanks are not required to release information on what sources of funding they receive. There is plenty of anecdotal evidence, however – widely reported in newspapers and talked about among Concertación and Alianza legislators – that the Instituto de Libertad y Desarrollo receives funding from companies and entrepreneurs associated with the most conservative positions within the Catholic church and with close ties to state companies privatized during the Pinochet dictatorship. The Instituto de Libertad y Desarrollo is the think tank most closely aligned with the neoliberal economic policies promoted by the Pinochet dictatorship. The Instituto Libertad, on the other hand, is comprised primarily of technocrats associated with RN. As a nonprofit corporation, Instituto Libertad gets funding from private sources as well. In addition, the influential Centro de Estudios Públicos (CEP) serves as supplier of policy positions for right-wing legislators. The policy positions announced and defended by the independent CEP occasionally serve as a signaling device for right-wing legislators. The CEP was originally created by the Matte family – one of the wealthiest family conglomerates in Chile with financial interests in forestry, electricity, and almost every other sector of the Chilean economy. CEP is funded by contributions from private donations – mostly private companies – and its nonparty ideology champions the defense of market-friendly policies and liberal capitalism. Occasionally, Concertación governments sought to negotiate policy agreements with CEP in order to obtain legitimacy before presenting legislative initiatives to Congress. Thus, the Concertación used CEP to bypass the think tanks more directly associated with the Alianza (Aninat et al. 2010).

Think tanks are also important for the Concertación. But since the center-left coalition has continuously occupied the executive power in Chile since the restoration of democracy, technocrats were often lured into government positions from Concertación-friendly think tanks. For example, after Michelle Bachelet was elected president, she appointed three ministers – including the finance minister – from among members of the liberal-leaning, Concertación-friendly Expansiva think tank. Similarly, in 1990, President Patricio Aylwin recruited many of his technocrats – including his finance minister, Alejandro Foxley – from the Cieplan think tank (Aninat et al. 2010).

Thus, Concertación think tanks have failed to remain permanent actors in the political arena. They form and, when successful, are rapidly recruited into the executive. Because the executive effectively controls the legislative agenda and drafts most relevant legislative initiatives, Concertación think tank technocrats have every incentive to join the government. As a result, Concertación think tanks are much weaker and more poorly staffed than Alianza think tanks. This adversely affects Concertación legislators, who have little technical support vis-à-vis the Concertación government when discussing policy reforms. Except for those legislators who develop a personal interest in specific policy issues, Concertación legislators can count on less technical support and expert advice when exercising their legislative role (Aninat et al. 2010).

8.6 The Virtuous Cycle of Democracy and Economic Development

In Chile, economic development and democratic consolidation occurred concurrently under the Concertación. As the Pinochet regime ended in 1990, the economy was showing strong and dynamic growth. The 1988 plebiscite was held under favorable economic conditions for the dictatorship. Yet the outgoing regime did not benefit electorally. When Aylwin won in 1989, the economy was growing at unprecedented levels. The sound fundamentals of Chile's economy made it easier for Aylwin to focus on strengthening social policy and alleviating poverty.

The rapid economic growth experienced during his tenure (7.8 percent annual average) and earmarked social programs helped reduced poverty dramatically from 38.6 percent in 1990 to 27.6 percent in 1994, Table 8.4. True, the government privileged poverty reduction rather than tackling inequality. Inequality only began to decrease after 2000. Still, the reforms first adopted by Aylwin set the country on an impressive path of poverty reduction that made Chile a successful case of poverty alleviation in Latin America (Meller 2005; Vega Fernández 2007).

In recent years, income inequality has also improved. As Table 8.5 shows, since 2000, the lowest income deciles have seen their income grow at higher rates than the top deciles. As a result of earmarked government spending, sustained economic growth, improvements in pensions for the elderly, and the entry into the labor force of new age cohorts with higher levels of education, income inequality has gone down. Naturally, as older cohorts with lower levels of education retire and new highly educated cohorts enter the

Table 8.4 *Poverty and extreme poverty in Chile, 1990–2006*

	1990	1992	1994	1996	1998	2000	2003	2006	2009
Poverty	38.6	32.9	27.6	23.2	21.7	20.2	18.7	13.7	15.1
Extreme Poverty	13.0	9.0	7.6	5.8	5.6	5.6	4.7	3.2	3.5
Gini Coefficient	0.57	.58	.58	.57	.58	0.57	0.55	0.54	0.55

Source: Encuesta CASEN, 2006, 2009.

Table 8.5 *Per capita income growth rate by income segments, 2000–2006*

Income Decile	2000–3	2003–6	2000–6
Lowest	10.2	22.2	34.6
2	6.5	17.5	25.1
3	5.7	16.4	23.1
4	4.7	15.7	21.1
5	3.3	14.7	18.5
6	3.3	13.5	17.3
7	2.6	12.7	15.6
8	1.8	12.3	14.3
9	0.2	11.2	11.4
Highest	0.1	0.6	0.7
Average	1.5	7.6	9.2

Source: Author with data from (Mideplan 2006).

labor market, income inequality should continue to improve and social inclusion should also advance (Torche 2005).

Concertación governments successfully combined a market-friendly economic model with a strong emphasis on poverty-alleviating programs. Poverty decreased in every administration since 1990. Moreover, recent data also shows that inequality has also began to decrease, as the Gini coefficient reached 0.54 in 2006. The policies championed by the Concertación proved successful, but were also electorally rewarding. In the 1993 presidential election, Frei obtained fifty-eight percent of the vote. Six years later, Lagos won a closely fought runoff election with 51.3 percent. Michelle Bachelet gave the

Concertación its fourth consecutive presidential victory with 53.5 percent of the vote in a runoff election.

The quality of Chile's democracy is far superior than that observed before 1973. The institutional setting is more strongly consolidated, there is more transparency and accountability from campaign funding to government spending, from lobbying and interest groups' influence, to access to government information. Though there are areas where there has not been sufficient progress, like plurality in the printed media (Dermota 2002) or citizens' groups and unionized workers (Olavarria 2003; Oxhorn 1995; Oxhorn and Ducatenzeiler 1998; Posner 2003; Posner 2008; Roberts 1998; Winn 2004), the depth and reach of Chile's democracy in the post-Pinochet era is commendably superior to that in existence before the authoritarian period.

8.7 Electoral Participation

Representative democracy is based on electoral participation. As Table 8.6 shows, only one in every three voting-aged Chileans cast ballots in the 1958 presidential election, but rapid enfranchisement almost doubled that number for the 1964 presidential contest. In 1970, when Allende was elected president, voter turnout decreased slightly, whereas in 1973, for the last election before the dictatorship, almost seventy percent of voting-aged Chileans cast valid votes.

After a fifteen-year interruption, interest in political participation was at its highest. Slightly less than ninety percent of eligible Chileans went to the polls in 1988 in a record-breaking turnout. As Table 8.3 shows, electoral participation has decreased since 1988, with presidential elections attracting more voters than other contests. Yet, in the most recent presidential election in 2009, only 56.7 percent of voting-aged Chileans cast valid votes, the lowest since 1970. Naturally, it would be foolish to expect the same high turnout levels reached in 1988. Decreasing interest in the political process could mean that people are fully satisfied, but there is evidence that the lack of interest corresponds to discontent with politicians and dissatisfaction with everyday politics. Table 8.3 also shows that, when measured as percentage of registered voters, electoral participation has remained remarkably stable and high since 1988. Nine of every ten registered voters cast ballots in each of the four presidential elections held since 1989. Among those registered, participation is fairly high – though there are no real penalties for those who fail to vote. Yet a growing number is not registered to vote. Thus, the real unique electoral participation phenomenon has to do

Table 8.6 *Electoral participation in Chile, 1988–2009*

Year	Voting-aged Population	Registered Voters	Voters	Valid Votes	Nulls, Blanks, Abstentions, and Non-registered	Voters/ Registered %	Valid Votes/ Voting-aged Population %
1988	8,062	7,436	7,251	7,187	889	96.6	89.1
1989	8,243	7,558	7,159	6,980	1,344	92.3	84.6
1992	8,775	7,841	7,044	6,411	2,345	81.9	73.2
1993	8,951	8,085	7,377	6,969	1,848	84.3	75.8
1996	9,464	8,073	7,079	6,301	3,085	76.6	65.3
1997	9,627	8,078	7,046	5,796	3,746	71.1	59.6
1999	9,945	8,084	7,272	7,055	2,890	90.0	70.1
2000	10,100	8,089	7,019	6,452	3,648	86.8	63.9
2001	10,500	8,075	6,992	6,107	4,393	86.6	58.2
2004	10,700	8,013	6,874	6,123	4,577	85.8	57.2
2005	10,800	8,221	7,207	6,942	3,758	87.7	64.3
2008	12,066	8,110	6,959	6,362	5,704	85.8	52.7
2009	12,226	8,285	7,186	6,938	5,284	83.7	56.7

Source: Navia (2004) and data from www.ine.cl and www.elecciones.gov.cl.

with a flawed institutional design. The constitution formally makes voting mandatory, but in practice, registration is optional. If registered, Chileans vote. Yet younger Chileans – those who turned eighteen after 1988 – are registered at lower rates. A natural solution would be to adopt automatic registration and hope that, when registered, voters will vote. Because the deadline for registration expires ninety days before an election, it is plausible that many unregistered Chileans who become interested in the political process during the official thirty-day campaign cannot vote. Polling data shows no difference in the depth and intensity of political views between those registered and those not registered.

Rather than discontent with democracy or the social order, low electoral participation seems to point to dissatisfaction with the political process, the lack of competitiveness in the electoral system, and the insufficient responsiveness by elected politicians. Yet those problems are also present in stable and industrialized democracies. Chileans might be unsatisfied with their politicians and the political process, but they are supportive of democracy as the only legitimate mechanism of exercising power.

8.8 Conclusion

The growth of a middle class since the 1990s has consolidated Chile as an LAO society. Yet as the middle class becomes stronger, the top-down structure of post-Pinochet democracy will face additional pressure to generate inclusion. Social and political inclusion must expand from poor to middle class to middle class to decision-making elite.

Paraphrasing former president Patricio Aylwin's famous dictum, Chile enjoys a democratic system to the extent possible. Aylwin's definition of transitional justice (*justicia en la medida de lo posible*) has extended into the fabric and institutions of Chile's twenty-year-old democracy. Democracy is today more consolidated and inclusive than before the military dictatorship or at any point since the center-left Concertación government came to power. Yet the 1973 coup and the seventeen-year Pinochet dictatorship remain a defining moment in Chilean history. After all, democracy has been built upon the foundations set in place by the 1980 constitution. Though amended several times – and most of its deadlock authoritarian provisions and enclaves now eliminated – the constitution reminds us that Pinochet is the father of today's Chile. Yet the Concertación coalition has been a deserving stepfather. Four consecutive Concertación governments have helped heal deep social and political wounds and have presided over Chile's most successful period economic growth, social inclusion, and democratic progress in the nation's history.

When democracy was restored in 1990, 2.8 million Chileans (seventeen percent) were less than ten years old. An additional 5.3 million (thirty-one percent) have been born since. In fact, less than forty-three percent of Chileans were born before 1973. Only three of every ten Chileans were at least eight years old when the military bombed the presidential palace and socialist president Salvador Allende committed suicide. When the new president – the fifth democratically elected since 1989 – took office in March 2010, Chilean democracy turned twenty years old. For most Chileans, it was the first democratic experience they knew. Because it has evolved within – and beyond – the constraints imposed upon it by the authoritarian constitution but also because it has evolved in a context of persistent levels of inequality combined with stable economic growth, Chile's democracy has evident strengths and unquestionable weaknesses. But it provides a good platform for future consolidation and offers opportunities to promote and bring about increasing levels of social and economic inclusion and to expand political rights.

Since its transition to democracy in 1990, Chile has made significant progress in economic development, poverty reduction, and democratic consolidation. The country enjoys a consolidated democracy as there is no fear of an authoritarian reversal. Chileans value democracy, and autonomous institutions with a working balance of power have made the political system stable. Elections are the norm and respect for individual rights is widespread. Yet, as do most democracies, Chile faces significant challenges. The success of the past should generate optimism about the country's ability to strengthen, widen, and deepen its democracy in the future. However, there are also some worrying signs. What proved successful in securing the transition and consolidating democracy in the 1990s might not work in the next phase. Chile needs to come up with a second generation of democratic reforms to meet the challenges of the future. As the country approaches its bicentennial, the success of its first two decades of postauthoritarian democracy have generated high expectations about what the country can do in the future. Moving forward in uncharted territory will not be easy, nor will it be inevitably successful. Yet Chile today enjoys a strong, vibrant, and consolidated democracy more so than ever before in its history.

References

Aguilar, M. I. (2002). "The Disappeared and the Mesa de Diálogo in Chile 1999–2001: Searching for Those Who Never Grew Old." *Bulletin of Latin American Research* **21**(3): 413–24.

Andrade Geywitz, C. (1991). *Reforma de la Constitución Política de la República de Chile de 1980*. Santiago: Editorial Jurídica.

Angell, A. (2003). "Party Change in Chile in Comparative Perspective." *Revista de Ciencia Politica* **23**(2): 88–108.

Aninat, C., J. M. Benavente , et al. (2010). "The Political Economy of Productivity: The Case of Chile." IDB Working Paper Series IDB-WP-105 (April).

Aylwin, P. (1998). *El reencuentro de los demócratas: del golpe al triunfo del no*. Santiago: Ediciones B Chile.

Aylwin, P., C. Briones et al. (1985). *Una salida político constitucional para Chile*. Santiago: Instituto chileno de estudios humanísticos.

Bacic, R. (2002). "Dealing with the Past: Chile – Human Rights and Human Wrongs." *Race and Class* **44**(1): 17–31.

Bardón M, Á., C. Carrasco A. et al. (1985). *Una década de cambios económicos*. Santiago: Editorial Andrés Bello.

Barros, R. (2002). *Constitutionalism and Dictatorship: Pinochet, the Junta, and the 1980 Constitution*. New York: Cambridge University Press.

Baxter, V. (2005). "Civil Society Promotion of Truth, Justice, and Reconciliation in Chile: Villa Grimaldi." *Peace & Change* **30**(1): 120–36.

Beyer, H. (1997). "Distribución del ingreso. Antecedentes para la discusión." *Estudios Públicos* **65**(Verano): 1–54.

Boeninger, E. (1997). *Democracia en Chile. Lecciones para la gobernabilidad.* Santiago: Editorial Andrés Bello.

(2007). *Políticas públicas en democracia. Institucionalidad y experiencia chilena 1990–2006.* Santiago: Uqbar editores.

Burgos, J. and I. Walker. (2003). "Hacia el parlamentarismo." *En foco (Expansiva)* **4**.

Cavallo, A. (1998). *Historia oculta de la transición.* Santiago: Grijalbo.

Cavallo, A., M. Salazar et al. (1997). *La historia oculta del régimen militar.* Santiago: Grijalbo.

Cristi, R. (2000). *El pensamiento político de Jaime Guzmán. Autoridad y libertad.* Santiago: LOM.

Cristi, R. and P. Ruiz-Tagle. (2006). *La república en Chile. Teoría y práctica del Constitucionalismo Republicano.* Santiago: LOM.

Dermota, K. (2002). *Chile Inédito. El periodismo bajo democracia.* Santiago: Ediciones B.

DeShazo, P. (1983). *Urban Workers and Labor Unions in Chile 1902-1927.* Madison: University of Wisconsin Press.

Drake, P. and I. Jaksic, Eds. (1995). *The Struggle for Democracy in Chile. 1982-1990.* Lincoln: University of Nebraska Press.

Drake, P. W. (1978). *Socialism and Populism in Chile. 1932-1952.* Urbana; University of Illinois Press.

Engel, E. and P. Navia. (2006). *Que gane "el más major." Mérito y competencia en el Chile de hoy.* Santiago: Editorial Debate.

Ensalaco, M. (1994). "In with the New, Out with the Old? The Democratising Impact of Constitutional Reform in Chile." *Journal of Latin American Studies* **26**(2): 409–29.

(1995). "Military Prerogatives and the Stalemate of Chilean Civil-Military Relations." *Armed Forces and Society* **21**(2): 255–70.

Espejo, N., Ed. (2008). *Informe Anual sobre Derechos Humanos en Chile 2008.* Santiago: Universidad Diego Portales.

Espinoza, V. (2010). "Redes de poder y sociabilidad en la élite política chilena. Los parlamentarios 1990-2005." *Polis, Revista de la Universidad Bolivariana* **9**(26): 251–86.

Fontaine Aldunate A., C. Larroulet et al., Eds. (2008). *Reforma de los partidos políticos en Chile.* Santiago: PNUD.

Fontaine Aldunate, A. (1988). *Los economistas y el presidente Pinochet.* Santiago: Zig-Zag.

Garretón, M. (1989). *The Chilean Political Process.* Boston: Unwin Hyman.

Garretón, M. A. and T. Moulián. (1983). *La Unidad Popular y el conflicto político en Chile.* Santiago: Ediciones Minga.

Garretón, M. A. (1999). *Balance y perspectivas de la democratización política chilena. La caja de Pandora: el retorno de la transición chilena.* A. Joignant and A. Menéndez-Carrión. Santiago: Planeta.

Geisse, F. and J. Ramírez. (1989). *La reforma constitucional.* Santiago: CESOC.

Gil, F., R. L. E. et al., Eds. (1979). *Chile at the Turning Point. The Lessons of the Socialist Years, 1970-1973.* Philadelphia: ISHI.

Heiss, C. and P. Navia. (2007). "You Win Some, You Lose Some: Constitutional Reforms in Chile's Transition to Democracy." *Latin American Politics and Society* **49**.3(Fall): 163–90.

Huneeus, C., Ed. (2006). *La reforma al sistema binominal en Chile. Propuestas para el debate.* Santiago: Catalonia.

Huneeus, C. R. (2007). *The Pinochet Regime.* Boulder, CO: Lynne Rienner Publishers.

Jocelyn-Holt, A. (1998). *El Chile perplejo.* Santiago: Planeta/Ariel.

Kaufman, R. R. (1972). *The Politics of Land Reform in Chile. 1950–1970. Public Policy Institutions and Social Change.* Cambridge: Harvard University Press.

Lagos Escobar, R. (2005). *The 21st Century: A View from the South.* London: First.

Larraín, F. and R. Vergara, Eds. (2000). *La transformación económica de Chile.* Santiago: Centro de Estudios Públicos.

Linz, J. (1990). "The Perils of Presidentialism." *Journal of Democracy* **1**(1): 51–69.

Linz, J., A. Lijphart et al., Eds. (1990). *Hacia una democracia moderna. La opción parlamentaria.* Santiago: Universidad Católica.

Loveman, B. (1976). *Struggle in the Countryside: Politics and Rural Labor in Chile, 1919–1973.* Bloomington: Indiana University Press.

(1988). *Chile. The Legacy of Hispanic Capitalism.* New York: Oxford University Press.

(1991). "¿Misión cumplida? Civil Military Relations and the Chilean Political Transition." *Journal of Inter American Studies and World Affairs* **33**(3): 35–74.

(1994). "Protected Democracies and Military Guardianship: Political Transitions in Latin America, 1978–1993." *Journal of Inter American Studies and World Affairs* **36**(2): 105–89.

(2001). *Chile. The Legacy of Hispanic Capitalism. Third Edition.* New York: Oxford University Press.

Loveman, B. and E. Lira (2000). *Las ardientes cenizas del olvido: Vía chilena de reconciliación política 1932–1994.* Santiago: LOM.

Martínez, J. and A. Díaz (1996). *Chile. The Great Transformation.* Washington: Brookings Institution.

Meller, P. (1996). *Un Siglo de Economía Política Chilena.* Santiago: Editorial Andrés Bello.

(2000). "El cobre chileno y la política minera" in P. Meller (ed.) *Dilemas y Debates en torno al Cobre.* Santiago, DOLMEN-CEA: 17–77.

Meller, P., Ed. (2005). *La paradoja aparente.* Santiago: Taurus.

Mideplan (2006). "Distribución del Ingreso e Impacto Distributivo del Gasto Social." Serie análisis de resultados de la Encuesta de Caracterización Socio-Económica Nacional (CASEN 2006) 2.

Ministerio de Planificación (2006). "Encuesta CASEN 2006." *Apuntes de Protección Social* **5**.

Navia, P. (2004). "Participación electoral en Chile 1988–2001." *Revista de Ciencia Política* **24**(1): 81–103.

(2005). "Transformando votos en escaños: leyes electorales en Chile, 1833–2003." *Política y Gobierno* **12**(2): 233–76.

Olavarria, M. (2003). "Protected Neoliberalism: Perverse Institutionalization and the Crisis of Representation in Postdictatorship Chile." *Latin American Perspectives* **30**(6(133)): 10–38.

Otano, R. (1995). *Crónica de la transición*. Santiago: Planeta.

Ottone, E. and C. Vergara (2006). *Ampliando horizontes. Siete claves estratégicas del gobierno de Lagos*. Santiago: Debate.

Oxhorn, P. D. and G. Ducatenzeiler, Eds. (1998). *What Kind of Democracy? What Kind of Market? Latin America in the Age of Neoliberalism*. University Park: Pennsylvania State University Press.

Oxhorn, P. D. (1995). *Organizing Civil Society. The Popular Sector and the Struggle for Democracy in Chile*. University Par: Pennsylvania State University Press.

Portales, F. (2000). *Chile. Una democracia tutelada*. Santiago: Sudamericana.

Posner, P. W. (2003). "Local Democracy and Popular Participation: Chile and Brazil in Comparative Perspective." *Democratization* **10**(3): 39–67.

(2008). *State, Market and Democracy in Chile*. New Yor: Palgrave McMillan.

Roberts, K. M. (1998). *Deepening Democracy? The Modern Left and Social Movements in Chile and Peru*. Stanford: Stanford University Press.

Rojo, E. (1995). *La otra cara de La Moneda. Los cuatro años de Aylwin*. Santiago; América, CESOC.

Roth-Arriaza, N. and J. Mariezcurrena, Eds. (2006). *Transitional Justice in the Twenty-First Century*. Beyond Truth Versus Justice. New York: Cambridge University Press.

Siavelis, P. M. and A. Valenzuela (1997). *Electoral Engineering and Democratic Stability: The Legacy of Authoritarian Rule in Chile. Institutional Design in New Democracies Eastern Europe and Latin America*. A. Lijphart and C. H. Waisman. Boulder: Westview Press.

Siavelis, P. M. (2002). "Coalitions, Voters and Party System Transformation in Post-Authoritarian Chile." *Government and Opposition* **37**(1): 76–105.

Stallings, B. (1978). *Class Conflict and Economic Development in Chile, 1958–1973*. Stanford: Stanford University Press.

Stallings, B. and A. Zimbalist (1975). "The Political Economy of the Unidad Popular." *Latin American Perspectives* **2**(1): 69–88.

Stein, E., M. Tommasi et al. (2006). *The Politics of Policies. Economic and Social Progress in Latin America*. Washington, DC: Inter American Development Bank.

Torche, F. (2005). "Unequal but Fluid: Social Mobility in Chile in Comparative Perspective." *American Sociological Review* **70**(3): 422–50.

UNDP, U. N. D. P. (2005). *Democracy in Latin America: Towards a Citizens' Democracy*. New York: UNDP.

Valdés, J. G. (1995). *Pinochet's Economists: The Chicago School of Economics in Chile*. New York: Cambridge University Press.

Valdés Prieto, S., Ed. (2000). *Reforma del Estado. Volumen I: Financiamiento político*. Santiago; Centro de Estudios Públicos.

Valenzuela, A. (1977). *Political Brokers in Chile: Local Government in a Centralized Polity*. Durham: Duke University Press.

(1978). *The Breakdown of Democratic Regimes: Chile*. Baltimore; John Hopkins University Press.

Valenzuela, A. and J. S. Valenzuela, Eds. (1976). *Chile: Politics and Society*. New Brunswick, Transaction Books.

Valenzuela, J. S. (1995). "The Origins and Transformations of the Chilean Party System." The Helen Kellogg Institute for International Studies at Notre Dame University Working Paper #215.

(2005). "Hay que eliminar el sistema binominal?" *Política* **45**(Primavera): 53–66.

Vega Fernández, H. (2007). *En vez de la injusticia. Un camino para el desarrollo de Chile en el siglo XXI.* Santiago; Debate.

Vergara, P. (1985). *Auge y caída del neoliberalismo en Chile.* Santiago: FLACSO.

Vial Correa, G. (2002). *Pinochet. La biografía. Volumen I y II.* Santiago: El Mercurio/Aguilar.

Walker, I. (2006). "Democracia en América Latina." *Foreign Affairs en Español* **6**(2).

Winn, P., Ed. (2004). *Victims of the Chilean Miracle: Workers and Neoliberalism in the Pinochet era, 1973-2002.* Durham: Duke University Press.

Zaldívar Larraín, A. (1995). *La transición inconclusa.* Santiago: Editorial Los Andes.

Zucco, C. (2007). "Where's the Bias? A Reassessment of the Chilean Electoral System." *Electoral Studies* **26**(2): 303–14.

NINE

Transition from a Limited Access Order to an Open Access Order

The Case of South Korea

Jong-Sung You

9.1 Introduction

During the second half of the twentieth century, South Korea (Korea, hereafter) transformed itself from a poor nation into a rich and democratic country. Although Korea relied heavily on American aid while endeavoring to emerge from the ashes of the Korean War (1950–3) in the 1950s, it has become a significant donor country.[1] Korea has demonstrated the long-term viability and strength of its economy by quickly overcoming both the Asian financial crisis of 1997 and the global financial crisis of 2008. Moreover, Korea has successfully consolidated its democracy since the democratic transition in 1987. The Korean people have made two changes of government through free and fair election, and Korea has seen no successful or attempted coup. Democracy has become the only game in town.

Many scholars have tried to explain Korea's success story of sustained economic growth. Few have, however, examined both the economic and the political development of Korea. Mo and Weingast (2012; Mo-Weingast, hereafter) is a notable exception. They applied the framework of transition from a limited access order (LAO) to an open access order (OAO) developed by North, Wallis, and Weingast (2009; NWW, hereafter) and North, Wallis, Webb, and Weingast (2007; NWWW, hereafter). As NWW and Mo-Weingast indicated, Korea is one of the three countries outside of Europe and the Anglo-American countries (Australia, Canada, New Zealand, and the United States) that have completed (Japan) or moved far along the transition to an open access order (Korea and Taiwan).

---

[1] Korea plans to increase its official development aid from 0.12 percent of GNI in 2010 to 0.25 percent by 2015.

NWW's conceptual framework of limited and open access orders provides a useful tool for a political economy approach that integrates developments in both the polity and the economy. NWW recognizes the interdependence of political and economic systems. Their theory of double balance posits that, over the long term, the degree of political openness tends to match that of economic openness and vice versa. Most developing countries remain locked in the equilibrium of limited access in both the economy and the polity, while advanced democracies are in the equilibrium of open access in both the economy and the polity. A limited access order contains violence by creating and distributing rents among powerful individuals and groups, while an open access order maintains stability by granting everyone equal access to political and economic opportunities. Substantial development occurs as an LAO matures from a *fragile* to a *basic* to a *mature* LAO as well as when an LAO transitions to an OAO.

This chapter attempts to explain the economic and political development of Korea by applying the lens of NWW and NWWW's framework as Mo-Weingast did. I will review the postcolonial history of Korean development, discuss several issues in applying the LAO–OAO framework to the Korean case, and make comparisons with Taiwan and the Philippines to explain Korea's transition to an open access order.

Mo-Weingast focus on three turning points in the postcolonial history of Korea: Park Chung-hee's military coup of 1961 and his establishment of a "developmental state," the democratic transition of 1987, and the financial crisis of 1997. In contrast, my account of Korean development starts with the land reform enacted around 1950. A crucial weakness of existing studies of Korean development is the inability to explain the origin of the developmental state, and I will demonstrate that the land reform played a critical role in laying the foundation for future development. My second turning point starts with the student democratic revolution of 1960 rather than the military coup of 1961 led by Park.

I will show that Korea developed from a *fragile* LAO (1945–8) to a *basic* LAO (1948–60) and then from a *basic/mature* LAO (1960–87) to a *mature* LAO with doorstep conditions (1987–97), and that Korea has been making a transition to an OAO since 1997. Also, I will provide an account of how successful control of violence has been established and how a different mix of rents for the dominant coalition has developed.

Although the focus of the chapter is Korea, I will briefly compare Korea with Taiwan as another successful case and with the Philippines as an unsuccessful case to explore what made it possible for Korea (and Taiwan) to make a transition to an OAO. Back in the 1950s, the Philippines appeared more promising in terms of economic and political development than did Korea and Taiwan. A comparison of these three countries provides insights about the distinct early features of Korea and Taiwan that positively influenced their subsequent development. The comparison illustrates the crucial role of sweeping land reform in Korea and Taiwan, which is rarely seen in other countries except Japan.

The chapter demonstrates the usefulness of NWW and NWWW's conceptual framework in explaining the postcolonial development of Korea. It also suggests that the doorstep conditions do not work the same way in today's developing countries as they did in the historical experiences of Western Europe and North America. The chapter closes with a brief discussion of the challenges Korea faces to complete the transition and consolidate its OAO.

9.2 History

9.2.1 Origin of the Korean "Developmental State"

Previous explanations of Korean development focused on the role of the state versus the market. While some studies emphasize the role of the market and trade liberalization (McKinnon 1973; World Bank 1987), the "developmental state" explanation became dominant in light of the mounting evidence for the interventionist role of the Korean state (Amsden 1989; Chang 1994; Haggard 1990). This group of scholars stresses the importance of an autonomous and meritocratic bureaucracy as the core of the developmental state, and the role of Park Chung-hee in establishing it. Mo-Weingast also follow the key arguments of the developmental state literature. They argue that Korea's transition to an open access order started with the developmental state under Park's leadership in the early 1960s. They characterize Syngman Rhee's regime (1948–60) as a "predatory state" in agreement with most of the developmental state literature.

A weakness in this literature is the lack of adequate explanation about the origin of the developmental state. What made it possible for Korea (and Taiwan) to establish developmental states unlike other developing countries? What explains the transformation from a predatory state (Rhee regime) to a developmental state (Park regime)?

Some scholars suggest a historical explanation: the Confucian tradition of bureaucracy and Japanese colonial experience (Woo-Cumings 1995).

Others suggest the role of security threat. These explanations are plausible, since they distinguish Korea (and Taiwan) from other developing countries, and Mo-Weingast subscribe to these explanations. The historical experience of Confucian statecraft and bureaucratic traditions helped to build coherent and meritocratic bureaucracy in Korea. The security threat from North Korea gave South Korean leaders incentives to pursue long-term growth rather than short-term rents. Neither explanation of the developmental state, however, can explain the differences between Rhee and Park's regimes. Why didn't the Confucian bureaucratic tradition and security threat lead President Rhee to form a developmental state?

In fact, Korea's conditions in the early 1960s were more favorable for economic growth than those of most developing countries (Benabou 1996; Eichengreen 2012; Mo-Weingast; Rodrik, Grossman, and Norman 1995). Korea had an unusually equal distribution of income and wealth and a high level of human capital when the Park regime began its export-led industrialization drive. These conditions were critical. As Rodrik et al. (1995) note, the exceptionally low levels of inequality in Korea (and Taiwan) made it possible for the state bureaucracy to remain autonomous and free from capture by powerful economic interests. As Eichengreen (2012) point out, Korea's high primary education enrollment and completion rate circa 1960 provided a labor force equipped with basic numeracy and literacy, which was well suited to the circumstances of a relatively poor, late-industrializing economy. Park's industrialization drive would not have been so successful without these favorable conditions.

These conditions were not inherited from the Japanese colonial period, but were the result of the land reform that occurred around 1950. The sweeping land reform dissolved the landed elite and produced an unusually equal distribution of wealth and income. It also helped to rapidly expand education by enabling most people to educate their children. These conditions in turn helped to establish a coherent and meritocratic bureaucracy by providing a pool of highly educated people to compete in higher civil service exams and by removing powerful landlords who could capture or corrupt the bureaucracy for their own economic interests. Thus, land reform contributed to widening economic openness.

9.2.2 South Korea, 1945 to the Present: Chronology

South Korea's postcolonial history (1945–present) can be divided into five periods. South Korea developed from a *fragile* LAO (1945–8) to a *basic* LAO (1948–60) and then from a *basic/mature* LAO (1960–87) to a *mature* LAO

Table 9.1 *From a fragile LAO to an OAO: South Korea, 1945–present*

Fragile LAO (1945–8)	• Liberation from Japanese rule; Occupation by the United States & the USSR (1945) • Establishment of two Koreas (1948)
Basic LAO (1948–60)	• Electoral democracy but authoritarian tendency • Land reform (1948–52) • Korean War (1950–3) • State monopoly of violence • Import substitution industrialization, dependence on U.S. aid
Basic/Mature LAO (1960–87)	• Electoral democracy (1960–1, 63–72), military rule (1961–3), authoritarian regime (1972–87) • Export-oriented, *chaebol*-centered industrialization
Mature LAO with Doorstep Conditions (1987–97)	• Democratic transition (1987) • Check on state violence, Decline of violent social movements • Firm civilian control over the military • Expansion of civil society organizations • Improving the rule of law • Economic liberalization • *Chaebols'* market power and moral hazard
Transition to OAO (1997–present)	• Democratic consolidation • Financial crisis and the change of government (1997) • Reform of *chaebol* and financial system • Economic liberalization • Improving the rule of law • Control of corruption

with doorstep conditions (1987–97), and has been making a transition to an OAO since 1997 (Table 9.1).

9.2.3 Fragile LAO (1945–8) and Basic LAO (1948–60)

When Korea was liberated from Japanese colonial rule in 1945, it was primarily an agricultural economy with few landlords and a vast number of peasants. The richest 2.7 percent of rural households owned two-thirds of all the cultivated lands while 58 percent owned no land at all. A radical land reform took place first in North Korea in 1946, which gave landlords no compensation and distributed lands to peasants for free.

The most important source of fragility and instability during the period of American Military Government (1945–8) was the land problem. Immediately after the liberation from Japanese rule in 1945, leftist forces had strong political influence as well as violence potential. By the time the South Korean state was established in 1948, these groups had weakened considerably partly because of suppression but also because of the government's commitment to land reform. Although partisan guerrillas fought in the mountains, they faced complete elimination during the Korean War. A state monopoly on violence was established and no powerful groups other than the military possessed serious violence potential that could threaten the state. Also remarkable was that the Korean peninsula maintained peace and the two Korean governments never attempted to launch another war despite the mutual hostility and tensions that continue to dominate inter-Korean relations to the present.

Land redistribution in South Korea was carried out in two stages: by the American Military Government (AMG) in 1948 and by the South Korean government from 1950 to 1952. In March 1948, the AMG began to distribute two hundred forty thousand hectares of former Japanese lands to former tenants, which accounted for 11.7 percent of total cultivated land. When the first election was held in the south in May 1948, all parties pledged to implement land reform and the constitution included a commitment to land reform. Syngman Rhee's government began to implement agrarian land reform in 1950, just before the Korean War broke out. Restricting the upper ceiling of landownership to three hectares, the government redistributed three hundred thirty thousand hectares of farmland by 1952. The landlords received 1.5 times the annual value of all crops in compensation from the government, and their former tenants were to pay the same amount to the government in five years.[2] In anticipation of the reforms, about five hundred thousand hectares had been sold directly by landlords to their tenants, the bulk in 1948 and 1949 (Hong 2001). In total, ownership of fifty-two percent of cultivated land transferred to tenants and the "principle of land to tillers" was realized. By 1956, the top six percent owned only eighteen percent of the cultivated lands. Tenancy dropped from forty-nine percent to seven percent of all farming households, and the area of cultivated land

---

[2] The price of land was very cheap in the Korean land reform, considering that it was 2.5 times the annual produce in the land reform in Japan and Taiwan. Moreover, Korean landlords had to see their compensation in government bonds to drop in real value because of hyperinflation.

under tenancy fell from sixty-five percent to eighteen percent (Ban, Moon, and Perkins 1980; Lie 1998; Putzel 1992).

Land reform profoundly transformed Korean society. The traditional *yangban* (aristocracy) landlord class was dissolved. Peasants became farmers (Lie 1998). Land redistribution and the destruction of large private properties during the Korean War produced an unusually equal distribution of assets and income in Korea (Mason et al. 1980; You 1998). Land reform opened space for state autonomy from the dominant class, as there was no organized privileged class or special interests immediately after the land reform, although the *chaebols'* growth and increasing economic concentration eventually became a concern. Although the markets were not fully open and competitive, land reform created a considerable degree of open access in the markets.

Land reform also contributed to the rapid expansion of education by making it affordable to a majority of the population. Enrollment in primary schools doubled between 1945 and 1955 while enrollment in secondary schools increased more than eight times and enrollment in colleges and universities increased ten times (Kwon 1984). Considering that the government's budgetary commitment to public education was minimal during that period, the speed of educational expansion would have been slower without land reform. Many farmers with small landholdings sold their lands to support their children's college education.

The spectacular increase in an educated labor force not only contributed to high economic growth, but also paved the road for the establishment of meritocratic bureaucracy. Although the higher civil service exam (*haengsi*) was instituted as early as 1949, only four percent of those filling higher entry-level positions came in via the exam under Syngman Rhee's government (1948–60). The higher positions were filled primarily through special appointments. This reflected Rhee's reliance on clientelistic ties as well as a shortage of highly educated people (Kang 2002). Park Chung-hee's government (1961–79), however, established a meritocratic bureaucracy manned by the supply of university graduates, although he allocated a substantial number of higher positions to members of the military who did not pass the highly competitive civil service exam (You 2012).

An important question regarding this period is why the Rhee regime chose to implement the sweeping land reform and why it was so successful in contrast to other developing countries (see Montinola's case study of the Philippines in this volume). The security threat from North Korea as well as the radical land reform in 1946 in North Korea made it imperative for Rhee's regime to court the support of peasants through extensive land reform (You

2012). Even the Korea Democratic Party that represented the interests of landlords did not openly object to land reform, but only tried to delay the implementation of the reform and to increase the compensation for the landlords. The position of the landed class in the National Assembly had been seriously weakened by the collaboration of large land owners with the Japanese. Rhee showed his strong commitment for land reform by appointing Cho Bong-Am, a former communist, as minister of agriculture, and he drafted a progressive land reform law with compensation of 150 percent of annual produce. Although there was an attempt to increase the compensation to 300 percent, the assembly passed the Land Reform Act with 150 percent of compensation and payment on February 2, 1950, and President Rhee signed it into law on March 10, 1950 (Kim 2001).

Land reform not only helped President Rhee to consolidate his political support among the rural population, but also contributed to stabilizing the country. Land reform removed the most attractive aspect of communism's appeal to the peasants, depriving communist partisan guerrillas of their support base in rural areas and helping to establish a legitimate state monopoly of violence.

Land reform was, however, not intended to create open access. Rather than promoting open access and competition in the economy, the Rhee regime used distribution of privileged access to state-controlled resources to consolidate its coalition. The *chaebols* began to emerge under the patronage of the Rhee regime, and they paid the regime back through illicit political contributions. The major sources of *chaebol* accumulation during the Rhee period were selective allocation of import licenses and quotas, bargain price acquisition of former Japanese properties, aid funds and materials, cheap bank loans, and government and U.S. military contracts for reconstruction activities (Jones and Sakong 1980: 271–2).

The sale of vested properties, formerly Japanese-owned industrial properties taken over by the American Military Government and subsequently transferred to the Rhee government, typically favored interim plant mangers as well as the politically well connected. The Rhee government set the price of the properties at twenty-five percent to thirty percent of the market value and offered the new owners generous installment plans. In return for their windfall gains, the new owners of these properties provided kickbacks to Rhee's Liberal Party. Vested properties provided the initial base for many *chaebols* (Lim 2003: 42).

The privatization of commercial banks in the 1950s provides another example of the irregularities in the disposal of state-owned properties. The government initially put banks up for sale in 1954 with provisions designed to prevent the control of financial institutions by industrial capitalists. When no bids satisfied these provisions, however, the government drastically relaxed the requirements. The result was the control of major commercial banks by a few *chaebols*, who were major contributors to Rhee's Liberal Party. Using political connections, they borrowed money from the banks in order to make bids for the ownership of the same banks (Lim 2003: 42).

The political system did not operate according to the principles of open access and competition, either. Although South Korea was established as a constitutional democracy, formal institutions of democracy did not always work in a democratic way. Universal suffrage as well as basic rights were granted by the constitution, but Koreans were not yet prepared to exert their political rights and civil liberties. Syngman Rhee's regime became increasingly authoritarian and corrupt over his twelve-year presidency (1948–60). The Rhee regime did not hesitate to suppress opposition and manipulate elections to perpetuate his rule. When Rhee wanted to amend the constitution from indirect presidential election by the parliament to direct presidential election in 1952, he faced opposition from a majority of members of the parliament. He successfully mobilized state terror and threats by imposing martial law to force the members of the parliament to agree to the constitutional amendment. The National Security Law, enacted in 1948, made both communism and recognition of North Korea as a political entity illegal and was used to suppress and persecute dissidents and left-leaning political leaders and groups.

Rhee's Liberal Party was essentially nothing more than his personal networks (Lee 1968: 71–6; Lie 1998: 35). It is notable that the Liberal Party did not have any class base, while the leading opposition, the Democratic Party, had as its initial base the landed class. Since the landed class was dissolved after the land reform and the Korean War, the political competition grew oriented toward personal appeals of leaders and distribution of patronage. Corruption scandals erupted in presidential election years, which involved exchanges of rents and illicit political contributions. Vote buying practices became widespread and fraudulent vote counting was common. Thus, the formally open access political system did not in fact guarantee open access and competition in political affairs.

9.2.4 Basic/Mature LAO (1960–87)

The people's demand for democracy increased over time from 1960 to 1987. Expansion of education produced anti-authoritarian forces among students and intellectuals. Industrialization and economic growth expanded the middle class and working class, and their voices and organizations grew. Student demonstrations in protest of election fraud in April 1960 led to the resignation of Syngman Rhee as president. The democratic opening was short-lived, however, as the military junta led by General Park Chung-hee overthrew the Chang Myeon government (1960–1) in May 1961. Although prodemocracy forces were growing, they were too weak then to contend with the military.

Park Chung-hee and Chun Doo-hwan ruled Korea formally as civilian presidents for most of the time, but they filled the bulk of the ruling party leadership and the bureaucracy with those from the military. Park created the Korean Central Intelligence Agency (KCIA) and the Democratic Republican Party to consolidate his power base before running for the presidency in 1963. The core leadership and the staff of the KCIA as well as the DRP came from the military. The KCIA, notorious for its persecution of dissidents and violations of human rights, began as a corps of three thousand officers dedicated to military rule (Kim 1971: 111–12). The DRP's major platforms included economic development and anticommunism. It did not have any class base, and the military officers that constituted the leadership of the DRP were from humble social backgrounds. Over time, however, the DRP forged an alliance with the *chaebols*. It was structured along a hierarchical, single command system with a large staff, modeled on the Kuomintang (KMT) in Taiwan. Park had to dispense patronage to military officers not only to utilize their loyalty for governing but also to prevent any revolt from within the military. As the single most powerful group with violence potential, the military enjoyed the bulk of appointments in the cabinet, to high-level government positions, and to positions in the KCIA and the DRP.[3]

Park ran very competitive presidential elections twice, in 1963 and in 1971, although the 1967 presidential election was not very close. There was speculation that Park could not have won the 1963 and 1971 elections without large-scale vote buying and vote counting fraud. He apparently concluded that democracy was too expensive and risky. He declared martial law, disbanded the National Assembly, and junked the existing constitution in 1972. The so-called *Yushin* Constitution abolished direct presidential election, which effectively guaranteed his life-long presidency. The *Yushin*

---

[3]   Interesting, the Park Chung-hee regime abstained from dispensing patronage jobs to economic ministries. Ministers and high-level officials in economic ministries were filled with technocrats, while non-economic ministries accommodated many military officers (Kang 2002: 85–90).

Constitution also gave him authority to nominate a third of the National Assembly members, which guaranteed an absolute majority to the ruling Democratic Republican Party. Park issued many emergency measures used to suppress criticism of the *Yushin* Constitution and his dictatorship.

Even when presidential and National Assembly elections were regularly held, they were far from open and competitive. Anticommunist rhetoric was conveniently used to suppress dissidents. The National Security Law was frequently abused to persecute dissidents, and the Korean CIA and police were used to suppress antigovernment activities. In addition, vote buying and fraudulent counting limited the scope of real contestation through elections. It is notable, however, that the anti-dictatorship student movement continued to grow in spite of harsh suppression; the major opposition New Democratic Party won the most votes in the 1978 general National Assembly elections, although Park's Democratic Republican Party still maintained a large majority in the National Assembly because of its advantage from the electoral system.[4]

After Park's assassination by KCIA chief Kim Jae-kyu in 1979, there was another short period of democratic opening, but the military junta led by General Chun Doo-hwan seized power through a two-stage coup and bloody suppression of the Kwangju democratization movement in 1980. After a short period of direct military rule, Chun became a civilian president through uncontested indirect election. It was not easy, however, to contain the ever-growing student and labor movements, particularly as student and labor groups became increasingly radical and militant. Student and labor movements were increasingly led by a radical nationalist camp that was often anti-American and pro-North Korea and another camp that emphasized class struggle and envisioned socialist revolution. While student movements used largely peaceful tactics before the Kwangju democratization movement, they more frequently utilized violent tactics such as the use of Molotov cocktails in the 1980s.

When hundreds of thousands of citizens, including students, blue-collar workers, and new middle-class white-collar workers, took to the streets in Seoul and all over the country in 1987, President Chun had to surrender to their key demands for democracy, including direct presidential election. President Chun considered using military force to suppress the demonstrations, but apparently he could not risk committing another massacre like the

---

[4] NDP got 32.8 percent of the total votes, while DRP's vote share was 31.7 percent. NDP and DRP obtained sixty-one seats and sixty-eight seats, respectively, out of the 154 seats from the nationwide two-member districts, and DRP added another seventy-seven seats from the president's appointment.

Table 9.2 *Growth of real GDP per capita, 1960–2003, for selected countries*

	Real GDP per capita (2000 dollars)			Average annual growth
	1960	1987	2003	1960–2003 (%)
S. Korea	1,458	7,374	17,597	6.05
Taiwan	1,444	9,396	19,885	6.34
Philippines	2,039	2,965	3,575	1.38
Mozambique	838	922	1,452	1.48
Senegal	1,776	1,474	1,407	−0.43
Mexico	3,719	6,595	7,938	1.84
Argentina	7,838	9,624	10,170	0.75

Source: Heston, Summers, and Aten (2006).

one that occurred during the violent suppression of the Kwangju in 1980. The United States urged Chun to refrain from using military force, perhaps alarmed by the increasing anti-American sentiments among Koreans due to U.S. support of the military crackdown of the Kwangju.

Although I've described this period (1960–87) as a long journey to democracy, the period is better known as a period of economic takeoff or export-led industrialization. Korea was poorer than most countries in Latin America and some countries in Africa when it began export-led growth in the 1960s. In 1960, Korea was much poorer than Mexico and Argentina and somewhat poorer than the Philippines and Senegal, but today it is much richer than any of these countries (Table 9.2).

Korea has enjoyed sustained economic growth with an average annual growth rate of six percent since 1960. Indeed, it has not experienced negative growth except for three years during this long period: slightly negative growth (-0.7 percent) in 1962 after the 1961 military coup led by General Park Chung-hee, -5.8 percent growth in 1980 in the midst of political turmoil after President Park's assassination and with the second oil shock, and -9.0 percent growth in 1998 during the financial crisis.[5]

The change of the Korean government's strategy from promoting import substitution industry to encouraging and subsidizing export industries contributed to boosting exports and raising productivity. To be sure, the economic system was nowhere near operating on the principle of open

---

[5] Korea was predicted to experience another negative growth in 2009 under the influence of the global financial crisis, but it actually recorded a positive (0.2 percent) growth that year.

access and competition, either internally or externally. Externally, imports were discouraged and strictly regulated with high tariffs and non-tariff barriers. Foreign direct investment was strictly restricted, although foreign loans were sought enthusiastically. Internally, the government owned and controlled commercial banks and distributed underpriced credit to favored firms and industries to reward export performance and in exchange for political donations.

Creation and distribution of rents was common not only under Syngman Rhee's regime, but also under Park Chung-hee and Chun Doo-hwan. Eradication of corruption was one of the key demands of the April student revolution in 1960, and Park initially listed anticorruption as a top priority, as Chun did in 1980 to justify the military takeover. Immediately after the coup of May 16, 1961, the military junta arrested *chaebol* owners on charges of illicit wealth accumulation, but the investigation ended with a negotiation of political and economic terms between the military and business owners. The junta reduced the fines for illicit wealth accumulation and provided financial subsidies for those industrialists who pledged to undertake specific industrial projects and to provide political funds (Kim and Im 2001). An important punishment, however, was confiscation of equity shares in commercial banks, which in effect renationalized the banks privatized in the late 1950s (Lim 2003: 44).

This episode shows that the military junta led by Park Chung-hee was eager to fill their "legitimacy deficit" that came from the overthrow of a legitimate democratic government by showcasing its will to fight corruption on the one hand and by forging a partnership with businesses to propel industrialization and economic growth on the other hand. After the student revolution in 1960, the short-lived Chang Myon government proclaimed its "Economy First" policy and prepared a launch of an Economic Development Plan (Lee 1968). Park realized that sustained military rule would not be possible without good economic performance and that he needed the business community as an ally for economic growth as well as a source of political funds. Since he did not want an equal partnership with the businesses, however, he seized firm control of the banks that would enable him to direct the incipient *chaebols* to invest in the sectors and industries according to the state's plans. Thus, a system of rent exchanges between the government, banks, and *chaebols* was formed during the early years of Park's administration that lasted until the East Asian financial crisis hit the Korean economy hard in 1997.

Under Park Chung-hee and Chun Doo-hwan, the most important forms of rents were allocation of domestic and foreign loans with low interest rates. The government favored *chaebol* firms and exporters in the distribution of rents in return for their political contributions, and often protected their monopoly by restricting the entry of other firms in specific industries. During the 1960s, export performance provided the government with a relatively objective criterion for underpriced credit allocation, while during the heavy and chemical industrialization drive in the 1970s, government support was based more on industry than on export performance. Since *chaebol* firms were primary exporters and pioneers in HCI drive, *chaebols* expanded rapidly under Park's regime and the problem of too big to fail began to emerge.

Typically, a firm that gets governmental approval for an industrial project will be financed by one-fifth equity and four-fifths foreign and domestic loans. It also receives other subsidies such as tax exemption. If the project succeeds, the firm starts a new line of business with the profits. Once again, the firm will not put up much equity but will rely heavily on external debt. The extension of this process leads to a group of firms, or *chaebol* (Jones and Sakong 1980: 273–4).

There were substantial differences in the importance of rent seeking and patronage between import substitution and export-oriented industrialization strategies, however. Under an import substitution policy, government protection and favors were decisive for the profitability of businesses. Under an export-oriented policy, firms had to compete in foreign markets. Although various forms of favors and subsidies helped the firms to compete in foreign markets, productivity and competitiveness became increasingly important. Also, the government's discretion was constrained, because it had to reward export performance, not just political loyalty and contributions. Thus, rent seeking and corruption were contained within certain limits, and the bureaucracy exercised discretion based on impersonal rather than personalistic or clientelistic criteria (Mo-Weingast).

As the size and power of the *chaebols* grew, the Chun Doo-hwan government (1980–7) began to take measures to promote gradual economic liberalization. The government liberalized imports gradually at U.S. request, but it also began to liberalize financial markets by reducing regulations of nonbank financial institutions, many of which had long been controlled by *chaebol* groups. In addition, measures such as the enactment of the Monopoly Regulation and Fair Trade Act were introduced to counter the market power of the *chaebols*, but these measures were not vigorously implemented. Interesting, *chaebols* grew even bigger and concentration increased further as a result of liberalization measures. Combined sales of the top ten *chaebols*, as a percent of GDP, grew from 15.1 percent in 1974 to 32.8 percent in 1979 to 67.4 percent in 1984 (Amsden 1989: 116, 134–7). Thus the Korean economy experienced increasing openness and competition on some dimensions, but increasing *chaebol* concentration and the collusion among political and business elites limited access and competition on other dimensions.

During this period, property right protection was not given to everyone equally. For example, President Park issued an Emergency Decree for Economic Stability and Growth to bail out the overleveraged *chaebols* in 1971, which transformed curb market loans into bank loans to be repaid over five years at lower interest rates, with a grace period of three years during which curb market loans were to be frozen. Out of 209,896 persons who registered as creditors, seventy percent were small lenders with assets in the market below 1 million won, or $2,890 (Kim and Im 2001; Woo 1991: 109–15). Thus the state ignored and violated the property rights of a large number of small creditors to save the *chaebols*.

Not all *chaebols* were treated equally, either. President Chun used the Industrial Rationalization to punish unsupportive *chaebols* and to favor the connected and supportive *chaebols*. The Kukje Group, then the seventh largest *chaebol*, was dissolved and Kukje's twenty-three affiliates were given to poorly performing *chaebols* that gave Chun large bribes or had family ties with him. Kukje Group's owner, Yang Jung-mo, was known to have refused to pay large bribes. The property rights of firms outside of the winning coalition, particularly firms whose owners paid few bribes or had ties with the opposition, were very insecure (Schopf 2004).

9.2.5 Mature LAO with Doorstep Conditions (1987–97)

The land reform and export-led industrialization not only contributed to opening access to economic activities but also created increasing pressures for political openings by expanding education and the middle class. In addition, the security threat declined as South Korea became far superior to North Korea in terms of economic and military power (including U.S. military support), and security could no longer be used to justify the authoritarian regime; the anticommunism rhetoric once used to suppress dissident movements also became ineffective. Although the first democratic transition in 1960 was followed by the Park coup in 1961 and the second democratic opening in 1979 was suppressed by the military junta led by Chun in 1980, the democratic opening in 1987 was more decisive and has not yet reverted back to authoritarian rule.[6]

After the democratic transition in 1987, Koreans enjoyed increasingly open access to political opportunities. Korea met the doorstep conditions that could lead to transition to an OAO. There were important developments with regard to civilian control of the military and checks on state violence, burgeoning of all forms of organizations, and improvements in the rule of law. In addition, there were attempts to increase the economic opening by further liberalizing markets and restraining the market power of the *chaebols*, although these efforts were not very successful.

Recall that the Rhee regime made a significant achievement with respect to the state monopoly of violence. The Korean War helped to eliminate militant leftist groups such as partisan guerrillas, and the land reform contributed to solidify political stability by removing sources of discontent and potential support for communism from the large peasant population. Thus, no powerful groups with violence potential except for the military and the police remained at the end of the war. However, military coups in 1961 and 1980 showed that the control of the military by the central government was shaky. During the Park and Chun presidencies, a large number of military officers were appointed as ministers and members of the National Assembly.

The democratic transition in 1987 brought an opportunity to firmly establish civilian control of the military. The military exercised self-restraint during the transition. President Kim Young-sam (1993–8) purged a group of politically ambitious military officers. Former presidents Chun Doo-whan and Roh Tae-woo were prosecuted and convicted of treason and corruption, which sent a strong message to the military that even successful coup leaders could be punished eventually. When the Koreans elected Kim Dae-jung, a long-time opposition leader formerly accused by the authoritarian regimes of being procommunist or pro-North Korea, as president in 1997, the military did not intervene. This proved the firm establishment of civilian control of the military. There has not been a single attempted coup for over two decades since the democratic transition.

Democracy also provided checks on arbitrary state violence such as torture, unexplained death, and violent suppression of protests. In parallel,

---

[6] Przeworski and Limongi (1999) found that no democracy failed in a country with a per capita income higher than USD 6,000 (1985 PPP). Korea was approaching that level of economic development when it made the democratic transition in 1987, as Korea reached USD 6,000 (1985 PPP) of per capita GDP in 1990 (Mo-Weingast). The Korean case may add evidence to their findings.

militant social movements declined, although they have not disappeared entirely. The rule of law improved as well. In particular, the Constitutional Court played an important role in protecting human rights and property rights. Various forms of organizations blossomed. Under authoritarian regimes, not only political organizations and labor unions but also business and professional associations were tightly controlled by the government. After the democratic transition in 1987, numerous civil society organizations in various fields were newly and freely created. Many of the industry associations, unions, and NGOs currently active were formed during the first three years of democracy (Mo-Weingast).

The rapid increase in political openings brought demands for further economic openings. On the one hand, business demanded deregulation. In particular, the *chaebols* sought to weaken or remove regulations such as the credit control system and restrictions on total equity investment, based on the Monopoly Regulation and Fair Trade Act. On the other hand was growing concern about economic concentration by the *chaebols* and collusion among political elites and *chaebols*.

When Park Chung-hee chose to favor the *chaebols* as a vehicle for export industry, the incipient *chaebols* were weak. The government was strong enough to direct their investment decisions, as the heavy and chemical industrialization drive of the 1970s demonstrated. Although the Park and Chun regimes increasingly relied on informal political contributions from the *chaebols*, they maintained strong government discipline on business. After the democratic transition, however, politicians' dependence on campaign funds increased *chaebols'* political influence and government discipline of large businesses weakened. The ruling party maintained close connections with the *chaebols*, and the opposition was often divided and lacked independent sources of political funds. The political parties were still weak in terms of presenting clear programmatic appeals, and political competition centered on personal appeals and regional cleavages that had formed from unbalanced regional development during the authoritarian era. In addition, the growth of the Korean economy in size and technology made it difficult for the government to control the private sector.

While the *chaebols* grew during the authoritarian era and continued to expand in economic and political influence after democratization, political and social organizations that could counterbalance *chaebol* influence were not so strong because of the stunted growth of civil society under the authoritarian regimes (Mo-Weingast). This imbalance of power led to an economic policy more responsive to *chaebols'* demands than to popular demand for *chaebol* reform. The government was unable to contain the *chaebols'* moral hazard, and their incentives to become too big to fail (TBTF) led to overinvestment and overborrowing, including excessive short-term foreign debt. The Kim Young-sam government's (1993–8) capital market account liberalization and deregulation of non-bank financial institutions (NBFIs) encouraged the *chaebols* to finance their overly ambitious investment through their affiliated NBFIs and international capital markets. Although the Korean economy was growing continuously after democratization, it became vulnerable to the East Asian financial crisis of 1997 after a series of bankruptcies of overleveraged *chaebols*.

9.2.6 Transition to an OAO (1997–Present)

The financial crisis of 1997 was a critical test of whether Korea would revert back to a more limited access order or make a full transition to an open access order. The economic crisis might have made Koreans blame the inefficiency of democratic political institutions and policy-making processes and revive nostalgia for authoritarian rule. Note that several countries in Latin America over the last century and a half moved closer to the doorstep conditions but moved away when crises brought a return of the military to politics or undermined rule of law (NWW).

In this regard, the election of Kim Dae-jung in 1998 as president in a closely contested race in the midst of financial crisis was a significant event. Kim had been a long-time opposition leader. Ten years later, Koreans made another change of government by electing conservative candidate Lee Myung-bak as president. These two changes of government, from conservative to liberal (1998) and from liberal to conservative (2008), satisfied the so-called two turn over test for democratic consolidation. As I noted earlier, the military exercised restraint in both elections.

President Kim Dae-jung pursued the "parallel development of democracy and market economy" and declared the end of government–business collusion or crony capitalism. He launched the so-called IMF-plus, a comprehensive reform program that went beyond the IMF-mandated reforms (You 2011). External liberalization, including a full-fledged opening of financial markets, selling off troubled financial institutions to foreign investors, lifting foreign exchange regulations, and radical liberalization of inward foreign investment was carried out. Structural reforms were carried out in the financial, corporate, labor, and public sectors. The *chaebol* reforms sought to enhance transparency and accountability in corporate governance and accounting practices. Financial reform strengthened the financial safety net and consolidated financial supervisory functions. Also, the government quickly expanded the social safety net such as unemployment insurance, health insurance, a national pension system, and public assistance for the poor.

These reforms increased openness and competition in the economy. It is probably too early to tell how much improvement has been made in the openness of the economy. On the one hand, Korea has experienced improvement in corporate governance and the protection of minority shareholders. Financial markets have been completely restructured. On the other hand, the powerful *chaebols* have resisted many reform measures, and the new conservative government of Lee Myung-bak has been weakening regulations on the *chaebols*.

Nevertheless, the sweeping economic reforms of the Kim Dae-jung government enhanced the basic institutional structure of market-based corporate discipline. Now, many new economic players such as banks, foreign investors, and institutional investors are acting independent from the government and the *chaebols*. In this sense, the degree of economic openness significantly improved after the crisis (Mo-Weingast).

The Kim Dae-jung government and the subsequent Roh Moo-hyun government (2003–8) increased openness and competition in the polity as well. Reforms in election and political financing laws increased transparency and promoted free and fair competition. Intraparty competition for nomination of candidates became more participatory and transparent as major parties introduced new processes similar to primary elections. Abuse of powerful agencies such as the prosecution, police, revenue, and information agencies for political purposes decreased remarkably, in particular under the Roh government. Rule of law improved further with the establishment of the Human Rights Commission. Many efforts were made to curb corruption, including the establishment of the Korea Independent Commission Against Corruption, the appointment of special prosecutors for several cases involving top-level officials, and the comprehensive investigation of presidential election campaign funds. Civil society organizations exerted substantial influence to hold the government, politicians, and *chaebols* accountable through negative election campaign against corrupt politicians and in support of minority shareholder activism.

After ten years of liberal rule, Koreans elected conservative and business-friendly Lee Myung-bak as president. The alternation of power between the liberal Democratic United Party and the conservative Saenuri Party and electoral contestation increasingly based on policy issues shows the development of the political party system in Korea.[7] Also, a few minor parties including the United Progressive Party have developed to incorporate a more diverse ideological spectrum. Although regional politics still dominate Korea's electoral landscapes, programmatic competition surrounding the issues of social policy and North Korea policies has increasingly affected voter choice.

There is a concern that the Lee Myung-bak government (2008–13) is retreating from the economic and political reforms of the previous governments. There are signs that rule of law is weakening recently as the legally guaranteed terms for public officeholders appointed under the previous government are not respected. Government intervention in the market is still occurring arbitrarily as in the case of attempted price control for necessary goods. Human rights groups such as Amnesty International have expressed concerns regarding the retrogression of freedom of the press and freedom of expression more generally under the new government. However, it is very unlikely that Korea will go back to the authoritarian era because the political system is competitive and civil society has grown strong.

9.3 Reflections on the LAO–OAO Framework and the Korean Case

Having briefly reviewed the postcolonial history of South Korea through the lens of the LAO–OAO framework, I will now examine a few key issues of the framework with regard to the Korean case.

9.3.1 Open Access and Economic Development

One of the disturbing facts about Korea's economic development is that the miraculous economic takeoff and sustained growth took place under the authoritarian regimes of Park Chung-hee (1961–79) and Chun Doo-hwan

---

[7] Both the major conservative party and the major liberal party have changed their names and gone through reorganizations including splits and mergers for the last two decades. The conservative Saenuri Party has developed from Chun Doo-hwan's Democratic Justice Party, which merged with the opposition parties led by Kim Young-sam and Kim Jong-pil in 1991. The Democratic Liberal Party created by a three-party merger changed its name to the New Korea Party, to the Grand National Party, and to the Saenuri Party. The liberal "Democratic United Party" developed from the Party for Peace and Democracy that Kim Dae-jung created before the 1987 presidential election. It has reorganized itself and changed its name several times to the National Congress for New Politics, to the New Millennium Democratic Party, to the Uri Party, to the Democratic Party, and to the Democratic United Party.

(1980–7). The authoritarian regimes not only suppressed the political rights of citizens but also heavily intervened in the economy. Only after Korea achieved substantial growth did political democratization and economic liberalization come. Does the Korean case suggest that economic growth comes first and transition to an open access order comes later?

It should be noted that Korea's economic growth was possible because of a series of changes in the structure of the dominant coalition. The association of landed elites with the Japanese occupation weakened their influence in the larger society and the polity. Land reform that might otherwise have been neutralized by landed elites was effective and dissolved the privileged landlord class, creating an unusually equal distribution of income and wealth. This, in turn, contributed to the rapid expansion of education. These constituted favorable conditions for the establishment of an autonomous developmental state. Land reform was not an expression of open access, but a reaction by a limited access polity to an external threat. Export-led industrialization limited the role of patronage and corruption because firms had to compete in the global markets. Allocation of government favors such as underpriced credit was largely based on objective criteria like export performance.

It is notable that the erosion of open access in the economy caused the financial crisis of 1997. The *chaebols* grew too big to fail during the authoritarian era and further increased their political influence after the democratic transition in 1987. The financial crisis, however, provided an opportunity for sweeping economic reforms. The comprehensive reforms undertaken by the Kim Dae-jung government increased openness in the economy, and the Korean economy continued to grow after a year of negative growth in 1998.

Also, we should note that democratization did not harm the economy. It is true that Korea achieved remarkable economic growth under the authoritarian regimes, with an average annual growth rate of 6.3 percent during the 1972–86 period. Korea's economic performance has not declined after the democratic transition, with an average annual growth rate of 5.9 percent during the 1987–2004 period (Heston, Summers, and Aten 2006; Table 6.2).

9.3.2 Theory of the Double Balance

NWW propose a theory of the double balance, which suggests that economic and political systems both tend to be open access or limited access. This implies that sustaining fundamental changes in either the economic or political system cannot occur without fundamental changes in the other.

They also emphasize that the formal institutions work differently depending on the social order in which they are embedded. When the institutional forms of an OAO are transplanted to an LAO, the logic of the LAO bends them to the purpose of rent creation to sustain the existing dominant coalition. This argument can be interpreted to imply that the formal institutions of democracy will not work well in a limited access economy and that formal institutions of the market economy will work differently in a limited access political system.

The theory of double balance sheds insights into our understanding of economic and political developments in Korea. The land reform produced a considerable degree of openness and competition in the economy. On one hand, the relatively open access economy produced pressures for open access politics. The movement for democracy grew until the democratic transition of 1987.

On the other hand, open access and competition in the economic system was restricted under the authoritarian regimes, because the limited access political system undermined open access and competition in economic activities. Although there were no big *chaebols* or powerful economic interests under Syngman Rhee's presidency, his authoritarian regime developed patronage politics and used distribution of rents such as allocation of foreign exchanges, former Japanese assets, and American aid to build up and reward political loyalty and illegal political contributions. Park Chung-hee and his successors' policy of favoring the *chaebols* created a triangle collusion of government-banks-*chaebol*, and the growing *chaebols'* market and nonmarket power increasingly limited access and competition in the markets. Although the Korean government has tried to limit the market power of the *chaebols* and promote competition since the passage of the Fair Trade and Anti-Monopoly Act of 1981, serious efforts to reform the *chaebols* did not take place until the financial crisis and change of government in 1997.

After the democratic transition in 1987, Korea came to have another imbalance: relatively more open politics and less open economy. This imbalance could produce forces to find equilibrium in either direction: toward more open economy or back toward less open politics. In the midst of financial crisis, Koreans chose the former. The post-crisis reforms made the Korean economy more open, and the double balance moved toward the direction of open access, both in the polity and the economy.

Another question is why the formal institutions of democracy did not work in Korea during the 1950s. It was not because powerful economic interests captured the political process. Korea was probably unprepared for democracy then. Open access political systems require citizens who share belief systems in open access and competition and vibrant civil society as well as political parties that can aggregate people's preferences (NWW). All these factors were lacking, and the authoritarian tendency of Syngman Rhee did not face much resistance until the short-lived student revolution of April 1960.

Indeed, the right question to ask is how Korea developed democracy in a couple of generations. And the answer is the relative openness in the economy, which was created primarily by land reform.

9.3.3 Rents and Corruption

NWW's key claim is that, in a limited access society, violence is contained by creating economic rents for powerful individuals and groups. They suggest that the types of rent as well as their effects on economic development tend to change from a fragile to basic to mature LAO and then to an OAO, in which Schumpeterian innovative rents dominate. They note that patronage and corruption will be more prevalent in LAOs than in OAOs, because creation and distribution of rents will involve patronage and corruption (Table 9.3).

Creation and distribution of rents by the government as well as corruption and rent-seeking activities were ubiquitous throughout the postindependence history of Korea. The most prevalent types of rent changed over time. During the 1950s, American aid was the most important source of rents. Allocation of import licenses and foreign exchanges was also important under the import substitution industrialization strategy.

During the early era of export-led industrialization centered on light industry in the 1960s and heavy and chemical industry in the 1970s, government-provided protection from internal and external competition, combined with various subsidies in the form of underpriced credit rationing and tax exemptions, was the most important source of rents.

Over time, monopoly rents became more important as the *chaebols'* market power grew. Land speculation also became an important source of rents as land prices tended to rise more than the overall prices. Last, Schumpeterian innovative rents have grown recently as the Korean economy is increasingly heading toward high-tech industry.

Table 9.3 *Different types of rent in different periods in South Korea*

Types of Social Order	Types of Rent
Basic LAO (1948–60)	Redefinition of property rights (land reform)
	U.S. aid, vested properties, import license, foreign exchanges
Basic/Mature LAO (1960–87)	protection (learning), credit rationing, monopoly, land speculation
Mature LAO (1987–97)	monopoly, land speculation,
	protection (learning), credit rationing, Schumpeterian
Transition to an OAO (1997–)	Schumpeterian,
	monopoly, land speculation

Different types of rents can have different effects on economic development. Apparently, the protection rents for infant industry largely translated to learning rents in Korea, as Khan and Jomo (2000) argue. Since protection from competition was not permanent, these protected firms eventually had to compete in global markets. Although the distribution of rents did involve corrupt exchanges, the degree of corruption was not too high because the government rewarded export performance rather than simply favoring high bribe givers. However, corrupt exchanges between the top of the government (including corrupt presidents Chun Doo-hwan and Roh Tae-woo) and the *chaebols* grew over time until the mid-1990s.[8] These corrupt exchanges and the government-bank-*chaebol* collusion led to inefficient overinvestment based on overborrowing, which brought several *chaebol* failures and contributed to the financial crisis of 1997. Recently, innovative rents have become increasingly important as Korean economy develops high-tech industry as well as culture industry. This development is consistent with the logic of an open access economy.

There is evidence that the overall level of corruption has decreased in Korea since the late 1990s (You 2009). The *chaebols'* informal political contributions have declined substantially, according to evidence from prosecutorial investigations of high-level corruption scandals. Experience of petty

---

[8] Prosecutorial investigations of high-level corruption scandals and journalistic accounts suggest that top-level businessmen's informal political donations steadily increased over time from the 1950s until the early 1990s. The amount of illegal political donations seems to have decreased only after the late 1990s (You 2009).

Table 9.4 *Trends of various measures of experienced corruption in Korea, 1992–2008*

Year	1992	1996	1999	2000	2001	2002	2003	2004	2005	2006	2007	2008
GCB bribery								6	4	2	1	2
SMG bribery			7.9	6.7	7.1	5.7	1.8	1.1	1.1	0.8	0.7	0.3
KIPA bribery (small businesses)				25.0	16.2			13.8	11.6	6.6	7.4	4.8
NEC vote buying	18.2	14.7		12.4				2.9				1.4

GCB bribery: Percentage of people whose family members bribed public officials during the last year, in Transparency International's Global Corruption Barometer
  Survey.
SMG bribery: Percentage of clients who bribed public officials of Seoul Metropolitan Government in the past year, in Seoul Metropolitan Government's Integrity
  Survey.
KIPA bribery: Percentage of small businessmen who bribed public officials in the past year, in the surveys of Korea Institute of Public Administration.
NEC vote-buying: Percentage of voters who were given money, gift, free tours, or entertainment by candidates or political parties during the National Assembly
  elections.

bureaucratic corruption has declined remarkably, according to surveys of businessmen and the general public. Vote buying practices have almost disappeared, according to the voter surveys (Table 9.4).

9.3.4 Doorstep Conditions

NWW and NWWW suggested that there are three (necessary but not sufficient) doorstep conditions for a transition to OAO: 1) rule of law for elites, 2) support for perpetually lived organizations for elites, and 3) centralized political control of organizations with violence potential.

As I noted earlier, Korea met these three conditions after the democratic transition in 1987.[9] Rule of law was weak even for elites, and support for perpetually lived organizations was inadequate under authoritarian regimes. Authoritarian rulers often ignored basic human rights of the dissidents (e.g., torture) and violated property rights of citizens (e.g., freezing of curb market). Even the seventh largest *chaebol* was dissolved when its owner did not bribe sufficiently and was suspected of having ties with the opposition. Industrial restructuring in the early 1980s shows that the Chun Doo-hwan government threatened property rights to extract further bribes from *chaebols* (Schopf 2004).

The development of rule of law and of support for organizations in Korea seems to differ from the experiences of Western Europe and North America. In the history of Western Europe and North America, rule of law and support for organizations developed for elites first and then expanded to the whole population. In Korea, however, rule of law and support for organizations developed for both elites and non-elites only after the democratic transition.

This difference may apply to many developing countries in which formal institutions of rule of law for everyone were introduced after independence but authoritarian rulers ignored the rule of law. Democratization in these countries means that formal institutions of rule of law for everyone cannot be violated by the rulers and that rule of law largely depends on the independence and integrity of the judiciary. Rule of law in Korea improved with the active role of the Constitutional Court, the Human Rights Commission, and special prosecutors appointed by the National Assembly and president to investigate high-profile corruption cases.

---

[9] Mo-Weingast seem to imply that the doorstep conditions were met much earlier, i.e. during Park Chung-hee's rule.

Conviction of two former presidents on charges of treason and corruption (1996) and the extensive investigation of presidential campaign funds (2003) also contributed to rule of law, because these events signaled that no person is above the law.

9.3.5 Consolidation of an OAO

NWW propose that an OAO is consolidated when open access in all systems is mutually reinforcing. Consolidation of an OAO requires not just formal institutions of democracy and a market economy but also citizens' shared belief systems on equality and inclusion, vibrant civil society, and competitive political parties.

Korea appears to be moving toward a successfully consolidated OAO. There seems to be a consensus that democracy is the only game in town. Civil society organizations have expanded rapidly. Political parties remain somewhat unstable, but they have been vying for control in competitive elections. Korea's peaceful transfer of power in 1997 from conservative to liberal, and in 2007 from liberal to conservative, demonstrates the working of open and competitive party politics. Korea's market economy is increasingly characterized by open access and competition, both internally and externally.

We also observe that open access in various systems mutually reinforces one another. Democratization has helped to invigorate civil society, and vibrant civil society has played an active role in promoting open access in politics as well as in the economic system. Civil society organizations pressured for anticorruption reforms and promoted women's rights and human rights of foreign migrant workers. Minority shareholder movements contributed to protecting minority shareholders and to reforming corporate governance.

However, restrictions to access in political and economic opportunities remain in place. The government sometimes intervenes in the market arbitrarily. The National Security Law still bans communism and prohibits even listening to North Korean radio. There also have been setbacks in the rule of law and freedom of expression under the new conservative government. The lack of progress and setbacks in these areas pose challenges to the consolidation of an OAO in South Korea.

9.4 What Made Korea's Transition Possible?

So far, I have interpreted Korea's postindependence history through the lens of the LAO–OAO framework and discussed some issues about the

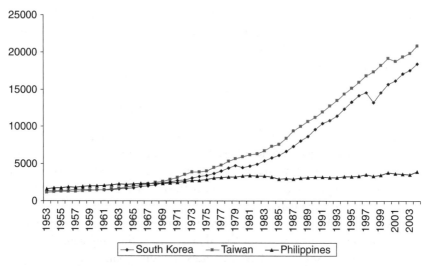

Figure 9.1 Real GDP per capita of South Korea, Taiwan, and the Philippines, 1953–2004 (in 2000 constant dollars).
Source: Heston et al. (2006).

framework. The big question is: What made Korea's transition to an OAO possible, while most developing countries failed to make such a transition? In order to answer this question, I will compare the postcolonial history of Korea with that of Taiwan and the Philippines. Finding similarities with Taiwan, another success story, and differences with the Philippines, a failure story, will give insight into this question. Note that, in the early period of independence, the Philippines was somewhat better off in terms of per capita income and educational attainment and looked more promising than Korea and Taiwan. Figure 9.1 shows that the per capita GDP of the Philippines was slightly higher than that of Korea and Taiwan until the late 1960s, but the stagnating long-run performance of the Philippines is sharply contrasted with the sustained high growth of Korea and Taiwan.

It is not just economic development but also political development that shows the inferior performance of the Philippines when compared to Korea and Taiwan. These countries all experienced democratic transitions in the late 1980s. Formal institutions of democracy seem to be working better in Korea and Taiwan than in the Philippines, however, according to the Freedom House's assessment (Figure 9.2). Freedom House ratings (political rights, civil liberties, and combined average scores) range from one (most free) to seven (least free). A combined average score of 1 to 2.5 is categorized as "Free," 3–5 as "Partly Free," and 5.5–7 as "Not Free."

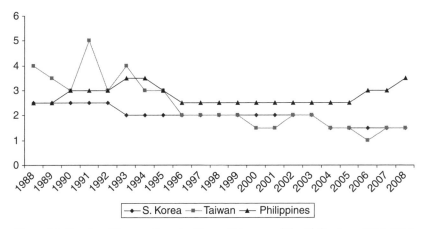

Figure 9.2 Freedom House ratings for Korea, Taiwan, and the Philippines, 1988–2008. *Source:* Freedom House.

Korea's combined average score of political rights and civil liberties has improved from 2.5 (1988–92) to 2 (1993–2003) to 1.5 (2004–8). The same score for Taiwan has also improved from "between 3 and 5" (1988–95) to "between 1.5 and 2" (1996–2003) to "between 1 and 1.5" (2004–8). However, the same score for the Philippines has worsened from 2.5 (1996–2005) to 3 (2006–7) to 3.5 (2008). The Freedom House changed the status of the Philippines from "Free" to "Partly Free" in 2006, and its political rights rating declined again in 2008 due to credible allegations of massive electoral fraud, corruption, and a spike in political killings specifically targeting left-wing political activists. While Korea and Taiwan have been successfully consolidating democracy, the Philippine democracy seems to have been deteriorating.

It is interesting to compare the levels of corruption in Korea, Taiwan, and the Philippines. Table 9.5 presents various indicators of corruption for these countries. Business International's corruption ratings for 1980–3 and Transparency International's *historical* CPI scores for 1980–5 and 1988–92 as well as average values for TI's CPI (1995–2008) reveal that Taiwan was the least corrupt, the Philippines the most corrupt, and Korea in between.[10] BI ratings range between 1 (most corrupt) and 10 (least corrupt), and CPI ratings range between 0 (most corrupt) and 10 (least corrupt). Both BI ratings (1980–3) and TI ratings for various periods (1980–5, 1988–92, and

---

[10] It is not appropriate to compare the *historical* CPI scores with the annual CPI scores that have been published by the TI since 1995, because the underlying data sources are different.

Table 9.5 *Various indicators of corruption in Korea, Taiwan, and the Philippines*

	BI 80–83	CPI 80–85	CPI 88–92	CPI 95–08	Problem 03–08	Bribery 04–08
Taiwan	6.75	6.0	5.1	5.5	3.0%	2.0%
Korea	5.75	3.9	3.5	4.6	5.4%	3.0%
Philippines	4.50	1.0	2.0	2.8	22.4%	17.8%

Notes:
BI 80–83: Business International's average perceived corruption ratings for 1980–3
CPI 80–85: Transparency International's historical data for 1980–5
CPI 88–92: Transparency International's historical data for 1988–92
CPI 95–08: Transparency International's average CPI for 1995–2008
Problem 03–08: Average percentage of businessmen who cite corruption as the biggest problem for doing business out of 14–15 factors, from World Economic Forum, *Global Competitiveness Report*, 2003–8.
Bribery 04–08: Average percentage of people whose family members bribed public officials during the last twelve months (%), from Transparency International, Global Corruption Barometer Survey, 2004–8.

1995–2008) consistently show that the Philippines to be much more corrupt than Korea and Taiwan. Korea was perceived to be somewhat more corrupt than Taiwan.

The average percentage of businessmen who cited corruption as the biggest obstacle for doing business from the World Economic Forum's Executive Opinion Survey (2003–8) is about three percent in Taiwan, five percent in Korea, and twenty-two percent in the Philippines. The average percentage of respondents whose family members paid a bribe to public officials during the last year according to TI's Global Corruption Barometer Survey (2004–8) is about two percent in Taiwan, three percent in Korea, and eighteen percent in the Philippines. These data all show that corruption has been extremely pervasive in the Philippines, while it has been much less of a problem in Korea and Taiwan. Korea seems to have had a slightly higher level of corruption than Taiwan. A closer look at various indicators of corruption, however, shows that Korea's level of corruption has been declining and converging to that of Taiwan recently (You 2009).

Korea and Taiwan have shown much better performance than the Philippines both in terms of economic development and in terms of democratic consolidation and control of corruption. While Korea and Taiwan appear to be making transitions to open access orders, the Philippines is locked in a limited access order. What enabled Korea and Taiwan to make transitions to OAOs but did not allow the Philippines to do so?

One answer could be the presence of developmental states in Korea and Taiwan and a predatory state in the Philippines. But that simply moves the question back one level to why Korea and Taiwan were able to establish a developmental state while the Philippines failed to do so. The biggest advantages that Korea and Taiwan enjoyed over the Philippines seem to be successful land reform and state monopoly of violence in the early period of independence.

Successful land reform reduced the influence of the landed class and laid the foundation for an open access economy in Korea and Taiwan, while in the Philippines the failure of land reform led to the continuing dominance of large landlords as well as high inequality in income and wealth. The failure of land reform helped the landed oligarchy to maintain and expand its wealth and power, and the economic policy machinery was routinely hijacked by the powerful landed and business elites. While the relatively more open access and competition in the economy spurred economic growth in Korea and Taiwan, the more limited access and competition in the economy hindered economic development in the Philippines.

In Korea and Taiwan, state monopoly on violence was established early. In both countries, land reform helped to produce political stability and to eliminate nonstate organizations with violence potential. In both countries, political control over the military was firmly established and there have been no attempted coups since their democratic transitions. In the Philippines, however, insurgencies based on peasant grievances have continued, including the Huk rebellion in the 1940s, the New People's Army during the martial law period, and decades of Muslim insurgency in the southern Philippines that continued until the 2008 peace accord. Also, militant landlords used to establish private armies. Even after the democratic transition, coup attempts recurred frequently and political killings increased. Failure of land reform was a major source of political instability in the Philippines.

The next question is why land reform succeeded in South Korea and Taiwan but failed in the Philippines. The key answer appears to be the existence or absence of urgent external threats from neighboring communist countries. In South Korea and Taiwan, communist threats from North Korea and mainland China gave the political elites little choice regarding land reform. It was imperative for them to win the hearts and minds of peasants through sweeping land reform. The landlords were discredited and lost political influence because of their collaboration with the Japanese during the colonial period. In the Philippines, there were no serious external threats, and internal threats from insurgencies were not so great as to force the political and landed elites to acquiesce to the peasant demand for land reform. Since their colonial master was the United States, the landlords' collaboration with the colonial ruler did not weaken their political influence (You 2012).

The security threat from North Korea as well as economic competition with North Korea has had enduring effects on South Korea's political and economic development. North Korea initially showed better economic performance than South Korea after the end of the Korean War, and South Korea's GDP per capita did not surpass that of North Korea until around 1970, according to the South Korean government's assessment (Seo 1993). Perhaps South Korean dictators could not afford to be too corrupt in the face of the North Korean threat. Even corrupt presidents Chun Doo-hwan and Roh Tae-woo were constrained compared to Marcos. On the other hand, the security threat was utilized to justify authoritarian regimes. Some restrictions on freedom of expression, notably the National Security Law, are still justified on the ground of the national security threat from North Korea.

9.5 Conclusion

This chapter demonstrates the usefulness of NWW and NWWW's conceptual framework in understanding the postcolonial development of Korea. The role of land reform in opening access to economic opportunities and establishing state monopoly of violence was critical to later economic and political development. The land reform also contributed to expanding education and establishing meritocratic and autonomous bureaucracy. The relatively open access economy not only brought about rapid and sustained economic growth but also created increasing pressures for open access polity, which led to the democratic transition of 1987. Although export-led industrialization helped to increase open access and competition in the economy, economic concentration by the *chaebols* and collusion between government and the *chaebols* increasingly limited access and competition. The 1997 financial crisis was a critical point at which Korea could have reverted back to a limited access order or continued to make a transition toward an open access order. Fortunately, post-crisis reforms enabled Korea to further open the economy and the polity.

My findings suggest that external threat and competition has played an important role. The communist threat from North Korea helped the land reform, and the fierce competition with North Korea helped to check extreme forms of rent seeking and corruption. The export-led growth strategy exposed the South Korean firms to global competition, which limited the importance of collusive rent seeking and promoted learning and inno-vation rents.

Comparison of the Korean experience with those of Taiwan and the Philippines reveals the critical importance of land reform. In Taiwan, the success of land reform under the communist threat of mainland China also helped to remove the privileged landed class and to develop the economy without excessive distributive struggle, which made the democratic transi-tion and consolidation processes smooth. In the Philippines, however, the initial failure of land reform in the absence of an external threat led to con-tinuous distributive struggles, which has made democratic consolidation difficult and helped the insurgencies to continue.

The chapter also suggests that the doorstep conditions may not work the same way in today's developing countries as they did in the historical expe-riences of Western Europe and North America. Whereas the rule of law was established for elites first and expanded to the broader population over time in the history of Western Europe and North America, it developed at the same time for both elites and non-elites in Korea.

References

Amsden, Alice H. 1989. *Asia's Next Giant: South Korea and Late Industrialization*. Oxford University Press.

Ban, Sung Hwan, P. Y. Moon, and D. Perkins. 1980. *Rural Development: Studies in the Modernization of The Republic of Korea: 1945–1975*. Cambridge, MA: Harvard University Press.

Benabou, Roland. 1996. "Inequality and Growth." *NBER Macroeconomics Annual* **11**: 11–92.

Chang, Ha-Joon. 1994. *The Political Economy of Industrial Policy*, New York: St. Martin's Press.

Eichengreen, Barry 2012. *The Korean Economy: Coping with Maturity*. Draft.

Evans, Peter. 1995. *Embedded Autonomy: States and Industrial Transformation*. Princeton, NJ: Princeton University Press.

Freedom House. *Freedom in the World* at http://www.freedomhouse.org/.

Haggard, Stephan. 1990. *Pathways from the Periphery. The Politics of Growth in the Newly Industrializing Countries*. Ithaca: Cornell University Press.

Heston, Alan, Robert Summers, and Bettina Aten. 2006. *Penn World Table Version 6.2*. Center for International Comparisons of Production, Income and Prices at the University of Pennsylvania.

Hong, Seong Chan. 2001. "Nongji Kaehyok Chonhuui Taejiju Tonghyang (Responses of the Landlords before and after the Land Reform)." In Hong, S. C. ed., *Nongji Kaehyok Yongu (Studies in Agrarian Land Reform)*. Seoul: Yonsei University Press.

Jones, Leroy P. and Il Sakong. 1980. *Government, Business, and Entrepreneurship in Economic Development: The Korean Case*. Harvard University Press.

Kang, David C. 2002. *Crony Capitalism: Corruption and Development in South Korea and the Philippines*. Cambridge, UK: Cambridge University Press.

Khan, Mushtaq H. and K. S. Jomo, eds. 2000. *Rents, Rent-Seeking, and Economic Development: Theory and Evidence in Asia*. Cambridge, UK: Cambridge University Press.

Kim, Byung-Kook and Im, Hyug-Baeg. 2001. "Crony Capitalism in South Korea, Thailand and Taiwan: Myth and Reality." *Journal of East Asian Studies* 1(2): 5–52.

Kwon, Byung-Tak. 1984. "Nongji Kaehyokui Kwajongkwa Kyongjejok Kiyo (Processes of Farmland Reform and Its Economic Contribution in Korea)." *Nongop Chongchaek Yongu (Korean Journal of Agricultural Policy)* 11(1): 191–207.

Kim, Se Jin. 1971. *The Politics of Military Revolution in Korea*. Chapel Hill: University of North Carolina Press.

Lee, Hahn-Been. 1968. *Korea: Time, Change, and Administration*. Honolulu: East-West Center Press.

Lie, John. 1998. *Han Unbound: The Political Economy of South Korea*. Stanford, CA: Stanford University Press.

Lim, Wonhyuk. 2003. "The Emergence of the Chaebol and the Origins of the Chaebol Problem." In Stephan Haggard, Wonhyuk Lim, and Euysung Kim, eds., *Economic Crisis and Corporate Restructuring in Korea*. Cambridge University Press.

MacIntyre, Andrew. 1994. "Business, Government and Development: Northeast and Southeast Asian Comparisons." In Andrew MacIntyre, ed., *Business and Government in Industrializing Asia*. St. Leonards, Australia: Allen & Unwin Pty Ltd.

Mason, Edward S., Mahn Je Kim, Dwight H. Perkins, Kwang Suk Kim, and David C. Cole. 1980. *The Economic and Social Modernization of the Republic of Korea*. Cambridge, MA: Harvard University Press.

McKinnon, Ronald. 1973. *Money and Capital in Economic Development*, Washington, DC: Brookings Institution.

Mo, Jongryn and Barry Weingast. 2012. *Political Economy of Korea's Transition, 1961–2008*. Draft.

Moran, Jon. 1999. "Patterns of Corruption and Development in East Asia." *Third World Quarterly* 20(3):569–87.

North, Douglass, John Wallis, and Barry Weingast, 2009. *Violence and Social Orders: A Conceptual Framework for Interpreting Recorded Human History*. Cambridge University Press.

North, Douglass, John Wallis, Steven Webb and Barry Weingast, 2007. "Limited Access Orders in the Developing World: A New Approach to the Problem of Development." World Bank Policy Research Paper, No. 4359.

Putzel, James. 1992. *A Captive Land: The Politics of Agrarian Reform in the Philippines*. London, UK: Catholic Institute for International Relations.

Rodrik, Dani, Gene Grossman, and Victor Norman. 1995. "Getting Interventions Right: How South Korea and Taiwan Grew Rich." *Economic Policy* 20 (April): 53107.

Schopf, James C. 2004. *Corruption and Democratization in the Republic of Korea: The End of Political Bank Robbery*. Dissertation, University of California, San Diego.

Seo, Jae-jin. 1993. *Nambukhan Kukryeok Choose Bigyo Yeongu (A Comparative Study of the Trends of National Powers in the South and North Koreas)*. Seoul: Minjoktongil Yeonguwon (The Research Institute for National Unification).

Woo, Jung-en. 1991. *Race to the Swift: State and Finance in Korean Industrialization*. New York: Columbia University Press.

Woo-Cumings, Meredith. 1995. "The Korean Bureacratic State: Historical Legacies and Comparative Perspectives." In James Cotton, ed., *Politics and Policy in the New Korean State: From Roh Tae-Woo to Kim Young-Sam*. New York: St. Martin's Press.

World Bank. 1987. *World Development Report 1987*, New York: Oxford University Press.

You, Jong-il. 1998. "Income Distribution and Growth in East Asia." *Journal of Development Studies* **34**(6): 37–65.

2011. "Political Economy of Economic Reform in South Korea." Draft.

You, Jong-sung. 2012. "Inequality and Corruption: The Role of Land Reform in Korea, Taiwan, and the Philippines." Draft.

2009. "Is South Korea Succeeding in Controlling Corruption?" Draft.

TEN

Lessons

In the Shadow of Violence

Douglass C. North, John Joseph Wallis,
Steven B. Webb, and Barry R. Weingast

Thinking of developing countries as limited access orders with their own social dynamic rather than as flawed or incomplete open-access societies affords new insights into the impediments and paths to development. The perspective distinguishes between two development problems that are normally conflated. The second development problem involves the transition of societies from LAOs to OAOs. The first development problem involves the movement of LAO societies toward forms of social organization that enable more economic output, reduced violence, stable political outcomes, and greater individual well-being. World Bank borrowers face the first development problem: developing as an LAO, from fragile to basic and from basic to mature LAO, while avoiding regression. The lessons we draw from the case studies presented in this volume are primarily concerned with enabling places like the DR Congo to accomplish social outcomes that more closely resemble Mexico or Zambia. We also draw lessons about making transitions to open access, but our primary focus is on the first development problem because it is first in terms of human priorities. Understanding better the logic of limited access societies and the dynamics of how they change holds out greater rewards in terms of reducing poverty and violence.

The control of violence is central to the logic of all LAOs and hence is central to the problem of development. The traditional economic development framework focuses mainly on the second development problem and fails to understand violence or incorporate an appreciation of the dynamics of violence into policy recommendations. Indeed, the Washington consensus of the 2000s was dominated by efforts to embed institutions of open-access orders – property rights, entry into markets, elections, or institutions of good governance – directly into limited access orders. Because these reforms ignore the logic of the LAO, they often fail to produce development and sometimes exacerbate the problem of violence. The traditional development perspective typically treats violence as a country-specific phenomenon and leaves dealing with violence for local police and courts. By doing so, this perspective fails to understand that LAOs are organized to prevent violence and that this often hinders traditional reform efforts.

What does it mean to become a better developing country, a better LAO? At the level of the population, the key outcomes are reduced violence, more predictability of law enforcement, increased income, better health, more equality, and more political participation. At the level of organizations, the key outcomes are more durable organizations in both the public and private sectors, an increasing reliability of public support for all organizations, and eventually the ability of elite organizations to operate outside the immediate circle of the dominant coalition. At the level of elites, key outcomes involve increasing confidence in access to unbiased rule of law for elites and eventually the provision of institutions that treat elites more impersonally, that is, that treat increasing numbers of elites in the same way. The cases show that feasible steps toward those outcomes on all these dimensions depend on each country's circumstances. What Mexico, Korea, and Bangladesh could do to enhance their LAOs in the 1990s was qualitatively different from each other and from what they did in earlier decades of the twentieth century, but there are commonalities.

This chapter summarizes the lessons from the cases; in doing so, it expands the framework summarized in the introductory chapter. In all of the case studies, the first steps at the fragile end of the LAO spectrum focused on making rent-sharing commitments among the organizations with violence capacity. Initially these agreements were on a personal level, as in the Philippines and Bangladesh. In India, the degree of rule-based institutions (versus personal) varies widely across states. Over time, personal elite bargains can be converted into rule-based institutions – more thoroughly, for example, in Korea than in Mexico. Holding competitive elections was a later step in these countries, and most of them still do not assure open economic and political access or competition.

The first section of this chapter highlights four areas of diagnostic insights that emerge from applying the LAO framework in the case studies and that can help us understand the political economy in developing countries: violence and the theory of rents; the dynamics of LAOs; the idea that similar institutions work differently in LAOs than in OAOs; and the pervasive influence of organizations based in OAOs. The second section identifies lessons with specific implications of the approach for development policy in four areas: rents and market constraints; organizations; democracy and elections; and organizations with violence capacity. We end the chapter with a discussion of the agenda for future research.

10.1 Diagnostic Insights

The World Bank's agenda for governance and anticorruption emphasizes explicitly what many have known for years, namely that designing programs to improve governance in a country needs to start with a good understanding of its political economy (World Bank 2007). This requires looking at the country through various lenses, including the limited access order framework emphasized here. The 2011 World Bank Development Report: *Conflict, Security, and Development* explicitly recognizes that violence plays a central role in the economic and political performance of developing countries all along the spectrum from fragile to basic to mature LAOs.

10.1.1 Violence and Rents

The efforts to reduce violence shape all LAOs, and all the cases, except Zambia, experienced periods of violence at a level that threatened or overthrew the government. These events cast a long shadow in people's memories and through the institutions that they created to constrain or discourage the violence. LAOs use rents, limited access, and privileges to reduce violence by granting privileges and rents to individuals and groups with access to violence and creating incentives to cooperate rather than fight. Powerful groups enjoy valuable privileges such as exclusive rights to trade, a monopoly on cement or telecoms, the exclusive right to hold a market in a given locality, or a monopoly on the importation of high-demand items. In the case of Mexico in the 1930s, India and Bangladesh after the partitions, and Mozambique coming out of its civil war after 1992, the allocation of rents to organizations with violence capacity helped to motivate the reductions in actual violence. As Bates (1983) demonstrates, many tropical African states used monopsonistic marketing boards to extract rents from farmers producing export crops. These countries used part of the rents from the marketing boards to keep food prices low, thereby placating urban workers who might otherwise riot and threaten to topple governments. Those with the power to create violence or disorder receive privileges – rents – while those who do not have this power have few rights and are often exploited.

Our approach to rents differs significantly from the literature that emphasizes rent-seeking (Buchanan, Tullock, and Tollison 1980; Krueger 1974) and directly unproductive policies or DUP (Bhagwati 1982), as detailed in the introductory framework chapter. Viewed from the LAO perspective, the rent-seeking/DUP approach ignores violence and implicitly assumes that the creation of rents is unrelated to the underlying nature of the society in which the rents appear. The LAO focus on violence and instability highlights the frequent tradeoff between raising hypothetical efficiency and creating stability with diminished violence. This perspective raises a question: When is it better to allow some costs to the economy, and perhaps to civil or political rights, in order to maintain or strengthen stability and prevent disorder? Our conceptual framework and the case studies show that the appropriate counterfactual about eliminating rents is often not a competitive market economy (as the DUP perspective suggests), but rather a society in disorder and violence.

To the extent that rent creation in LAOs is the means of creating stability, then rents are a symptom of the development problem, not the cause of it. Attempts to remove institutions and policies that support economically unproductive rent creation and corruption need to be done in ways that avoid the recurrence of instability and violence, which derails development in an LAO. Often it is not done right, as in Bangladesh during the emergency government of 2007–9 or in the Philippines under Marcos and then under Aquino, causing the LAO to regress. Other examples in our cases show how key organizations with violence potential can be sufficiently satisfied so that they remain in the ruling coalition while still allowing space for dynamic parts of the economy to open up: The army in Chile has kept its ten percent of the profits from the state-owned copper mines, while private firms were allowed to also enter the sector and now account for the majority of output. Most of the unions in Mexico have kept or solidified their power in Mexico since the political opening in the 1990s, but NAFTA and other reforms also opened many opportunities for new firms to emerge.

10.1.2. Dynamics of LAOs

Although the patterns of social dynamics within LAOs are persistent, LAOs are not static. As circumstances change, so too do important features of each LAO, even while they remain within the general LAO logic for decades and even centuries. Changes occur in response to both exogenous and endogenous factors. Changing relative prices, climatic events, technological change, globalization, and violence from neighbors are all exogenous events, beyond the explanatory potential of the LAO framework. Economic growth or recession within the country, changes in the nature and distribution of rents, the membership in the dominant coalition or asymmetric growth (including violence potential) among these members, and the nature of public policy are all endogenous changes. The LAO framework, although it does not explain everything, helps us understand how these endogenous factors interact with each other and with the exogenous ones.

All the cases exhibit significant change while remaining LAOs. On the negative side, as the Philippines case shows, Marcos used the threat of violence to impose martial law on what had been an LAO with electoral democracy. Some years later, the Marcos regime fell, in part because the fall in commodity prices reduced the total rents available to Marcos so that his support coalition fell apart. Electoral democracy returned, but as under Marcos, the new regime perpetuated limited access in both economics and politics, so the Philippines remains an LAO. Similarly, the PRI enjoyed a long-term hegemonic political position in Mexico (roughly 1930 through 1990). The PRI lost its monopoly on government in the 1990s, culminating in the election of an opposition leader as president in 2000. The changing regime altered the distribution of rents among political parties but less so among economic organizations. Mexico remains an LAO.

On the positive side, South Korea and Chile have moved to the doorstep conditions and, in South Korea's case, into the transition to open access. Mozambique has progressed as an LAO since 1992, expanding the range of socioeconomic groups in the Frelimo system and for much of the past two decades building expectations that no major group will be totally excluded from rents. In contrast, the DR Congo has fallen into disorder, as Mozambique did in the 1980s, and Bangladesh exhibited problems following the attempted election in 2007. India and Zambia have exhibited greater stability, although India still experiences episodes of extreme organized violence. LAOs often exhibit episodic crises and regression rather than continuously moving forward. Some move from mature to basic LAOs, such as Chile in the 1970s, Bangladesh in 2007–9, Venezuela under Hugo Chavez, or Russia under Putin. Crisis and disorder in the DR Congo since the decline of Mobutu and in Mozambique in the 1980s pushed these societies from the basic back to the fragile range of the LAO spectrum. The more fragile LAOs usually had fewer self-correcting mechanisms to adjust policy in the face of new challenges. Even where LAOs replace their leaders or ruling parties, the need to maintain the dominant coalition through rent creation means that the new leadership often simply redirects rents. The high likelihood of violence in LAOs makes it hard to create pacts and new policy bargains that solve a crisis. Many elites will fight to maintain their privileges in the face of crises, especially when the proposed solutions to crises involve reducing or removing these privileges.

We conceive of LAOs as spread along a spectrum with the fragile and mature ranges at the least and most developed ends. Basic LAOs are in the middle, with less sophisticated organizations than the mature and more state organization and control than the fragile LAOs. All of the nine cases were basic LAOs for at least part of the time, but they also differed substantially in their characteristics as basic LAOs. The nature of the governments varied from military juntas (at times in Korea, Chile, Bangladesh), to formal single-party governments (Zambia 1972–90, Mozambique 1975–94, Bangladesh 1971–5), to single dominant party (Mexico 1930–90, India 1950–70s, Mozambique post-1992), to competitive clientelism (India, Zambia, and Bangladesh at times since the 1990s), and to formal two-party and multiparty electoral democracies (Philippines 1946–72 and 1986 to the present). There is not a clear distinction between basic LAOs with competitive clientelism and mature LAOs; stable competitive clientelism can gradually change into independent political and economic organizations.

Furthermore, as we think about the maturation of LAOs along several dimensions – control of violence, the scope of relationship subject to credible rule of law, and the durability of organizations and agreements beyond the lives of the individuals creating them – we see that the pace and direction of change is not the same on all dimensions. While progress or failure on one dimension tends to reinforce the others, they often move in different directions in the same country during any decade. As elaborated later, all LAOs have had to deal with the questions of how to define the inner circles of elites and how to deal with outside groups that aspire to gain access via economic success or mobilization of violence capacity.

10.1.3. OAO-type Institutions Function Differently in LAOs

LAOs often copy institutions from OAOs, especially since the mid-twentieth century – and international donors have encouraged these countries to do so as part of reform packages – but these institutions operate differently in the LAO context and thus have different effects than in OAOs.[1] For instance, most LAOs have banks and many have stock markets, but these fail to become a means of pooling savings from large numbers of citizens, investing capital in enterprises, and making business opportunities open

---

[1] For the historical LAOs discussed in NWW, there was not a world of OAOs, richer and more powerful, from which the LAOs of 1800 like Britain, France, and the United States could copy institutions. Now, however, elites in LAOs often get their education in OAOs and bring back ideas for (or against) adopting OAO institutional forms at home (North et al. 2007).

to all citizens. Capital markets (banks in particular) are underdeveloped, typically making loans to insiders, elites, and the government while failing to finance new entrants and entrepreneurs. On paper, banks and stock markets in LAOs may look like OAO institutions – and some firms in LAOs may even be subsidiaries of OAO corporations – but they act as parts of the LAO system that keeps access limited. The discussion of capital markets in the Mexican case shows this most clearly. A similar observation holds for laws and other political institutions, notably, legislatures and elections, discussed in detail in the next section. The wording of legislation such as social insurance policies and corporate law seems to replicate similar OAO polices. Nonetheless, the implementation and enforcement in corrupt courts means that the laws and programs in practice become another source of privileges. Mexico's antipoverty program during the Salinas government (PRONASOL) illustrates this effect, although the successor program, Progresa/Oportunidades, has had relatively impersonal criteria.

10.1.4 Third-party Enforcement from OAO-based Organizations

The issue of third-party enforcement by OAO countries and organizations takes us beyond the original framework. All LAOs face the problem of creating a reliable third party to enforce agreements. In the first movers to OAO – Britain, the United States, and France, as described in NWW – the problem motivated the development of the institutions that brought about the transition to open access. LAOs in the world have often used third-party enforcement from organizations based in open-access countries – multilateral organizations, bilateral donor organizations, international banks, and other corporations – and this pattern seems to have increased since 1950. Usually these organizations come in as partners with members of the local elite coalition, and they share the rents. This may bring medium-term gains in productivity but it also reduces the incentive for elites in the LAO to develop indigenous institutions for providing third-party enforcement of institutions that could eventually benefit wider circles of domestic firms and households.[2] Our cases show a wide variety of arrangements and their effects, some positive and some not.

The UN has intervened to maintain the territorial integrity or restore order in three of the countries in our sample. In South Korea, UN intervention stopped the invasion from North Korea after a hard war. Continued international military presence for six decades has helped sustain the

---

[2] For a discussion of the role of third-party involvement in LAOs see Handler (2010).

external borders. The internal effects are not obvious, as the foreigners did not overtly meddle in Korean politics, but the omnipresence of foreign (mostly U.S.) troops had indirect effects, such as discouraging the use of the Korean army against prodemocracy demonstrators in 1987.

In Mozambique, the white minority regimes of Southern Rhodesia and South Africa supported the anti-Marxist Renamo insurgency that launched a decade-long civil war in the 1980s. (The UN international framework may have deterred any more direct intervention from Southern Rhodesia and South Africa.) In the early 1990s, the Vatican brokered a ceasefire, leading to the entrance of a UN peacekeeping mission that monitored an election in 1992. Regular elections have followed since. Although the Marxist Frelimo Party has won these with increasing margins of victory, the country has become the recipient of and dependent on large aid flows from OAO countries, so it has pursued its aims within a Washington consensus framework, including respect of property rights.

In Zaire/DRC the UN rules and interventions have helped maintain the nation's borders on paper, but have not stopped internal violence or foreign military incursions. Without the UN framework and interventions, the neighbors would probably have dismembered the country to appropriate its valuable mineral resources. Some regions might have benefited from this, but it is not clear if the country as whole would have.

Being able to use the international banking system and its guarantee of property rights for depositors has been an important benefit for elites in most of our cases, except perhaps India and Korea, which developed adequate domestic banking sectors. In the DRC and the Philippines and to a lesser extent in Zambia and Bangladesh, elites have used the international banking system to move ill-gotten assets offshore. In Mexico, the domestic banking sector has been repeatedly raided since the 1920s, as it did not find a way to protect itself through rent sharing (Haber et al. 2003); since the mid-1990s Mexico has had a small banking system almost entirely composed of foreign banks and not providing much service to the non-elites.

Foreign direct investment in mineral extraction has played a major role in the economies of many LAOs, including the DRC and Zambia in our sample. Both cases have experienced cycles of foreign investment, with especially favorable terms during the more welcoming phases, in which some members of the local elite shared benefits. The mining ventures were mostly enclaves, and the internationally linked institutions that provided some third-party enforcement for the mineral sectors did not spread benefits to the rest of the economy. Mexico is unique in having expelled foreign firms from its oil industry early in the twentieth century – in the 1930s – and maintained a monopoly for the government-owned company ever since. PEMEX and its union became major players in the Mexican political economy, with mixed effects on the rest of the economy. (For a discussion of mineral extraction in other LAOs of Latin America, see Webb 2010.)

A notably beneficial targeted international intervention in our sample was the Multi-Fiber Arrangement (MFA) that created an export-oriented time-bound subsidy for Bangladesh's textile/clothing industry. Most governments have had trouble credibly limiting the duration of subsidies for infant industries, because the program creates a strong lobby for extending the subsidy. With the MFA, however, the international community had set the timetable, out of reach of Bangladeshi lobbying, so the industry knew that it had to achieve competitiveness quickly.

10.2 Implications for Development Policy

Our discussion of concrete policies starts with the policy areas that are of most direct concern to the World Bank and to its governance and anti-corruption efforts. The discussion then broadens to include other related issues. We begin with rents and competition constraints, then move to organizations, elections, and democratic reforms, and finally to violence and the military.

10.2.1 Rents and Constraints on Competition

As discussed earlier, rent creation and limits on competition can have good as well as bad effects, depending on a country's level of development. Practical policy recommendations, therefore, need to be more nuanced than just eliminating constraints on entry and competition. In an LAO, the primary concern is to reduce violence, which is a prerequisite for any economic development. When rents are eliminated, the relevant counterfactual alternative often is not a competitive market economy but a society with disorder and violence. For the medium-term developments in an LAO, it matters whether the rents create incentives for learning, increased efficiency, and accumulation of productive capacity. We see positive effects of rents on production (besides discouraging violence) in many of the case studies: Chile, Korea, at times in Mexico, Bangladesh, and India.

These economically productive rents in our cases have two characteristics: they do not last forever, and they have some link to the performance of the firm getting them – augmenting the market rewards (see also Khan and Jomo 2000). When the competition for rents becomes a zero-sum or negative-sum game, as in the Philippines and Zaire/DR Congo, then the decline of the aggregate pool of rents at the disposal of the government puts increasing, perhaps unbearable, strains on the ruling coalition. Limits to access (so as to create rents) that have particularly negative efficiency effects, such as the trade restrictions and state's telephone monopoly in Mexico and Chile in the 1970s, must be considered in light of how much the rents can be reduced without destabilizing political equilibriums that keep the peace. In contrast, South Korea slowly transformed the rents to larger firms (*chaebols*) from patronage in the 1950s and 1960s into incentives based on success in increasing exports. In Mexico and other cases those collecting rents have still done well even when there was substantial opening and growth of trade, because then a small percentage rent could be collected on a much bigger volume. Furthermore, economic progress may open new areas for accruing rents. While rates of trade tariffs have come down in India, there is no evidence that the percentages of rent collection have in general declined; corruption appears to have dramatically increased around many government activities, which have also become more valuable, like the auction of communications spectrum licenses.

As societies move toward the mature end of the spectrum of limited access orders, rents are increasingly distributed according to impersonal rules. In Korea, for example, import licenses and subsidized credit were distributed in the 1960s and 1970s mainly according to firms' demonstrated export performance. On the other hand, as a society moves toward the fragile end of the LAO spectrum, durable organizational rent creation is gradually supplanted by more personal and less durable rent creation, as occurred in the Philippines, Bangladesh, and more extremely in the DR Congo.

The cases show, not surprisingly, that redistribution of ownership and control over productive property – and rents from it – have major effects on growth and the transition from privilege to more impersonal and equal citizens' rights. The effects are more likely to be positive if the redistribution encourages entrepreneurs and the creation of real assets. The effects are more often negative if redistribution encourages political dependencies. The cases illustrate this with respect to land reform. In South Korea and Taiwan, land reform increased access to economic opportunity for the lower half of the income distribution. Land reform in the Philippines did not happen, because the old pattern of land holdings provided rents to so many politically powerful interests, including U.S.-owned plantations. In Mexico, land reform followed the revolution but did not succeed in opening opportunities for poor peasants; instead it encouraged inefficient land utilization, tying peasants to the land and making them dependent on largess distributed by the PRI at election time.

The distribution of rents in the commercial and industrial sides of the economy also plays a key role in motivating political stability. Commercial and industrial rents have a mixed history in promoting positive economic development. In Bangladesh, the rents from the final years of the regime of quotas on textile exports led, with assistance from a Korean firm, to the creation of a successful textile export industry. In Korea, even though the *chaebol* concentrated the control of the industrial economy in a few hands and benefited from government protection of their oligopoly position, they did accumulate capital, improve their technology, and, most importantly, succeed in competitive international markets. Later the government trimmed back the special economic privileges it gave to the *chaebol*, although they retained great market power in the economy. In India, Mexico, and the Philippines, on the other hand, powerful domestic corporate interests have maintained their personal links with politicians in power, and with illegal organizations at times. Similarly, when countries rely on international corporations to run major sectors of their economy, like mining and banking, these have needed protection from electoral populism or other local forces (and sometimes the military) and have provided reciprocal economic benefits to those in power, as seen in Zaire/DR Congo, Zambia, and the Philippines.

10.2.2. Organizations, Parties, and Personalities

Organizations play a central role in the LAO framework. The spectrum of fragile, basic, and mature limited access orders is defined in terms of the nature of organizations within a society. All types of organizations matter: political, economic, social, religious, military, and educational. In countries toward the fragile end of the LAO spectrum, organizations are tied closely to personal identities, and their leaders are connected directly into the dominant coalition. The ability of leaders and organizations to survive and thrive depends on constantly changing conditions.

The cases provide new lessons for the framework. The DR Congo, Bangladesh, the Philippines under Marcos, and Zambia 1964–91 show the importance of organizations based on personality, which attempted to balance interests in an uncertain environment. In other cases, such as West Bengal under the CPM and Mexico under the PRI, the main political organizations were less oriented to personalities, which seems to have made the LAOs more stable.

How should development policy treat organizations? What organizations and rules for interacting among them should be supported? As with rents, the cases show that the value of organizations for improving the political economy of an LAO depend on each country's circumstances. When the countries struggled to reduce violence, consolidating political control and limiting economic access was the common outcome. The aim was to make more credible the commitments for distributing rents. Military governments worked temporarily, with their effectiveness in promoting development depending on how disciplined they were as organizations, being effective in Chile and Korea, less so in Bangladesh and the Philippines, and least in the DR Congo. Minimizing the military's role in directing the economy seemed to help.

Exclusive single-party governments (Zambia 1972–91, Mozambique 1980–90, Zambia/DR Congo 1965–90, and Bangladesh 1971–5) did not do well, with problems in maintaining stability and promoting development. The successes of China and Vietnam in the last three decades show, however, that a single-party government can succeed. The Bangladeshi and Zambian cases in the 1970s and 1980s reveal two reasons why an all-encompassing single party may fail to restore order: i) if the dominant coalition (party membership) cannot be defined to include all the organizations that have access to violence capacity; or ii) if too many of the member organizations in the party demand excessive shares of a fixed rent pool (and they are not themselves generating rents from productive growth). Dominant (but not legally exclusive) single parties in Mexico and Mozambique succeeded at times in maintaining order and promoting growth. Eventually, however, the single or dominant party approach becomes a hindrance to the sophisticated and impersonal commitments needed for further economic development.

As societies move from the fragile toward the basic range of the LAO spectrum, organizations become more durable, eventually to the point that some live longer than their leaders. The organizations themselves come to take on important roles in balancing interests, even as some remain linked to individual personalities. The organization becomes the framework in which long-term relationships are embedded, and organizations develop longer-term relationships between each other. The early Korean *chaebol*, the army in many cases, public/private organizations in Mexico (such as PEMEX, Telmex, and the PRI) are durable organizations that provide a stable framework for political and economic interaction, even as they manifest limited access and rent creation. These organizations are closely tied to the government and to the balance of interests in society, yet they are more durable than the personal identity of their leadership.

The movement from basic to mature limited access orders involves organizations substantively independent of the government. The extent to which Korean *chaebol* have become independent of the government is a question raised by Jong-sung You's essay. In Chile, the outgoing Pinochet regime put clauses in the 1989 constitution intended to entrench and secure the position of the conservatives. One might have expected, given the course of events in Chile over the previous twenty years, that when the center-left alliance attained power it would rewrite the constitution and restructure basic government organizations like the legislature. Instead, when this coalition came to power, it kept the conservative constitutional rules for a considerable time, including rules that guaranteed the independence of political organizations from ongoing manipulation and interference. As Navia concludes, Chile is not an open-access order yet, but it is a mature limited access order that appears to moving toward the doorstep conditions.

For concrete policy applications, helping LAOs to make their organizations more durable and rule-based is more useful for development than trying directly to promote the appearance of fully open economic and political competition in societies where threats of violence perpetuate limited access arrangements.

Recent research has advanced our understanding of organizations, their extent across different societies, and something of their structure (De Soto 1989; World Development Report 2003, etc.). Attempts have been made to estimate the difficulty of forming a business, getting a license, or obtaining a corporate charter. Typically the World Bank and OAO donors have emphasized the ease of starting a business entering at the bottom, but the LAO lens calls more attention to the institutions that facilitate or hinder the growth of an enterprise to achieve a scale that is politically and economically important. We also have long known that corrupt courts in many LAOs fail to provide basic services for organizations, such as enforcing contracts or collateral agreements in bank loans. Efforts to address these problems should be extended, both conceptually and empirically, an issue we return to later. For the moment, we lack well-defined ways to measure the structure of organizations across countries and how that changes over time. Such measures have not been developed even for OAOs such as the United States.[3]

---

[3] See, for example, the historical work comparing the structure of corporations in Britain, France, Germany, and the United States: Guinnane, Harris, Lamoreaux, and Rosenthal (2007).

The case studies offer clear examples of movements along the spectrum from fragile to mature. Korea moved away from personal treatment of powerful organizations, like the *chaebol*, as unique and idiosyncratic organizations, even while the *chaebol* remained as important organizations in the dominant coalition. Over time, Korea came to treat them more impersonally as a class of organizations, and in recent years, to just one of a general type of organization (although *chaebols* still possess enormous market power). In contrast, organizations in the Philippines moved toward more personal and idiosyncratic privileges. Montinola documents the close personal relationships of the Marcos regime with economic leaders. For countries that have achieved stability for two decades or more, the cases point to the value of widening the range of organizations they support, not only at the initial entry phase but also in increasing the ability of the organizations to make sophisticated commitments internally and with each other, commitments that firms need in order to grow to elite status.

The case studies demonstrate that societies do not inevitably move to more impersonal and credible support for organizations. Although institutional economics has given us a deeper appreciation of institutions as the cause of economic and political outcomes, it has devoted less attention to how institutions evolve as the result of economic and political influences. The LAO/OAO conceptual framework helps us think systematically about these problems.

10.2.3 Democracy and Elections

In the twenty-first century Washington consensus on governance, elections have become the signature OAO institution to export to LAOs. Viewing the nine cases through the lens of the LAO framework, however, provides two implications about elections: first, holding elections in an LAO differs considerably from democracy in the OAO sense; and second, elections in LAOs sometimes, but not always, serve useful purposes, even if they are not free and fair.

The traditional consensus in the donor community has been that democracy is good because it represents the fundamental means of ensuring political freedom. This consensus further implies that countries should move quickly to hold elections and implement democratic reforms. After all, who can be against enhancing freedom and citizen control over government? Many examples in our cases show that this agenda often ignores reality. Moving too quickly to democracy may undermine social stability in a country. In other cases, elections can be useful stabilizing rituals, even if the elections do not express the will of the people or hold the government accountable. The tradeoff between stabilizing and moving toward democracy is especially problematic for fragile LAOs that have recently emerged from disorder (Collier 2009).

For example, Keefer and Vlaicu (2008) show that implementing elections in societies where political organizations are dominated by patron–client networks – that is societies with highly personal forms of political organization – is likely to produce an outcome in which the patrons use votes as another medium of exchange. Clients trade their votes for privileges and other services. Elections in this setting may help stabilize an LAO by providing a visible and widely acknowledged means of assessing the relative strength of disparate groups, as Khan shows in the case of Bangladesh (see also Cox 2009 and Magaloni and Kricheli 2010). In this sense, elections can increase the likelihood that adjustments in power among those with access to violence occur peacefully, making the LAO more stable and preventing downward spirals into violence. Nonetheless, elections of this type fail to produce OAO-style democracy; rather, they perpetuate limited access orders. Keefer and Vlaicu see this result as failure. The LAO conceptual framework, on the other hand, suggests that it is inevitable and could be part of a beneficial process of maturing as an LAO.

The relevant question is whether the election in a particular situation facilitates the economic and political development of the society within the LAO spectrum. As elaborated later, the case studies illustrate the varied effects of elections: to destabilize the political system (Chile 1973 and Bangladesh 2007–9), to consolidate and reassert political control (Mexico 1930–90, Philippines 1946–72 and 1986–present, and Zambia 1972–90 in a formally one-party setting), to ratify a peaceful transition to power sharing (Zambia 1992, Mozambique 1994, Mexico 2000, India 1977, Chile 1989–90), or to make genuine choices between well-defined alternatives (Chile after 1990). South Korea moved relatively slowly toward democracy, and Chile regressed to dictatorship in the 1970s; now both are among the successful instances of long-term economic and political development.

Elections, even if not free and fair, can be useful as stabilizing political rituals in LAOs. Examples in our cases include the PRI-dominated elections in twentieth-century Mexico, national and state-level elections in India, Zambia 1972–90, and post-Marcos Philippines. Sometimes they are salient steps in advancing a LAO country's development on the political side – as with the elections of 1990 in Chile and 1987 in South Korea that restored civilian rule, the 1994 election in Mozambique that ratified the peace agreement, the 1977 election in India that ended the years of undemocratic rule by Indira Gandhi, and the 1991 election in Zambia after which Kaunda accepted defeat peacefully. As Khan emphasizes in the case of Bangladesh, good election outcomes in an LAO are those that reflect the balance of power between competing groups on the ground, even if the elections themselves did not follow a free and fair process.

Elections may be part of the regular political ritual of stability in an LAO regime, as with Mexico in the years of PRI dominance, and Zambia in the years of Kaunda's dominance. An unswerving adherence to free and fair elections on Western terms may undermine the role of elections in an LAO. Elections that occur when the rules to carry out the results of an election are sufficiently institutionalized (i.e., that the incumbent party will willingly step down) or when elections produce outcomes that are unacceptable to the existing distribution of economic power often bring on periods of unfortunate instability and violence, such as Chile in 1973 and Pakistan-Bangladesh in 1970. The lesson from cases like Bangladesh, the DR Congo, and Korea around 1960 is that the governance agenda should not always push for elections now, but should recognize the prior need to have adequate institutions in place to carry out the election and its results, even if unfair by OAO standards.

Competitive elections in some LAOs make politicians more dependent on donations from major economic organizations (big firms, etc.), which weakens (or keeps weak) the will and ability of the government to curb monopolistic practices and assure more open access on the economic side. Mexico since the 1990s and Korea after 1987 illustrate this effect, where business concentration has remained high or even increased. India and Bangladesh are more complicated. Politicians clearly protect the big businesses that pay them but the economy as a whole is becoming more open simply because the number of players is increasing. And the same is happening in the political sphere of the South Asia cases, where new organizations are setting up more freely.

10.2.4. Violence

In most LAOs, the military and police force(s) are part of the array of organizations with violence capacity. Seen through the LAO lens, a Weberian state with a monopoly on violence is not a policy outcome achieved by striving for it directly, but is rather an outcome of an historical process that is not on the immediate horizon for most LAOs. Helping a weak LAO government achieve a strong military and police force is no panacea for development problems; in many cases, this strengthening allows greater repression and extraction of rents from opponents, hindering development. In other cases, the effort fails completely. The strengthening of government forces, which work in OAOs as coercive threats to deter criminal use of violence, cannot be easily carried over to LAOs as a way to reduce violence, since LAO governments usually cannot prevent their military and police from rent seeking on their own.

The key insight is that successful LAOs limit disorder mainly by creating incentives for organizations not to use violence; these incentives for peace rarely involve the state assuming a monopoly on violence. The DR Congo is the most obvious situation where strengthening one faction and calling it the government did not lead to the other factions reducing their use of violence. The cases of Bangladesh, the Philippines, and Mozambique also illustrate the intertwined relations between the formal military and police and other organizations that have violence capacity but are not under full control of the government.

Although violence is central to the internal dynamics of every limited access society, it is only recently that the World Bank has given attention to violence as a policy concern. Problems of crime and violence have been treated as something outside the state; societies with widespread violence are classified as failed states or postconflict states. The Bank's assistance has traditionally aimed to support rebuilding efforts and deals much less with the causes and remedies for ongoing armed conflict. The WDR 2011 and the present research represent new efforts of the Bank to look more deeply at the problem of violence. The cases here, with perhaps the exception of the DR Congo, show how countries have successfully reduced violence, although not eliminating it entirely. The LAO framework can help to sort out which of the country experiences in this set is relevant to another particular country circumstance.

In open-access orders, control of military and police is lodged with a responsible political system effectively constrained by political and economic competition. In limited access orders, however, the government rarely controls all of the organizations that can or do use violence. The formally organized military and police have been active participants in the political process at various times in most of the cases, with exceptions being Zambia, India, and Mexico since the 1930s. In South Korea, Chile, Bangladesh, Philippines, and the DR Congo the army (or armies) were at some point or still are primary players in both the polity and the economy.

Rather than an organization under the control of the government, the military in these societies is one among several organizations vying for control of or influence over the government. In Mozambique since independence in 1974, there has been little separation between the military and the ruling Frelimo party.

The role of the military is only one facet of the complex balance of powerful organizations whose interaction results in stability or instability in an LAO. The creation of rents through limited access is systematically connected to maintaining the balance of power and influence. Governance policies in LAOs cannot be divorced from the ongoing problem of balancing powerful interests when those interests are capable of bringing down or taking over the existing formal government or of obstructing the economy with the threat or actuality of violence. All of the countries (except Chile) have or had nonmilitary organizations (some legal and some not) with serious violence capacity that have played a role in the allocation of political power and economic wealth.

Table 10.1 lists some of the organizations with violence potential in the nine country cases. In OAOs, politics is also about balancing powerful interests, but in the absence of any serious threats to alter the government through the use of violence.

In historical European cases, the military and police established a monopoly on violence as a result of the long-term development of other social, economic, and political organizations that could credibly limit the military (NWW 2009). First, monopoly control evolved as part of a larger development process that moved these states to the doorstep conditions, helping organizations and the state itself to be perpetual lived and capable of implementing impersonal rules, including control over the military and police. Second, an important feature of the monopoly in the historic cases afforded government control of a military with sufficient capacity to defend the nation from external enemies while simultaneously withdrawing the military from the internal allocation of rents. This happened in over several decades in Korea after 1950, although the Korean CIA was more involved in domestic enforcement of the military dictatorship. In Chile the military had a good professional (nonpolitical) reputation dating back to the nineteenth century, which was only partially lost in the Pinochet years, since the military restrained its involvement in the day-to-day governing. The inability of civilian politics to control the military also comes through in the cases of Bangladesh, the Philippines, and the DR Congo, although not in Mexico, Zambia, or India.

Table 10.1 *Nonmilitary organizations with violence capacity*

Country	Organizations inside the state or legally recognized	Informal or Illegal organizations
DR Congo	Regional militias and police	Foreign military
Mozambique	None	Renamo rebel group
Zambia	Unions	Ethnic groups
Bangladesh	Political Parties	
India	Political Parties	Maoists (including Naxalite and insurgencies); organizations based on religion, caste, and tribal origin.
Philippines	Unions, student groups	Communist Party (CPP), New People's army (NPA), Moro Islamic Liberation Front (MILF), Abu Sayyaf
So Korea	Unions, student groups, Korean CIA (before 1987)	Partisan guerilla groups (until the Korean War)
Mexico	Local Police, Unions	Drug cartels, Zapatistas,
Chile	None	None

10.3. Agenda for Further Research

The lessons we have learned from the cases both expand and deepen the conceptual framework. Much remains to be done, however, to improve the framework and to improve policy advice. The most promising areas for future research seem to be:

- A deeper understanding that the principal development problem is making improvements within the LAO framework. Compared with the transition to open access, improving LAOs does more to improve the lives of people in terms of proportionally increasing income and reducing incidence of violence. The first development problem focuses on the movement of LAOs from fragile to basic, from basic to mature, and from mature into the doorstep conditions. Attempting to skip these steps and focus instead on the transition from an LAO to an OAO is more likely to fail than succeed.
- Simply taking elements of OAOs and transplanting them into LAOs – including open access to markets, new legal systems, and

democracy – does not seem to work. The framework explains why such policies do not work; these institutions work very differently in the limited access context than they do in an open access one. The case studies suggest some insights into the first development problem, but far more understanding is necessary.

- Rents pose another central set of conceptual issues, particularly the distinction between rents that facilitate development and those that do not. We also highlight the critical relationship between rents and incentives to maintain peace. Progress on the first development problem in low-income and middle-income countries requires that we obtain a clearer understanding of the ways in which rents be changed without increasing the risk of violence.
- The framework emphasizes organizations and their role in the development process. Several directions exist to facilitate organizational power and productivity, including improving access to organizations, improving the legal and other tools used by organizations to maintain themselves, and improving the tools that organizations have to maintain relationships and contracts with each other. We know too little about the tradeoffs between facilitating organizations and undermining the rents they generate that produce stability in LAOs.
- The role of outside organizations, including official aid agencies and NGOs, needs more thought. Outside organizations hold the potential to reduce the threat of violence, and may serve to enforce agreements, pacts, and even constitutional provisions; yet doing so may require that these organizations operate differently than they do now. We need to know more about how these organizations can work within the LAO framework to facilitate incremental improvements. Handler 2010 uses game-theory analysis to provide some insights about the role of an outside player.
- Because violence is so central to the structure of LAOs, so too is the issue of limiting violence. As is obvious, preventing LAOs from undergoing violence and its attendant problems makes people in these societies better off. The LAO lens provides new insights into how violence can be and is limited. Nonetheless, we need to learn more about the processes by which governments in different contexts can discourage violence, perhaps without attaining a monopoly control on violence, and along with measures that reduce extortion and abuse of citizens. Facilitating an LAO government's monopoly power over violence may simply grant it even stronger abilities to limit access and create rents.

- The cases illustrate the great diversity among LAOs, even those we place on similar points along the fragile to mature spectrum. We need greater conceptual understanding of how this diversity links to the framework's key concepts, such as violence potential, rents, and organizations.
- The framework reorients policy recommendations for LAOs. This conceptual and practical transformation is just a beginning.

Finally, the countries in our project suggest other cases to examine. The French Development Agency (AFD) has already initiated studies on China, Vietnam, Burkina Faso, Cote d'Ivoire, Ghana, Kenya, Turkey, Pakistan, Tamil Nadu, and Gujarat (states in India). The World Bank currently has over fifty political economy assessments under way, funded by a multi-donor Government Partnership Facility. This will give us a richer understanding of how the framework applies in places that remain LAOs despite dramatic changes.

Most of the countries that have made that transition to open access or at least achieved the doorstep conditions are in Europe or European colonies. The Nordic countries and the Low Countries probably made the transition before the First World War. After serious regressions to basic LAOs between the wars, Germany, Austria, Italy, and Spain made their transitions to OAOs in the second half of the twentieth century, within the context of the European Union. Japan is also an important case. The EU has also provided the context and rules of the game for Eastern European countries to move to the doorstep and perhaps make the transition to OAO. Examination of a selection of the EU accession cases could help us understand better the requirements for progress in LAOs in the rest of the world and how the international development community could offer relevant support.

Recent events in the Arab world, the Arab Spring, highlight why the perspective offered by the LAO framework is so important. A wave of popular uprisings, beginning in Tunisia in January of 2011, resulted in revolutionary changes in governments in Tunisia and Egypt and the onset of civil war in Libya. Similar protest movement arose throughout the Arab world, creating sympathy and hope in the developed world. But as of late 2011, these events have produced few changes in regimes. Throughout the world these revolutionary movements were hailed as popular uprisings that would lead to democracy and development, but the ensuing reality presents a muddier picture.

Arab societies are limited access orders, typically dominated by a coalition of military, political, economic, and religious organizations. While the mix varies from country to country and some coalitions are dominated by strong leaders, all the countries have dominant coalitions and limited access. The events in Tunisia, sparked by the self-immolation of Mohamed Bouazizi in December 2010, were couched in terms of the lack of dignity and respect that the Ben Ali regime showed to the Tunisian people. What ensued as a result of the crisis sparked by the popular protests was a reorganization of the dominant coalition.

In Tunisia, Ben Ali lost the support of the army and the security forces, and he was quickly asked to leave. Members of his family and close associates were arrested and imprisoned. In Egypt, the police failed to quell the protests; when the army responded to the call to restore order in the streets, it did so but refused to shoot. The negotiations that followed between the elements within the dominant coalition of Egypt eventually led to Mubarak stepping down. The uprising produced a reorganization of the LAO coalition, not a removal of all the powerful players. Egypt and Tunisia are undergoing revolutionary changes, but changes within the framework of limited access orders. Open access is not just around the corner, and modern democracy and economic development are not likely outcomes of a revolutionary struggle. The LAO framework and case studies suggest that the next steps forward for both countries involve the creation and sustaining of more durable organizations independent of the dominant coalition. This includes political, economic, and social organizations. In Libya, the dominant coalition fractured, and the result is civil war. The framework here cannot predict any details of the outcome, except to say that it will be another version of an LAO.

The Arab Spring created an opportunity for change, but did so by also creating circumstances that are not easy to deal with. If leaders in Tunisia and Egypt are expected to produce open-access societies immediately – expectations often voiced by their own citizens and the international community – they are bound to fail to meet those expectations. The natural reaction to increased violence in a limited access order is to make arrangements that are more personal, to tie the arrangements that bind powerful individuals and organizations more closely to rents threatened by violence and lack of coordination within the coalition. Holding Arab leaders to unrealistic expectations for change will not help with the first development problem: increasing the performance of a limited access society. A more nuanced and realistic view of the first development problem may be a precondition for realistic and productive expectations about the changes that are possible and will move the development process forward. We hope that the framework and these case studies are a step in the right direction.

References

Bates, Robert H. 1983. *Markets and States in Tropical Africa*. Berkeley: University of California Press.

Bhagwati, Jagdish. 1982. "Directly-Unproductive Profit-Seeking (DUP)" *Journal of Political Economy* **90** (October): 988–1002.

Buchanan, James M., Robert D. Tollison, and Gordon Tullock. 1980. *Toward a Theory of the Rent-seeking Society*. College Station: Texas A & M University.

Collier, Paul. 2009. *Wars, Guns and Votes: Democracy in Dangerous Places*. New York: Harper Collins.

Cox, Gary W. 2009. "Authoritarian elections and leadership succession, 1975–2004." Unpublished Working Paper, Department of Political Science, Stanford University.

De Soto, Hernando. 1989. *The Other Path: The Invisible Revolution in the Third World*. New York: Harpercollins.

Guinnane, Timothy, Ron Harris, Naomi Lamoreaux, and Jean-Laurent Rosenthal. 2007. "Putting the Corporation in its Place." *Enterprise and Society* **8**(3): 687–729.

Haber, Stephen, Armando Razo, and Noel Maurer. 2003. *The Politics of Property Rights: Political Instability, Credible Commitments and Economic Growth in Mexico, 1876–1929*. Cambridge, UK: Cambridge University Press.

Handler, Scott Paul. 2010. *Wolves in Sheep's Clothing: Understanding Modern State-Building (and Counterinsurgency)*. Ph.D. Dissertation. Stanford University.

Khan, Mushtaq H. and K. S. Jomo, eds. 2000. *Rents, Rent-Seeking, and Economic Development: Theory and Evidence in Asia*. Cambridge, UK: Cambridge University Press.

Keefer, Philip and Razvan Vlaicu. 2008. "Democracy, Credibility and Clientelism", *Journal of Law, Economics and Organization*, October **24** (2): 371–406.

Krueger, Anne. 1974. "Political Economy of the Rent-Seeking Society," *American Economic Review* **64**: 291–303.

Magaloni, Beatriz, and Ruth Kricheli. 2010. "Political Order and One-Party Rule," *Annual Rev. of Political Science*. **12**: 123–43.

Mittal, Sonia. 2010. "Constitutional Stability in a Changing World: Institutions, Knowledge, and Adaptive Efficiency," Working Paper, Department of Political Science, Stanford University.

North, Douglass C. 2005. *Understanding the Process of Economic Change*. Princeton: Princeton University Press.

North, Douglass, John Wallis, Steven Webb, and Barry Weingast. 2007. *Limited Access Orders in the Developing World: A New Approach to the Problems of Development*. World Bank Policy Working Paper.

Webb, Steven. 2010. "Political Economy and Mineral Wealth in Latin America and the Caribbean", World Bank. processed July 19.

World Bank. 2003. *World Development Report: Sustainable Development in a Dynamic World: Transforming Institutions, Growth and Quality of Life*. Washington DC. 2007. *Governance and Anticorruption Strategy*. Washington, DC.

Index

Abu Sayyaf group, 187–88
accidental rents. *See* rents
ADF (Allied Defense Forces), 81–82
AFDL (*Alliance des forces democratiques pour la liberation du Congo/Zaire*), 79–93
Afghanistan, as fragile LAO, 11
Africa, regional comparisons, 20–21
African National Congress (ANC), 134
agrarian relations. *See* Court of Agrarian Relations
Agricultural Land Reform Code of 1963, 165
agricultural monopolies/monopsonies, 171–73
Agricultural Tenancy Act, 165
agriculture, sector shares/growth rates, 36, 55, 214–17
aid, international, 103
Akbayan Citizens' Action Party (Akbayan), 186
Albania, institutional quality, 144
Alessandri, Arturo, 264–65
Alianza para el Campo, 253, 273, 274–84
Allende, Salvador, 263, 266, 268
Alliance democratique des peuples, 80
Alliance des forces democratiques pour la liberation du Congo/Zaire (AFDL), 79–93
Alliance for the Presidential Majority (AMP)
  composition of, 92–93
  in electoral process, 104–6
  formation of, 103
  infrastructure development and, 96
  Kabila and, 71, 90–94
  region-center dynamics and, 99
Alliance pour la majorite presidentielle. *See* Alliance for the Presidential Majority (AMP)

Allied Defense Forces (ADF), 81–82
allocation of rents. *See* rents
Al-Qaeda, 187–88
Alston, Lee, 2–3
American Military Government (AMG), 298, 300
AMP. *See* Alliance for the Presidential Majority (AMP)
ANC (African National Congress), 134
ANEF (National Federation of Public Sector Workers), 279–80
Anglo American Corporation, 126
Angola
  AFDL and, 80–81
  CIAT mandate of, 89–90
  Kabila government and, 87
  security concerns in, 82
anti-corruption cases/reforms, 62–63, 311. *See also* corruption
April Revolution (Korean), 305
Aquino, Benigno (Ninoy), 176–78
Aquino, Corazon, 177–78, 185. *See also* Philippines, in post-Marcos era
Arab countries, as basic LAO, 11–12
Arab Spring, 348–49
arbitration, in garment industry, 56–58
Argentina, GDP growth rates, 304
Arroyo, Gloria Macapagal, 185, 189
Asian financial crisis (1997), 310, 313
Asset Privatization Trust (APT), 189
authoritarian clientelism. *See* Bangladesh, authoritarian clientelism phase
Autonomous Region of Muslim Mindanao (ARMM), 187

Awami League. *See also* Mujibur Rahman,
    Sheikh
  BNP and, 49
  in military authoritarian phase, 39
  one-party state creation, 41–43
  in populist authoritarian phase, 40
Aylwin, Patricio, 270, 272, 275–77, 283–85,
    287

Bachelet, Michelle, 270, 276–77, 282–83
BAKSAL (Bangladesh Krishok Sromik Awami
    League), 41–43, 45
"banditry," in Mexico, 258
Bangladesh
  authoritarianism, turn towards, 205–6
  governance reform agenda, 25
  on LAO spectrum, 332
  organizations, role of, 338–41
  partition of, 24
  regional comparisons, 20–21
  rents in, 25–26, 336–38
  sector shares/growth rates, 36, 55
  third-party enforcement agreements, 335
  violence capacity, 345–46
Bangladesh, authoritarian clientelism phase.
      See also garment industry (Bangladesh)
  BNP formation, 47
  decentralization in, 48
  dominant coalition in, 47–48
  overview of, 28–30
  privatization/nationalization in, 50–51
  rent distribution/allocation in, 48–50
  ruling coalition in, 49
  social order evolution, 27
Bangladesh, competitive clientelism phase
  anti-corruption cases/reforms, 62–63
  caretaker government under, 62
  elections/electoral process, 60–61, 65
  judiciary in, 66
  LAO framework under, 63–65
  long-term investment projects in, 65–66
  overview of, 30–31
  ruling coalition in, 61–62
  social order evolution, 27
Bangladesh, constitutional crisis phase, 26, 27,
    31–33
Bangladesh, military authoritarian phase
  Basic Democracy system in, 39
  financial institutions in, 35–36
  governance capabilities, 37
  industrial capitalist class in, 37
  overview of, 26–28

  political stability in, 33
  rent-seeking groups in, 33–34
  social order evolution, 27
  state-created rents, 34–35
  violence organizers in, 34
Bangladesh, populist authoritarian phase
  asset privatization/nationalization, 46–47
  capitalist class emergence, 44
  career paths/organizational chains, 45
  economic performance in, 47
  leadership's control of rents, 44–45
  one-party structure in, 41–43
  overview, 28
  political entrepreneurs in, 40
  rent allocation in, 43–44
  social order evolution, 27
  violence in, 40–41
  zero-sum rents in, 45–46
Bangladesh Garment Manufacturers and
    Exporters Association (BGMEA), 56
Bangladesh Krishok Sromik Awami League
    (BAKSAL), 41–43, 45
Bangladesh Nationalist Party (BNP)
  Awami League and, 49
  elections/electoral system and, 29, 60–61
  formation of, 47
"barangays," 153
Bardhan, Pranab, 224
Basic Democracies Order (1959), 39
basic LAOs, 11–12, 14. *See also specific
    countries*
Bates, Robert H., 330
Bayan Muna, 186
behavior, rents and, 6–7
Belgian Congo. *See* DR Congo
Belgium, CIAT mandate of, 89–90
Bell Trade Act, 153
Bemba, Jean-Pierre, 73–75, 90–92
Benedicto, Roberto, 171–73
Berlin, Isaiah, 144
BGMEA (Bangladesh Garment Manufacturers
    and Exporters Association), 56
Bhagwati, Jagdish, 6
Bharatiya Janata Party (BJP), 205, 208–9, 216,
    217–22
Bhutto, Benazir, 204–5
BNP (Bangladesh Nationalist Party)
  Awami League and, 49
  elections/electoral system and, 29, 60–61
  formation of, 47
Bolsa Mexicana de Valores (BMV), 249
Bombay Presidency, 220

Borras, Saturnino M., 182
Brazil, OAO economies and, 9–10
bribery. *See* corruption
Buchanan, James M., 6
bureaucratic quality, measurement of, 145
Burma, as basic LAO, 11–12
Buscayno, Bernabe, 166, 178–79

CAFGU (Civilian Armed Forces Geographical
    Units), 185–86
Calles, Plutarco Elias, 252
Cámara Chilena de la Construcción (CChC),
    279
cane prices (India), 211–14
Cárdenas, Lázaro, 245–46, 247
'carnation revolution' coup, 130–31
CARP (Comprehensive Agrarian Reform
    Programme), 181–82
caste hierarchy/politics, 206–7, 217–22.
    See also Other Backward Classes
    (OBCs)
Catholic Church, 240–41, 248
Central Bank (Mexican), 249
Central Bank (Philippine), 161, 168–69,
    170–73
Centro de Estudios Públicos (CEP), 282
chaebols, in Korea, 299, 300–1, 309–10, 313
Chang, Myon, 305
chibalo labor system, 130
Chile
    on LAO spectrum, 332
    organizations, role of, 338–41
    regional comparisons, 20–21
    rents in, 8, 336–38
    violence capacity, 345–46
Chile, as limited access order
    under Concertación governments, 272–73
    constitutional reform, 273–74
    dominant coalitions in, 262–65
    doorstep conditions, 263
    economic issues/indicators, 270, 271, 276–62
    electoral participation/system, 265–75, 286
    income growth/growth rates, 263, 284–86
    ISI policies, 266, 267
    mining industry, 267–69
    nationalization, 268
    OAO transition, 261–63
    under Pinochet, 270–72
    political inclusion/exclusion, 263–66
    poverty in, 284
    rents in, 262–65, 266–67
    transition to OAO, 275–77
    violence potential, 269–70
    vote/seat distribution, 274–84
Chile, democratic institutional system
    business/political party networks, 279
    Communist Party and, 280
    constitutional reforms, 277–78
    economic development/policies, 278,
        283–85
    electoral participation, 285
    labor unions, 279–81
    legislature, 278
    political inclusion/exclusion, 287–88
    presidential system, 277–78
    socio-economic actors, 278–79
    think tanks and, 281–83
Chiluba, Frederick, 123–24
China
    DR Congo and, 96
    as mature LAO, 12–13
    OAO economies and, 9–10
Chinese Communist Party, 13
Chinese *mestizos*, in Philippines, 154
Chissano, Joaquim, 135
Christians/Muslim conflicts, 174–76
Chun, Doo-hwan, 302, 303–4, 305–7, 308, 309,
    312–13
CIAT (*Comite international d'accompagnement
    a la transition*), 89–90
Cinq Chantiers (Five Construction Sites), 92
civil war, in Mozambique, 133–34
Civilian Armed Forces Geographical Units
    (CAFGU), 185–86
CNC (*Confederación Nacional Campesina*),
    251–52
CNRD (*Conseil National de resistance pour la
    democratie*), 80
CNS (*Conference National Souveraine*), 82,
    86, 103
Coal India Ltd, 204
CODELCO (National Copper Corporation),
    268, 279–80
Cojuangco, Eduardo, 171–73
Collier, Paul, 2, 11
Colombia, on LAO spectrum, 13
colonial rule/colonialism, 116–20, 128–31,
    236–37
Communism, in Bangladesh, 41
Communist Party, in Chile, 280
Communist Party of India Marxist (CPM),
    200, 220
Communist Party of the Philippines (CPP),
    166, 178–79, 186–87

Communist Party of the Philippines (PKP), 164–65
competition, constraints to, 336–38
competitive clientelism. *See* Bangladesh, competitive clientelism phase
Comprehensive Agrarian Reform Programme (CARP), 181–82
Concertación governments, 272–73, 274–85
Conditional Cash Transfer Program (*Oportunidades*), 253
Confederación de la Producción y el Comercio (CPC), 279
Confederación de Trabajadores de México (CTM), 252
Confederación Nacional Campesina (CNC), 251–52
Confederación Regional Obrera Mexicana (CROM), 252
Conference National Souveraine (CNS), 82, 86, 103
Conflict, Security, and Development (World Bank), 3, 330
Confucian tradition, 295–96
CONFUSAM (Health Professionals and Health Workers Unions), 280
Congo. *See* DR Congo
Congress Party
    under Ghandi, 203–5
    in Maharashtrian state politics, 208–9
    Muslim political elites and, 32
    in Nehruvian period, 201–11
    political coalitions and, 199
    Shiv Sena and, 216–18
    voter composition, 217–22
    in vulnerable maturity period, 201–11
    in West Bengal, 221–22
Conseil National de resistance pour la democratie (CNRD), 80
Constitutional Congress. *See Conference National Souveraine* (CNS)
constitutional crisis. *See* Bangladesh, constitutional crisis phase
Consultative Councils, 135
contract enforcement, in garment industry, 56–58
copper mining. *See* mining/mining sector
corruption
    anti-corruption cases/reforms, 62–63, 311
    Business International ratings, 321–22
    indicators of, 322
    rents and, 315–18
    trends in, 317–22

Court of Agrarian Relations, 165
CPC (*Confederación de la Producción y el Comercio*), 279
CPP (Communist Party of the Philippines), 166, 178–79
crime syndicates/underworld, 209, 218
Cristero War (Mexico), 241–42, 258
CROM (*Confederación Regional Obrera Mexicana*), 252
Crowther, William, 162
CTM (*Confederación de Trabajadores de México*), 252
Cuba, as basic LAO, 11–12

Daewoo, 52–53
Dante, Commander, 166
De Leon, Teresita O., 186
debt burden, of DR Congo, 78
Decree Law 600 (FDI Statute), 269
Dee, Dewey, 176–77
definition/description, of key concepts
    dominant coalitions, 4–5
    limited access, 5
    limited access orders (LAOs), 3
    open access, 16
    open access orders (OAOs), 16
    organizations, 12
    rents, 5–6
democracy, elections and, 341–43
Democratic Alliance (DA), 164
Democratic Labor Party (Korean), 311–12
Democratic Party (Korean), 311–12
Democratic Republican Party (DRP), 302
Desh Garments, 52–53
Development Bank of the Philippines, 169–70
development indicators, after colonial rule, 116–18
Dhlakama, Alfonso, 135–36
Díaz Ordaz, Gustavo, 245–46, 247
Diaz-Cayeros, Alberto, 245
directly unproductive rent seeking activities (DUP), 6
Disini, Herminio, 168
dominant coalitions
    authoritarian clientelism and, 47–48
    in Bangladesh, 47–48
    in Chile, 262–65
    definition/description of, 4–5
    efficiency wages in, 7
    in LAO framework, 4–5, 11, 12–13, 33
    in Maharashtra, 228–29, 230
    in Philippines, 152, 161–62

rents/rent allocation in, 7, 20, 44
rule of law and, 17
in West Bengal, 220, 228–29, 230
doorstep conditions. *See also* Philippines,
  doorstep conditions
in Chile, 263
in Korea, 318–19
in Mexico, 233
for OAOs, 17–19
'double balance' hypothesis, 114, 313–15
DR Congo. *See also* Kabila, Joseph; Kabila,
  Laurent; Mobutu, Joseph-Désiré
armed groups, 79–93
FLAO narrative of, 11, 71–72, 73–75
GDP (per capita), 71
growth, collapse of, 71
growth rates, 72
independence of, 70
international resources and, 70–71
on LAO spectrum, 332
organizations, role of, 338–41
political parties, 92–93
regime traits, 72–73
regional comparisons, 20–21
regional security concerns, 81–82
rents in, 8, 336–38
third-party enforcement agreements, 335
violence capacity, 345–46
DR Congo, as limited access order
AMP coalition in, 104–6
elite coalitions, 100–1
governance/rule in, 102
historical milestones, 103
pro-development outcomes, 101–2, 106–7
region-center dynamics, 99–102
rent-seeking elites and, 106–7
resources as rents, 95–97, 99
security sector reform, 97
state capacity, 103
DRP (Democratic Republican Party), 302
drug trafficking, 259
Dunning, Thad, 256
DUP (directly unproductive rent seeking
  activities), 6

East Asia, regional comparisons, 20
East Asian financial crisis (1997), 310, 313
Echeverría, Luis, 246, 247
economic development, 1, 8–10
economic institutions, 118–29
economic organizations (EOs), *14*
"Economy First" policy, 305

Ecuador, on LAO spectrum, 13
efficiency wages, 7
Eichengreen, Barry J., 296
ejidos, 241, 246
elections/electoral system
AMP and, 104–6
in Bangladesh, 29, 60–61, 65
in Chile, 265–75, 285, 286
democracy and, 341–43
in Mozambique, 137
in Philippines, 155, 157, 167, 180–81, 188
in South Korea, 302–4
sugar industry and, 210
elite bargains, role for, 3
elite organizations, perpetual lived forms of,
  17–18
elite privileges, basic LAOs and, 11–12
elites. *See also* dominant coalitions
relative power of, 14–15
rule of law for, 17, 189–91
Emergency Decree for Economic Stability and
  Growth (Korea), 307
Enrile, Juan Ponce, 177–78, 180
Ershad, Hussain Muhammad, 28–29, 48, 49
Escobido, Gema Maria O., 186
Espinoza, Vicente, 279
Estado Novo, 130–31
Estrada, Joseph, 189
Ethiopia, institutional quality, 144
EU (European Union), 187
Europe, as OAO, 9–10

FAC (Forces Armees Congolaises), 84, 85–86, 87
Fair Trade and Anti-Monopoly Act (1981), 314
FARDC (*Forces Armées de la République
  Démocratique du Congo*), 97–98
Faruq, Ghulam, 35
FDI Statute (Decree Law 600), 269
FDLR (*Forces democratique pour la liberation
  du Rwanda*)
description of, 79–93
Interahamwe fighters and, 87–88
Kabila's power base and, 104–5
mining operations and, 96–97
security sector reform and, 96–97
Federation of Free Farmers (FFF), 165
financial development. *See* stock market access
Five Construction Sites (*Cinq Chantiers*), 92
Food for Work programmes, 39
Forces Armees Congolaises (FAC), 84, 85–86, 87
*Forces Armées de la République Démocratique
  du Congo* (FARDC), 97–98

Forces Patriotique Rwandais (FPR), 79–80
Foxley, Alejandro, 282–83
fragile LAOs, 11, *14. See also specific countries*
Freedom House ratings, 320–21
Frei, Eduardo, 263, 266, 270, 276–77
Frelimo
    civil war and, 133–34
    as dominant political party, 139–40
    governance equilibrium and, 134–36
    Marxist-Leninist ideology and, 131–33
    power/rule of, 131
Front for the Liberation of Mozambique
    (Frelimo). *See* Frelimo

Gallagher, Mark, 158–59, 160
Gandhi, Indira, 203–5
garment industry (Bangladesh)
    contract enforcement, 56–58
    emergence/growth of, 30, 51, 66–67
    export growth, 54
    investors/investment in, 52–53
    labor market flexibility, 58–59
    learning rents in, 54–55
    rent strategies/allocation, 59
    success of, 55–56
GATT (General Agreement on Tariffs and
    Trade), 51–52
GDP (per capita), *5–10*, 214–17, 304
Gecamines, 71, 83
generics market, in India, 203
GFIs (government financial institutions), 169–70
Ghana, institutional quality, 144
Gizenga, Antoine, 91
governance features
    of Mozambique, 129
    of Zambia, 118–29
government
    basic LAOs and, 11–12
    violence capacity and, 18
governments, organizational support by, 16
Grand National Party (Korean), 311–12
Grindle, Merilee S., 2
growth, neoclassical assumptions for, 1–2
Guebuza, Armando, 135, 137
Guerrero, Amado. *See* Sison, Jose Ma

Haber, Stephen, 237, 248, 252, 257
Habib Bank Limited, 35
Haiti, as fragile LAO, 11
Hardie, Robert S., 164–65
Health Professionals and Health Workers
    Unions (CONFUSAM), 280

Herdis Management & Investment Corp., 168
Hindu/Hindutva politics, 206–7
Hindustan Antibiotics Ltd., 203
Hirschman, Albert, 147
HMB (*Hukbong Mapagpalaya ng Bayan*),
    164–66
Huks (*Hukbo ng Bayan Laban sa mga Hapon*),
    164
Human Rights Commission (Korean), 311
Huntington, Samuel P., 2
Hutus/Hutu refugees, 79–80, 81, 86

IEC (International Election Commission),
    89–90, 106
impersonal relationships
    doorstep conditions for, 17–19
    economic development and, 339
    for elites, 329
    implementation of, 345
    in open access societies, 16–17
    rent distribution and, 337
    stock market access and, 234
Import Substitution Industrialization (ISI),
    235–36, 241–42, 266, 267
IMSS (*Instituto Mexicano del Seguro Social*),
    253
India. *See also* Congress Party; Left
        Front government (West Bengal);
        Maharashtra; West Bengal
    authoritarianism, turn towards, 205–6
    cane prices in, 211–14
    coalition governments/politics, 205, 207
    economic/political compromises, 198
    growth rates, 214–17
    industrial licenses issued, 222
    institutional quality, 144
    LAO framework/characteristics, 198–99,
        200–11
    on LAO spectrum, 332
    as mature LAO, 12–13
    nationalization drive, 204
    OAO economies and, 9–10
    political fragmentation, 206–7
    political violence, 207
    regional comparisons, 21
    rents in, 199, 206, 336–38
    technology industries, 203
    violence capacity, 345–46
India, limited access order evolution
    Nehruvian period, 201–11
    transition period, 64–65, 201–11
    vulnerable maturity period, 201–11

Indian Drugs and Pharmaceuticals Ltd., 203
Indonesia, 9–10, 73, 144
Industrial Development Bank of Pakistan
    (IDBP), 35–36
industrial growth rates, 214–17
industrial investment, in Pakistan, 38
Industrial Peace Act, 162–64
Industrial Rationalization, 307
Industrial Relations Act, 121
industry
    flight of, 224–25
    sector shares/growth rates, 36, 55
INFONAVIT (*Instituto Nacional de Fomento
    de la Vivienda para los Trabajadores*),
    253
information technology, in India, 203
institutional quality, of low-income countries,
    144
institutions, in economic/political
    development, 1
Instituto de Libertad y Desarrollo (LyD),
    281–82
Instituto Mexicano del Seguro Social (IMSS),
    253
Interahamwe militia, 79–80, 81, 87–88
international aid, role of, 103
International Election Commission (IEC),
    89–90, 106
International Monetary Fund, 78–79, 310–11
investment, in Pakistan, 38
investment projects, in Bangladesh, 65–66
Iraq, as fragile LAO, 11
ISI (Import Substitution Industrialization),
    235–36, 241–42, 266, 267
Islam, Nurul, 46–47

Jamaat-i-Islami, 60
Janata Party, 204–5
Jatiyo Rakkhi Bahini (JRB), 42
Jatiyo Shomajtantrik Dal (JSD), 43–44
Jinnah, Muhammad Ali, 32
Jomo, K. S., 2–3, 316
judiciary, in Bangladesh, 66
Juntas de Conciliación y Arbitraje, 252

Kabila, Joseph
    AMP, political alliance with, 90–94
    election of, 90–95
    international community and, 70–71, 88
    peace accord of, 88–89
    regime of, 73–75
    rise of, 80–81

run-off election share map, 91
Rwandan peace accord and, 87–88
transition government of, 89–90
Kabila, Laurent
    assassination of, 88
    foreign allies of, 87
    government of, 82–83
    Interahawme and, 87–88
    international community and, 86–87
    regime of, 73–75
    regional security concerns of, 84–86
    rent seeking and, 83
    security forces of, 84
Kagame, Paul, 87–88, 104–5
Kamitatu, Olivier, 92
kasama system (Philippines), 151–52
Katumbi, Moise, 100
Kaunda, Kenneth, 117–20, 121
KBL (Kilusang Bagong Lipunan), 180
Keefer, Philip, 342
Khan, Ayub, 34
Khan, Mushtaq H., 2–3, 224, 316, 342
Khan, Nurul Quander, 52–53
Kim, Dae-jung, 308, 310–12
Kim, Woo-Choong, 53
Kim, Young-sam, 310
Korea. *See* South Korea
Korea Independent Commission Against
    Corruption, 311
Korean Central Intelligence Agency (KCIA),
    302
Korean War, 298
Kornai, Janos, 255–56
Krueger, Anne, 6
Kukje Group, 307
Kuomintang (KMT), 302

labor market flexibility, 58–59
labor regulation/unions, 235, 251–54, 278,
    279–81
labor system/policy, 130
Lagos, Ricardo, 270, 273, 276–77
Lajous, Adrian, 254
Lakas, formation of, 188–89
Lalvani, Mala, 212
land reform
    Agricultural Land Reform Code of 1963, 165
    Land Reform Act of 1955, 165
    in Mexico, 234, 245–48
    in Philippines, 155, 164–66
    in South Korea, 297–300, 323
    in West Bengal, 223

Land Reform Act of 1955, 165
Lande, Carl H., 152
landownership, in Philippines, 151–52
Latin America
  mature LAOs and, 12–13
  regional comparisons, 20–21
law. *See* rule of law
LDP (Laban ng Demokratikong Pilipino),
  188–89
learning rents. *See* rents
Lee, Myung-bak, 310–12
Left Front government (West Bengal)
  agricultural growth under, 223–24, 225–26
  basic LAO version of, 221–22
  failure, explanations for, 227
  industrial promotion, 226–27
  industry's flight under, 224–25
  land reform measures, 223
  Moaist movement and, 227
  Panchayati system and, 222–23, 224
  rent allocation system, 224
  rent-creation strategies, 225
Leopold II, King of the Belgians, 74
Levy, Santiago, 253
LGC (Local Government Code), 181
Liberal Party (Korea), 301
Liberal Party (Philippines), 157, 177–76
limited access, described, 5
limited access orders (LAOs). *See also* open
    access orders (OAOs); *specific countries*
  change over time of, 20
  competitive clientelism and, 63–65
  conceptual framework for, 2, 3
  definition/description of, 3
  development within, 14–16
  'double balance' hypothesis, 114, 313–15
  efficiency wages in, 7
  GDP (per capita), 10
  OAOs, distinction from, 112–13
  organizations in, 19–20
  regional comparisons, 20–21
  rents in, 20
  transplanting OAO institutions to, 314,
    346–47
  types/progression of, *14*
  violence in, 19
limited access orders (LAOs), diagnostic
    insights
  competition constraints and, 336–38
  democracy and elections, 341–43
  development problems, 328
  key outcomes, 329

military, role of, 345
non-military organizations, 345–46
OAO-type institutions and, 333–34
organizations, role of, 338–41
rent-creation, 331
research agenda, 346–49
social dynamics, 331–33
third-party enforcement agreements,
  334–36
violence capacity/control, 328–29, 330–31,
  343–45
limited access orders (LAOs), logic of
dominant coalitions in, 4–5
economic development in, 8–10
leadership, 4
rents in, 5–8
social arrangements, 3
uncertain dynamics in, 8
limited access orders (LAOs), spectrum of
basic LAOs, 11–12
fragile LAOs, 11
mature LAOs, 12–13
types/progression of, 10–11, 13
Local Government Code (LGC), 181
Lumumba, Patrice, 74, 91
LyD (*Instituto de Libertad y Desarrollo*),
  281–82

Macapagal, Diosdado, 157, 165
Magsaysay, Ramon, 157, 165
Maharashtra. *See also* India
  business/government arrangements, 217–16
  caste composition of voters, 217–22
  characteristics of, 207–8
  crime syndicates/underworld in, 209, 218
  dominant coalition, 228–29, 230
  formation of, 209
  growth rates, 214–17
  industrial growth, 229
  LAO features/evolution, 199–200, 219–20,
    228–30
  political fragmentation, 208–9
  real estate prices, 217–18
  regional comparisons, 20–21
  rent allocation, 208
  Shiv Sena, rise of, 216–18
  sugar lobby in, 209–15
  violence specialists in, 229–30
Maharashtra Industrial Development
    Corporation (MIDC), 213
Mai Mai militia, 84, 98
Malaysia, OAO economies and, 9–10

Malegaon Sugar Factory, 210
manufacturing growth rates, 36, 214–17
Mao Zedong, 166
Marcos, Ferdinand. *See also* Philippines, under
    Marcos
  acquittal of, 171
  new rents and, 8
  PD 27, 173–76
  violence under, 332
Marx, Karl, 2
Marxist-Leninist limited access order, 131–33
mature LAOs, 12–13, *14*, 15–16
Megaloni, Beatriz, 245
Mexican Revolution, 234, 237–38, 241, 258
Mexico
  as basic LAO, 11–12
  democratization of, 233
  doorstep conditions, 233
  foreign/domestic investment, 243
  GDP growth rates, 304
  labor regulation, 235, 251–54
  land reform, 234, 245–48
  LAO perspective/framework, 235–36,
    256–57
  mining companies in, 248–49
  OAO and, 9–10
  oil rents, 235
  organizations, role of, 338–41
  political competition, 243–44
  privatization in, 243
  public finance, 235, 241, 243
  regional comparisons, 20–21
  rents in, 8, 244, 336–38
  social arrangements, 233–34
  social structure, 235
  socio-economic/political equilibrium,
    234–35
  State Owned Enterprises, 242–43
  stock market access, 234
  violence capacity, 345–46
Mexico, as limited access order
  after 2000, 238
  under colonialism, 236–37
  fragile vs. mature periods of, 239–38
  in Mexican Revolution, 237–38, 241, 258
  "mixed" economy model, 239–40
  oil revenues, 254–56
  persistence of, 244–45
  political arrangement, 238–39
  private/public organization balance, 240–43,
    257
  stock market access, 248–51

violence issues, 257–59
War of Independence and, 237
MFA (Multi-Fibre Arrangement).
    See also garment industry (Bangladesh)
  accidental rents and, 30, 66
  as international intervention, 336
  learning rents and, 54–55
  quota rents and, 51–52
Miba (*Minieres de Bakwanga*), 71, 83
MIDC (Maharashtra Industrial Development
    Corporation), 213
MILF (Moro Islamic Liberation Front), 176,
    187
military authoritarianism. *See* Bangladesh,
    military authoritarian phase
military groups, Congolese, 97
military power, consolidated control of, 18
Mining Law of 1982, 268–69
mining/mining sector
  in Chile, 267–69
  in DR Congo, 95–97
  in Mexico, 248–49
Misuari, Nur, 175–76
MLC (*Mouvement pour la Liberation du
    Congo*), 73, 79–93, 94
MNLF (Moro National Liberation Front),
    175–76, 187
Mo, Jongryn, 293–94, 295–96
Moaist movement, 227
Mobutu, Joseph-Désiré
  economy under, 77
  external debt burden under, 78
  fall of, 78–80
  institutional legacy and, 76–77
  patronage system of, 76
  regime of, 70, 73–74
  Zairianisation process of, 77
Mobutu, Nzanga, 92
Mobutu Sese Seko. *See* Mobutu, Joseph-Désiré
Mohammadi Steamship Company, 35
Monopoly Regulation and Fair Trade Act
    (Korea), 309
Montemayor, Jeremias, 165
MONUC (United Nations Mission in the
    Congo), 70–71, 89–90
MONUSCO (United Nations Organization
    Stabilization Mission the Democratic
    Republic of the Congo), 103
Mookherjee, Dilip, 224
Moore, Mick, 2–3
Moreno, Honorata, A., 168–69
Moro elites, 174–76

Moro Islamic Liberation Front (MILF), 176, 187

Moro National Liberation Front (MNLF), 175–76, 187

Mouvement pour la Liberation du Congo (MLC), 73, 79–93, 94

Movement for Multi-party Democracy (MMD), 123

Mozambican National Resistance (RENAMO). *See* Renamo

Mozambique
  colonization of, 114–15
  development indicators, 116–18
  economic growth, 115
  GDP growth rates, 304
  governance features of, 129
  institutional changes, 113–14
  on LAO spectrum, 332
  regional comparisons, 20–21
  rents in, 8
  third-party enforcement agreements, 335
  violence capacity, 345–46

Mozambique, as limited access order.
  See also Frelimo
  civil war and, 133–34
  colonial policies and, 128–31
  electoral outcomes, 137
  foreign aid/investment, 136
  governance equilibrium, 134–37
  institutional features of, 128
  Marxist-Leninist ideology and, 131–33
  public expenditure, 136
  risk factors for, 137

MPLA (*Mouvimento Popular para a liberacao de Angola*), 82

MRLZ (*Mouvement revolutionnaire pour la liberation du Zaire*), 80

Mujib. *See* Mujibur Rahman, Sheikh

Mujibur Rahman, Sheikh
  assassination of, 47, 204–5
  national party creation and, 41–43
  opposition to, 28
  resource control, lack of, 45

Multi-Fibre Arrangement (MFA).
  See also garment industry (Bangladesh)
  accidental rents and, 30, 66
  as international intervention, 336
  learning rents and, 54–55
  quota rents and, 51–52

Mulungushi Declaration, 119

Museveni, Yoweri Kagua, 81–82

Muslim League, 32, 35

Muslim political elites, 32

Muslim separatists, 174–76, 187–88

Nacionalista party (Philippines), 156, 157

NAFTA (North American Free Trade Agreement), 243, 254

NALU (National Army for the Liberation of Uganda), 81–82

Namibia, 87

Nation Building Companies, 35

National Army for the Liberation of Uganda (NALU), 81–82

National Awami Party, 42

National Copper Corporation (CODELCO), 268, 279–80

National Democratic Front (NDF), 186–87

National Federation of Public Sector Workers (ANEF), 279–80

National Front coalition (India), 206–7

National People's Army (NPA), 166

National Security Law (Korea), 301

Nationalist Congress Party (NCP), 208–9, 210, 217–22

nationalization, of assets, 46–47, 50–51, 204, 268

nativist movements. *See* Shiv Sena (SS)

Naxalite movement, 222

NBFIs (non-bank financial institutions), 310

NCP (Nationalist Congress Party), 208–9, 210, 217–22

NDF (National Democratic Front), 186–87

Nehru, Jawaharlal, 32, 202–3

Nehruvian period, 201–11

New People's Army (NPA), 178–79

Ngandu, Andre Kisase, 80

NGOs (non-government organizations), 181

Nicaragua, institutional quality, 144

Nindaga, Anselme Masasu, 80

non-military organizations, 345–46

North, Douglass
  basic LAO features, 139
  framework of, 1–2, 235–36, 256–57, 293–94
  institution/organization histories, 228
  OAO doorstep conditions, 184
  on social arrangements, 238–39
  Violence and Social Orders, 112, 233

North American Free Trade Agreement (NAFTA), 243, 254

North Korea, as basic LAO, 11–12

NPA (New People's Army), 178–79

Nyamwisi, Mbusa, 92

oil rents/revenues. *See* rents
open access, described, 16
open access orders (OAOs)
  consolidation of, 319
  definition/description of, 16
  doorstep conditions for, 17–19
  'double balance' hypothesis, 114, 313–15
  LAOs, distinction from, 112–13
  transition to, 16–17, 19
  transplanting institutions to LAOs, 314,
    346–47
  types of, *14*
Oportunidades (Conditional Cash Transfer
    Program), 253
Organization of the Islamic Conference (OIC),
    187
organizational support, LAO maturation and,
    16
organizations
  basic LAOs and, 11–12
  definition/description of, 12
  fragile LAOs and, 11
  in LAO framework, 19–20
  mature LAOs and, 12–13
  perpetual lived forms of, 17–18
  rents in, 7
  role of, 338–41
Other Backward Classes (OBCs), 206–7, 216

"pacto de retro" (money lending practice),
    154
Pakistan. *See also* Bangladesh
  authoritarianism, turn towards, 205–6
  institutional quality, 144
  as model of economic growth, 36–37
Pakistan Industrial Credit and Investment
    Corporation (PICIC), 35–36
Pakistan Industrial Development Corporation,
    35
Pakistan Industrial Finance Corporation,
    35–36
PAL (Philippine Airlines), 182–83, 184
PALU (*Parti Lumubiste Unifie*)
  elite coalitions and, 105
  Kabila and, 90–92
  leadership of, 92–93
  region-center dynamics and, 99
PAN (*Partido Acción Nacional*), 256
Panchayati system, 222–23, 224
Papanek, Gustav F., 35, 36–37
Park, Chung Hee, 294, 295–96, 301–3, 305–7,
    309, 312–13

*Parti du people pour la reconstruction et le
    development* (PPRD), 92–93
Parti pour la revolution populaire (PRP), 80
Partido Acción Nacional (PAN), 256
Partido Lakas Tao formation, 188–89
Partido Revolucionario Institucional (PRI), 234,
    237–38, 245, 247–48, 251–52, 332
Patino, Patrick, 186–87, 188
Patrick, Hugh, 168–69
patron-client organizations, 43–44
Pawar, Sharad, 210
Pax Hispanica, 236–37
Pax Porfiriana, 237
PCGG (Presidential Commission on Good
    Government), 170–71
PD 27 (Presidential Decree No. 27), 174
Pelzer, Karl J., 153–54
PEMEX (*Petróleos Mexicanos*), 254–56
People Power Revolution, 177–78
perpetually lived organizations, 17–18, 188–89
personal elite bargains, 329
personal forms of political organizations,
    342
personal identities, 338–41
personal relationships/loyalty, 4, 76
personal rent creation. *See* rents
personality
  of coalition membership, 71–72
  of leaders, 8, 11
  organizations and, 338–41
Philex (Philippine Exchange Company),
    171–73
Philippine Airlines (PAL), 182–83, 184
Philippine Coconut Authority (PCA), 171–73
Philippine Independence Act, 155–56
Philippine Tobacco Filters Corporation, 168
Philippine Trade Act, 153
Philippines
  Chinese *mestizos* in, 154
  comparison with South Korea, 319–24
  corruption indicators, 322
  Freedom House ratings, 321
  GDP in, 304, 320
  organizations, role of, 338–41
  regional comparisons, 20, 21
  rents in, 8, 336–38
  third-party enforcement agreements, 335
  violence capacity, 345–46
Philippines, as limited access order
  change/continuity in, 150–59
  economic indicators, 183
  restoration of democracy and, 150

Philippines, at independence
  economy status, 151
  land reform measures, 155
  landownership, 151–52, 153–55
  overview of, 191–92
  ruling/dominant coalition, 152
  social justice program, 156
  social structure, 153
  Tydings-McDuffie Act, 155–56
  U.S. economic dominance, 153
  voting/elections, 155
Philippines, democratic government
  agricultural monopolies, 173
  credit subsidies/allocation, 160–61, 170–73
  dominant coalition in, 161–62
  electoral costs, 167
  foreign exchange controls, 158–60
  import subsidies under, 158
  internal/external debt, 166–70
  labor/wage issues, 162–64
  land reform measures, 164–66
  manufacturing wages, 163–66
  politics/elections, 157
  rent-sharing agreements, 166
  U.S. transfer of sovereignty, 156–57
Philippines, doorstep conditions
  control over violence potential, 184–88
  to obtain OAO, 184, 192
  perpetually lived organizations, 188–89
  rule of law for elites, 189–91
Philippines, in post-Marcos era
  banks/banking law, 182
  civil-military relations, 185–86
  communist insurgents, 186–87
  coup attempts, 185
  deregulated sectors, 182–83
  economic performance, 183–84
  election-related violence, 188
  elites, elections and, 180–81
  land, redistribution of, 181–82
  military factions, 179–80
  Muslim separatists, 187–88
  NGO participation, 181
  ruling coalition composition, 178–79
  Supreme Court, 189–91
  tariffs/exchange rates, 182, 189
  vigilante groups, 188
Philippines, under Marcos
  coalition collapse, 176–77
  credit allocation, 168–69
  elite families, 167–68
  GFIs, 169–70

  martial law, 167
  monopoly rights/control, 171–73
  Muslim separatists, 174–76
  opposition suppression, 173–76
  preferential treatment, 168
  rent beneficiaries, 170–71
  ruling coalition, 149–50
  violence, use of, 332
Philippines Supreme Court, 189–91
Pinochet, Augusto, 268–69, 270–72
PKP (Communist Party of the Philippines),
  164–65
PMO (Privatization and Management Office),
  189
political entrepreneurs, 40
political institutions
  of Mozambique, 129
  of Zambia, 118–29
political organizations (POs), *14*
political rights/civil liberty scores, 320–21
populist authoritarianism. *See* Bangladesh,
  populist authoritarian phase
Porfiriato, 240–41
Porfirio Diaz, Jose de la Cruz, 240–41, 257
PPRD (*Parti du people pour la reconstruction et
  le development*), 92–93
'praetorian' basic LAO. *See* Bangladesh,
  military authoritarian phase
Presidential Commission on Good
  Government (PCGG), 170–71
Presidential Committee on Human Rights
  (Philippines), 178–79
Presidential Decree No. 27 (PD 27), 174
PRI (*Partido Revolucionario Institucional*), 234,
  237–38, 245, 247–48, 251–52, 332
'primitive accumulation,' 28.
  See also Bangladesh, populist
  authoritarian phase
principal elites
  of Mozambique, 129
  of Zambia, 118–29
privatization, of assets
  in Bangladesh, 46–47, 50–51
  in Mexico, 243
  in South Korea, 300–1
  in Zambia, 125–26
Privatization and Management Office (PMO),
  189
Procampo, 253
PRP (*Parti pour la revolution populaire*), 80
Public Sector Unit (PSU), 213
Putzel, James, 165

Quezon, Manuel L., 156
quota rents. *See* rents

Rahman, Mujibur. *See* Mujibur Rahman,
   Sheikh
Rahman, Ziaur, 28–29, 53
Rally for Congolese Democracy. *See* RCD-K/
   ML (Rally for Congolese Democracy-
   Kisangani-Movement for Liberation)
RAM (Reform the Armed Force Movement),
   177–78
Ramos, Fidel, 177–78, 185, 188–89
Rassemblement Congolais pour la Democratie.
   See RCD-K/ML (Rally for Congolese
   Democracy-Kisangani-Movement for
   Liberation)
Razo, Armando, 257
RCD-K/ML (Rally for Congolese Democracy-
   Kisangani-Movement for Liberation),
   79–93
Reagan, Ronald, 54
Reform the Armed Force Movement (RAM),
   177–78
Renamo, 133–34, 135–36, 137
rent seeking. *See* rents
rents
   accidental rents, 30, 66
   allocation of
      in dominant coalition, 44
      in garment industry, 59
      in patron client organizations, 43–44
      in 'praetorian' basic LAO, 26–28
   competition constraints, 336–38
   creation/structuring of, 5–8
   definition/description of, 5–6
   in LAO framework, 20
   learning rents
      MFA and, 54–55
      in 'praetorian' basic LAO, 26–28
      sector growth rates and, 36
   oil rents/revenues, 235, 254–56
   personal rent creation, 337
   quota rents, 51–52
   redistributive, 206
   rent seeking
      DUP activities, 6
      in Kabila government, 83
   rent sources/extraction
      in DR Congo, 95–97, 99, 106–7
      of Mozambique, 129
      of Zambia, 118–29
   state-created rents, 34–35

violence and, 330–31
   zero-sum rents, 45–46
research, agenda for, 346–49
resource extraction, in DR Congo, 95–97
RFP (Rwanda Patriotic Front), 87
Rhee, Syngman, 295–96, 297–300, 301
Ricardo, David, 6
Rodrik, Dani, 2, 296
Rogaly, Ben, 224
Roh, Moo-hyun, 311
Roh, Tae-woo, 308
rule of law. *See also* doorstep conditions
   for elites, 17, 189–91
   in Korea, 318–19
   LAO maturation and, 15
ruling coalition. *See also* dominant coalitions
   authoritarian clientelism and, 49
   competitive clientelism and, 61–62
Russia, on LAO spectrum, 13
Rwanda
   AFDL and, 80–81
   relationship with Kabila, 84–86
   security concerns in, 81
Rwanda Patriotic Front (RFP), 87
Rwandan genocide, 79–80, 81, 86, 87–88

SADC (Southern African Development Com-
   munity), 87
Savimbi, Jonas, 82
security sector reform, in DR Congo, 97
Seguro Popular, 253
Senegal, 144, 304
services, growth rates in, 55, 214–17
Shirley, Mary M., 2–3
Shiv Sena (SS), 208–9, 216–22
Simango, Daviz, 137
Sison, Jose Ma, 166, 178–79
Slim, Carlos, 243, 250
Smith, Adam, 6
SNA (*Sociedad Nacional de Agricultura*),
   279
SNTE (*Sindicato Nacional de Trabajadores de
   la Educación*), 252
social arrangements, 1–2, 3, 233–34, 238–39
Social Weather Stations (SWS), 190
Socialist ideology, in Bangladesh, 41
sources/extraction of rents. *See* rents
South Africa
   CIAT mandate of, 89–90
   as mature LAO, 12–13
   OAO economies and, 9–10
South Asia, regional comparisons, 20–21

South Korea
 anti-authoritarian forces, 301–4
 banking, privatization of, 300–1
 Communist threat, 323–24
 corruption ratings/trends, 317–22
 developmental state origins, 295–96
 economic growth, 304–5, 309–10
 economic/political development, 293–95
 educational expansion, 297–300
 electoral system, 302–4
 Freedom House ratings, 321
 GDP in, 304, 320
 industrial property, 300
 land reform, 297–300, 323
 on LAO spectrum, 332
 MFA and, 52
 organizations, role of, 338–41
 political rights/civil liberty scores, 320–21
 political system in, 301
 regional comparisons, 20, 21
 rents in, 8, 305–7, 316–17, 336–38
 security threats/military power, 307–8, 324
 third-party enforcement agreements,
  334–35
 violence capacity/potential, 308–9, 323,
  345–46
South Korea, LAO-OAO framework
 as basic/mature LAO, 301–7
 corruption, rents and, 315–18
 doorstep conditions in, 318–19
 double balance theory, 313–15
 economic development, 312–13
 as fragile/basic LAO, 297–301
 as mature LAO, 307–10
 periods in, 297–304
 transition/consolidation, 310–12, 319
Southern African Development Community
  (SADC), 87
Soviet countries, as basic LAO, 11–12
Spanish American War, 154
State Owned Enterprises (Mexico), 242–43
state-created rents. *See* rents
stock market access, 234, 248–51
strike activity, 163–66
student revolution. *See* April Revolution
  (Korean)
Sub-Saharan African countries, as basic LAO,
  11–12
sugar industry (in Maharashtra)
 business/political arrangements, 213
 cane prices, 211–14
 electoral politics and, 210

MIDC and, 213
 price support policies, 210–11
 rents generated by, 209–10, 212–13
 sugar lobby, 211–12
Supreme Court (Philippines), 189–91
SWS (Social Weather Stations), 190

Taiwan
 comparison with South Korea, 319–24
 corruption indicators, 322
 Freedom House ratings, 321
 GDP in, 304, 320
Tanzania, institutional quality, 144
Tata Group, 203
Telefonos de Mexico, 243
Telmex, 250
think tanks, Chilean, 281–83
third-party enforcement agreements, 334–36
Tollison, Robert D., 6
"too big to fail" (TBTF), 310
transplanting, OAO institutions to LAOs, 314,
  346–47
Tullock, Gordon, 6
Turner, John Kenneth, 257
Turner, Thomas, 76
Tutsis, 79–80
Tydings-McDuffie Act, 155–56

UDEMO (*Union des Democrates Mobutistes*),
  92–93
UDPS (*Union pour la democratie et le progres
  sociale*), 92–93
Uganda
 AFDL and, 80–81
 institutional quality, 144
 relationship with Kabila, 84–86
 security concerns in, 81–82
underworld/crime syndicates, 209, 218
Union National (UN), 90–93
unions. *See* labor regulation/unions
UNIP (United National Independence Party),
  117–20, 121, 122–23
UNITA (*Uniao para a independencia total de
  Angola*), 82
United Coconut Planters Bank (UCPB),
  171–73
United Nations Mission in the Congo
  (MONUC), 70–71, 89–90
United Nations (UN), 334–35
United States
 CIAT mandate of, 89–90
 as OAO, 9–10

'untouchables,' 206–7. *See also* Other Backward
    Classes (OBCs)
upazillas (tier of government), 48

Vedanta Corporation, 126
Velasco, Djorina, 186–87, 188
Venezuela, on LAO spectrum, 13
Vertical Political Integration, 237
Vietnam, 9–10, 144
Violence and Social Orders (North, Wallis and
    Weingast), 112, 233
violence/violence capacity
    in Chile, 269–70
    developing countries and, 1–2
    government control and, 18
    in LAO framework, 12, *14*, 15–16, 19,
        343–45
    in Mexico, 257–59
    non-military organizations and, 345–46
    problem of, 3
    rents and, 330–31
    security sector reform and, 97
Vlaicu, Razvan, 342

wages, manufacturing, 163–66. *See also* labor
    regulation/unions
Wallis, John Joseph
    basic LAO features, 139
    framework of, 1–2, 235–36, 256–57,
        293–94
    institution/organization histories, 228
    OAO doorstep conditions, 184
    on social arrangements, 238–39
    Violence and Social Orders, 112, 233
Walsh Sanderson, Susan, 245–46
War of Independence (Mexican), 237
Weingast, Barry R.
    basic LAO features, 139
    framework of, 1–2, 235–36, 256–57, 293–94
    institution/organization histories, 228
    Mexican land reform, 245
    OAO doorstep conditions, 184
    on social arrangements, 238–39
    Violence and Social Orders, 112, 233
West Bengal. *See also* India; Left Front
    government (West Bengal)
    Congress government in, 221–22
    dominant coalition, 220, 228–29, 230
    formation of, 220
    growth rates, 214–17
    industrial growth, 229
    LAO features/evolution, 199–200, 228–30

organizations, role of, 338–41
regional comparisons, 20–21
rent allocation strategy, 220–21
violence specialists in, 229–30
Workers and Peasants Awami League.
    See Bangladesh Krishok Sromik Awami
    League (BAKSAL)
World Bank, 3, 344
World Bank Development Report, 3, 330

Young, Crawford, 76

Zaire. *See* DR Congo
Zairian debt crisis, 78–79
Zairianisation process, 77
Zambia
    colonization of, 115
    development indicators, 116–18
    economic growth, 115
    governance features of, 118–29
    institutional changes/quality, 113–14, 144
    on LAO spectrum, 332
    OAO economies and, 9–10
    organizations, role of, 338–41
    regional comparisons, 20–21
    rents in, 8
    structural features of, 114–15
    third-party enforcement agreements, 335
    violence capacity, 345–46
Zambia, access order approach
    citizen participation, 142
    dominant leader/party in, 146–47
    elite bargaining in, 138, 145–46
    globalized engagement, 141
    institutional quality, 143–45
    investment deal transparency, 142–43
    openness in, 138–39
    policy reforms, 141–43
    public administrative capacity, 142
    strengths/weakness in, 139–41
Zambia, as 'competitive clientelistic' LAO
    characterization of, 127–28
    copper mine privatization, 125–26
    elite bargaining in, 126–27
    institutional order/arrangements, 123–24,
        125
    rent-seeking and corruption in, 124–25
Zambia, one-party LAO phase
    civil-service jobs, 120
    copper prices, 122
    economic policies, 121–22
    patronage resources, 122–23

Zambia, one-party LAO phase (*cont.*)
  political failures, 122
  political logic of, 120–21
  price-controls in, 121
  state controls, 121
  worker organizations, 121
Zambia, political economy
  colonial bequest phase, 117–20
  goals of, 116–17
Zambia Congress of Trade Unions (ZCTUs),
  121

Zambia Industrial and Mining Corporation,
  121
Zepeda, Guillermo, 246
zero-sum rents. *See* rents
Zia-ul-Haq, Mohammad
  BNP and, 29–30, 47
  coup attempts under, 49
  garment industry support, 53
  as 'investor-friendly', 52
  political organizers and, 48
Zimbabwe, 87